DATE			

THE BEST
OF FRIENDS

THE BEST OF FRIENDS

Martha and Me

MARIANA PASTERNAK

HARPER

An Imprint of HarperCollins*Publishers*
www.harpercollins.com

HarperCollins books may be purchased for educational, business, or sales promotional use. For information, please write: Special Markets Department, HarperCollins Publishers, 10 East 53rd Street, New York, NY 10022.

FIRST EDITION

Designed by Cassandra J. Pappas

Library of Congress Cataloging-in-Publication Data
is available upon request.

ISBN: 978-0-06-166127-3

10 11 12 13 14   OV/RRD   10 9 8 7 6 5 4 3 2 1

For my daughters

CONTENTS

PART III • DEATH OF THE HEART

PART IV • THE END OF THE AFFAIR

THE BEST
OF FRIENDS

Prologue: August 1997

IN THE WANING days of summer, Martha came to visit me at the cottage I rented every year in an old-fashioned family camp on Golden Pond in New Hampshire. It was shortly after our respective birthdays, which fell just a few days apart. She had spent hers in Maine with her friends Memrie and Charlotte. I had spent mine, as usual, on the lake, with my daughters, Monica and Lara, and my friends Angela and Linn, who came with their children for a week to celebrate with us.

The girls and I loved the place. We had some of our best times there: beautiful, uncomplicated days with family and friends, golden sunsets, and nights of loon calls and shooting stars. The water was calm for a lake that large, strewn with islands, most of them wildlife sanctuaries. Motorboat restrictions made it a paradise for canoeing and swimming, and the water was so clear you could see six or seven feet down, and so warm that it felt like slipping inside a second skin.

An ash as large as the Norse World Tree guarded the dirt driveway. A weathered birch-bark camp sign with wood-burned lettering marked the entrance to Walhalla, as the summer camp was called.

The center-chimney Adirondack Camp–style cottage had been in the same family for generations. The screened-in porch overlooked the lake. Flecks of mica found along hiking trails in the surrounding mountains shimmered at night, making it easier to see the contours of the path between the cottage and the private dock.

The cottage was homey and clean, with knotty-pine paneling, rustic arts-and-crafts furniture, and walls lined with elm-wood shelves chock-full of classic novels and volumes of poetry, many of them early twentieth-century first editions. "1905"—the year the house was built—was carved into a corner of the impressive granite hearth of the large fieldstone fireplace. On its generous mantel were old copper kettles that we filled with cut flowers, an eclectic collection of candlesticks and oil lamps, and an antique toile-patterned tin box filled with matches to light the fire during the chilly evenings.

The kitchen was simple but our meals were delicious and the mood joyful. We had no dishwasher, yet my friends and I never complained about doing dishes, what with the sounds of happy children playing in the living room, the well-deserved glass of wine for the mother on kitchen duty, and the cross-stitch sampler that hung above the sink:

> *Thank God for dirty dishes; they have a tale to tell.*
> *While others may go hungry, we're eating very well.*
> *With home, health, and happiness, I shouldn't want to fuss;*
> *By the stack of evidence, God's been very good to us.*

I was grateful to Martha for my happiness there. I owed it to her influence that I had acquired the capacity to make summers by the lake such a fabulous part of our family life. By example, she helped me recognize that I loved the physical effort that went into it. And Martha's fearlessness gave me the courage to go live with small children in the woods. I was still married when I began taking my daughters there, thinking that if I gave my husband the space he so much seemed to want, I might save our marriage. However, the only men I invited to

Walhalla were my friends George and Michel, who came with us on our first visit there, a weeklong celebration of my fortieth birthday.

Now Martha had come to tell me she was in love.

During Martha's trip to Maine, Memrie Lewis, a tony landscape designer, had introduced Martha to the upper crust's upper crust. Memrie had also introduced Martha to Skylands, the former home of Edsel and Eleanor Ford, a grand estate on a bluff soaring nearly four hundred feet over Seal Harbor, Maine. Once Martha saw the place, she knew she had to have it. Swept up by its pillars and post, she did what she was so good at doing: she quickly converted her larger, shapeless longings into a much more manageable mansion-yearning. From the moment Memrie and her fiancé, Charlie, landed their plane to drop Martha off with me, she could not stop talking about Skylands.

Side by side in two Adirondack chairs, sipping red wine from glass goblets, we watched the scenic expanse of the lake in the light of a waxing moon, and listened to soul-stirring calls of the loons. As we sat on the dock, late that August night after my children had gone to bed, we spoke in low voices about how Martha might carry off the acquisition of Skylands. I had a highly successful real estate career, and I knew what moves she needed to make to pull off this larger-than-life scheme.

Most of the time, Martha decided where we would eat, which movie we would see, what countries we would vacation in. "Let's do—," "Let's see—," "Let's go—," she would say. And, most of the time, I followed. This was one of those rare moments when Martha needed my opinion to make the grand decision.

It had happened once before that year, when she told me about her daring plan to buy her company back from TimeWarner, the corporation that held all of Martha Stewart Living Enterprises magazines, books, and a mail-order catalog. It was February, and we had seen a movie, and then stopped for our usual late-night bite at the Sherwood Diner. Martha didn't like to eat in diners, but there weren't many options for decent, clean food close to home at that hour in Westport, our sleepy Connecticut commuter town. It was there that Martha confided to me a high-stakes strategy that she and Sharon Patrick, who for the past few years had been helping Martha reorganize her company, had been devising behind closed doors: a strategy that would show my friend Martha at her best. She always had the ability to sit back, ponder, plan, and then choose her actions in ways that were at once creative and astute.

On that cold winter night, Martha seemed calm, composed, and her eyes had the sparkle I knew so well. This was the sparkle that came when Martha had a line of attack, when she saw the curve coming and no one else did, and I loved her for it.

"So tell me what you think," I recall her saying, leaning in toward me across the table. And then she told me about the meeting she and Sharon had planned for the following day. It was not so much a meeting as a daring venture that, if successful, could bring Martha's career several steps forward.

Early the next morning, she and Sharon were going to present Time-Warner with a request for further investment in several new magazines that Martha wanted to launch. If they refused, as Martha and Sharon expected they would, Sharon, with her diplomatic silver tongue, would ask them to allow Martha to buy herself out. Sharon felt certain that TimeWarner would take the offer, but Martha wasn't so sure. We ate our Greek salads, sipped chamomile tea, and wondered. If they did agree to a buyout, she would be free. But who would catch her if she fell?

I understood her concerns, the "what ifs."

"I think it's a brilliant idea," I said. "It's exciting, Martha! You know what your readers want much better than TimeWarner does. They judge your magazines based on the publishing business as a whole."

"Which is dismal. The magazine business is tanking."

"So buy yourself back cheaply and get those guys out of your life."

The next day, after the meeting, Martha called me as she was getting in the car with Sharon. Martha's voice was totally ebullient. It had all worked out as Sharon predicted. Martha was a free woman.

"Congratulations!" I said. "You did it."

We laughed, Martha harder than I.

* * *

SO NOW, IN mid-August, a few weeks before her TimeWarner deal was due to close, Martha came to Golden Pond with a new plan.

Knowing how she could be blinded by love at first sight, Martha wanted to bring me to see Skylands, this wondrous property, immediately. We both knew that, because of the buyout, it was not the best time for Martha to buy a house, especially a fifth expensive house. Since February, Martha and Sharon had been scurrying to raise about $75 million of what Martha called "internally generated capital" in order to complete her TimeWarner deal.

Martha also knew that I understood the symbolic value of her owning Skylands—it would give her social credibility in the rarified world to which she aspired. She needed someone whose opinion she trusted, someone who loved her enough to tell her when she was making a mistake. Because by then, with all the fame and power she had accumulated, only the few who really loved Martha still dared to be frank.

I listened to her long recitations filled with collections and details of Skylands' appointments, and each time she recounted another extraordinary feature, I nodded in understanding or acquiescence. The twelve-bedroom, three-story house was made of pink granite, and had large patios and terraces surrounding it. The property included several outbuildings, notably a guesthouse, a playhouse, a stable with upstairs maids' quarters, a mechanic's garage, and a desanctified church large enough to host a sizeable wedding. All of this nestled on more than sixty acres of woodlands overlooking the harbor.

"And Mrs. Ford's Orange Fitzhugh china looked like a service for twenty," Martha said.

Near midnight, the wind began to blow, and the lake responded, its waters going choppy. We shivered, and pulled the single blanket we shared tighter around us.

"Listen," I said then. She turned toward me, expectant, as if I were about to make some pronouncement regarding her acquisition dreams, but I shook my head: no. Listen. From deep in the center of a New

Hampshire night, we heard the loons again, only this time with a ratcheted up intensity of furious trilling and guttural tremolos.

"Threatened nest. Calling for its mate," I whispered.

Skimming the inky surface of the lake toward the loon-laughter coming from Squaw Cove, our gaze stopped at a scene of high drama. Near the shore of an island, in a pool of light cast by the low-hanging, chunky moon, were two loons rising upright in the water. They were facing each other, seemingly engaged in a dance and a dissonant duet of spine-chilling yodeling. Our eyes glued on the eerie performance, we watched as the birds, like ballet dancers changing step, went from their confrontational "penguin-dance" to "rowing" across the lake propelled by their large wings, following each other, splashing along as they gained speed.

Then the moon glided beyond the cliffs of the White Mountains, and the magic show disappeared in the dark, leaving behind the haunting echoes of scuttering sounds. Out of the shadows, the long, lupine howls of a loon trying to locate its loved one pierced the night.

Where are you? Come to me!

The answer reverberated across the distance with the mate's loud wailing: *Here I come.*

After a volley of questions and replies, the loon pair began a nocturnal chorus of sustained tremolos, and from some place we could not see we heard the awesome flapping of immense wings. They would, we assumed, meet at the nest.

Martha's attention was divided, half on the house she wanted, half on the loons. "I'm listening," I remember her saying, as a bright Perseid meteor streaked across the moonless, starry sky. "I'm listening."

And indeed she was, leaning slightly forward in her seat, as though stretching toward the sound with a longing I know something about. We were two divorcées who had pledged to wait it out, because somewhere across some lake sat our soul mates, and we wouldn't settle for anything less. In the meantime, we had each other.

Part I

First Encounter

1

Martha at the Gate

THE ATTRACTIVE BLOND intruder, wearing a conservative button-down shirt and pleated khaki shorts that came to just above her knees, stood next to her bike in front of our garden gate and peered in. My fiancé and I were having a Memorial Day party on our Westport grounds, two acres with a large lawn, landscaped gardens, old and new trees, a covered loggia, and a garden terrace. Enclosed by stone walls, the property could be entered via the main gate or the garden gate, which was open under a cascade of fragrant wisteria blossoms. The preppie-looking lady walked her bike right through.

Two other couples, friends from Manhattan, had come to spend the long weekend. It was Sunday afternoon, and warm in the East Coast way of May, the summer perennials putting out petals and the tips of green leaves, coaxed ahead by the sunny soil. There were bees fat from early bee balm, and good-fortune ladybugs plump with aphids. We had just finished lunch and were lounging on comfortable chaises, sipping chilled Chablis Premier Cru, passing back and forth sections of the Sunday *New York Times*, the discarded pages in a fluttering heap under the glass-topped terrace table. Our new puppy, Attila the Hun, an adorable golden brown Vizsla—all legs, ears, and personality—had fallen asleep on my lap.

I put him down and walked toward our new visitor. As I approached, she stared at me. I had never seen a woman's eyes look at me with such intensity—her gaze seemed to reflect a masculine dominance, feminine competitiveness, and a child's curiosity all at once. I saw her eyes sweep across my body, take me in, process me, my youth, my shorts, my high heels. I had colored my copper-chestnut hair a brave bright blond and wore my long locks down, or in a carefree twist held to my head with a found stick. While most of the American women I knew in the early 1980s sported preppie outfits that suggested "proper," I was more interested in "chic." I was comfortable with my body and, like many European women of my age, I grew up inspired by images from French-Italian cinema and influenced by the British Mod subculture of the hyper-cool.

I saw the slightest shadow ripple across her face, and then just as quickly she brightened up. "Hi," she said with willful cheerfulness. "I'm Martha. Your neighbor. Thought I might stop for a glass of water before biking up the hill to my house."

I invited her to sit down with us, but she declined. I called out, "Everyone, this is our neighbor, Martha," then went inside to get her some water. When I came out, she was still standing rigidly near the gate, holding her bike with one hand, with everyone watching. By that simple act of staying where she was, she had managed to disrupt our party and make herself the focus of everyone's attention.

She sipped her water and then said, "I'd heard a handsome bachelor doctor had just moved in here. I thought I might come by to meet him."

That handsome bachelor doctor, of course, was my fiancé. Now I understood why she had been appraising me.

She began listing her accomplishments as though she were reading from a curriculum vitae, and loud enough for everyone on the terrace to hear her. She told us she was married, but her husband was away (*lonely*, I thought), and that she ran a catering business and was about to have a cookbook published.

I remember thinking that her sudden appearance was somehow surreal, like a blue-sky window in a René Magritte painting. Researchers have found that first impressions play a huge role in whom we will later choose for friends, employees, even mates. If this is so, then my experience contradicts these findings. If you had told me this woman would become one of my closest friends for twenty years, that she would be the driving force behind a lifetime's worth of adventures, that her signature would become so intertwined with mine that even now, the friendship over, my name is impossible to disentangle from her shadow, I would have said, trying out my American slang, "No way."

Yet I heard myself ask, "Would you like to join us for dinner this evening?"

Martha turned to look at me and I saw in her luxuriously velvet brown eyes a deep longing combined with something swift and sharp as she graciously accepted the invitation. Her voice had a silky slide to it.

She drained the last of the water, then held the glass out in the air, as if expecting one of the men to take it from her. Long seconds passed as none of them made a move, so I relieved her of the glass, conscious of saving an awkward moment. I had no idea how many times I would see this scene with the glass replayed, how typical it was of Martha.

The party had gone silent during her brief visit, but as soon as she left it was as if some spell had been lifted and our friends kicked back into action, whooping with laughter—*She came to meet the handsome bachelor doctor!* To my fiancé, they said, *What's the diagnosis for women seeking to quench their thirst at the new neighbor's house when her own house is just a few doors up the street?*

But my fiancé looked thoughtful and embarrassed. He scratched the side of his chin, then cracked a grin. "Just what the world needs," he said. "Another cookbook."

• • •

WHEN MARTHA CAME back that night, she was dazzling in her finest pearls. She was dressed as if out for a night at The Ritz, a bit too fancy for our informal Sunday-night dinner party.

We served coq au vin with a delicious Burgundy. When Martha asked if I'd made the dinner, my fiancé gave his standard answer, "Mariana is the spice, I am the cook." Our friends laughed and raised their glasses. Despite a strong breeze that night, Martha seemed completely unruffled; not a single strand stirred on her head. Yet her eyes seemed to devour the scene with great concentration. Her smile seemed too carefully carved. In the flickering candlelight, her too-white teeth made me think of ivory chessmen on a board, moving in a game of skill and strategy rooted in war. Yet there was nothing the least bit bellicose about Martha. She was friendly in a girl-gabby kind of way. She told us that she was alone over Memorial Day because Andy, her husband, was in Patagonia.

This caught my attention. Patagonia! Despite the fact that I was, for all intents and purposes, living in a distant land, less than two years in America after fleeing Communist Romania, I hadn't lost my wanderlust. While I enjoyed the privilege that came with living in Westport, and was in love, I already felt stifled by suburbia and I secretly longed to escape the confines of ordinary life. So ardent was that longing that not for a moment did I think of the legendary lesson taught to us by Faust, whose desire for wonder and discovery led him to enter into the infamous pact that brought him temptations and ruin. Over lunch at my job, as I bit into my crusty bread and pâté de foie gras, I would fantasize about the wild lands I wanted to explore, the ruins and temples I yearned to walk through, the woodland streams I might drink from, where the water was cool with mountain-melted snow and tasted of treetops lost in layers of clouds.

While people in Westport certainly traveled, they did not go, as a rule, to places like Patagonia, and so I immediately knew I wanted to meet Andy Stewart, who seemed like a remarkable person well before I ever laid eyes on him. Born into a wealthy and highly educated American family, a graduate of the Yale School of Law, he was a partner at the publishing house Stewart, Tabori & Chang. The company had recently been founded by former executives at Abrams, a respected illustrated book publisher where Andy had been president.

"Patagonia!" I said, and looked at Martha across the table. She nodded, and smiled slowly.

"Patagonia," she said again, looking not at me but above me, her gaze sad and searching, as if perhaps trying to locate her man wherever he was.

THE WEEK AFTER Memorial Day went by fast. In the mornings my fiancé and I went off to the hospital where we had met and continued to work. We left at different times, according to our separate schedules. I would soon discover the downside of working with a soon-to-be-spouse—the clash of our intimacy on the one hand with the forced formality of demanding occupations on the other, he as a vascular surgeon and I as a biomedical engineer. Our paths rarely crossed during the day, for he was operating in brightly lit surgery rooms in one part of the hospital, and I toiled in computer labs in another, analyzing the data his patients' tests produced.

I loved my job. It called on my greatest strengths and fierce concentration. Although I had a wide range of interests from fashion to the arts to evolutionary psychology, writing computer code that expressed no emotion but contained within its structure amazing possibilities for detection, theory, point of view captivated my imagination. During the day, I was consumed with my work, which, as time went by, expanded to contain analyses of blood gases, ratios of respiratory functions, the structuring of computer programs to screen out cancer's false hot spots and, simultaneously, to find their real ones.

I saw cancer cells that were bunched tightly together, as if packed in a floral ball. I studied hot cores, bright scatters, elongated knots of tumors clustered like stars among interstellar clouds in close-up pictures of faraway galaxies, their density directly proportional to the frailty of the patient who bore its brunt.

In our free time, my fiancé and I did lots of things together, so I was busy with *doing* and *being*. I lived in a free country, I read whatever I wanted, I traveled, I had amazing friends, and most of all, for the first time in my life, I was in love in the right place at the right time.

A week after the Memorial Day dinner party, almost to the day, the phone rang. It was Martha. Her husband, Andy, was back from Patagonia. *Dinner. Would you like to come? We would love to!*—and, best of all, I would get to meet Andy.

We pulled up the short, straight drive at Turkey Hill. Getting out of the car on one of those light lavender evenings peculiar to summers on the East Coast, I could smell, coming from somewhere, the scent of a garden, made all the more seductive by its elusive trail. I looked around, trying to find the flowers, but I could not see them at first.

Little did I know how many sources for these aromas there were. Turkey Hill was no ordinary Westport abode. After they purchased it as a dilapidated farmhouse in 1972, the Stewarts had made the place their own work of art, washing this cherished canvas with color after color in search of just the right hue, swiping away any mistakes with the equivalent of an artist's oil-soaked rag, and starting again, brush by brush, brick by brick, garden upon garden upon orchard upon orchard. We were not dining with our neighbors *in* their home, we were dining with neighbors who *were* their home. The Stewarts were one with Turkey Hill.

Because it was the beginning of June when we first went to dinner at Turkey Hill, the long day cast a soft pink light over the gorgeous property. The place could properly be called an estate, bringing to mind the setting of Eugene O'Neill's *Mourning Becomes Electra*. Like the Mannon residence on the outskirts of a small New England seaport town, Turkey Hill had extensive grounds, a greenhouse, an orchard, and large flower gardens (which I got to see the following morning when we were invited back for a daylight tour of the place, with its pool, barn, and chicken coop that Martha, with charming humor, referred to as the *palais du poulet*).

Most flower gardens, despite the images propagated by gardening magazines, are less a show of color than a display of life and death, with some perennials blooming too early, others too late, the coordination promised in the planting packets never quite coming through. Not Martha's. Her flowers were magnificent, in concert, and bloomed before anyone else's, as though there were some isolated precocious microclimate at Turkey Hill. It may have been the property's position on the hill, or just Martha's luck that caused her peonies—some of my favorite flowers—to put on such a show. Her tree peonies were three to four feet tall and had the largest blossoms I had ever seen: some deep red, almost black, and fragrant, with silky petals that formed a delicate crown for the large cluster of golden yellow stamen; the dramatic fuchsia ones with a subtle fragrance; and pink Hanakisoi. As we toured Martha's garden in the cool of the evening, she showed us all her plants, pronouncing every name correctly, like Hah-nah-khi-soy, their lush heads drooping as though doped, the ruff of pale petals mysteriously supported by the verdant cluster of leaves.

The setting was splendorous, even theatrical, but when the door swung open and we stepped inside the house, I felt claustrophobic, as if I were in a museum. Homes have hearts, and one need not venture very far into them to hear how they beat. The heart of the Stewart home, in contrast with the lively gardens outside, beat slowly, and low, like a fog horn on a day thick with drizzly mist.

Or so I thought. Several seconds into my first visit, Martha and Andy's home revealed itself to have several hearts, each with a beat distinct from the next. If the main pump had a somewhat sad sound, the peripheral pulses in the array of rooms that sprawled throughout the farmhouse had somehow clung to their own unique rhythms, thus making color, fun, laughter, even love possible in certain spots.

But I didn't dwell much on the Stewarts' abode, because a house is ultimately a shell. I was curious about the sort of people who might make their shelter into a museum, the mandate of which, above all else, is to not touch.

I TOOK TO Andy Stewart immediately. He was a love of a man, keenly intelligent but with a generosity of spirit so strong you could bask in his knowledge and never once feel inadequate, or afraid of asking a question that would reveal your ignorance. Andy opened the door for us that evening, ushered us in, and I could immediately sense his energetic spirit. Successful entrepreneur, world traveler, he was still so much more than the sum of these accomplishments. There exist in the world a few extraordinarily special people and Andy was one of them.

Andy led us down a hallway into the kitchen. As soon as we stepped over the threshold, it was as if we had stepped into a whole new house. Leaving behind the stark, formal, and chilly abode, we found ourselves in an open kitchen suffused with a warm glow, a table elegantly set in front of the large, dark stone fireplace where a fire was crackling away, and above the mantel a Hudson River Valley painting. Martha was cooking at the stove, stirring with a huge wooden spoon. Above and around her, hanging from hooks, were copper pots, their bottoms lustrous in the low, rich light. From another part of the ceiling hung baskets, and on the shelves were displays of clay pots, pretty dishes, and Depression glass. As I took domesticity for granted and lived on love, not food, I had little appreciation for all that luxury and refinement. It was so beautiful it seemed staged, and an odd feeling came over me. I felt outside, detached, unreal.

"I feel," I said to Andy, "like we are in a Soutine painting."

I was thinking of his *Carcass of Beef*, for which Soutine kept a rotting animal carcass in his studio, much to the displeasure of his neighbors. And indeed the kitchen had a gleam of abstract expressionism. Andy looked at me with his warm eyes and nodded, and then he told a tale about Soutine, one of many painters he knew a lot about.

I listened to Andy talk. He was the first person I met in America who shared my liking of the Russian writer Mikhail Bulgakov's *Master and Margarita*. He lent me his copy so I could read it in English. The sheer volume of his knowledge convinced me, right then and there, that of the four of us, he was the most impressive.

I heard the whisking of Martha's stirring spoon. I heard the wind walking through the trees beyond the open windows. Suddenly the evening was alive with good food and good hosts and good fun. The meal was excellent, as delicious as watching its preparation had been. Andy was taster supreme. Martha used the dinner party as an occasion to try out recipes for her upcoming book, *Entertaining*. Holding long-handled spoons out to her husband, spoons brimming with rich red broths or tasty stewed juices in which floated tender hunks of choice meats, Martha would patiently wait while Andy took the spoon from her hand and, touching his lip to the spoon's edge, take in the complex matrix of flavors. I could almost hear him deconstruct in his mind: *pepper, parsley, nutmeg*. Martha waited for his assessment, which she trusted so completely it was endearing.

"Salt," Andy finally pronounced. "It needs more salt." Or just a smidge more thyme, a sprinkling of rosemary, a slice of shallot, a mince of garlic—no, not the store-bought kind. The Stewarts grew their own garlic, and Martha could pull a fresh bunch of bulbs from one of her many pantries, and, after splitting each one with the side of her powerful fist, expertly wield her knife and sever the cloves so delicately that every segment fainted flat on her cutting board.

I watched, fascinated. I noticed that my fiancé, standing next to me, was equally taken in. This was unlike anything I'd ever seen between a couple before. We were witnessing the intimacies of a marriage, and more. We were witnessing two artists at work. For me, who had always pooh-poohed cooking as work for women under domestic duress, that night was transformative.

The abundance of spices, the tangy sauce took me back to the scented shadow of the apricot tree that grew in the perennially blooming flower beds of my childhood home. Those gardens were even more magical than Martha's, for my grandmother had resurrected every shredded peony, each torn tulip from the bomb-blackened ruins of World War II, which had turned my Romania into a landscape of charcoal and chiaroscuro. In my grandmother's hands, flowers parted their petals and melons yielded their flesh—plus all their seeds, which she scooped from the cut halves and then flung back over the loam, yielding her still more fruit, more flavors, year after year, and long past the time when the Communists came. They could not take away my grandmother's secret ways with seeds or sauces, or the fact that even the most ravaged soil loved her touch. As did I.

In some strange way, just as the survivors of World War II returned to their homes with so much hope, and the keenest caution, so too, after that first night, I was drawn back to the Stewarts' kitchen, so I might watch (and taste) what I had long thought a menial chore rise up to the ranks of art. In secret, I thought of the Romanian word *dor*: the feeling of nostalgic longing for something that, or someone who, might be forever lost.

On a tour of the house, Andy described the renovations they had made over the years. I met their cats, draped like minks over couches, or shooting from hidden corners. During dinner, Harry, Martha's impressive and leonine chow chow, with his ruff of silky, shaggy fur, his cinnamon-colored coat, and his impressive purple-black tongue, lay on the floor near my feet. I reached down and scratched his head, feeling the contours of his skull.

Back in the kitchen, I commented on the beauty of the pots Martha was using, glazed clay pots of simple form with flat bases and flaring rims. And that is when she started talking, her words working on me like a spell. I listened to the stories of the pots that Martha and Andy had brought home from the Moroccan markets. I could smell the kabobs, hear the humming of traffic, see the stand of the potter who molded the soil into shapes, and then covered his creation with glazes of exotic traditions.

We sat at their beautiful kitchen table in front of the fireplace, and Martha and Andy took turns throughout the meal entertaining us with tales of their world travels, from Morocco to Japan to France. I told the story of my escape from Romania. My fiancé told the story of his service in Vietnam.

Having finished his surgical training in England, he had come to the United States for advanced training in cardiovascular surgery at the Mayo Clinic. The Vietnam conflict was still raging. Since the American military had an urgent need for surgical staff, he was called to service as soon as he arrived in the country. But he was determined to complete his advanced training and petitioned the local Selective Service Office in Rochester, Minnesota, for a deferment, vowing to volunteer for service in Vietnam as soon as his training was finished. To his amazement, the deferment was granted. As my fiancé explained that night, this great country had so much respect for individual preferences that it even respected someone who was not yet a citizen. Once he completed his surgical training, he went to Vietnam.

As we sat around their kitchen table in front of the fireplace with our empty dinner dishes, he said, "I had a premonition." What? I looked at this man I would soon marry, and I understood there is so much you cannot know about another human being.

"I had a premonition," he said, "that I would not come back alive. I ordered a handmade tuxedo so I could be buried properly, and packed it with my favorite book and a bottle of bourbon."

The room had fallen into a hush.

Then Martha spoke, her voice cracking the mood.

"Did you eat dog meat over there?" she asked.

The question jarred me. It was, at the very least, wildly out of context.

"Dog meat," Martha said again, her countenance cool, almost cruel, especially because she could see the pain in his eyes. She went on to explain how the Vietnamese have many culinary delights made with dog meat.

"And the dogs," she said, "are sometimes tortured before slaughter."

Andy then stepped in to save the evening. "Come," he said, breaking the awkward silence that followed, his voice the color of sun-thickened honey.

He led us from room to room, and suddenly the Stewarts were doing their duet again, charming us, enchanting us with stories of their travels, story after story, country after country, the whole globe, it seemed, spilling from their lips.

They showed us their dining room chandelier. As a discrete object, it surpassed loveliness. Yet for me that chandelier was a revelation not just because of its innate beauty, its stateliness and self-composure as it hung, so still, from the dining room ceiling, at once radiating light and at the same time drawing its glow back into its body. For me it was the Stewarts' showing off their chandelier that was inspiring.

The handsome crystal chandelier had been given to the couple by Andy's mother. Most people, upon pointing out a favored object in their home, would have simply communicated this shred of history and stopped there. But Martha, who began the story of the light, continued, standing in its hand-cut glass-and-crystal glow as she described the story of this light with obvious passion. With Martha pausing at points that seemed almost rehearsed so that Andy could step in and pick up the trailing root of her sentence, they told us why that particular fixture was absolutely appropriate for the historicity of their home. They had sought out the perfect fixture, bypassing hundreds of gorgeous chandeliers that were somehow not "quite right." The "right one" had to fit the original architecture of their 1805 colonial-style farmhouse and its elegant simplicity. It had to have a cast-bronze frame, and be magnificent but not very large, to suit the proportions of the dining room. It had to have a certain kind and quality of leaded crystals, prisms, and hand-blown bobeches. And behold, here it was.

We then came to a large oil painting hanging on their dining room wall. The Stewarts told the story of how they had found it in an antique gallery in France, how Martha had purchased it, only to then learn that the French government was loath to let them take it from France due to export laws that forbade cultural treasures and antiquities from being carried out of the country.

The fact that the Stewarts prevailed through what must have been an intense negotiation was testimony to their drive, and perhaps their canniness. They'd cleared all the obstacles and gone through the trouble and expense of shipping the painting across the Atlantic. They'd gone, if not through hell then certainly high water, to bring this eighteenth-century canvas to their walls, where it now hung center-stage, a statement for sure.

But what really surprised me was the subject of the picture itself: Jupiter, in the form of a cloud, embraces an ecstatic Io. The scene, copied from Correggio's *Jupiter and Io*, was inspired by Ovid's classic *Metamorphoses*, in which the god and philanderer Jupiter, hoping to hide his love affair from his ever-vigilant wife, turns the world to fog and mist, which then becomes the blanket for his and princess Io's illicit lovemaking. Io is clearly enraptured, her eyes fixed on her lover. Jupiter, having left his wife, comes down, feathery, to touch Io's glowing rosy flesh.

"I fell in love with the painting," Martha said, her voice oddly flat.

It was late now. Time to go home.

"Is it strange," I said as we got back into the car, "to make infidelity the focal point of your home with your husband?"

I don't remember his reply. We were tired. We were intrigued with our hosts, a bit wary but impressed, not only with Andy's vast oceans of knowledge but by their home and their flair.

And the dinner had been delicious.

2

Coming to America

ON THE DAY I met Martha, I'd been in this new country not even two years. In that short time, I had undergone a transformation from Romanian political refugee to biomedical engineer and mistress of a lovely home in Westport, Connecticut, one of New York's most exclusive suburbs. My fiancé and I had begun living together not long before our Memorial Day gathering. Our house was not typical of Westport. Built in the 1930s by the American ambassador to Italy, it was almost an ode to the magic of Tuscany; everything from its stucco arches to its sun room wall fountain exuded the romance of loggias and villages and Puccini's *Messa* under the domes of the world's most gorgeous churches. I was blessed. I'd come to the States with nothing but had wound up with a job I loved and a man I loved more, a handsome doctor, himself having emigrated from Poland some twenty years before. I felt I was living the quintessential if somewhat clichéd American Dream.

There was no traffic in Westport, no smoke or soot or subways. The houses, many of them anyway, had the kind of poshness only the really rich can afford. Westport was filled with two kinds of wealth:

the venture-capital kind and the more bohemian kind accrued by successful artists, filmmakers, and writers. The homes of the businessmen were very different from the homes of the artists, but they all had one thing in common: a lawn.

I had never seen one in Romania. We had grass, and it grew where it rightly should, in meadows or pastures or mountain crevasses, and we had patios or terraces made of veined slabs of stone. A lawn, a controlled and chemically treated fabric of green that unrolls from front steps to curb, tended to with fume-spewing, gas-guzzling, hellishly noisy machines—I found that very odd. But I would come to admire them and cultivate my own, despite the continuing ambivalence about the exorbitant environmental price we pay to enjoy their beauty.

I'm sure the elegance I was surrounded with was heightened by its stark contrast with my past.

I came to America in 1979 and watched through the 1980s as the country feasted on its wealth: me, Mariana, an escapee from a Communist country where a ripe apple or piece of fresh cheese had become as rare as rubies, or freedom. Here I learned what freedom could smell like. Freedom smelled like the popcorn in movie theaters showing any film you might like to see. Freedom smelled like a library book, on its inside cover a pasted tab stamped with dates suggesting all the hands that have held it. Freedom smelled like the glorious main branch of the New York Public Library on Fifth Avenue in Manhattan, with its muscular pillars and the starch-white statues of the guardian lions Patience and Fortitude, or like my small suburban library where the wood flooring preserved beneath the polyurethane glowed gold. I could read anything in America: books by Freud or Nabokov or Ionesco, or even *Communication with Extraterrestrial Intelligence* by Carl Sagan. My first years here, I devoured books like M&Ms.

I had escaped Communist Romania, but had to leave behind my entire family, my heritage, my friends, my loves, my life, the country where I had joyously played as a child in my grandfather's fields while the peasants labored, sometimes bringing us luscious wild strawberries gathered in the forest, a voluntary token of their respect for my grandfather.

The last kings of Romania were long gone by the time I was born. Land reforms of 1945 resulted in the confiscation of the aristocracy's lands, and King Michael abdicated under pressure from the Communists in 1947. I grew up thinking of the intelligentsia, often the children of the expropriated aristocracy, as being the nobility. In my schema, there were old noble families here, peasants over there, workers on the other side, gypsies at the outskirts of town. Not a perfect place, Romania, but it was my place. It was where I savored my mother's love, where I saw my first snow, blown by the winds that came from the Siberian plains and made our winters long and sharp as shards of glass. Romania has some of the only old-growth forests left on this planet, with towering trees and silver streams—a delicious surprise as they emerged from the carpet of thick moss when I hiked through the woods when I was twelve years old, with my sister and cousins on our way to sleep at the old stone monastery, where the monks chanted to a great god, in a great land, in a time before Communism came.

Communism did not come all at once, but rather like a fever, bit by bit. The primary objective of the Soviet-imposed Communist government that came to power in 1945 was to eliminate the opposition. The war contributed to the new government's successful accomplishment of this goal, as many of the old regime's ruling elite had either been killed in action or emigrated to the West. During World War II, the Axis armies marched across Romania, toward Russia, then after its defeat in the Battle of Stalingrad in the winter of 1942–1943, when the front turned, many of the surviving aristocracy left with the retreating German forces as the Red Army approached. Some escaped overseas, others got out through convoluted strategies, like my boyfriend Dan's parents did. His father had held a position in the Romanian government before 1945. Having just found out that she was carrying a child, Dan's mother, a medical doctor, convinced her husband not to take a chance at sharing the fate of his colleagues, but instead leave Bucharest with her to live in a remote village where no one knew them. Using her maiden name, she went to work at a faraway hospital, to which she commuted several hours every day via three different buses for the rest of her career. Many among the elite who stayed became political prisoners: writers, scientists, lawyers, priests, students, superior officers of the Royal Army and Air Force, and members of former political cabinets. The process was swift: false accusations, summary judgments, incarcerations, executions. Between 1945 and 1964, the number of political prisoners in Romania surpassed 1,000,000. It was common knowledge that the prisons for political detainees were planned and organized for slow and deliberate extermination through physical and psychological torture. By the time I was born, in 1953, most members of the intellectual and upper classes had been murdered or had gone missing, and the Communist government had confiscated houses, land, mills, farms, and forests.

Before I was born, my father worked in a coal mine for one year to "prove" his allegiance to the working class in whose name the Communists asserted their power. But in a veiled attempt to voice his pro-American position on the Cold War, my father named me, his firstborn, after the Mariana Islands, the place in the Pacific Ocean from where the Americans had deployed the atomic bomb. However, by the time the 1956 Hungarian revolution against the Russian occupation was bloodily smothered by Soviet tanks, my name was all that remained of my father's anti-Soviet protest. By then a family man responsible for his wife and two daughters, he had traded in ideological aspirations for survival, and became a member of the local Communist Party in order to secure a job commensurate with his professional qualifications. Yet we were still watched. When I took piano and ballet lessons in elementary school, my father was reprimanded for it, and told he should put more emphasis on teaching me conformity. Throughout my childhood, there were arrests, killings, political detentions, or deportations of those resisting nationalization, expropriation, forced collectivization, crop and livestock requisitions. When collectivization was finished in 1962, the impounding of horses began, by which the animals were seized from their owners, brutally killed, cut up, and fed mostly to pigs. Millions of horses were murdered, as the noble equines represented to the Communist government the old, feudal way of life.

For much of the 1950s, however, it was still possible to find a privately owned store, and one might still have a housekeeper if one called her "comrade." My grandfather was able to retain part of his farmland in the historical Romanian province of Moldavia near the eastern Carpathian Mountains. I looked forward all year to spending summers with my grandparents at the old family compound, and riding in my grandfather's phaeton—a carriage as glamorous as a royal coach, dark green with tan leather upholstery and brass fittings—going with him when he brought food to the peasants who worked his wheat fields. Then came the summer when I was told that we no longer had a carriage, or horses, or crops in the field, or peasants to feed.

"But they are ours. Why don't you get them back?" I asked.

"A great man once said that if a donkey kicks you, it would be silly to kick it in return," my grandfather replied in that tone adults used when much more was on their minds but they did not want to tell us what it was.

Ideological indoctrination, which emphasized conformity and anti-individualism, encompassed all aspects of life, dictating correct behavior in everything from dress to personal beliefs, and was systematically imposed through the education system. It formally began at age nine, with political and patriotic training in Pioneers, and continued during high school and university, with compulsory membership in the Union of Communist Youth and enforced extracurricular activities. We were required to study interpretations of Marxism-Leninism that served the Romanian political agenda ordered by the Communist Party's Central Committee and articulated through the endless pronouncements of demagogical speeches delivered by the country's tyrant president, Ceausescu.

All publishing and media were nationalized and operated under strict control by the state, which decreed that all art and journalism must be rendered with a Marxist-Leninist perspective, and denounced the "polluting" impact of "Western propaganda." Radio Free Europe was deemed illegal for its "corrupting" messages, but I was highly influenced by the informative cultural commentaries by journalist Monica Lovinescu as I developed a passion for politics and freedom.

When I was accepted into the highly selective program of Mathematics Informatics at the University of Bucharest, and the extremely competitive Academy of International Relations, my parents were proud of me, yet they tried to dissuade me from going to study in Bucharest. Like parents the world over, they feared the nefarious effect a metropolitan city might have on their child. Bucharest filled my mind and fueled my desires. It was in Bucharest that I planned my escape.

All college classes were dictated by Communist curricula, and I refused to learn those lessons. Instead, I fell in love with a beautiful boy named Dan, who shared my love of music, literature, theater, the bold primitivism of Gauguin, the stylized figures of Brancusi and Modigliani, and generally subscribed to Chekhov's opinion that "there is nothing more awful, insulting, and depressing than banality."

Dan was doing his residence training in psychiatry at a well-known hospital in Bucharest. The official state doctrine condemned psychoanalysis, but it was still practiced, as long as it was disguised by the innocuous name of psychotherapy. We were desperate to get our hands on anything written by Freud or Jung, who were banned along with almost every other Western great, devouring and discussing these forbidden volumes as a prelude to our lovemaking.

We could hardly wait to find each other's arms at the end of the day, after Dan parted with his patients and I walked away from classrooms and notebooks. We went out to eat every night, then for a walk, talking late into the night, never in a hurry. Somehow, we had time for everything. Most of our favorite restaurants were old establishments in elegant downtown Bucharest, places where artists, writers, journalists gathered in a casual, party-like atmosphere.

On the chilly evening of March 4, 1977, Dan and I went out for dinner at the Berlin Restaurant, a vibrant meeting place for Bucharest's bohemian community, for our favorite, Wiener schnitzel. Suddenly, the entire place was trembling: people, tables, silverware, porcelain, the walls and the ceiling. Someone called out: "Earthquake!"

Dan lifted me off the ground and moved us away from under the heavy crystal chandelier. The elegant-looking crowd began a stampede down the stairs toward the front door. "We are not meant to die like this," Dan said, and smiled with that wonderful kindness of his. Bracing each other, Dan and I withstood the pushing and shoving of the crowd, as the cracking sounds grew louder and louder and the building shook violently up and down and side to side. We learned later that the earthquake, which lasted for seventy seconds, registered 7.2 on the Richter scale. When it stopped, we were among a handful of people standing inside the restaurant among fragments of fine porcelain and crystal sparkling in the light of an ominously huge, blood orange, full moon that shone through the broken windows. We made our way outside to a horrifying spectacle of ruins, sirens, screams, and unrecognizable city streets veiled in a dusty, murky light. More than fifteen hundred people died, more than eleven thousand were wounded, and thirty-three of Bucharest's historic buildings collapsed. The total damage was estimated at more than $2 billion.

One evening a few months later, we were walking the cobblestone streets of downtown Bucharest when we ran into an old acquaintance of mine from the university, an architectural student. He was missing his right arm and a piece of his left ear, and he looked very thin. As we found out, he had tried to escape by swimming across the Danube to Yugoslavia through the rapids near Iron Gates—gorges whose waters were so treacherous that fewer patrol squads walked their banks—when a Romanian sentry spotted him from a tower on the limestone cliffs and began shooting. Hit in the arm, he continued to swim, hoping to be taken prisoner by the Serb border patrols on the other side. Instead, they gave him back to the Romanians.

My friend was arrested, joining the ranks of political detainees estimated to have numbered by then between half a million and two million people. Before the secret police agents shoved him in the back of a filthy van to be taken to the Department of State Security, also known as the Securitate, for interrogation, they used him as a human punching bag. A bloody mess, but having survived the grilling at the station—which many did not—he was taken to prison, where the torture continued. Every day, he said, they came to interrogate him.

His arm began to swell with gangrene, the bullet still lodged inside. He was isolated in a cage in a cavernous subterranean corridor chained to a ring fixed to the stone floor, without clothes on his body or shoes on his feet. He was obligated to stand up day and night because, at intervals, and without warning, salt water filled up the cavern to the height of his chin. When he realized that he wasn't going to be given medical treatment for the arm, he conned one of his torturers by daring him to cut his arm above the gangrene and burn his flesh at the cut. Which the brute did. The "surgery," as he called it, healed without infection.

Over time, my friend pretended to go insane, and began calling the rats that crawled through his cage by human names, holding long conversations with them when he knew he was being watched. He petted the rats, even as they nibbled at his ear, and fed them from his meager food ration. He made a big fuss about one of the rats going missing and accused his persecutors of having stolen his friend. He was eventually released, a warning to others who thought of attempting to escape the country.

A while after that encounter, Dan made a generous offer. We'd get married and I would go to medical school. Later, if I still wanted to leave, I would have a profession to count on. But by then, I was being targeted myself by the secret police.

In January 1977, a civic initiative known as Charter 77 of Prague was organized in Czechoslovakia. It called for respect of the Soviet pledge to permit exercise of "human rights," per the 1975 Helsinki Agreements between the USSR and the United States. Among the

Charter 77 organizers was Václav Havel, the playwright who two decades later became the first president of the post-Communist Czech Republic.

On February 10, Radio Free Europe read an open letter of solidarity with Charter 77, written by the writer Paul Goma. He was the leader of a nonviolent dissident movement in Romania known as *The Goma Movement for Respect of Human Rights*, which publicly condemned the regime's violations of human rights. Among the intellectuals who signed the appeal were two doctors, Dr. Ion Vianu, who was Dan's supervisor at the hospital where he worked, and Dr. Ion Ladea, who was our friend, a charismatic renaissance man with an amazing mind and a long history of political detention for his antiestablishment outspokenness. Ladea's letter of support, addressed to Paul Goma, was read by Radio Free Europe on March 17.

On April 1, Goma was arrested and detained as a political prisoner, as well as denigrated for his alleged indifference to the disaster that faced the nation after the earthquake. In response to pressure from an international campaign that included intervention from President Jimmy Carter, Goma was freed from prison and went into exile in France. Dr. Vianu was subjected to public abuse, dismissed from his professional positions, and his young son, a student, was assaulted by a Securitate agent on school premises. Dr. Ladea was detained and endured a savage beating by his interrogators. When he was released, I lent him my apartment until he recovered while I stayed at a friend's house.

I knew, of course, that by giving Ion shelter I was putting myself at great risk. If not everyone was aware of the horrors to which people were subjected during political arrest it was because most of the detainees never came back. But I had already met my university friend who was the living proof of what happened. However, I believed in the cause of Goma's movement for human rights, I understood Ladea's support for Goma, and I admired his principles. To help him I was willing to defy the law and the government and the possible consequences.

Shortly after that, the secret police began to follow me. At the beginning they were just shadows, never revealing their faces. Then, for a while, they stopped, so I thought they had decided to leave me alone. Judging by Radio Free Europe reports, the Securitate had more important things on their hands. In August, 35,000 miners went on strike to protest food shortages and new regulations that forced older workers to retire with reduced benefits. On November 18, in Paris, there was an assassination attempt on Radio Free Europe's Monica Lovinescu, which left her in a coma.

By the fall of 1978, the secret police were no longer shadows following me. They had become more brazen and their faces became familiar. I knew that they could appear at my door any moment of the day or night, search my home, and find incriminating evidence, each item carrying a separate sentence: American dollars, foreign books and magazines, clothes with foreign labels, undeclared luxuries that brought some sparkle to the drab days, perfumes that came from flowers in foreign lands.

I was twenty-five years old in February 1979, when I visited my childhood home one last time to tell my parents about my imminent plans to leave. To protect them, I gave few details. They did not reproach me but the sadness in my mother's eyes and the piercing looks I got from my dad betrayed their suspicion that I might not be telling them the whole truth. Although they knew me well enough to guess that nothing would have changed my mind, my parents, of course, were worried. Over the years, they had acclimated themselves to their country, with its impositions, limitations, and straightforward brutality. They would never have considered running away from the land of their ancestors. But they came to terms with the fact that I wanted to live my own life.

As a child, before Communism had gained such force, I would dance around my mother, whose face was faded from fatigue, and whose mouth was full of pins she plucked out one by one, fixing the hem of some beautiful dress she was making. A manager of the local fashion salon and a homemaker, my mother worked two jobs and knew rest, if at all, as something she read about in the novels she devoured in the snatches of time between her stitches and her cooking.

Food, which permeated all aspects of our family life, was filled with hearty family recipes, saucy and mouthwatering, exuding intoxicating aromas of a pinch of this, a dash of that, and a lot of love. The indulgence of sweet desserts was vital, fragrant rose-petal preserves, froth-topped Turkish coffee bubbling in the hand-hammered brass-and-copper *ibrik*. My mother, despite her love of cooking, had refused to teach me the domestic arts, since she believed they brought subservience to women. "If you know how to make coffee," she would say, "it's enough to get married!"

"You'll live to regret raising a daughter who's outspoken and can't cook!" my father would say, half-joking. "Who'd marry her?"

I tried to take in the sounds and smells of our family home. With my parents' hospitality, my mother's superb cooking and my father's delicious wines, life had seemed like a continuous celebration, with ad-hoc parties of friends and relatives, just as it was on that last day, even though food was scarce and we now lived off the black market.

Protected from the cold by her beautiful paisley shawl, my grandmother had come outside with me to watch the last rays of sun warm up the wintry sky. By the way she stood, it seemed she knew that those were likely to be the last moments we'd ever spend together. Yet, besides the essential bit I shared with my parents, I couldn't spill the secrets of my escape to my grandmother or anyone else close to me. One doesn't have to live behind the Iron Curtain to understand that the less others know about one's crime, the better it is for them.

In an effort to squeeze in every moment of time with me, my mother accompanied me on the evening train back to Bucharest. My parents and I decided that my father had to stay behind and keep the party going, pretending to pay no more attention to my departure than usual. I was to send home a telegram from the Vienna train station. The mere fact of receiving it would let my parents know that I had succeeded while its content would reinforce their claim of not having known about my plans to flee the country. We knew that a few days later the secret police would call my parents for interrogation and accuse them of not having snitched on me, which was the legal obligation of every Romanian citizen. I knew that the authorities would declare me a "traitor to the motherland."

I BRIBED MY way onto a three-day group tour traveling to Budapest, the capital of Hungary, where a non-Romanian friend of mine and I arranged to meet. Our agreement included my also paying for her travel expenses, which incorporated the price of train fare from Bucharest to Vienna, via Budapest. It was, in fact, a two-way ticket—an extra expense that I deliberately incurred thinking it would make my cover story more convincing, since I would be the one to continue the trip from Budapest to Vienna on that ticket. I was to leave Budapest with her passport, which had her picture and stated that my brown eyes were blue. My friend, who also added her student ID to my travel document package, was supposed to go to the police station in Budapest, or to her country's consulate, where she would declare her documents lost or stolen once my train had reached Vienna.

On a Friday in mid-February 1979, after resolving some unexpected glitches in our plan, I parted with my friend and rushed to catch the last train to Vienna. I had to leave my luggage behind in the hotel room in order to allay the suspicions of my roommate from the group tour. I had only a large tote handbag and the clothes on my back, which, except for the Hermès scarf given to me by my grandmother, were not much different from what other European girls of my age wore at that time: lightly starched white cotton shirt, tight Italian jeans, knee-high, black stiletto-heeled leather boots, a wool-and-silk foulard, and a car-length shearling jacket.

Once on the train, I'd barely sat down before the compartment door opened and a man in uniform said something to me in Hungarian. I could not understand a word but, given his polite demeanor and the ornate uniform, I presumed he was taking orders for the restaurant car. I smiled and said, in French, "Thank you. I don't want anything."

I could not make out his answer. I looked inquisitively at the elderly gentleman who sat next to me, and he said, in German: "Papers."

I pulled the train ticket out of my handbag and gave it to the man in uniform. His face began to harden and his voice climbed a few octaves. Confused, I again solicited my neighbor for help. He told me that I was being asked to show my passport. So I did. The man in uniform, who was, in fact, a border guard, opened it. I did not need to understand his words in order to know why his voice was thundering inside the small compartment, but I pretended not to comprehend what was going on and kept asking the frightened old gentleman to translate.

Two large men posted themselves on each side of the officer's small frame, blocking the door to our compartment. I kept my eyes on my neighbor's face as he interpreted the requests for me to stand up, open my bags, and show another picture ID. I answered the officer's passport questions by reciting the data I had memorized in the taxi on the way to the train station. The elderly man's expression seemed to tell me that I was crazy to not accept the writing on the wall, but, as he kept translating, I had the impression that he wanted me to succeed.

I insisted that I was the person on the passport, and looked only at the kind Hungarian gentleman, grateful for the excuse to avoid direct confrontation with the guard. As his voice took on a nastier and nastier tone, I stopped listening and tuned him out, concentrating on the prayer I kept saying in my mind, asking God to save me. The shouting border guard and his giant companions eventually left our compartment.

Remembering that my Romanian identity card was hidden in a zippered pocket of my handbag, I went to the restroom at the end of the corridor and locked myself inside. Once alone, I could no longer restrain the torrent of tears. I worked a pair of nail scissors through the letters of my name, my place and date of birth, and the trusting smile on my photo.

I was back in the compartment, reading, when I realized that the train had not been moving for a while. Through the glass panes of the compartment door, I could make out a train station, so I walked out and found a space between the bodies of people standing in the corridor. I looked out on a crowd of people swarming the platform, and had to bite my lip to hold back a scream at the sight of soldiers hitting civilians with the stock of their guns, pushing them toward the station building. Some were being dragged. I saw the disbelief on a woman's face as her hand, which held what appeared to be banknotes, was struck with the butt of a gun. A young man was rolling on the ground, a trickle of blood slipping from the corner of his mouth. An angry-faced uniformed man kept kicking the fallen body with his boot.

Suddenly, the train gave a little shudder and began to move. I kept watching as the scene at the station disappeared into the distance.

Occupied with abusing the people on the station platform, the border patrol had let me slip by. Although I would never know them, I owe these people, who were to suffer countless acts of brutality for having sought their own freedom, my life.

I watched as the train approached the silhouette of what appeared to be some kind of crisscrossed fence made of spindly tree trunks. When we got nearer, I thought I saw barbed wire. The train slowed down a bit as it chugged through a gap. Tears ran down my face as I thought of the millions of people condemned to live and die as prisoners of Communism, held back by that flimsy-looking fence.

I got off the train in Vienna. Like most Czechoslovakians, Bulgarians, East Germans, Hungarians, Poles, Romanians, and Russians who escaped from behind the Iron Curtain, I knew nothing of what a person was supposed to do as a fresh escapee. I saw three young Yugoslavian men who had been in the corridor watching the horrific scenes of abuse at that last station in Hungary with me. They were the only people I knew in the West, and the first people I confided in about my escape. They were shocked, but they helped. One of them called a friend who said I should go to the police for foreigners. Another came with me to send a telegram to my parents. He offered me his arm to lean on, which I gratefully took because my knees were shaking.

After a weekend inside the Red Cross facility at the train station, I was taken with several others to the Traiskirchen Refugee Camp, which came as a shock. I was not aware that the moment I touched Western soil I had first to become a refugee before I could become an émigré.

In the camp, they took my vitals. I was measured, weighed, made to undress and dress, photographed front and profile, my manicured hands smeared with dark ink for fingerprints. Then I was given an aluminum bowl and cup, and a spoon.

I would remain there for six months.

I found the lumps in my breast while in the camp. I saw the camp physician, who, after a quick examination, gave me a pass that entitled me to leave the grounds, which were guarded day and night by uniformed men with guns, and go into Vienna to the city's large free clinic. There, inside an examination room, surrounded by the guttural sounds of German, I was instructed to unbutton my shirt. A shadow passed over the specialist's face when he had examined me.

"Must be taken out," he said to me.

"You mean an operation?" I asked.

"Immediately."

The specialist was staring at me. In that moment I saw all the "operations" of the recent German past, plus piles of shoes and combs and bones.

"No!" I said, and pulled away. I buttoned up my shirt. "No operations!" The specialist looked surprised, so much so that I felt guilty for what I had just thought. But *No* it was.

The pass allowed me to wander the streets of Vienna with some freedom, and I did, thinking all the while of the cancer I feared was growing inside me. I went to the Belvedere Museum to see Gustav Klimt's "The Kiss." It made me feel lonely. I thought of Dan, my friends, my family, our home, and Grandfather's favorite horse, Lucina, the beautiful mare with a large white star on her forehead. I went looking for the Winter Riding School's Lipizzaner horses, born with dark coats that turn snow-white with time. If only I could see these pure white horses, I might somehow become pure too, free of any illness. I found them at the Training Arena and watched eight noble stallions perform stylized walks and canters, show off their Spanish steps, dance pirouettes, and make dramatic leaps to the sounds of Bizet's "L'Arlésienne Suite."

I continued to use the medical pass to take trips to Vienna. One morning at the beginning of August, as I was getting ready to leave the camp, four uniformed men appeared before me. I was suddenly, without explanation, escorted to an imposing flight of stairs inside the camp headquarters. At the top, a well of shadow turned out to be a dark door opening into a large attic room. Inside, a man sat at a long desk in semidarkness, his desk lamp illuminating a sheaf of paper.

"Approach," he said.

The man stood up and shook my hand across the desk. He announced, "You are leaving on a transport to America on August 9."

It was August 6. Three days until I turned twenty-six. Happy birthday to me! For three straight days I heard the sound of singing.

I could have chosen to remain in Europe. I was a political refugee, and the Austrian government had granted me asylum in their country, so I could have settled down, gotten a job, and made a living in Vienna or thereabouts, not far from my family and friends in Romania. But my instinct told me that as an immigrant in Western Europe I would always be a second-class citizen. Only in America, it seemed, could I live on equal footing with all her citizens, who are or were all immigrants, too. Thus I was flying to "Oh beautiful for spacious skies for amber waves of grain" with a ticket funded by Amnesty International, money I promised to pay back as soon as I could. (And I did.)

Seven hours later, I landed at Kennedy Airport, where I was greeted by my sponsor, Constantin, who had agreed to host me for a year. He picked me up at baggage claim and we were off. The car sped over the roadways and highways, carrying me to his home in Connecticut, where he lived with his wife, Wanda, and their two small children, Valerie and Simon. Hello, America.

I passed my first few weeks in America in a state of what felt like limbo. *What had I done?* Even my taste buds were confused. When Constantin and Wanda took me out to eat, I ordered a frappe expecting a *café frappé*, an iced coffee drink that my friends and I often savored at elegant patisserie-brasseries of Bucharest, where it was topped with a two-inch-thick layer of froth and served in tall, chilled glasses. The milkshake I received clogged the straw, and, although embarrassed to be wasteful, I left it on the table, not even one-quarter done.

Wanda was, like me, an uprooted city girl, living in the Connecticut suburbs, a long way away from theater, concerts, dance floors, and art galleries. We spoke French, smoked cigarettes, and drank coffee. She seemed to like my company; I found her presence reassuring, and was grateful for the things she taught me. As I struggled to understand what it was that caused me such existential angst those first few weeks in America, my despair so odd since it came when my deepest wish was granted, Wanda explained that shopping is therapy, so we should go to the mall.

Wanda, who was from Toronto, thought that watching soap operas with her would help me learn English. And it sort of did. The soaps had given her ideas about how to decorate an American home, and make her table look pretty. Wanda cooked a meal for each day of the week, so every Thursday was tuna casserole. She used a lot of ingredients but, somehow, the foods smelled and tasted so different from those in my mother's kitchen. If Martha had been known then, Wanda would not have had to search so hard, and she'd have had many options, through Martha's decorating and cooking books, magazines, and television shows, to learn how to make her home prettier and her food taste better.

Trying to find my way, I collected all the possible clues about American life. Not long after I arrived, Wanda invited me to the beach. I dutifully donned my bathing suit, determined to enjoy the surf on this side of the Atlantic. I came out of my bedroom, shorts on, the top portion of my bathing suit securely tied around my neck and back.

"Mariana," she said upon seeing me, near panic in her voice. "Your bathing suit. Your . . . bikini—"

"What is it?" I asked. "What is wrong?"

She blurted out, "Youcannotwearabikiniatthisbeach."

No bikini? At that moment I thought that she was telling me my bikini was wrong because in America one did not wear bathing suits on the beach. I thought this, perhaps, because in Romania many beaches were informally divided into areas where people wore bathing suits and areas for people who preferred nudity.

"Good. I can't stand wearing a bathing suit, and having to check all the time, making sure you are not peeking out of it," I said to her, reaching up to loosen the neck-knot of my bikini in anticipation of taking it off when we reached the beach.

"Listen, Mariana," she said, her hand held out like a policeman, the white flash of her palm pressing on me despite the distance. "In America we do not go *na-ked* in public places."

Tears stung the edges of my eyes. "I'm sorry," I said.

And I was.

I couldn't help but feel a pang of guilt thinking that the family and friends I had left behind would sooner or later become faded memories. I could not contact them for the rest of my life. They could no longer risk knowing me. Correspondence from abroad was censored in Romania. The smallest trace of communication between us would have been used to compromise or even imprison them. The realization that my life was to forever happen in places where I knew no one and about which I knew nothing was starting to dawn on me.

It was on a Sunday that August that I began to unravel the roots of my initial bewilderment upon my arrival in the States. That was when I went to church for the first time in America.

"E-piscopal," Wanda enunciated. "Anglican."

"Oh! The Church of England. Henry the Eighth . . . " I was full of anticipation. I expected that in church I would be transported back to the land I had lost with my exile.

The exterior of the building was fieldstone and wood. The church's stark interior did not smell of holy oil and myrrh. The choir was accompanied not by an actual organ but by a boom box only half-hidden in the shadows. The priest wore a white collar and black cassock but no caftan, no priestly robes embroidered with symbols, no vestments draping over his shoulders, no monastic hat. I tried my best to follow, but the arrangement seemed to only further deepen what was already my impressive alienation. The priest's English words were lost on me, and with no Greek or Latin being spoken during mass, no chanting of "Thrice Holy," which, according to Byzantine Rite, opens the Eastern Orthodox prayers, I didn't even realize that the service had started.

But Father Loring proved to be an unusually gifted listener, and I learned, or confirmed, that faith and connection do not depend on icons or architecture. He spoke about many issues with me, and reminded me to reflect on the meaning of grace. He helped me through an English version of Kierkegaard's *Fear and Trembling*, as well as that philosopher's definition of faith: a willingness to go forward in the face of despair.

When the question of where I was from came up, it was Mrs. Loring who asked me, so gently and politely that it was easy to talk about myself. I didn't feel like an exotic beast as I sometimes did when strangers, on hearing my accent, demanded a recital of my life story while I would never dream of grilling them about theirs.

Father Loring also did me the more secular but equally important favor of introducing me to a group of people he thought I might like and with whom it would be easy to communicate since many of them spoke French and German and all knew Latin. He told me they belonged to a club called MENSA. I had no idea about the club's association with supposed "genius." Had I known this, I would never have gone, for I am as close to genius as Einstein was to stupidity. But the people in the MENSA group reminded me of my university days in Bucharest, and being in their presence was more salve than I could possibly say. Day by day, colors came out of hiding, streaks of pink, caramel yellows, the sun setting on Manhattan's smoggy skyline, igniting the skyscrapers. I started, slowly, to see.

As my spirit returned to me, so did my desire for education. I wanted to go to school. Instead of spending years negotiating with the Romanian government to get my college credits transferred, I decided that I would start all over and matriculate as a freshman.

"You cannot possibly pass the entrance exam. You can't speak English," my sponsor said to me.

I finally convinced him to let me try. He took me to the exam at a local community college. The fact that I passed was due entirely to my knowledge of the universal language of math and science and my ability to decode written English by relying on Latinate roots. I had no idea how impoverished was my background knowledge of American culture and history, but I moved forward unafraid.

At school I studied hard and well, learning English in addition to many computer languages, at which I was quick and adept. Less than one year into my curriculum, I was offered a job by Cadbury Schweppes, writing computer code for cost/profit analyses, and I dropped out. The money allowed me to leave my sponsor's home and to move closer to my job, which meant farther from New York City and the cultural opportunities I coveted. I lived in a bland apartment building with wall-to-wall carpeting the color of masking tape. I learned that without culture one loses one's dreams, and without one's dreams, one dies, or starts to. I began to believe I would never achieve for myself the laughing, loving family I had always expected I would have. I could not imagine finding a man in America with whom I could fall in love.

Since the job came with health insurance, I had no excuse for not seeing a doctor and confirming what I had been told by the doctor in Vienna. I made the appointment.

The doctor's office was in New Haven, a college town with theaters, concerts, great bookstores, good restaurants, and beautiful New England architecture. I'd bought myself a gas-guzzling Oldsmobile with my work money, and, stepping out of it after maneuvering it in what could be called "parallel parking" only out of kindness, I immediately felt cheered by the street life. Students were walking to and fro, dangling their book bags, too immersed in talk to see me and so swerving around me, saying, "Oh sorry!" before plunging back into Proust or physics. I stood on the sidewalk and watched them, the doctor's address crumpled in my hand. A kind of longing uncoiled inside me, and with it a voice: *Mariana, you do not want to die.*

I found the doctor's office and climbed the flight of stairs thinking about the men and women who had marched through fears worse than even this, marched with guns at their heads, mumbling their Baudelaire before the Romanian Communists shot them dead. They had gone down, so we heard, their heads held high even as the stems of their necks crumpled. What was this compared to *that*?

The doctor was an elderly man with palms as clean and dry as talc. I had expected machines, probes, test tubes spinning serum as cells were sucked up through a straw, but there was none of that. I lay on the table, he pressed on my chest, and said, "Nothing. Mariana, you are fine."

I sat up. "FINE?" I pressed my own chest, my fingers finding their way to the nodules.

"You need not check up on yourself like that," the doctor said, turning from me and starting to wash his hands in the sink.

"I assumed—"

"Don't assume anything. You should," he said, as if reading my mind, "lead a normal life."

I nodded. He nodded back.

"I had given up," I said, "on living a normal life. On finding a man with whom to have a family. Men in America . . . the good ones I met are either married or old," I said, and then stopped, recognizing that I was speaking, after all, to an American man, elderly and probably married.

"Can you help me?" I said. I had never really explicitly asked for help before, and now, having done it, I realized what an intimate and cherished act it was. I told him how my life's mission was to study biomedical engineering and make a social contribution. I told him this all in one swift garble, and as I spoke I knew that the words were true.

He found me a volunteer job in the ER at Saint Vincent's Hospital in New Haven, and my world opened up. Suddenly I was surrounded by fiercely intelligent people, dedicated to a cause. Many of the young doctors were fresh from Yale, as were the interns and the social workers, a lot of whom I met as I ran through the rooms holding bags filled with fresh cells or blood. I met a Romanian doctor who introduced me to his fiancée and their friends, and when a paying position at a nearby Connecticut hospital came up, the Romanian doctor cut out the ad, which led me to make the phone call which led to the interview which led to my first job in the United States as a biomedical engineer. I fell in love with that job, because it offered me the opportunity to begin a life in America, worthy of the risks I took when I escaped from behind the Iron Curtain.

And now, as a biomedical engineer at that Connecticut hospital, when I got up and dressed for work, it was with some of the flair I had had in Romania. While I had little money, I bought a few fine things. I was doing serious work at the hospital, and thus earned the high praise of my medical manager, so I tried to ignore it when my technical manager would pull his chair too close to mine. However, the way he let his eyes land in the barely visible cleft between my breasts instead of on the pages of Fourier analyses annoyed me, especially since he insisted that I teach him those intricate math formulas coded into complicated lines of computer language.

And then came the day when the lechery became too much. I stood up and kicked back the rolling office chair. "Learn Fourier analysis yourself," I said, and walked out.

Lucky for me, the elevator was there. I stepped in, only to find myself face to face with a doctor I had seen in the hallways.

"Helloooo," he said, as the doors slid shut.

"Hello," I said curtly, and then I turned to look at the panel.

He kept talking, all friendly and confident. The doctor was handsome and had a comma of blood near the neck of his surgical scrubs under his white coat. He told me he was a vascular surgeon, and while I knew this meant cutting open a human body to repair the blood vessels, I pictured him holding a human heart in his hands. He asked for my number. I felt a mix of interest and dislike, for he was as cocky as he was persistent. I agreed to a dinner, three weeks hence, and was surprised when the meal turned out to be home-cooked. We ate that night while listening to Brahms's Piano Concerto no. 1 in D Minor. I didn't think of Bucharest. I just listened to Brahms, the long opening movement, the descending line, and felt at home.

I met him in January 1981. By April, we had a puppy and were living together in his Westport home, and by May I had fine-tuned a fresh pesto recipe and was sufficiently settled to host a Memorial Day weekend celebration.

3

Martha, Matron of Honor

DURING THE FIRST two years of our friendship with the Stewarts, Martha and I were still eyeing each other from a distance. Meanwhile, Andy opened his arms wide and welcomed my fiancé and me into their world; his energy, kindness, and intelligence drew us in. We'd sit around the table by the fireplace in the lovely Turkey Hill kitchen that would become Martha's laboratory for all her business ventures, tasting Martha's cooking and talking late into the night. We talked about our desires and ambitions. We looked at the world through the Stewarts' eyes and their amazing attention to details. Andy's knowing observations about spices—he'd acquired his great palate from being exposed, as a child, to the exquisite delicacies of the grand restaurants of the world—made it clear to me that I was lacking information in a very important area, and I was eager to learn more.

My friendship with Andy was strengthened by very subtle shared traits, like the desire for connectedness with the world by which every living experience has an artistic quality that evokes a whole gamut of nuanced feelings.

When Andy told a story, I always found something in it that fascinated me. He told us about their trip to Japan, and how they came back inspired to turn the bathroom in their barn into a serene, Japanese-like bath, a place to relax and rejuvenate. While he showed us the deeply sunken rectangular bathtub with a built-in seat so the bather could soak in neck-high water, Andy described the etiquette of Japanese bathing in natural *onsen* hot springs. He explained how that custom is connected to rituals of Buddhist cleansing and to the *sento* of the Japanese public bath, an experience sought out for its pleasant respite from the pressures of daily life. Andy told us about sixteenth-century Japanese feudal lords who created a new type of castle architecture— fortresses that were opulent in décor and so expansive in scale, they were town-castles. But their warring lifestyle left those town-castles in ruins by the beginning of the 1600s, and during the following two and a half centuries of the refined Edo period, when Japan was closed to foreigners for about a hundred years, the new shoguns built castles impressive not in size but luxuries, with lavish decorations, lacquered bathing rooms, and tea-ceremony houses overlooking scenic gardens where plum trees and azaleas blossomed in the spring, and autumns were colored cinnabar by Japanese maple trees. And I wanted to go there and experience those ancient ruins. My fiancé shared my wanderlust but I knew that his emotional response to old monuments and temples and ruins was not as strong as mine, or as Andy's.

Nor did Martha seem to share our "pleasure of ruins," to borrow from Rose Macauley's book of the same name. I liked Martha from the start, but she would not have been my first choice of company for traveling to an exotic place. In fact, when it came to Martha, my instincts warned me toward caution. What gave me pause the most was that, after having lived and worked in Westport for about ten years before we met, Martha seemed to have very few friends, especially for a mother who had raised a child in the suburbs. Or perhaps it was because of her tendency to talk only to men. One of my best friends would often joke about this trait of Martha's, which amused but also annoyed her. A superbly talented decorator, my friend and her husband owned a beautiful 1930s waterfront stone house, which they renovated and decorated with the best of French Provincial antiques and tapestries. Each time they invited her to a party, Martha would compliment the husband on some superb detail, even though she knew it was my friend who was responsible for choosing and incorporating the element into their house.

Yet, when we were just the four of us together, I felt completely at ease. We all loved nature, hiking, cross-country skiing, bicycling, theater, music. As we saw a lot of each other, our friendship as couples became very close. I remember the four of us reading Robertson Davies's *Deptford Trilogy* at the same time and realizing that we were all attracted to Jungian ideas like those conveyed in *The Manticore*. We discussed magic energies, subatomic physics, Eastern mysticism, psychology, collective unconscious. I never felt the slightest discomfort in asking Andy a question, no matter how ignorant that might have made me appear. I trusted him as much as I might have trusted a brother.

We often went to the movies as a foursome and discussed what we saw at great length. Movies provided Martha and me with the opportunity to communicate without words. I later read Neil Gabler's book *Life: The Movie*, and came to believe we shared what I thought of as a "Life: The Movie" syndrome, in which the screen influenced our real life so that, without consciously knowing we were doing it, we sometimes conspired together with gestures and language we'd picked up from a movie or a book.

Sometimes I tried to decipher Martha's true feelings through what she said about a given movie. She once said that one of her old favorites was *Black Orpheus*, a 1959 retelling of the Orpheus and Eurydice myth set in Rio de Janeiro during Carnaval. I couldn't help but wonder if Martha yearned for the kind of husband who loved his wife so much that he would be willing to descend to Hell to bring her back despite the terrifying certainty that by doing so he will face unlimited horror. But mostly, Martha was inscrutable to me in the early days, and no matter how much I tried, I could not quite figure her out. One incident about six months into our friendship had been especially perplexing.

The four of us were coming back from celebrating my fiancé's birthday in New York City. Andy was driving. It was a rainy, unpleasantly cold mid-November night, the sky split with the occasional jagged line of lightning, the windshield wipers squealing the whole way. Just as we got on the exit ramp toward home, we felt an altered rhythm to the ride, and Andy pulled over to the side of the road. The tire was flat.

Andy and my fiancé got out of the car to change the tire. Each time lightning struck, I could see them working out there in the dark. I worried they would get sick, with that freezing rain beating down on them. When Martha lowered her window, I thought she shared my concern. But to my dismay, her harsh, raspy voice roared above the rumbling thunderstorm and the noisy highway, berating Andy for not changing the tire fast enough, for keeping her waiting when she was tired and wanted to go home. Andy, like a swan under deluge, stood still and unfazed, not letting her torrent of insults ruffle his feathers.

"Take off your coat!" Martha screeched. "I just paid *six hundred dollars* for that coat. You are ruining it already."

That's when Andy finally raised his eyes from the tire and for a brief moment he looked at her, his face empty of expression, his eyes reflecting nothing but the headlights from a passing car.

THAT NIGHT CAME as such an unpleasant surprise that had it not been for Andy we might have never wanted to visit Turkey Hill again. But we liked Andy very much, so we continued to see each other, as couples.

For our second Christmas together, Martha gave me a copy of her book *Entertaining* as a gift. She had inscribed it, *For Mariana, Be Entertaining Always. I love you, Martha*, in her childlike script. Although *Be Entertaining Always* was her standard signature message for that book, it was the first time Martha said "I love you."

Andy and Martha also gave me Timothy Ferris's *Galaxies*, published by Andy's company, Stewart, Tabori & Chang, earlier that year. It had stunning photographs and excellent descriptions of the stellar universe. I remember unwrapping the present and opening the big, beautiful book on my lap. The Christmas tree was lit in blues, reds, and purples, gorgeous globes spangled with gold dangling from its splayed branches. Martha, dressed for the holiday, looked lovely, as she always did.

"Thank you," I said, my eyes meeting Andy's. "Thank you."

"You're welcome," he said, nodding once, which was all he needed to do to show he understood how moved I was by the choice. I thanked Martha too, and then we went on talking, exchanging gifts and gab.

Martha may have chosen the gift, but what I felt for Martha, and from Martha, at that time was far more primitive. We circled and sniffed each other like animals, a tentative touch, a quick withdrawal. I was more carefree and less guarded than she, maybe because she was twelve years older than me, with a nearly grown child by the time we met. Even so, as opposites, we learned from each other. There was much I admired in Martha, in her fresh face and perpetual industriousness, how she figuratively spun so much yarn to silk. I can say with less certainty that there were things she admired in me.

I copied Martha in taking up cooking, which, within four or so months of meeting her, I was doing with gusto, having bought Wolfgang Puck's *Modern French Cooking for the American Kitchen* and studying the mouthwatering *Recipes from the Cuisine of Ma Maison*. By the first winter of our first year as a foursome, Martha and I were adopting each other's behaviors and styles all the time.

I was the fashion-conscious European girl who didn't leave home without layers of foundation, eyeliner, mascara, artfully twisted tresses, the latest outfits, and spike heels. With her glowing complexion, even when she did not wear makeup, Martha was the All-American fresh-scrubbed Breck girl who wore low heels and sneakers, Laura Ashley dresses, or carefree sportswear.

I started to try on her style, her Heartland look, stepping from the steam of my shower and casually tossing on a sundress, scrunching my hair, and glossing my lips with petroleum jelly instead of the dark

Chanel Red Red that was my signature color. But you can only wear another person's style as costume, and until no-lipstick became part of my own look, my mouth felt naked and exposed. Under Martha's influence, I let my blond-colored hair grow back to its natural reddish copper and introduced some "sensible clothing" to my wardrobe.

Martha, whom I regarded as the living example of that singularly American combination of energy, freedom, and can-do attitude, motivated me to change careers and climb the corporate ladder, and soon I was the manager of development for International Playtex, a Fortune 500 company.

While I tried her on, she tried me on. We were girls in Grandma's dressing room, trading old-fashioned brooches and pearls. On occasion, she would add some sophisticated pieces to her wardrobe, which echoed what I would wear: a simple monotone sweater, sandals and shoes instead of sneakers and clogs. Her natural elegance shone through. She experimented with what she called "Mariana pedicures," which were nothing more than French pedicures. As I helped Martha discover the seductive magic of high heels and couture, she sometimes imitated my stride: "I'm doing the Mariana walk," she would say, laughing, looking at me over her shoulder to see my response.

I was flattered to be imitated by a woman as handsome and poised as Martha was, and yet every imitation had about it the feel of awkwardness, of dress-up, the way a child wears her mother's high heels and wobbles as she walks. Martha could not do my walk because she was not me. As well dressed and attractive as she was, and despite having modeled more actively than I did during college, personal style proved to be somehow out of reach for her. I was happy to see her experiment and I hoped she'd come into her own and find her way. But it wasn't easy for her despite her sophistication in so many other areas.

Likewise, it wasn't easy for me to find my way among the myriad things Martha was excellent at. She instilled her love of estate sales in me, but in the beginning, the very *idea* of spending a Saturday combing through the belongings of some dead person sent shivers through my spine. Often the homes we visited had been occupied by the wealthy, by people who would have been seen in Communist Romania as landed gentry or the aristocracy, and entering these places brought back images of my past that I did not want to revisit: the expropriated mansions and overgrown grounds of aristocrats killed in ways no one discussed but everyone feared, the windows covered with vines, the chimneys crumpling as the mortar eroded from weather and neglect.

"I don't want to go," I told her the first time she suggested it, the summer when our friendship began, though I didn't tell her why. But she coaxed me, leading me over the thresholds as one might lead a horse with a cube of sugar.

The first time I went with Martha to such an estate sale was a bit of a shock. We got up before dawn, drove down dark country roads to the address on the cut-out newspaper ad, which Martha gave me to hold, and waited in her Suburban as lines of treasure hunters snaked behind us on the estate grounds.

Hours later, in bright daylight, we rushed inside the graceful late-eighteenth-century colonial house to get our hands on the treasures that Martha coveted. With no apparent interest in the historic details of the house, Martha headed straight for the dining room. She grabbed a large silver candlestick off the magnificent and not-for-sale Rhode Island Chippendale dining table only to look up and see an antiques dealer who was already holding the candlestick's mate. Martha called to him across the table, demanding he give up his piece. In the silence that befell the room, the man, clearly familiar with Martha's as yet still local Westport catering fame, said, "Okay, La Martha. You be the proprietor," and let her have the second candlestick. Without much of a reply, my friend turned to me and placed the multi-branched decorative silver pieces in my arms. Then she reached for the bowl at the center of the close-grained mahogany surface. She scanned the hairline fissure in the fine porcelain for only a moment before she clutched the large vessel close to her chest, telling me we couldn't put down these heavy things because someone might swipe her booty.

Eventually, I learned to relax inside these homes and even began to enjoy myself, seeking out the treasures of strangers whose hands you could still feel holding the objects. For Martha, it was Depression glass; silver trays with edges scalloped or straight; antique furniture both primitive and ornate; pretty dishes; large, tulip-shaped café au lait mugs, their porcelain thinning from the base to the top so the mixture stays hot at the bottom without burning one's lips; gorgeous molds and millwork; old print blocks that left letters on the page in a long-lost font; simple boxes and baskets gone golden and speckled with time. I started to collect art pottery and art glass, picture frames and antique books. We traded our treasures and studied each other's taste.

MARTHA WAS VERY, very busy. *Entertaining*, which came out just before Christmas 1982, was a smashing success, a best-selling cookbook that catapulted her beyond the borders of Westport and the East Coast onto a national platform. There were radio shows, talk shows, TV interviews, *Good Day* this and *Good Night* that; it was all very exciting. Martha made so many media appearances that she ran out of things to wear. I remember lending her the luxurious new turquoise cashmere wrap sweater that I had just brought home from London.

But fame fades faster than lipstick and must be continually reapplied in order to retain its color and sheen. It is such a shame that just when a person has finally reached his or her most-hoped-for peak of success, there is no enjoyment. Almost immediately, it seemed, Martha began working on a new book about food and living the good life, only this time she herself was ravenous for the subject, which consumed her as she consumed it. As she worked nonstop, often short-tempered, her body took on a rigid new mien, the spring in her step faded, her waist thickened, and her hands seemed permanently clenched as though always grasping for something.

Nothing was spontaneous in Martha's life anymore. It was all designed, all for show, all filmed, all forced, all exploited by her for her growing success. Her mind was always three steps ahead of her fast-working body, and her ability to compartmentalize was her key coping mechanism. She had cubbyholes for everything, including tasks and relationships. For this reason it wasn't entirely surprising to me that she was able to simultaneously cater my gorgeous wedding and serve as my matron of honor.

When my fiancé and I told Martha and Andy of our plans to get married and have children, Martha immediately asked to be godmother to our firstborn. We had by then seen how Martha behaved with her husband, their daughter, Alexis, and other people. My fiancé and I were both immigrants without family in the United States. Our children's godparents had to be people whom we would trust to raise our children in case something happened to us. Trying to preempt future discomfort when we were certain to refuse Martha's offer, we decided to ask her to be our matron of honor instead.

May 1, 1983, was a glorious day. Our wedding was in the afternoon at our home in Westport. In the garden, the rhododendrons and azaleas were in bloom. I had decorated the house with urns filled with hundreds of long, flowering quince branches with coral-orange red blossoms that reminded me of the Japonica bushes in my grandmother's garden. I put gardenias in small vases on all of the tables. I had fallen in love with the gardenia, a flower with velvety petals and a delicate fragrance that I encountered for the first time in America, having previously read wonderful descriptions that still could not conjure the flesh-fact of that flower and the scent gracing the afternoon when we made our vows.

It was Peter, my groom's best friend from surgical training at the Mayo Clinic, not my father, who gave me away. Not one person from my family was there. Romania was still a Communist country ruled by a dictator and his treacherous secret police. My family was far away. But in my mind I could see my mama and papa; my younger sister, married by then to a man I only knew from the few photographs that escaped the censors; my tall grandfather, his skin so ancient, his face shattered by time and trials; my uncles, aunts, cousins; and my Romanian friends.

While my groom, Martha, and the local justice of the peace were waiting in our living room with the wedding party, my friend Christine helped me get ready. My "something old" were the white high heel sandals that had been among the few things I could pack in the carry-on bag I took with me on the escape train to Vienna. They had been custom made by a shoemaker in Bucharest, who used a mold of my feet that he had sculpted and kept in a box with my name on it in a room lined with such boxes. My "something borrowed" was a luxurious London couture dress lent to me by my friend Lois. Made of ivory pure silk taffeta, and cut with exquisite simplicity, it showcased my neck, décolletage, and the lustrous pearls that were my "something new." Pinching a gardenia from a vase, Christine fastened it in my shoulder-length hair. Then she removed her diamond-and-sapphire-studded Van Cleef clips and put them on my ears. "They are the perfect 'something blue' for your big day," Christine said.

My arm in his, Peter walked me into the living room.

The music started. We chose to have a romantic concert harp playing at our wedding reception. The gorgeous soloist, whose profile resembled a pre-Raphaelite painting, began her melodic repertoire, filling the room with the harp's lyrical harmonics.

The only family members who could come were my groom's mother and her husband. My groom's father had died many years before and his brother, a professor at Warsaw University, lived in Poland and was not allowed to leave the country. However, we tried not to be saddened by the scarcity of family members in attendance, because there were so many friends who had come to celebrate our wedding with us, like our friend Jim and his wife RoAnn, my very best friend since I came to the States four years earlier, who would become godmother to our first child. Martha, in her stylish light beige afternoon party dress and pearls, stood out looking beautiful even among the elegant crowd of attractive guests, some of whom had traveled a long distance to be at our wedding, like Maxine, my talented modernist sculptress friend, who came from California with her husband, Ray, and my eccentric friend Jenie, who lived in Mexico City when she wasn't traveling the world.

Although Martha no longer did much catering, since the success of her first book, concentrating mostly on parties that she photographed for her publishing projects, she had graciously agreed to cater our wedding party. We consulted with her on the menu, but it was Martha who suggested, arranged, and prepared everything. She ordered the rentals and the flowers. She chose the maître d', a bartender, and one chef who came from New York. Lisa the flower designer, the two waiters, and the three kitchen helpers were local, and so was the other chef, Necy, the wonderful Brazilian woman who did housekeeping for Martha and for me, and also worked for Martha's company, Martha Stewart, Inc., Entertaining and Catering. So talented was Necy that she later became a set stylist for Martha's television show.

The glowing copper trays were from Martha's kitchen, and the French cotton lace doilies with which she lined the trays were mine, collected from our estate sale escapades. Elegant waiters carried the flower-decorated serving trays, presenting our guests with delicious hors d'oeuvres including the heart-shaped English cucumber slices topped with decoratively piped smoked-salmon mousse—my favorite Martha-signature appetizer.

While standing by my side as my matron of honor, Martha also directed her catering crew. She orchestrated their comings and goings with barely noticeable body language and discreet disappearances into the kitchen, and was quick to materialize back among the guests, all smiles and hostess-friendly gestures, next to Andy, who walked around the crowd taking pictures. Martha said I should also have a rose, and, pulling one out of Lisa's arrangements, she bit off the stem and added the opening rosebud to the gardenia in my hair.

In our dining room and sunroom, Martha's crew had set up eight round tables, with fine white lightly starched cotton damask tablecloths and napkins, tasteful silver, beautiful water goblets, and thin-stemmed wine glasses and champagne flutes.

The entrée was plump, deboned Cornish hens stuffed with thyme-flavored wild rice, glazed with crab-apple jam, and served with sautéed beets, carrots, and radicchio. The plates were beautifully arranged in the kitchen and served at the table though I couldn't help but feel a sudden pang of longing for the "Meissen Rose" porcelain with a hand-painted rose in a bouquet of forget-me-nots that had graced our family's festive tables since my great-grandparents' wedding.

Martha outdid herself with the stately, four-layer French orange almond wedding cake, its Grand Marnier meringue buttercream frosting applied in a perfect basket weave and decorated with coral rose-buds, white lilac, Stephanotis blossoms, and crystallized violets she had asked Andy to bring, fresh, from Paris. It was so gracious of her and I was so grateful.

I was on cloud nine, celebrating my wedding with all my new friends, but also pining for my old friends and my family, who were excited to learn that by the next evening my new husband and I were to be honeymooning at the Ritz in Madrid. We would go to the Prado and visit several other beautiful places in Spain. We would be on European soil, still so far yet so much closer to them.

Back home, Martha's catering invoice was the first bill we looked at together as a married couple, and I thought it was funny how differently we reacted to it. While my husband was bemused by how promptly Martha had sent us the bill on May 7, although she knew we were still on our honeymoon, I noticed that Martha had designed her stationery with a folk art–type drawing of a black cat with an arched back and a bushy, upraised tail, and underneath it the word "TOTAL," in the left margin, between the closing "Very cordially" and her signed and printed name. I wondered if Martha had chosen the Total cat as some enigmatic symbol, like James Abbott McNeill Whistler, who signed his paintings with a butterfly.

Part II

The Best of Friends

4

A Friendship Grows
in Westport

I N THE EARLY years of my marriage, our lives became increasingly intertwined with the Stewarts'. I admired them, two such complex people who had kept their marriage vital for a quarter of a century. Despite all their differences and crises, they still had fun together, at least when we were around. I had seen people who after a number of years as a couple seemed to have nothing to say to each other, but Andy showed Martha tender attention and a lot of deference and respect, although she often was less than friendly to him, and I always believed that friendship between partners is the key to a relationship. We attended parties, concerts, and theater together, shared movies, books, and music. We went out to restaurants, or met at our place or theirs. The atmosphere was warm, fireplaces glowed during the cold seasons, the Stewarts' tastefully minimalistic pool was welcoming in the summer. So passed the next few years, a blur of new Martha books and then my first baby.

The summer of my first pregnancy, I swam at the Turkey Hill pool almost every day, grateful for the cool clasp of water even as the pool's ominous black bottom, the cats who skittered too close to the cement sides, and the swarms of bees buzzing around the beautiful blooms in the surrounding garden spooked me.

And, by knowing Martha and Andy, I was given an opportunity to meet many extraordinary people. In 1984, Andy published astrophysicist Dr. Joseph P. Allen's *Entering Space: An Astronaut's Odyssey.* Dr. Allen was an astronaut who had flown two space missions, as well as a superb photographer whose glorious views of the Earth and the Moon and the mysterious celestial world were taken on board the space shuttles *Columbia* and *Discovery.* These were gathered in his book.

Dr. Allen came to dinner in the glass-paneled porch at Turkey Hill one evening when the stars were visible in the smudged way they are near a major city. That night, talking to that extraordinary man, I felt a little like an astronaut myself, as though I had found life on another planet far, far away.

I asked the guest of honor as many questions as I could, and he obligingly answered all of them. I recall asking Dr. Allen if planets and constellations look the same from space as from Earth.

"Personally, I shall never forget the view of Earth," he said.

Andy told us that the one memory most etched in his mind was looking at the stars with Alexis when she was a child, her delight in learning about the constellations. The love and tenderness in Andy's voice made me think of July 21, 1969, when I watched *Apollo 8*'s historic moon landing on TV with my family and friends. Remembering how I had held my breath when Neil Armstrong stepped out of the *Eagle*, put his left foot in the grayish dust, and took those first human steps on lunar soil, then the three American astronauts planting the Stars and Stripes in the Sea of Tranquility.

I said, "Their legacy was so inspiring to me. I was already in love with the idea of freedom, but it was that image that sparked my wish to live in America."

As I soaked up the astronaut's descriptions of the stars, the light, and looking at Earth from hundreds of miles away, I became conscious of the fact that I was talking face-to-face with an actual American hero. In that exclusive club of those who had walked in space, Dr. Allen was one of only a handful of astronauts who had ventured away from their shuttle untethered to a safety device. At that moment, in his presence, I realized for the first time that as a newly naturalized American citizen, I had truly begun another life. So *this* was America.

It was my grandfather who had shown me how to string stars into the shapes of constellations, tracing scenes from mythology across the night sky. I remember searching for Orion, the hunter with a belt of three lined-up stars; Cassiopeia, the queen showcased by a W of five heavenly glitters; and, across the Milky Way, the Big Dipper, whose bright stars at the tip of the bowl point you to Polaris in the handle of Little Dipper, the polestar that glitters due north and around which rotate our starry skies. Those stars had certainly smiled on me.

I was happily married, we had a baby girl, Monica, soon to be one year old, and we had fun together whether doing things alone or with friends. That fall, my husband and I took a ride with Martha and Andy to watch the leaves changing in the New England countryside, and stumbled upon an auction at a reputable gallery. Andy bid on a painting and, as a lovely pair of aquamarine earrings came up for sale, my husband and Martha started bidding against each other. Martha won in the end, but she was angry with my husband for forcing her to bid too high. My husband was no less upset for having lost, as he had wanted to buy the earrings for our little girl because the aquamarines would look so pretty with her blue eyes when she grew up. Martha promised to give the earrings to our daughter when she turned sixteen. And she did.

In early 1985, we were invited to lunch at Turkey Hill with environmental sculptor Christo and his frequent collaborator, his wife, Jeanne-Claude. Christo had recently completed his *Surrounded Islands* project, the encircling of eleven man-made islands in Biscayne Bay near Miami with two-hundred-foot-wide sheets of flamingo-pink polypropylene fabric, which he described as his version of Monet's water lilies. We discussed the meaning of packaging in Christo's installations, all of which are objects bundled, draped, or, to put it plainly, *wrapped*. Are the wrappings sculpture, landscape architecture, or social art therapy? Are they minimalism, pop art, or are they more theoretical?

The avant-garde artists, who gave no concrete explanations, alluded to the fact that the packaging was simply to skewer our packaged perceptions, that by wrapping familiar objects the artists were, in some sense, asking us to see what was there by making it not there. The conversation reminded me of a discussion among my friends in Romania about the psychology of human perception, and how psychological experiments have shown with great certainty that people see only what they expect to see so that if, at a football game, a gorilla runs down the field, the fans engrossed in the game will fail to notice the gorilla. The brain simply ignores deviations from the norm. In fact, my experience with Christo in some sense proved Christo's point. I had by then been eating Martha's superbly rendered lunches for months and months, the sheer repetition thereby making the extraordinary ordinary. So absorbed was I in Christo's words that I cannot recall what she served. I had ceased to see that which was always in front of me.

Christo mentioned that he fled Communist Bulgaria as a stowaway aboard a medical supply train to Austria. I told him I had also escaped to Vienna, but it felt inappropriate to talk much about my experience to Christo, who never abandoned the high ideals of his youth, while I had quickly become at ease with the comforts of materialism.

As Christo and Jeanne-Claude gracefully indulged us with answers to our questions, their faces became animated by that interior sparkle shared by children and geniuses. Christo could have passed for a brilliant scientist, while Jeanne-Claude, with her radiant smile, deep-red lipstick, and flamboyant hairstyle, looked unmistakably like a free-spirited artist despite her self-effacing attitude. Yet, the combination of the two transformed them into a richly textured entity that was there for all to see, a couple closely bonded and vibrating with friendship.

When asked about the various materials Christo and Jeanne-Claude used to wrap their objects, they said: "Fabric, like clothing or skin, is fragile. It translates the unique quality of impermanence."

I imagined wrapping my husband in satin sheets, bestowing artful touches on my subject, then, as his eyes widened at the recognition of naughtiness in mine, unfurling him with that wondrous passion we shared in our early years together.

We drew comparisons to the ancient Egyptian practice of wrapping mummies, but Christo rejected any symbolism we tried to ascribe to their massive installations. He insisted his work was purely aesthetic, creating new ways of seeing the familiar world. It occurred to me that Martha was also creating new ways of seeing the familiar world. She had done it for me, and her escalating fame was the proof that her work was appreciated by more and more people.

Christo and Jeanne-Claude were preparing to leave for Paris, where they were going to wrap the Pont Neuf. I thought about the possible meanings of wrapping the oldest and longest bridge in Paris, the city of lovers. I tried to imagine what it would look like draped in folds of cloth outlined by terra-cotta-colored ropes, if it would resemble antique statuary or appear smothered in golden sandstone silence, restrained, like Martha, who was very quiet that day. Each time she came from the kitchen to sit with us on the sun-bathed porch, Martha looked out at her property, her eyes flashing in a way I had become so used to, when her mind was absorbed in calculations and planning. I was amused to think that Martha, the artisan, was engrossed with her earthen plans— maybe new designs for her gardens—while the artists were consumed with their ethereal ideas of a bridge.

"What would you most like to wrap in the entire world?" Andy asked.

"The Reichstag, in Berlin," Christo said.

"So your *Sturm und Drang* is wrapping the very symbol of historical unrest?" I asked, referring to the German expression "Storm and Stress," coined by Goethe to describe the unease of man with his contemporary society.

"Wrapping the Reichstag has been on my mind for almost twenty years," Christo answered, avoiding a political discussion, which was just as well, since we could not have envisaged then that on November 9, 1989, the Berlin Wall would fall, and with the crumbling of that Cold War shrine the Soviet Bloc system would collapse. What I might have foreseen was that while the other countries emerged from the ruins through a "velvet revolution," a thousand peaceful demonstrators in Bucharest would be senselessly murdered, and that my native country would be the last in Eastern Europe to shed its Communist chains.

It took still a number of years, but after the fall of the Berlin Wall Christo got his wish. I followed *Wrapped Reichstag, Project for Berlin* in the press as best I could. In June 1995, Christo, Jeanne-Claude, and their many assistants, together with a hundred mountain climbers, wrapped the edifice in thousands of yards of artfully folded silver fabric shaped by blue ropes. The *New York Times'* Holland Cotter wrote that the project "can be viewed as the bandaging of old wounds." Christo's installation, which lasted about two weeks, was viewed by millions of people. When it came down, the German government went ahead with plans to remodel the building to house the newly unified German parliament.

IN THE AUTUMN of 1985, a few months after Christo came for lunch at Turkey Hill, my husband and I were leaving on a hunting trip. It was a beautiful sunny day, so Martha and Andy decided to join us and take a long nature walk.

It had been four years since I went on my first armed hunt. I never held a gun until shortly prior to meeting Martha. I had decided to learn how to shoot so I would be good company to my fiancé, who liked to hunt, as his father had before him. I'd learned by shooting clay pigeons at Trap and Skeet target practice. Then, after completing requirements for a Connecticut hunter education program, I got my hunting license.

Our first fall together, when my fiancé and I went hunting for pheasants, I discovered I was a good shot. We often took out fewer birds than the "bag limit," which was about two pheasants per hunter, depending on local regulations meant to protect species from overhunting, but I enjoyed our weekend-long trekking in the fields with our dog.

Attila's breed, the Vizsla, are prized pointer-retriever gun-dogs, said to trace their line back to the hounds brought by the Huns to what is today Hungary. On our first hunting trip, when he was barely a year old, our pooch hid his face against my knees each time he heard gunfire. But before long our Vizsla figured out how to stand staunch and hold a picture-perfect point on a pheasant instead of chasing it. As for the retrieving, well, we did it ourselves because Attila didn't quite get that part.

I am sure my fondness for the sport was enhanced by having my surgeon husband do the field dressing for both of us. His expert hands neatly harvested the lean meat, which we took home to eat, leaving the carcass in the field for scavengers to feed on, a common practice among hunters.

My preparation of the gamy delicacy improved a lot over time, and we served tasty pheasant dishes at our dinner parties. Some of our friends hunted with us, most often Carlos, who was one of my husband's best friends, and also couples, like my graceful friend Delphine and her husband, Frank.

On that Indian summer weekend of October 1985, Martha, Andy, my husband, and I, all wearing sage, green, and brown hunt-chic Barbour and classic British casuals for the woods, got in the car with Attila, and drove to Mashomack Fish and Game Preserve, a club in Dutchess County, New York, where my husband and I had been members for a few years.

A couple of hours later, when we arrived at the 1800s Greek Revival clubhouse overlooking Halcyon Lake, Martha was instantly won over by the charming surroundings, excellent atmosphere, and welcoming company. Daniel Daly, Mashomack's refined founder and president, was an accomplished outdoorsman of indomitable spirit, and visiting with him was part of what I loved most about those trips. Dan introduced the Stewarts to a number of club members and their guests.

Soon, hunting parties dispersed among the nearly two thousand acres of beautiful nature preserve that made up the club's land. Each group was assigned hunting grounds by David, the club's personable and competent managing director and cofounder. Men and women wearing blaze-orange safety vests on top of their hunting jackets, carried Beretta, Remington, or Winchester stack barrel shotguns, muzzles pointing away from their companions and themselves as they walked behind club guides, heading out into the wilderness to hunt for upland birds.

Andy was opposed to hunting. He confessed his concerns regarding man's power over nature. But according to our original plan, he was going to come along and limit his shooting to his camera.

Martha perhaps, as I once did, needed to weigh her ambivalence about killing the birds with the justification that they ended up on the table, like chickens that are sold and bought in grocery stores. But I suspected that her decision to hunt was also inspired by the scene at the club, which was reminiscent of movies and novels depicting the sport as a country-lifestyle hobby popular with the upper crust. Besides, Martha loved the thrill of the chase. I had clearly seen it while she was bargain-hunting. So I wasn't surprised when Martha said that she wanted to hunt.

In 1982, my then-fiancé had given me for my birthday a beautiful 20-gauge shotgun with exhibition-grade walnut and hand-checkered stock. It had a between-the-hand balance that was perfect for me. When we honeymooned in Madrid a year later, we got matching leather gun casings from Diana Turba, at that time a fashionable place for elegant hunting gear. I took my gun out of its case and offered it to Martha with a box of cartridges. She slipped the ammo in her jacket pocket and was ready to learn how to walk while holding the gun. Because we were going to hunt in terrain where there was no thick brush, and since Martha and my husband were to walk ahead, in line, while Andy and I would be behind their shooting party, I thought it was safest for all of us if Martha side-carried the gun. So I showed her how to hold and carry the shotgun in her right hand, with the stock tucked between her body and her elbow. Also, for safety, when we got to the hunting grounds, my husband shared the field with Martha, deciding she would track and shoot the birds on the right side, and he on the left.

While I started Martha off on the hunt, Andy walked behind us alone. I was showing her how to break, load, check that the safety is on, find the groove at the shoulder to steady the gun, hold the firearm expecting the kickback when shooting, when we noticed that Attila had stopped his nose-down zigzagging of the field and stood still holding point on a thicket in Martha's zone of fire.

As we hurried stealthily toward the spot, I whispered: "Raise your gun up. Higher! Don't shoot my dog. Aim higher than a man, Martha."

I glanced at my husband, who was approaching from our left, eyes on the scene, holding his gun with both hands, muzzle upward, at ready-carry. I knew he was preparing for the event that Martha wounded but did not kill the bird, when he would end the bird's suffering with a clean, rapid shot. I watched the concentration on Martha's face and the posture of her body. She looked like a pro.

"Safety off. Put your finger on the trigger," I said.

We were so still I could hear Martha breathe next to me. Suddenly a beautiful rooster flushed from the ground cover that Attila was pointing at, taking wing with a burst of loud cackles.

"Aim ahead of the bird, Martha. Swing smoothly, don't jerk the gun. Shoot only if you're sure to hit!" I said as the bird flew in that oblique-and-up way pheasants do when they go for the trees.

Martha may have never shot a gun in her life before, but she aimed to kill, and she did. I heard the smack of the shell entering the plumage and felt the usual sadness.

From that day on, I shared my gun with Martha, until years later when, one morning, as my husband and I were preparing to go pheasant hunting, our second-born daughter, Lara, who was about four years old, reached up, her little hand tugging at my jacket: "Mommy?"

"Yes, my darling," I answered and bent down, my face level with hers.

"I don't want my mama to kill," she said, her doe eyes looking at me expectantly. I didn't know how to talk to her about hunting to procure food, or about the realities and paradoxes of the meat we eat, so I said: "Then I promise I shall not hunt for as long as you don't want me to."

We looked at each other for some moments, after which Lara put her thumb back in her mouth and sealed our pact with an affirmative nod of the head.

I continued to go on our hunting trips but I did not shoot. After a while, my husband got increasingly frustrated and eventually sought out new hunting buddies.

As for Martha, each time she went hunting with her friend Dan and his entourage, she asked to borrow my shotgun and I lent it to her although I was often reminded by my husband about the dangers and risks I ran when giving someone else my firearm. But by then we were good friends and I trusted that Martha would never involve me in a crime.

That glorious autumn day when Andy and I walked together for hours as he took pictures, while Martha and my husband hunted ahead of us, we planned to dine on their catch the next day at our place. I was to cook the pheasants and Martha would bring dessert.

As I usually did when we gave dinner parties, I took advantage of my toddler's afternoon nap to organize my food preparation, put out the wines, and set the table, which took a while, since I liked to spoil my guests with our Baccarat glasses, our wedding Limoges porcelain, my husband's family silver, white linen napkins. New beeswax candles and fresh flowers were on the table, the platters of canapés and various *amuse-gueules*—the bite-size morsels I liked to serve as appetizers—arranged, when I realized that I was out of the juniper berries for my pheasant recipe. I could have perhaps gotten away with using some good gin but I wasn't going to take chances with the precious pheasant meat, which can easily get stringy and dry.

Once I had learned my first steps from Wolfgang Puck, cooking proved to come quite naturally to me. I made delicious meals from ad hoc recipes. Influenced by Martha's fresh and simple cuisine, I followed my inspiration in combining ingredients from our refrigerator and pantry, which I always kept well-stocked. But game can be tricky, and to prepare the pheasant I closely followed our secret family recipe given to me by my mother over the phone from Romania, which suited my husband's palate as it required no cream. The only change I made was to replace my mother's homemade kirsch with Cointreau or Grand Marnier. I ran over to Turkey Hill for a few juniper berries. Martha's kitchen smelled heavenly. She was baking a tarte Tatin to bring over for dessert, and had just opened the oven to check on the pie. I watched Martha lift the pastry crust for which she had made her own pâte brisée. As she checked on the golden browning of the apples, the aroma of caramelizing sugar and butter made my mouth water.

Andy was out, visiting with the family of Martha's sister, Laura, who lived in Weston, a neighboring town. Martha was running between the pie and the landscapers who were winterizing her bushes outside.

"Wait till you see," she said. "You'll like it."

And then I saw. Martha had added a new dimension to the cold weather design of Turkey Hill. Taking rolls and rolls of burlap, she had the landscapers wrap her bushes not in the ordinary protective way one does in the winter. Instead, she fabricated custom-made winter wraps for the bushes, extending the burlap along the driveway and walkways, following the property's softly sloping hill and dropping down by the gardens, through the orchard, toward the barn and the *palais du poulet*.

The effect that Martha had created was noticeably Christo-inspired. It looked to me like a cross between his *Running Fence* installation in the hills of Sonoma and Marin Counties and the *Valley Curtain* stretched across Rifle Gap in the Colorado Rockies.

And Martha was right. I loved the way she winterized her garden with Christo effects. Many people commented on Martha's cleverness; the burlap-wrapped bushes looked good in their tailor-made winter wear. I never heard Martha mention Christo. And perhaps he didn't care.

After all, Martha was famous by then.

5

All Good Things

*E*NTERTAINING BECAME A best seller.

Martha had dedicated the beautifully illustrated guide to cooking, decorating, and entertaining, which featured Turkey Hill, to Andy, to her father, and to her daughter, Alexis.

With Andy's knowledge of the book industry and Martha's innate talent for self-promotion, Martha's good taste, style, and savoir-faire in the domestic arts won her national recognition. I was sure that Martha's stupendous success, which was greater than any one of us might have predicted, played a large role in the massive shift in her demeanor. But it was not at all clear if the change was due to a shift in her internal landscape or because of the relentless spotlight that followed her every move.

A few years before we met the Stewarts, Andy had become the president of Harry N. Abrams, Inc., bringing to publishing his vast education and his experience with corporate law. Soon thereafter, his company released a *New York Times* best seller, the English-language edition of *Gnomes* by Dutch authors Wil Huygen and Rien Poortvliet. Andy's publishing success received much attention, and *People* magazine ran a story on him. The piece also featured his wife, mentioning that she catered parties for Robert Redford, Paul Newman, and other famous Westport area residents. At the *Gnomes* book release party, Andy, who had contracted Martha's catering company to provide the food, introduced his gifted hostess to Alan Mirken, the president of the Crown Publishing Group. He suggested she write a book about cooking and entertaining.

Andy negotiated Martha's book contract with Crown and supported her entire publishing effort, from sharing his expertise with best-selling illustrated lifestyle books right down to serving as taster for her recipes. Sophistication also seemed to have entered Martha's life with Andy, whose stylish mother, Ethel, and sister, Diane, Martha aspired to emulate.

At the beginning of our friendship, the elegant lunches and dinners at Turkey Hill had often resulted from Andy's career and the various dignitaries, scholars, and artists whom his work as owner of the successful publishing company Stewart, Tabori & Chang put him in touch with. After *Entertaining*, and increasingly with the success of her following books, the elegant lunches and dinners stemmed from Martha's media ties. The first of these was the *Entertaining* publication party in Westport.

We watched as the cameramen held their large silver discs this way and that, Martha sitting on a stool, her feet demurely crossed at the ankles, as makeup artists flitted around her, snapping open clamshells of compact powder, making over her mouth again and again. Cameras flashed on Martha's friendly wholesome good looks and photogenic smile. "Could you look straight but turn your face a little to the right? Chin slightly down?" Flash. Click. "What do you think of . . . ?" In some ways, the questions were often lost opportunities. Her answers revealed little of her sharp mind, her up-at-dawn-have-to-have-it treasure-hunt spirit. She began to sound muted. Calm. Before our eyes, we watched an icon born in the place of a person struggling to be.

After the success of *Entertaining*, Martha was on a roll, releasing book after book: *Martha Stewart's Quick Cook* in 1983, *Martha Stewart's Hors d'Oeuvres* in 1984, *Martha Stewart's Pies & Tarts* in 1985. She wrote newspaper columns and magazine articles, gave countless interviews, and made appearances on national television programs. Martha apparently thought she needed an empire, but then once she had it and all eyes were on her—the books, the fame, the cameras—then came Martha's *Sturm und Drang*.

Perpetual publicity and fame piled on her the uneasiness that Martha handled with a masterful show of composure. However, in private, Martha didn't cope as well with the strain of rampant consumerism and increased pressures. It was often quite awkward to be around her, but I never lost the sympathy that she had inspired in me the first time we met. I didn't think her unpleasantness was a principal characteristic, so all I could do was guess at the reasons for it, like, perhaps, Martha's insatiable desire for power, which I thought came from her father, a pharmaceutical salesman who obviously meant a lot to Martha and who had passed away a couple of years before we met. In a voice filled with pain, Andy once said that the best way to describe Martha's father was as the quintessential Willy Loman. I figured that comparing him to the tragic character from Arthur Miller's *Death of a Salesman*, whose pride in being well liked and whose dreams of success ended with family estrangement and disillusion, was Andy's way of inspiring sympathy for a man who had also been a domineering father. I felt so blessed to have had a father who was jovial and charismatic, who spoiled me and my younger sister and instilled in us a sense of comfort with power, not cravings and fears.

I WANTED TO raise my child myself, so I quit the corporate ladder and became a consultant, working as a computer research analyst for a local firm, Marketing Corporation of America, and doing volunteer fund-raising for Paul Newman's Hole in the Wall Gang Camp, a nonprofit summer camp for children with serious illnesses.

At MCA I became friendly with Norma Collier, a sophisticated lady and respected analyst. In a matter of weeks, we were spending work breaks together. Norma had had a thriving career as a high-fashion model, lived in Paris for a while, married a man who was successful in the art world, had children, divorced, went for an MBA, and was now raising two girls as a working single mother. One day, months after we met, Norma said she had decided I should know that years earlier she had been friends with Martha.

While she was at Barnard, and shortly before her marriage to Andy, Martha entered *Glamour* magazine's 1961 Best Dressed College Girls contest, which had launched Norma's successful modeling career after she won the previous year. The magazine's editors were hoping to duplicate that success with Martha, and assigned Norma to accompany Martha when she got the award. That is how they met.

I once asked Martha if *Glamour* photographers had followed her around the Barnard campus without her knowledge, as she went about her life, a beautifully dressed coed. It turned out that there were no candid cameras involved. The reason she got to be known as the best-dressed was because Martha had cleverly staged a winning portfolio: she had sewn herself several outfits, borrowed a few pieces from friends, then dressed up and posed for pictures that she used to enter the contest. There was nothing accidental about her winning. She made it happen. Martha's resourcefulness then was entirely similar to her staging of the picture-perfect entertaining poses that graced her books, those ideal images of life that inspired her audience with dreams for living.

After having modeled in Europe for a while, Norma returned to New York and renewed her friendship with Martha, who by then had married Andy, had a child, and become a stockbroker with the firm of Monness, Williams, and Sidel. Norma gave Martha a share of her life savings to invest. It was a good chunk of money representing a lot of Norma's hard work, so Martha assured her she'd be very careful, and would only buy stock that she'd put her own money in. Martha did just that when she invested Norma's money in Levitz Furniture in 1970. But by 1972, the company was in trouble, and the stock price plummeted. Norma said she was left with a huge loss. Yet I could only imagine something like that happening to Martha if it were totally out of her control.

"Wasn't the whole stock market in bad shape in the Watergate era?" I asked. "I was still in Romania, but I understood it was one of the worst markets in American history."

Norma agreed, but what she couldn't answer was why Martha had unloaded her own shares yet didn't sell Norma's Levitz Furniture holdings before the stock lost so much of its value. Norma also said something about unreturned calls and Martha's subsequent departure from the brokerage company.

I found that confusing, primarily since in the four years I had known her, Martha had always been prompt at calling back. According to Andy, Martha became a stockbroker not long after she got married, and had done very well. Martha had also talked about her job, and how much fun it was to be a smart, beautiful woman, dressed in a miniskirt, doing lucrative work on the floor of the New York Stock Exchange. One of her coworkers with whom she remained friends was a tall, charismatic man named Brian Dennehy, who would go on to become an award-winning actor.

And she must have done well, judging by the real estate the Stewarts owned. They had bought their weekend home, a late nineteenth-century schoolhouse in Middlefield, Massachusetts, when Andy was fresh out of law school. It was a modest house with no heat or running water, but it came with fifty or so bucolic Berkshire acres, and a stream that ran on the property. My husband and I went there with them a few times. They told us the story of their yearlong renovation of the place, with Martha planting her "Williamsburg" gardens in front of the open porch and Andy exploring the overgrown property, exhilarated each time he discovered a mossy patch, a bunch of ferns, a beautiful clearing where one could imagine the fairies and gnomes, or the textured skin of a majestic tree trunk he disentangled from killer vines. Andy seemed more attached to Middlefield than Martha, but the work they did there explained the Stewarts' skill and resilience when later they spent three years restoring Turkey Hill while they lived in it with their small child.

Dilapidated as it may have been at the time they acquired it, the Stewarts' place on Turkey Hill was a significant investment. By the time they bought it, Andy was a high-powered corporate attorney, and Martha had left Wall Street to dedicate herself to family life in Westport. I never heard her talk of trouble or of having lost money before she resigned as a stockbroker, so when Norma told me that Martha had lost her investment, it occurred to me that she was perhaps making too much of it. Martha, in fact, mostly spoke of the Turkey Hill renovation, and her catering, showing me the basement where she started that business. She often mentioned her writing for *Mademoiselle, Bon Appetit, Good Housekeeping, Country Living*, and *House Beautiful*.

But while I was thinking of all that, not knowing exactly how to respond to Norma, whom I had known for only a short time while I had been friendly with Martha for years, Norma had more surprises for me. She told me how she had been Martha's partner in her first catering business, the Uncatered Affair. I had, until then, been under the impression that Martha did the catering all by herself and that she had acquired her local fame without anyone's help. I remembered Martha proudly telling me about the clever name, but I had never heard her mention Norma, or having had a partner, or much at all about that period of her career. Norma gave me some details. The twist lay not only in how they used the title of that movie, *The Catered Affair*, starring Bette Davis, but also in the fact that they did all the preparations then disappeared before guests arrived, making it seem as though no caterer had been involved and the hosts who hired them had done it all. I thought of how much fun my two friends must have had coming up with that, but didn't interrupt Norma, who went on to say how the business required both women to work long, hard hours baking biscuits and brisket and stepping over polished thresholds with armloads of puff pastry, the butter in whipped dollops sitting on ice in the Suburban waiting to be fetched.

The business grew as they lugged elegant lunches and dinners onto people's summer porches, whipping up froths of this or that in one of the several blenders they carried in huge packs, straining their backs. Then there was the day, Norma said, when she overheard Martha tell Andy that she deserved the lion's share of the revenue. "I'm the one with the bigger talent. My vision is the greatest contribution to this company!" Already upset that Martha had booked catering jobs on the side without her, Norma confronted Martha, who didn't take it well.

In response, Martha tossed Norma's belongings outside in the rain. Norma took the high road and, shortly afterward, left the business. It didn't seem to matter. Martha just soared, powered by her will, determined to succeed; however tough the going got, it seemed nothing could fell her. Martha took a job managing Market Basket, a Westport gourmet food store that she transformed into a great success. She also developed Martha Stewart Inc. Entertaining and Catering, under which she had catered our wedding.

I was bothered by Norma's Martha story and wanted to give Martha a chance to explain her side. Without denying it, she essentially said that the reasons their association ended were a disparity in business acumen and Norma's jealousy of Martha's marriage.

I chose to pass no judgment and stayed friends with Norma at work and with Martha at home. I never talked with Norma or Martha about the other again, although I did invite both of them to our dinner parties where it was nice to see my two girlfriends and Andy behave cordially.

My grandmother used to say, "Whenever you feel like criticizing anyone, just remember that all the people in this world haven't had the advantages that you've had." Or as F. Scott Fitzgerald wrote in *The Great Gatsby*, "I'm inclined to reserve all judgments." Yet, as I watched Martha, Norma, and Andy exchanging private jokes and old memories, it crossed my mind that Martha had not achieved her success entirely on her own, as much as she might have wanted to. However, while she was apparently quite adept at getting a leg up and riding on someone else's shoulders, Martha did it with charm, and I was already under her spell.

• • •

THE FIRST TIME I witnessed Andy's seminal role in the making of Martha was that first night we had dinner at their home in the summer of 1981. As Martha cooked and Andy tasted, and added and subtracted spices, he appeared in every respect a husband who was not only not threatened by his wife's ambition, but supportive of it. Indeed, as I witnessed it, Andy was the vital spark, the soul, in Martha's career, and, as I understood it, it was Andy's energy, his contribution to the blueprint, that permeated every aspect of what would multiply and come together years later to form Martha Stewart Living. The whole that the Stewarts made together was greater than the sum of the parts. Through that union, the Stewarts created the image of Martha as a symbol of perfection, an icon who could single-handedly lead prosperous Americans to an elevated lifestyle and a more fulfilling American Dream. Andy and Martha created, in effect, a social movement.

Their cooperation was the perfect example of the synergy that businesses so often aspire to: "A product or line of products is marketed cooperatively across multiple advertising and media outlets so that the sum of the various outlets—for example, television, publishing, and retailing—provides greater marketing power than any one medium in isolation," as an Internet biography of Martha put it. One example of Martha and Andy's synergy that I observed up close was *Outdoor Pleasures: Picnics, Parties, and Portable Feasts* by Elizabeth Sahatjian, a beautiful illustrated book that Andy published in 1985. Now that Martha was a best-selling author, Andy used her name to market his company's book. She wrote a delightful and informative introduction, and there was an entire chapter devoted to Martha as the consummate hostess, with a photo spread of one of Martha's annual garden parties in which she simultaneously entertained a group of women friends and orchestrated a "baby shower" and birthday party combined. The illustrations included Nina, the beautiful painter wife of Andy's friend JC, a full-page photo of Martha's elegantly set tea-table in the foreground and, in the background, nine ladies dressed in flowing white dresses and my thirteen-month-old daughter Monica sitting in a wicker armchair, me on one side fussing with my baby, and on the other side, a few paces away, Robyn, a young, petite brunette who worked with Martha as a flower consultant and all-around assistant.

Martha's name was prominently displayed on the front cover, mentioned twice on the inside jacket, and several times inside the book with respect to her expertise. Several of Martha's books were mentioned along with her catering business in Westport, and, of course, she was given credit for her recipes. I thought it was a masterful technique by which to capitalize on and simultaneously propagate name recognition, another way to market Martha's image as an authority on the subject of entertaining while also marketing *Outdoor Pleasures* to Martha's audience.

Martha had made her first TV appearance on the *Today Show*—one of hundreds she would make over the next two decades. The film crew went to Turkey Hill to show Martha making a Thanksgiving feast with Andy in front of host Willard Scott and a national audience. By the fall of 1986, she had her own special, "Holiday Entertaining with Martha Stewart," for which she again made a sumptuous Thanksgiving dinner for her family on camera. Crown was delighted with the chance to distribute a mail-order video of the show.

Martha was also working on a new book, *Weddings*, scheduled to be published mid-1987. At the Stewarts' house one day, I met Elizabeth Hawes, the writer who had worked with Martha on *Entertaining*. She wasn't at all the way I had imagined. I had expected a Julia Child type, but Elizabeth looked like she had just stepped out of a Henry James novel. When she left, I commented on her solemn beauty. Andy agreed with me, but all Martha wanted to talk about was how to phrase Elizabeth's credit on the title page of her new book. Elizabeth had gotten "Text with" credit in *Entertaining* but Martha seemed to have issues with giving her "Text by" credit for *Weddings*. I suggested that perhaps it wasn't as big a deal since, as I confessed, I thought that Elizabeth's writing and style in *Entertaining* was superior to the writing in the books Martha had published since.

Then Andy looked at Martha; and I recall him saying, gesturing toward me, "See? It's not just me. Your reader also thinks Elizabeth is the best writer for you."

The photography for *Weddings* was sure to be spectacular, as the Stewarts, in one of their joint coups, had found Christopher Baker, a fine photographer whose work appeared in numerous glossy American and European publications. He was also contributing his distinct artistic talent and sensibility to *The Natural Cuisine of George Blanc*, by the chef and owner of Mère Blanc, the renowned Michelin three-star restaurant in Bresse, Burgundy, a book to be published by Andy's company.

Andy's sharp mind never stopped helping Martha plot her career moves—from picking the feminine Laura Ashley dresses she wore for the cover shots of *Martha Stewart's Quick Cook* and *Martha Stewart's Hors d'Oeuvres* to devising big plans. One evening in the Stewarts' kitchen, we learned that Andy had been negotiating a deal that could bring Martha millions of dollars if she worked as a lifestyle consultant with Kmart, a great opportunity for Martha to get national exposure, sell a lot of books, and eventually develop her own lines.

My husband asked, "Why do they want Martha?"

"I think that Martha can help them elevate their image," Andy said.

"What would Martha have to do?" I asked. "Would this be like a desk job?"

"No. She'd continue writing her books and would consult with them, pitching their home products. I also got them to agree on how much publicity they'd give Martha."

Andy's voice was calm but he was unusually stressed out. He obviously had worked hard on the deal, and since he was, as always, two steps ahead of everyone, there wasn't one thing he hadn't thought of on Martha's behalf. However, when the Kmart contract was ready to be signed, Martha didn't seem to see the value of it. Evidently Andy was trying to enlist our help in convincing Martha to sign, but she shot him a "don't air the family's dirty linen in public" glare, which Andy disregarded, especially since Martha had by then done plenty of that in front of us.

To my thinking, the deal was one of those rare instances when Victor Hugo's famous observation pertained: "There is nothing more powerful than an idea whose time has come."

"You can sell domesticity and make millions, Martha! What's wrong with that?" I asked.

"Have you ever been to a Kmart store?" Martha said, her voice tinged with offense, her eyes filled with reproach.

"No, you know I hate to shop."

"You go to Hermès!"

I knew Martha had high aspirations, but being in a Hermès boutique is as different from shopping as going on a trip to Paris is from taking a spin around the block.

We ate in silence for a while.

"Would Martha have to share the profit from her books with Kmart?" my husband asked, attempting to get the conversation going.

"No. They'd sell her books in their stores," Andy said. "Nationally," he added with emphasis, while looking pointedly at Martha. "But she wouldn't pay Kmart any royalties for that, it would be just part of the relationship."

Minutes later, the Stewarts started to argue. Martha resented the plan because she did not want to be associated with a lowbrow chain such as Kmart. She accused Andy of thinking her unworthy of a loftier business image.

Andy turned to me. "Mariana, do you know who Jaclyn Smith is?" As I must have looked clueless, he added, "The actress from *Charlie's Angels*. The brunette."

I nodded. Although I didn't watch much TV, I had seen some episodes of that detective series.

"She launched her clothing line at Kmart," Andy said, defending his position.

"Wow! Martha, she's beautiful. And glamorous. Nothing wrong with that image," I said.

"You'd be hands-on—"

Martha cut him off. "What if it doesn't work out? What if Ralph Lauren wants me?"

"You can make another deal with anyone else. I told you that. We can go over the contract again. I'll show you where that is," Andy said.

But that night Martha's ego seemed to be greater than her understanding.

It was the first time since I'd known Martha that I read signs of insecurity in her. Instead of seeing how Andy was offering her the chance of a lifetime, Martha perceived his action as a deliberate attack on her grand fantasies.

WHEN MARTHA TRAVELED, which was more and more often, her assistant Robyn took care of Turkey Hill and all the pets—the Persian cats, the chow chows, the colorful chickens. Martha had taken Robyn, whom she believed to be a talented painter, under her wing. I liked that about Martha, the way she gave talented people like Robyn and Necy the opportunity to support themselves on the way to becoming a painter and a set stylist, respectively. While pet-sitting and housekeeping were not glamorous positions, Martha said that she had herself worked as a cook and a housekeeper for some ladies in Manhattan when she was a college student. Besides, she also gave the women who helped her the opportunity to use their artistic skills, Robyn doing flower arrangements and Necy designing beautiful sets for Martha's catering jobs and book photographs, which they were doing right then for Martha's upcoming book *Weddings*.

One evening in the summer of 1986, Andy and Martha had given a small dinner party in honor of Roger Vergé, a renowned French chef and owner of the famous Moulin de Mougins, a Michelin three-star restaurant near Cannes, whose new cookbook Andy had just agreed to publish.

One of the guests that evening was Robyn, who, I noticed, was returning Andy's looks rather flirtatiously while Martha killed herself to impress the famous guest and his charming wife, Denise. When I found myself alone in the kitchen with Martha, I told her my suspicions.

Martha raised a dubious eyebrow. "Do you believe a man would leave his tall blond wife for a short brunette?" she asked.

I bit my tongue as I watched Martha's dexterous hands put the finishing touches on a delicate dessert and wondered whether she had an excess of self-confidence because she was so brilliant and successful, or because she was just oblivious to the subtleties of human behavior. But then I recalled how my boyfriend Dan, the Romanian psychiatrist, used to say that there are always reasons that some information is hidden from the Ego. In that light, Martha's blond superiority theory might have been just a screen to keep her from seeing the power of a sultry petite brunette, "though," as James Joyce put it, "her rosebud mouth was a genuine Cupid's bow, Greekly perfect." And then, for the first time, I felt protective of this woman who was taller than I, older than I, more experienced than I, but somehow lacked elementary feminine instincts.

After that hushed tête-à-tête in her kitchen, Martha and I became closer by virtue of our first shared secret. But I felt that I was balancing my loyalty to Martha on the one hand, and to Andy on the other. Their marriage, which had been in so many ways a gift to me and my husband, was deteriorating rapidly. Their fights rang out, sharp and shrill, and evenings at their home now felt like being on the set of *Who's Afraid of Virginia Woolf?* Although, unlike Elizabeth Taylor, whose passionate film performance twisted her beautiful features, Martha expressed her anger with a sulk disguised as self-possession.

One evening during the Christmas season, we arrived at Turkey Hill to pick up the Stewarts on our way to a holiday party. We went to the festively decorated glassed-in porch. On the large table in the center of the room was a beautiful serving dish filled with Ossetra caviar, a silver-handled mother-of-pearl spoon set invitingly for scooping out precious dollops of the greenish-gray delicacy to enjoy with just-made blinis and crème fraîche.

Andy opened champagne and served the four of us, as it fizzed in perfectly proportioned flutes. We raised our glasses and the Stewarts put on a show of happiness, but Martha's face had that hardened look I'd seen the evening when Andy wanted her to sign the Kmart contract. Like then, she said nothing, and it was Andy who told us what the fuss was about.

He had given Martha a gift and she didn't like it. Knowing that Martha always wished he'd give her jewelry, Andy made sure to get her something truly special that year, and put great effort into finding it. He had brought it for her from London. Andy was willing to return it, which would surely be a pain, but all he wanted was for Martha to tell him why she didn't like his gift.

Then he opened the lyre-shaped antique jewelry box and we looked inside its luxurious interior of gray silk and cut velvet. It was an elegant Georgian demi-parure worthy of a princess—a magnificent rivière-style necklace and matching elongated earrings, set with impressive, natural Siberian amethysts and mounted in gold. The necklace was made of many large, graduated, oval-shaped cabochon amethysts. Similar stones were set in the top of the earrings from which dangled sizeable pear-shaped amethyst drops. They were breathtaking.

Martha refused to explain why she didn't like the present, and abruptly ended the conversation by smacking the opened jewelry box with the back of her hand, sending it sliding across the table in a crystalline jingle of purple sparkles. Andy lurched to the far side of the table and, with his sure tennis forehand, stopped the box at the edge of the table from crashing to the floor.

Between a sense of disappointment, which Martha vented freely but which was perhaps deeper than she could even admit to herself, and the cascade of demands from a public that craved what she offered—the combined pressures made Martha furious. Yet Andy seemed to put up with her volatility. I was convinced they were a well-matched, strong couple, and I thought they would weather the difficulties after having been together almost thirty years.

However, there had been signs early on of something gone awry.

At one point, Andy had started to wear a Walkman—in part, I'm sure, to drown out Martha and her rules, but also because he was the sort of person who wanted to bring beautiful music as close to his soul as he could. "Rude Man," Martha started to call the Walkman that made her as furious as it must have made Andy calm.

She could not stand to see her husband plugged in, plugged up, away from her. "AN-DY," she would scream. I once saw her give him a hard time when he stopped the tractor he'd been working on to take a break. I was there, rustling about in their garden, picking vegetables they were always kind enough to offer their family and friends. Andy was in the orchard. I could see the pool glimmering in slices of steel-blue through the branches.

I was grasping the coiled head of a fennel when Andy, motioning to me, held the Walkman out.

"It's Handel's 'Water Music.'"

"I don't really like the Baroques," I said. "Too solemn for me."

"You must hear this," he insisted in that Andy manner, always wanting to share.

The music filled my ears and then flowed down my neck, spreading like liquid into my limbs and my lungs, so when Martha started to run toward us, her hands beating the air, her voice was muffled. I thought she was waving, so I waved back, but when I looked at Andy I saw his face fall and realized she wasn't saying hello. I pulled the headphones off of my ears and handed them back to him.

"Useless," Martha was screaming, red-faced and shaking with rage. "You are useless."

As I walked away through the garden gate, I heard the sound of the tractor gunning, Andy beginning to garden again.

• • •

MEANWHILE, MY HUSBAND and I had a very active social life and shared our time with many other friends. Some of them we saw often as couples. Our friends Andy and Maggie lived close by, while Jim and RoAnn, as well as Peter and his wife, lived three hundred miles away, but we all spent many weekends and holidays together. RoAnn had her first baby soon after me, an adorable little boy, James. The two of us, playing with our babies and watching them grow, spent weeks together at RoAnn's summer home on Fishers Island, New York.

I also had a few close women friends who, like me, had taken a hiatus from professional positions and dedicated themselves to raising their children, all about Monica's age. We came to cherish our little ones' playdates, as they were times for us to have fun and learn from one another about child-rearing, baking cookies, and making Halloween costumes. We talked about Gymboree classes and Suzuki lessons, and shared our dread of that stubborn five-pound baby fat one seems to struggle with after giving birth. We also discussed books we'd read, and helped one another keep up on current events. We talked of Diane's plans for a political career, Rene's progress on the memoir she was writing, Cherry's part-time antiques business, my project-to-project consulting jobs, as well as various pro bono work that we were each involved in.

Still we saw a lot of Martha and Andy.

As both my husband and I grew closer to the Stewarts over the years, the final vestiges of formality melted away, allowing us to enter and exit our respective abodes with just a knock and a brief "Hellooooooo," which was always answered with a similarly relaxed "Come on in." We came on in with the ease of children who live on the same block.

It had been over five years since we first met when, one sunny day, Andy came to our door, his face strained, his eyes crumpled with fatigue. More and more often the victim of Martha's well-aimed barbs, Andy began to look bent with grief.

"I am thinking of leaving Martha," Andy said to me. "I don't want to

spend the rest of my life . . . I thought that once she got the book published things would be better."

Not knowing exactly what to say, I asked him, "Would you like a
drink?" But he didn't seem to hear me.

"You know, when I met her, Martha was a perfectly charming girl."

"Can you talk to her about this?"

"I tried," Andy said. "My trip to Patagonia was to give us some time
apart from each other. The chance to start again. You've known her since."

"She has many qualities . . ." I tried.

"Tell me honestly. Would you live with someone who treated you so
badly?" Andy asked.

"What will she do?" I replied. "You're such a big part of her life."

His answer: "She's a survivor."

"I think," I said, "I think she's angry at herself for having had that
hysterectomy so soon after Alexis was born. I think that might have
affected her a lot. She told me many times how much she now wished
she could have another child."

"Did she also tell you how she'd make Lexi help with her catering
business? How Martha once woke her up late on a school night demanding that Lexi make a new batch of cookies because the ones she
had already made weren't perfect?"

Yes, she had. In fact, Martha told me she wished she hadn't done it,
that she had just come home from a long day, having catered late into
the night, and was worried about the next day's job. She had checked
the cookies—I think she said they were madeleines—and their edges
were a bit dark. And Alexis was in middle school, I think. And she
made a mistake.

I thought of that evening about three years earlier, soon after my
first baby was born. We had invited Martha and Andy for dinner at our
house, but I spent most of the evening attending to my colicky baby
who only settled down when I brought her and the baby swing into the
dining room—not exactly a picture-perfect *Entertaining* scene. When

I finally joined the dinner party, Martha began to give me some advice on handling children. Andy interrupted her, anger flushing his face, and said that when it came to mothering, I should use my own instincts.

"Did you talk to Alexis about . . . this?" I asked him.

"I've been trying to. I can't seem to find the right moment."

"Andy, I am worried that if you leave her, Martha will be destroyed."

"No one destroys Martha," Andy answered. "She will destroy herself."

A FEW WEEKS later, Martha's beloved chow, Harry, wandered away from Turkey Hill in a manner totally unlike him. He was a loyal dog, long in his years, most comfortable in his plush dog bed. He probably went down the hill, through the tick-infested woods of the neighboring bird sanctuary, and, his old eyes filled with cataracts, kept wandering the streets until, confused, he got to the highway. I doubt he knew what hit him.

He was found dead. Martha brought his mangled body back to the house. She was distraught, and then beyond distraught. Her grief was wild, fierce.

And then something strange happened. Shortly after Harry's death, in the midst of a sadness that must have been boundless to her, Martha pulled me aside.

"Mariana," Martha said, leaning toward me as if about to impart something revelatory. I could see the pink limning her tired eyes, and I wanted to touch her then, lay a single finger on her impossibly distant face. "You know Harry," she said, and I nodded. "Harry was not accidentally hit by a car! He couldn't take it here. So he committed suicide."

"Martha! Dogs don't—"

She waved her hands: "Stop it!" She would not hear it. "Harry committed suicide." It was clear there was to be no discussion of the matter, not with me, not with Andy, not with anyone else. "Harry has killed himself."

6

After Andy

EARLY THAT YEAR, our families vacationed together on St. Barth, one of my favorite places on Earth. We stayed with mutual friends at their luxurious villa, Cap au Vent, built high on a picturesque cliff overlooking the sea on the tip of Pointe Milou. There we enjoyed balmy breezes under azure skies, watched sensational sunrises with cappuccinos and fresh-baked croissants, and drank perfectly chilled champagne as we took in the dramatic views of the sun setting over the Caribbean behind the high mounds of Colombier on the western end of the island.

On our last afternoon, we went to the beach at Grande Saline. We walked by old saltpans inundated with opaque water and swarming with birds. We hiked the rocky hillock path bordered by fragrant flowering knotty frangipani, anaconda trees with red-orange blossoms, and majestic palms, and then the view opened up as we approached the pristine seaside, where most of our group undressed down to the topless norm of St. Barth beaches and rushed into the surf.

Martha offered to look after Monica, my three-year-old daughter, so I tucked my two-month-old baby girl, Lara, in my arms under the shade of my wide-brimmed panama hat and took her with me on a walk along the mile-plus stretch of the world-renowned Saline beach.

Back from my walk, I took a few photographs of Martha, who was building a sandcastle with Monica, catching sea foam to make tall turrets with tear-shaped drippings of wet, white sand as fine as powdered sugar. I was grateful for Martha's interest in my toddler. I picked up a fat cushion starfish that had washed up on shore and, baby asleep under the beach umbrella, I joined them in decorating their masterpiece, while Martha and I took turns teaching Monica about starfish.

"You can cut one of those creatures in half and the animal will still survive," Martha said.

"Sometimes they split themselves in half to grow two new starfish," I added.

"Poor starfish," Monica said, sadly considering the short-legged orange creature, its body covered with knobby spines.

"It heals its own wound," Martha declared.

Normally, I would have regarded those words as one of the extravagant statements Martha liked to make, but under the circumstances it made a situation I knew about, and Martha did not seem to, all the starker. I had to look away for fear she'd see the secret in my eyes.

The day before, Martha had flawlessly prepared an assortment of delicacies for lunch while simultaneously helping a group of children do a shell project at the breakfast bar, and conferring with our host and his friends, true wine connoisseurs, on the perfect bouquet to be uncorked from our stash of French vintages. Martha was in a great mood and she gave instructions to the gregarious swarm of guests gathered on the covered dining terrace as they set the tables and swayed to the rhythm of Grace Jones's "I Need a Man." Every now and then, Martha called out to our hostess, Maggie, who was steps away on the limestone terrace chatting with her sister and brother-in-law, Beth and John, and keeping watch over the kids splashing about in the spectacular infinity pool.

Alexis, in her early twenties by then, had largely kept to herself on this trip. With no siblings and no one her own age, she was stuck among the older adults and the small children. She stood in the center hall, apart from all the prelunch commotion, taking in the ocean view, the same one Martha would later pose in front of for the cover of *Martha Stewart's Quick Cook Menus*. That beautiful photograph, taken by Chris Baker, depicted Martha smiling behind an invitingly set table. In the hazy blue background of that shot was the island of Frégate rising from the caldera of the submerged volcano said to have made St. Barth.

It was my husband's turn at toddler duty, so I had taken my baby away from the hub of the house to nurse her on the east-facing terrace, with its view of the open ocean and the island La Tortue, said to be circled by sharks. But from the comfort of Cap au Vent all I saw was the splash of a manta ray and the swoop-glide of a West Indian frigate bird pirating another bird's catch.

My baby had fallen asleep by the time Andy, who was to fly home for a business meeting early the next morning, before our outing to Saline beach, came and sat in the chaise next to mine. Since he had his camera, I pointed to the group of small ocean islands and reefs on our left: "Take a picture of Toc Vers Island!" By the way Andy smiled I realized I'd been quite a pest on the photo front, reminding everyone not to take pictures of me that vacation since I wasn't back in shape after the pregnancy yet.

"I read that there is a—fortunately rare—cactus on that island," I said, trying to lead the conversation away from my concerns. "It attacks those who come near by tossing sharp spine-covered leaves at them, leaving behind agonizingly painful barbs in your flesh."

"I am not going home for business," Andy said with so much sadness in his voice that my eyes instantly turned to look into his. "I am leaving Martha."

The news came as such a shock that, although I heard Andy say that he had just told my husband of his plans, it took me a while to process what he meant before I replied, slowly, "It sounds so . . . final, Andy."

"My mind is made up."

"It is going to be very hard for Martha."

"Please take care of her. She'll need you."

"I'll do my best," I said.

As he reached over to gently squeeze the hand with which I supported the weight of my baby, I realized that Andy really meant what he was saying and that he was truly leaving behind all of what he and Martha had been and had made together.

"She's such a good baby!" he said.

"I thank God every day," I replied, but all I could think of was how much I would miss him. I felt my eyes burn with tears. I knew once Andy walked out that door that our connection would be difficult to maintain. Given that the nature of our friendship was as a foursome, it would be almost impossible for us to remain close friends when they were no longer married.

The whole thing—the separation and the secrecy that was required in order for Andy to enact it—felt like a punch in the solar plexus, yet one does what one must do for friendship. Ever since we met the Stewarts, Andy, who treated me like a kid sister, had been a closer friend to me than Martha, whom I couldn't really read and whose competitiveness I sometimes found tiresome. But my participation in his scheme, although it required no more than silence, put me in a hopeless position, not only because I was faced with having to choose between them or lose both, but also because I knew that I would never abandon a woman in distress. So, in fact, the choice was already made for me, and Andy knew that when he said, "Please take care of her. She'll need you." He was saying good-bye to me. I figured Andy's leaving in such a secretive way was to avoid a scene with Martha.

As I watched Martha build sandcastles at Saline beach with my daughter on that last day, I worried about how she would survive what was coming. She was getting so famous, so popular. Many people, once the news hit, would wonder how a man could leave a woman as accomplished as she.

However, Martha seemed to suspect nothing. During those days on the island, before Andy left, her moods changed on a dime as they always did, so a sour face and a cruel comment might very well be followed a moment later with an enthusiastic bid for an adventure. One day it was hiking the narrow donkey-trail to Colombier beach through a forest of giant torch cacti and along the windy slopes of Anse Paschal where silent pelicans dove acrobatically; another day it was a sunset drink and exploring the cobbled streets in the historic harbor town of Gustavia, where tax-free boutiques have elegant window displays and sport the names of exclusive shops from Paris to New York; or she'd entice us to spoil ourselves with exotic lobster delicacies and exquisite atmosphere for dinner at the superb restaurant at the Hotel Eden Rock. Being with Martha could make one's head spin, or one simply got tired of relentless activity, the way one does when minding a toddler who has just learned to walk and runs awkwardly around, while you, with your arms out, step this way and that, following his jerky path, hoping to avert the crash.

When we returned from St. Barth, I imagined Martha walking into her home alone, maybe calling "Aaaandy," and then, only when she heard the walls' echo in reply, would she sense something was wrong. "Aaaandy!" Maybe a few more shouts, then the curve of a question mark: "Andy?"

I imagined her wandering through the perfectly decorated empty rooms, the heat coming on slowly, gurgling in the belly of the boiler as she flicked on light switch after light switch—the kitchen, the library, the front parlor, the dining room, the glassed-in porch, their bedroom upstairs, the two spare bedrooms. She'd be serpentining up and down her glorious hallways, flooding them with light, one room after the other, waiting for some sign of him somewhere, and finding none. Soon the whole house would be blazing like a birthday cake and would seem, from outside, like a glorious beacon of radiant warmth in winter.

After parting ways with Martha when we got home from the airport, my husband and I were on alert. I suspected that once the reality at Turkey Hill hit her, she would reach for the phone and call me, not because we were dear friends but because I was one of the few women she was at least closer with.

And sure enough, not long after we had stepped inside, put the baby in her crib, and I was taking Monica to bed, the phone rang. My husband took our sleepy child from my arms.

"I'm sure it's Martha. You take it," he said.

I picked up the phone with an uncertain "Hello."

"Andy left. He's not coming back." Her voice, which at first sounded flattened by sadness and disbelief, suddenly peaked in a contemptuous snicker: "He didn't have the courage to face me. He left a letter!"

I imagined her finding that thinnest slice of white paper, perhaps lying tucked between the plump pillows on their bed, reading it, going to the closet to see. He did not take much, just a suitcase, but I pictured her opening the closet and seeing that it had lost some of its soul, and then turning to see their bed, vast now, as for the first time in almost thirty years Martha was to sleep there alone.

"I'm so sorry, Martha."

"It's impossible," Martha said. I didn't know how to respond to that, because Martha seemed to have forgotten her terrible behavior toward Andy, and in front of so many people. She must have known what consequences to expect. "He can't leave me," Martha howled. "Not now!"

I knew what she meant. Martha's next book, *Weddings*, was to come out in just a few short weeks, a book celebrating nuptials in general and her own specifically, the entire introduction a nostalgia-laced look back at the ceremony she and Andy had when they were barely out of their teens. Martha had shown me their beautiful wedding picture, which she picked for the book. They looked so happy. The dedication for the book read:

To my husband Andy:
Our wedding will always remain my favorite
and to my daughter Alexis,
whose wedding I look forward to with pleasure.

I could hardly think of anything less serendipitous than being a public figure publishing a book memorializing her union, months of book tour awaiting, while her "better half" had just walked off. How would she explain this to the ABC anchor on *Good Morning America*? Or any of the audiences scheduled to attend Martha's appearances across the country, part of the elaborate book promotion program already arranged by Martha's publicist, Susan Magrino. I could only imagine all the gossip and the gloating. Yet, I didn't think that it should matter to her audience, who would no doubt make *Weddings* a success.

"You want me to come over?" I asked.

"I'll call around. He's probably at his sister Diane's," she said.

"I'm here if you need me."

And Martha did. She began to call me several times a day, time not healing the wound but opening it wider with every infectious tick-tock of the clock. Every day that passed was God laughing in her face because Andy had not come back. Regardless of her treatment of Andy and her apparently mixed motives for wanting him back, they had built a home together, raised a child together. One needn't listen hard to hear the pit of pure pain at the center of her hysterics.

My woman's instinct to reach out to another in need kicked in and I reached out to help as best I could. I had made a promise to Andy but aside from that, I genuinely felt sorry for Martha, particularly a couple of days later, when Martha learned her husband had not flown the coop by himself but rather as part of a pair. I was truly surprised to hear that. Although the other woman was none other than Robyn, the small brunette I'd warned Martha about at the Roger Vergé dinner months before, Andy had never so much as implied there might be another woman.

At first, Martha's rage was so raw it was shocking. The nightly emergency calls seemed to come more often from Martha than from the hospital where my husband was frequently on call.

"Martha again." My husband handed the receiver to me.

"I can't stand it. I must see Andy. I'm driving to New York!" Martha sobbed hysterically.

"Wait! I'll be right there."

"How long is this going to last?" my husband asked. "I want my wife here, with me. You have small children. You need your sleep."

"I'll be right back, I promise." I kissed his arm and he let my wrist go.

When I entered Martha's driveway, she was running out of the house, pulling at her hair with both hands, heading for her car. I barely had time to jump in with her and slam the car door shut before we flew past the gate and down the street.

"Please, Martha, slow down!"

She let go of the steering wheel and started to hit her thighs, head, and arms, the dashboard. I defended my chest as her flying fists also came at me a few times, while the car dangerously careened into the left lane and over the grass toward a huge tree.

"What are you doing? Are you mad?" I yelled.

I fended off her blows with my left arm and leaned forward to grab the steering wheel with my right hand, straightening the car barely a second before it crashed. Then the engine abruptly cut off. Martha banged her head against the steering wheel and went through all the motions of crying without any tears.

"Why did he leave me? Why won't he talk to me? He's afraid to see me. He knows I'll get him back."

"Why don't you send him a letter?"

"I did. He didn't read it. I have to see him."

There were actually times when we made it, in her car, into the city, Martha in a manic mindless rage, perhaps precipitated by news that Andy had been seen—"He leaves his droppings," she used to say—with his new partner in this or that café, bar, theater, having good times. Robyn had rented a painting studio in the city, and her work was being shown in SoHo galleries. We went to his building on the Upper West Side, so late that most of the city lights were off. She called out his name, threw whatever objects she found on the side of the street at his window, once broke some glass. It went this way for months without her ever seeing him.

I lost confidence in my ability to give comfort. Martha's screams had turned guttural. She must have been all black-and-blue from punching herself. Slowly, I stopped offering advice. There was nothing left to say. We filled the silence with movies. Sometimes, in the dark theater, I saw Martha, her profile rigid, her mouth a knot, occasionally her fist swinging out in response to some interior image.

BY JULY, WHEN Martha was perhaps the only one who still hoped that Andy would come back, *Weddings* was published. It was a great success.

Before he left, Andy had taken as many precautions as he could to help Martha project the image of domestic happiness and protect her professional success. By the time news of their split became public, the Kmart contract was well under way. When the deal was announced, the tongues wagged, for a while. But as they say, he who laughs last, laughs best. Martha's contract with Kmart, which proved to be extremely profitable for her, was eventually credited for its brilliance. I was surprised to see how so many journalists regarded Andy as just a husband who had left his famous millionaire wife for a younger woman. It made no sense to me that his role as the mastermind of Martha's career was simply disregarded.

In addition to working with Kmart, Martha gave numerous magazine interviews, made several television appearances, and continued to write books, like *The Wedding Planner* and *Martha Stewart's Quick Cook Menus*, published in 1988.

But in private it took a long time, as these things do. Like those of a very young child, her first words were exclamations: "I'll write a book! *The Good Wife*! I'll show everyone how he cheated on me and I forgave him and then he found another one to run away with!" I let Martha ramble on but it really got me when she'd say, "I wish he'd die!"

"Oh, Martha, don't say that!" I responded meekly one day, although her anger frightened me. My words didn't make a dent in her verbal deluge but rather gave her anger more impetus.

"Don't SAY that? How would you like it if your husband slept with Erica Jong?"

"Who is Erica Jong?" The last name, with its peculiar pronunciation, got stuck in my throat.

Martha looked at me, and for the first time in weeks I saw an emotion other than anger or despair take over her face. Surprise.

"Who is Erica Jong?" Martha said incredulously. "Didn't you read *Fear of Flying*?"

"I remember," I said, mentally sorting through my stash of books, "reading a book about a woman pilot, she was English and lived I think in Kenya. She flew solo over the Atlantic . . . had many affairs . . ."

And then Martha's surprise vanished, overtaken, I suppose, by my ignorance.

"Erica Jong," she said, somehow managing to make a sibilant hissing sound out of a name with no sibilant qualities whatsoever, "Erica Jong, whom Andy had an affair with, writes about having sssex!"

I was profoundly uncomfortable hearing this news, and yet the source of my discomfort was not the information itself—that Andy (according to Martha, anyway) had been disloyal. How was I to know if it was even true? I did not dismiss her comment, nor did I accept it.

I had the queasy feeling that Martha was telling me this to manipulate my feelings for a man she knew I had loved. Martha's tidbit, which had a sort of surgical precision to it, brought the strident image of that beast wearing a cauldron on its head, swallowing the damned and dumping them into a hole in the ground near the coin-excreting human posterior in the third "Hell" panel of Hieronymus Bosch's painting *The Garden of Earthly Delights*. The image to me defied all explanation, although I read somewhere that it's a portrait of instinctive fears.

Then Martha began to act. First, she deleted Robyn's photos from all reprints of all of her books, like the full-page picture showcasing Robyn creating the *Weddings* flower arrangements. Second, she refused to give Andy copies of the family photos when he asked. I disliked Martha's penchant for revenge, and I abhorred the lengths she went to in her vengefulness, yet I did not walk away. Perhaps I was flattered that Martha Stewart was crying on my shoulder; by then Martha was one of the Western world's biggest stars, and in many ways larger than life. But what I am sure of is that while taking care of Martha, I began to care for her as a friend, for herself alone, not for Martha who was part of a couple. And, although I don't believe that loving means indulging bad behavior, I thought Martha had learned her lesson by the time when, after making statements concerning Andy's ability to father children, she then acknowledged lying in public.

IN THE FALL of 1987, when there was no denying that the voluptuous petite brunette had clearly captivated Andy, Martha told me that she had come up with a plan to get him back. The Ebenezer Banks Adams House, built in 1838 and located on a well-traveled corner in Westport, had just come up for sale. Martha said that when she and Andy were working together to restore Turkey Hill, they often drove by the "handsome flat-roof entrance portico with Doric columns and pilasters" of the "five-bay, two-story house in Grecian taste" with "six-over-six windows," as the State of Connecticut Historical Commission described it. Time and again the Stewarts talked about that house, which had so many features similar to theirs that they were pretty sure it had been built by the same hands that built Turkey Hill. Martha convinced herself to buy the Adams House, apparently believing that she would get Andy to come back and they would work on that dilapidated, overgrown house and be happy again. A well-spent near-half-million dollars.

Martha and Andy had bought Turkey Hill together in the early 1970s, when their daughter, Alexis, was still in grade school. It might be fair to say there were two Turkey Hills. One is accessible to all and has become in many ways an American symbol of domesticity; indeed, it was the model for the TV show Martha would develop a few years later. A second, secret Turkey Hill contained in the horsehair plaster the simple story of a young couple. The woman, a Breck model as a young girl, became a shining Barnard student and then a stockbroker whose grit was fascinating behind her flawless complexion, forthrightness, and a mind on the move. The man was a young Yale Law School graduate with an impeccable pedigree and an intellect to match, a real renaissance man who fell in love with this shining girl and married her in 1961. Together, as equals, they bought a dilapidated farmhouse on the outskirts of New York City, and over the years painstakingly restored it to the point where the home itself had become their joint palette.

That house had become a part of me too, as my husband and I had grown closer to the Stewarts over the years. How often, after their initial separation, did Martha tell me that the best time of her marriage had been in restoring Turkey Hill? That house had done what no marriage counselor could ever do.

7

Starting Over

*E*NTERTAINING HAD SET Martha on course to become a superstar, the way a star's explosion marks the birth of a supernova. As millions of stargazers watched in awe, Martha transformed whatever inspired her at Turkey Hill into homemaking ideas that revolutionized the manner in which Americans entertained at home. Once Martha designated an idea to be It, enough people were persuaded that it was It, that it de facto became It.

While Martha never lost her tight grip on her business empire, the ugly dissolution of her marriage dragged on. Abandoned, dejected, and angry with Andy, Martha refused to accept any blame for the relationship's failure. She avoided dwelling on her personal tragedy by waging legal challenges over each detail of the divorce and taking every possible step to forestall dividing the possessions that she and Andy had amassed over the years. To Martha, material success meant the world, so securing what she saw as her rightful share was a high priority.

The Turkey Hill paradise became the lair of the dragon lady. Like the legendary Dragon Empress who erected China's largest theater, Martha spared no expense in renovations of "the farm" to make a model home in which she lived alone and used as a dream world to showcase for her television viewers.

The Easter after Andy left, Martha gave a wonderful lunch party at Turkey Hill. Soon after we arrived, Martha opened the Easter hunt and my daughter Monica, carrying the basket she and I had fun decorating the day before, joined the crowd of adorable children in their Easter Sunday best, looking for eggs that Martha had hidden around the property early that morning—probably at dawn.

The heart of the party was the outside kitchen, which had recently been reconstructed, but the look of Turkey Hill had not yet changed so much from when Andy lived there; this was to happen soon thereafter, when all the outside trim was painted an elegant but severe emu-egg green. Martha had transformed the center island into a celebratory buffet table, covering its surface with an abundance of festively presented, traditional Polish Easter dishes. Martha had made many of them herself and the rest had been prepared by members of her family: hams that came from their favorite butcher in New York, oven-roasted smoked kielbasa and beets with grated horseradish came, I think, from her sister Kathy, a teacher who lived in Old Greenwich with her husband and two sons. I remember that Martha's mother, Big Martha, as we called her, had made the cabbage pierogi, those pillowy semicircle-shaped dumplings we wolfed down as she watched us with a wide-open smile.

Martha's celadon-green Fire King dinner plates, an assortment of glasses—many of them the Depression glass she liked to collect—and cheerful flatware with Bakelite and painted-wood handles individually wrapped in linen napkins were invitingly set on the counter next to her always sparkling kitchen sinks.

The breakfast table by the door to the original greenhouse was a picture-perfect Easter display. Marble-shell eggs, which Martha had dyed herself, and oval cookies, their rose-trellis and garland icing as pretty as jeweled Fabergé Imperial eggs, hung from an Easter tree. Exquisite serving trays were arranged with a variety of madeleine cakes shaped as lambs, rabbits, and chickens, which Martha baked in her vintage molds and glazed with chocolate icing. Among the cakes were delicately hued hand-painted large duck eggs and larger goose eggs, as well as naturally pale aqua eggs from Martha's rare Araucana chickens. The golden-brown almond and raisin babkas were made by Martha's youngest sister, Laura, their brother, George and his wife, Rita, who worked as Martha's business manager, brought their two toddlers. Also among the large group of guests were some longtime friends of mine and my husband's, many of whom Martha had met while she was still with Andy.

It was a glorious, cool, sunny day. Everything was still in bud, with only the grape hyacinths in full bloom. Children ran up and down between the peach, cherry, and apple trees in the orchard while some of the guests strolled the pebbly paths of Martha's garden. The arbor that stood near the middle created a focal point that seemed to divide the garden into two outdoor rooms— a formal upper garden and a more casual lower one. I loved exploring the garden by the path that started near the door of the outside kitchen. I knew that, whichever way I walked, I would discover some plant I hadn't seen before. Sometimes Martha and I went there to share a secret, a few moments of silence, or a cappuccino. Over the years, I often took my girls to her garden, trying to impart in them the sense of wonder I felt in the rose-and-clematis-covered arbor that appeared to both separate and join two worlds.

While everyone missed Andy, Martha perhaps most of all, we had a wonderful Easter, and enjoyed a feast that only Martha—the hostess with the mostest, as I used to call her—could give.

MARTHA WAS ALWAYS polishing her domestic skills and her image. Cameras followed her around celebrations and festivities for her TV specials, like her 1989 *At Home with Martha Stewart this Christmas*, in which she smilingly described her step-by-step secrets of the arts of home decorating, cooking, and entertaining. She painted nuts, fruits, leaves, and pinecones in gold, and baked Christmas cookies in front of the television cameras, surrounded by a group of six children, four of whom were my five-year-old Monica and three of her friends from school. Having met Martha on several occasions at our house, the children's parents agreed to let the kids be on her show (for fun, of course, not for money). And indeed they had fun with frosting, spatterware, and dot decorating, and eating Martha's delicious sugar cookies. My husband and I even appeared as guests at her televised party, with a hostess gift and an opportunity for a hospitality hint—"Mariana always finds an extraordinary ornament for the tree."

Martha marketed the show with Kmart, who did distribution, and simultaneously published a companion book, *Martha Stewart's Christmas, Entertaining, Decorating and Giving*, which included the show's recipes and crafts, pictures of Monica presenting a bowl of festive potpourri; our friends' children—Katharine, Olivia, Christen, and Peter—preparing popcorn balls with Martha. My friends were also included in a second Christmas party that Martha gave at the Turkey Hill barn, in order to stage photographs for the book.

The pictures of the main house were a testimony to both Chris Baker's talent and Martha's determination that Turkey Hill and its adornments would be hers after the divorce. A gingerbread house she made for the Christmas book was a "copy" of her "own Turkey Hill Federal farmhouse." The full-page photograph shows the "gingerbread mansion" on a sideboard in the dining room, lit by the chandelier from Andy's mother, under the large painting Martha described in the caption as "my 18th-century copy of Correggio's *Jupiter and Io*," which, as Martha had told me, she was determined to keep.

After being photographed and filmed as props, the lavish meals she created were transported in cars and planes for festive dining with family and friends. Sometimes Martha offered them as hostess gifts. Sometimes they just ended up as chicken feed for Martha's exotic poultry.

Off-camera, when she was not engaged in endless sparring with lawyers, Martha cooed at her color-point Persian cats and chow chow dogs. She hung out with her fancy new acquaintances, as well as with a handful of personal friends. She relied almost exclusively on me as her "companion in grief."*

The fact that Martha had so few old close friends often gave me pause. But I accepted the fact that politics, not commitment, guided her. I stood by Martha, even when she was very clear with me about her expectation that our friendship should rule out my keeping in touch with Andy. By then my compassion for Martha prevailed and it was too late for me to ponder her edicts. I had already undertaken trying to help her heal her gaping emotional wounds. Martha was often charming and down-to-earth, a challenging but interesting person to have as a friend. Despite the reasons I had for caution, we became confidantes.

I liked some of Martha's irreverence, like her not falling prey to what William Allen Butler called "the pitiful wail of 'Nothing to Wear.'" I figured that, after having publicly flaunted tradition for so long, Martha reveled in ignoring convention even when it came to the code of evening dress. Whenever Martha would invite me to a fancy evening, I would think nothing of sporting "just a little black dress" because I knew that Martha might change her shoes or earrings for the occasion but was otherwise likely to wear business attire. Nonetheless, at each of those formal social events, it was Martha who stood out above the crowd of beautiful women in their finest bejeweled couture.

It was exciting to be around Martha. Everything became an adventure. In the beginning of June 1988, she and I went to London, the first time I took a trip without my husband. Martha was invited to visit the elegant Booth-Clibborns. I had met this couple a few times and liked Julia, a very proper lady, and her husband, Edward, an interesting gentleman and esteemed publisher of high-quality books. They had been

---

*Aristotle wrote in *Nicomachean Ethics*: "Friends are sought in times of both good fortune and bad fortune. Friendship is more of a necessity in times of bad fortune, but it is more noble in times of good fortune, because in times of bad fortune friendship is based on usefulness while in times of good fortune it is based on virtue. Better men avoid sharing their grief with their friends, because they don't want to cause sorrow to their friends. But weak men enjoy to have others as companions in grief."

the guests on *A Formal Dinner Party*, the debut video in Martha's *Secrets for Entertaining* series produced with Kathy Deutch Tatlock when Andy still lived at Turkey Hill.

After Andy left, Julia and Edward were among the few friends who remained loyal to Martha. They had just had their second baby, Augustin, so I wasn't sure I should come along, but Martha insisted, reassuring me that we were both invited. She was excited that Edward and Julia had accepted her offer to be godmother to their newborn son.

Julia graciously received us and hoped that indeed, as Martha had told her over the phone, we didn't mind sharing the small guest room in their beautiful London flat, since the larger one was occupied by the baby's nurse. However, when we realized that we were to sleep together in an exquisite but narrow period bed, we decided to spend most of our nights lingering over long dinners out.

We went to a well-regarded restaurant that Martha had heard about, an impeccable place with a clubby English atmosphere, where elegant patrons were seated at tables placed at a comfortable distance from one another. One of the guests was Joan Collins, the actress, perhaps the most beautiful woman I'd ever seen up close. A man who dined alone came to our table and, after introducing himself as Terry O'Neill, began an amusing barrage of "you look like models"–type compliments. I responded with my coldest polite smile. Martha, on the other hand, was friendly and forthcoming, and, to my dismay, invited him to sit down with us.

As he did, our gregarious new companion turned to me and said, "You are married." Then he looked at Martha, and said, "You are not."

I resented being made a party to such an obvious pickup, but seeing that he was clearly attracted to Martha, I let my guard down and we ended up having a great evening. Terry shared little about himself, besides telling us that he was a photographer. As funny as he was handsome, he had us both laughing and we even told him about our splurging on dinner because there was not enough room in bed for us to sleep.

After dinner, Martha dropped me off at Julia's and went off with

Terry. I was grateful for the sleeping space and appreciative of Martha's talent at finding solutions for all kinds of problems, but her impulsivity made me uncomfortable, if only because I was afraid that she might get hurt. But Martha came back by five o'clock next morning, saving me from further worry about her disappearance with this stranger. I then learned that he had not been Jack the Ripper, as I feared, but the ex-husband of Faye Dunaway, a woman as beautiful, tall, and blond as Martha.

I followed Martha's energetic lead to the London flea markets, to catch the peddlers as they unpacked small and large treasures beyond the mounds of fresh fruit perfuming the chilly morning air. My happiest find was Turkish coffee in a copper pot called an *ibrik*, made just the way we prepared it in Romania. Martha bought lots of plant seeds and tons of beautiful vintage and antique ribbons.

But the best discovery Martha and I made while browsing the flea markets was that we were great travel partners. As many women eventually become aware when traveling without men, it's not easy to find well-matched companions among one's friends. We had enormous fun traveling together. We went to antique galleries and flower markets, visited museums, and saw Chekhov's *Uncle Vanya* with a superb cast, including Greta Scacchi and Jonathan Pryce, at the Vaudeville Theatre in Westminster.

However, I didn't feel right being away from my family and I was happy to go back home. My children loved the gifts I picked up for them during our quick stop at Harrods. I didn't say a word about Terry to my husband, as by then I was keeping Martha's secrets to protect her from his judgmental comments.

Terry came to Turkey Hill for a visit when Martha was filming a tag sale for her TV show. If at first he appeared to find it strange, Terry appreciated the quaintness of Martha's glamorizing her longtime fad. He teased her no more for that than for her cohort of felines. Martha had just been given a pair of kittens to complete her already large troupe of Himalayan cats: Mozart, Verdi, Vivaldi, Bartok, Beethoven, and Berlioz.

Terry named the new ones Teeny and Weeny. Terry had a fabulous sense of humor, so he saw the funny side of the hole in his sweater as the new kittens indulged their passion for chewing cashmere. When Terry visited some years later, Martha kept her new collection of live birds in beautiful antique cages placed on side tables in the glassed-in porch where her dogs patiently observed how easily the menagerie of cats could stick their paws between the bars. Terry mirthfully said that Martha had designed the arrangement to strengthen character in her canaries.

Good things happened after our trip to London. Martha and I grew closer, and the Andy storm stopped as abruptly as it started. It was as if Martha had simply pushed some button inside of her. She no longer raged or wept or pulled clumps of hair out of her head. She shook herself off, stepped up, and set about finding herself a mate.

Martha launched into her new single life with gusto and a touch of desperation. I stood back and watched Martha stumble into sex as one might watch one's child learn to walk, covering one's eyes as the stairs loom into view. She had an attractive girlfriend, Zacki, also a former model. They had met in the 1960s, when Martha did ads for Tareyton cigarettes and Breck shampoo. Lovely and well-connected, Zacki, who now worked as a stylist and image consultant, introduced Martha to many desirable bachelors, including Charlie Rose. I also recall a witty journalist, tall and handsome. When she brought him for dinner at our house a few times, the women guests crowded around him. I thought he was very attractive. But after a short game of seduction, the journalist only returned Martha's calls to see her platonically. She wasn't crushed, but she was quite upset and said that, although she only wanted a very rich man for a husband, she might have married him had he asked.

My husband and I gave many parties. We invited Martha each time, and, as she met our friends and their friends, someone introduced her to Dan Shedrick, a sports marketing wizard with a multimillion-dollar company that produced baseball trading cards. Dan, who soon became a regular companion, recently separated from his second wife, with whom he had two small children. Sometimes Dan would forget that he had made a date with Martha, and she would be left waiting for him. When he didn't show up, Martha would try finding him at his mansion in Fairfield, a couple of miles from Turkey Hill, but the evening usually ended with her calling me every few minutes, and when I couldn't think of any more excuses, I would take Martha out to console her. Eventually, she got used to Dan's disappearing act, perhaps because he charmed her with his good looks, his leonine mane of black hair, and his disarming smile, or simply because he was funny and fun to be with. Martha went duck-hunting (I gave her my shotgun) with Dan and his old school-buddies from Fordham, somewhere down South. They went on safari in Africa together, although she had little nice to say about that trip. Dan stayed around, off and on, for several years. He was an interesting dinner partner, who escorted her to fancy New York benefits, and also looked good on camera, like when he sat on Martha's right at her 1994 Thanksgiving dinner TV special.

Martha worried that she might not find another husband. She was Martha Stewart the star, but when Andy left, she no longer knew who she was. For a while, she behaved like so many women who are afraid of getting old—so eager to look younger they wear miniskirts, hoping to recapture their youth. The result, unfortunately, was best described by F. Scott Fitzgerald in *The Last Tycoon*: "It's like actors, who try so pathetically not to look in mirrors. Who lean backward trying—only to see their faces in the reflecting chandeliers."

I couldn't tell Martha that she had become a recurrent motif for arguments at home. My husband, who I thought was perhaps jealous of our close friendship, found many reasons for criticizing Martha's looks and her sexual escapades.

"She's a beautiful woman, youthful and alive!" I said, but I could not persuade him to accept my theory that Martha was just catching up on skipped homework, that because she had married her Prince Charming before having learned harsher lessons, this was simply her way of growing up.

Sometimes I wondered if, had he been less critical of Martha, I would have felt better about our marriage. At first I thought yes, but then, as time wore on, the answer came: No, I would not. By belittling Martha, my husband had unwrapped a new part of himself, and I didn't like what I saw.

As for Martha, her life crisis greatly undermined her image of herself. I tried to persuade her to seek professional help but she refused. Then I came up with an idea. I had heard of this man in Weston, a psychologist, who was supposed to be a great counselor. I proposed that we should both go to him. I thought that my offer to join her might reduce the stigma of not being able to deal with her problems. I also needed answers about my slowly disintegrating marriage.

The counselor was a kind man with a gray beard, a cross between Freud and a hippie. Martha wanted me to be in the first session with her and after that we went to see him separately a few more times. He might not have given us many answers, but he gave us both some glimmer of hope.

Martha and I talked on the phone every day and I developed the habit of stopping by Turkey Hill with my children. I kept Martha company at her photo and TV shoots, I was in her filmed holiday specials, and photographs of me and my daughters appeared in her books and, then, magazines. We went together to the market, the beauty salon, the movies, garden-shopping, and did a lot of bargain-hunting and antiquing.

Before we met the Stewarts, my then-fiancé and I had redecorated our house. After that, we had continued to search antique stores and auctions in New York and around New England for the pieces we wanted. Meanwhile, inspired by Martha's example, I had studied and learned much about decorating and antiques. I also adopted her idea that every piece of furniture, each fixture and ornament should fit multiple criteria, like the dining room chandelier at Turkey Hill. My husband and I enjoyed our treasure hunts, and did so much of it that any time we stopped at an antique store or auction gallery, the backseat of our car echoed with our daughters' calling, "Antiques? Not again!"

Eventually, it was Martha with whom I did most of my antiquing.

We went to one auction where she wanted to bid on some dishes. We got there minutes before they closed the preview, yet in enough time for me to notice a very beautiful Persian rug. It was an elegant, early-twentieth-century "palace-size" Tabriz carpet. What I loved about that rug was that it had an unusual amount of turquoise in the rosette of its large central medallion, in the escutcheons at its sides, and along the borders and bands, livening yet softening the scarlet red flowers and palmettes of the *herati* motifs.

Based on what I had learned from books, museums, and show rooms, and having also recognized a few rug dealers in the audience, I deduced that there were some good rugs there and that by the way the dealers bid I'd find out if the one I liked was among them. Since my husband and I had been talking about finding a larger and better rug for our living room, I decided to bid on it and bring it home as a surprise. But it cost many thousands of dollars, a sum I had never before spent without consulting first with him. Also, it wasn't like bringing home a picture frame or a vase, but a very large rug for the place where we spent every evening of every day. So although I was really happy with my purchase, I felt a bit unnerved by the thought that he might not like it. I could tell that Martha felt my anxiety.

When we arrived home, we found that my husband had cleared the living room of furniture and was in the process of unrolling the Persian rug that he had just bought from a dealer in New York. It was, as I remember, a fine room-size Kashan, with silk weft and a suffusion of rubia reds. It also had a lot of deep indigo blue, a color that, I remembered having read somewhere, signified solitude.

It was an awkward moment. After complimenting his find, Martha and I helped my husband carry ours, which weighed a ton, out of her Suburban. The rugs, for which we had paid similar price, were of the same vintage, similar in quality and condition, both done with beautiful vegetable dyes, yet very different in pattern and mood. Martha, who didn't have Orientals and mostly lived with stenciled floors, declined to be the arbiter. I thought my rug fitted the room much better, but I let my husband decide which we should keep. His response was as of late a familiar one when it came to my ideas: first he ridiculed, then attacked, and finally adopted them once it became blindingly obvious they were valid. So it was that the Tabriz stayed to spend evenings with us as we read different books, spoke less and less, and paid no attention to the fact that antiquing was yet another activity we no longer liked doing together.

Meanwhile, Martha, who loved the society scene, did not miss one social occasion. Since Martha felt betrayed if she was not invited, my husband and I asked her to come with us every time we went out, to festive gatherings with our friends or even just for a movie or quick dinner. She often wanted us to accompany her to parties where she was a guest. Like a veritable people junkie, Martha accepted all invitations. Her favorite audience was people she perceived to be successful in ways she was not, especially those with happy family relationships and those whose enormous wealth overshadowed her own fortune.

Ironically, Martha rarely seemed to enjoy herself at parties and did not bother to pretend otherwise. She was usually laconic in her social exchanges but she could become abrupt or even doze off at the dinner table, mortifying the other guests. When Martha was late, left a dinner party before the last course had been served, or sometimes didn't show up at all, she did it with an unabashed lack of apology. My husband found such behavior unmannerly, but I always came up with an excuse: Martha was a very busy person, and so clever that she probably could have trademarked breaches of etiquette for a profit if she wanted. Secretly, though, I felt mutinous admiration for Martha's couldn't-careless attitude. While doing a lot to please those around me, I worried about becoming dependent on their approval. I feared I might lose my true self and grow to be one of those seething, enraged women.

After a while, my husband started to turn down the evenings out with Martha. Perhaps he didn't want to share my company with her, but certainly our marriage grew increasingly strained. More and more often, after our family dinners and evening rituals with my children, I went out with Martha alone.

By then, although Martha's social circles were constantly widening, she relied almost exclusively on me for close friendship and sought my company. If I became a hostage of her entertainment routines, it was mostly because being with her was fun. My husband and I had begun living parallel lives. While he was educated and bright, his interests were limited to cold book-learning, quite the opposite from Martha and me, who sought all kinds of knowledge. To her, everything was information, so if I told her of having read about a brilliant physicist, John Wheeler, who, to the best of my understanding, said that there is no "out there" out there without us, Martha would not tease me as my husband would but actually listen. She may have even filed the thought away for future inspiration, somewhat like Wheeler's "idea for an idea." Gradually, my friendship with Martha started to make up for what was lacking in my marriage, making me feel like a more complete human being with a life of my own.

In some ways, Andy Stewart may, possibly, have allowed my marriage to continue for as long as it did because he filled pockets of thought that my husband simply could not. After all, it was Andy who had not only read my favorite books but also delighted in them. It was Andy who had an implicit understanding of one of my favorite quotes, from the British geneticist J. B. S. Haldane: "The universe is not only queerer than we suppose, but queerer than we can suppose." Exactly.

As Martha and I allowed our emotional longings to surface, and even lead our adventures, it never once crossed my mind that our relationship might mimic the beginning of a *folie à deux*, what Merriam-Webster calls "the presence of the same or similar delusional ideas in two persons closely associated with one another." Although it did occur to me later that perhaps our attempted escapes from the confines of ordinary life were part of a shared *Life: The Movie* delusion. However, our escapes were more like a magic show at *Master and Margarita*'s Variety Theater or the Devil's Midnight Ball. I don't recall if we spoke about it first, or we just did it, but by the spring of 1988, a year after Andy left, Martha and I had entered our pact for wonder and discovery. We went to restaurants and parties. We hooked arms and held our perfumed pulses up to one another's noses.

Our adventure may have begun on Walpurgis Night, known as the "other Halloween," a night of magic spells, evil craft, and witches on broomsticks, celebrated on April 30 since the times of the Vikings and Valkyries. It is the night about which Winifred Hodge writes in *Wael-burga and the Rites of May* as a time "for seeking deep roots of life-knowledge and life-mysteries . . . for almost all the elements of what is called 'women's magic.'" It is also the night Goethe's Faust met Mephistopheles, but if I recalled that at all when Martha and I went out that night, it was because it reminded me of my happy student years in Bucharest, when we fêted both famine and feast with poetry, and I was sure to have understood the verses from *Faust*.

WHILE MARTHA AND I went out by ourselves, we were hardly ever alone. Most of the time, Sam Waksal, a man as gracious as he is erudite, led us through the "small" and "great" worlds of New York. We met Sam in December 1987. It had been a stormy year for Martha, who had been terrorizing Andy with the ferocity of the jilted woman played by Glenn Close in the movie *Fatal Attraction*. Martha was still finding it hard to accept that Andy would not return to the relationship they had. As holiday time came, she felt especially lonely.

My husband and I invited Martha and her daughter, Alexis, to our family dinner on Christmas Eve. Martha, who was excited about having met that afternoon the man Alexis had been dating for a few months, suggested she ask him to join us. We welcomed the idea and Sam agreed to come. I was curious to meet him in person after all the stories Martha had told me about him.

Sam's conservative appearance masked his flamboyant and kind spirit. His sharp gaze registered every nuance and his superb mind processed every detail. He won me over from the start with his intelligence, his charm, and that protective concern a woman can read in some men's eyes. I felt a bit blue myself that Christmas. Although I was the happy mother of a little girl, and thrilled about my new baby, I also was the wife of a dynamic, successful man whose all-consuming nature rivaled Martha's. In addition, I carried in silence that pain which underlies every celebration in an immigrant's life, the absence of the family and friends left behind in another corner of the world.

After that evening, Sam became a dear friend of Martha's and one of her most trusted advisers. Sam proved to be a dashing and charismatic businessman, a scientist and a scholar, a moving spirit in Martha's life, a man of the world who knew everybody and was known to everyone in New York's social circles. Over the next decade and a half, Sam and I would be Martha's closest friends. He and I kept in touch through our bond with her, and knew a lot about each other, since Martha kept every one of her friends au courant with events in the others' lives. Even after he and Alexis were no longer dating, Sam remained friends with both mother and daughter.

MARTHA'S GROWING SUCCESS brought her new wealth, and she used her millions to buy a co-op on Fifth Avenue and a house she dubbed Lily Pond, in East Hampton. Both became wonderful homes as well as great investments. In fact, Martha made only one not-great purchase of real estate: the Adams House in Westport. Not only had Andy not succumbed to her plan to win him back with the house, nothing Martha planned to do with the Adams House worked smoothly. She sold it after Andy moved to Vermont and, by that time, it had undergone extensive repairs and been on the market for a while.

Lily Pond, located on one of the best streets in the exclusive seaside town of East Hampton, was once called Divinity Hill. Martha completely renovated the late nineteenth-century, three-story shingle-style house, and transformed it so that it had six bedrooms, six or seven full baths and a few halves, a huge steam-shower room, a massage room, a "thinking cage," a couple of fireplaces, and a fabulously designed feast-and-live-in kitchen with celadon-aqua Mexican tile floors and her collection of dozens of blue- and green-glazed tall McCoy vases on the wide sills of the all-window walls around a custom-made, marble-top kitchen table so long that it comfortably fitted fourteen matching chairs. The house had many doors, lots of tall, bright windows, and an overflow of collections. She filled the beautiful library with the best gardening books known to man.

I once slept the night in the library. Martha was already asleep in her room, and her dog ZuZu, whom I had known and loved since she was a puppy, scowled at me from the top of the stairs when I attempted to go up to my room. Growling, her small deep-set eyes filled with warning, her black ruff standing on end, she bared her teeth every time I touched the bottom step to go up. I knew she did it simply because she was a chow chow. Her ancestors, as Martha loved to tell, had guarded Chinese emperors. Concerned that ZuZu might wake Martha, I gave up and slept downstairs that night. When she found me in the library the next morning, Martha thought it was very funny, especially since I was the one who could get her dogs to come back inside at night when she couldn't; somehow they would always respond to my call.

On the Lily Pond terraces and covered porches—arranged with tables, chairs, and many large turquoise-glazed earthen pots—Martha served delicious lunches and her famous frothy margaritas. Just beyond was the new pool Martha had put in, the cottage-style guesthouse, and many elaborate gardens that bloomed spring, summer, and fall. All of that on the one acre of "dead soil," as Martha called the land when she bought it.

Martha had planted countless blue hydrangeas, a beautiful shade garden with specimens inspired from the long list of flora at Pocantico, the Rockefeller garden at the Kykuit estate—a list which Martha had generously shared with me—and a few thousand tulips, of which she herself planted at least three hundred one weekend we spent together at Lily Pond. Martha had said we should go to bed early the night before so that we could plant those bulbs the next morning. When I woke up, I saw from the balcony off my bedroom that Martha was already working in the garden, so I scurried to go help her. All that was left to do was to hand her the watering hose, because by then Martha had already planted the three hundred tulip bulbs by herself.

I was often Martha's houseguest at Lily Pond, mostly with my girls, rarely alone, and never with my husband. Somehow he always found a good reason not to come with us, and, of course, as a doctor on call, he had a supremely unarguable excuse. My girls loved going there and we always had fun. We all loved the beach. At the house, Monica and Lara mostly liked being in the pool or we read books and played games sitting on Martha's deep-cushioned porch chaises or among the flowers on my favorite of Martha's antique iron garden benches, designed with a motif of gracefully curved large fern fronds and painted that aqua teal color predominant at Lily Pond. Martha's housekeeper, Marie, watched the girls while Martha and I went riding on her "old-lady" bikes, as she called them, or in the evenings when the two of us went out partying.

Sometimes we drove separately out to East Hampton, but time and again the girls and I got in Martha's Suburban together with her dogs. We went so often partly because Martha needed my company and would get visibly sad whenever I turned down her invitations and partly because my children and I had such a good time with her. Without my even realizing it was happening, I saw very little of my best friend, RoAnn, and less of my husband. Before I knew it, I was spending most of my free time with Martha, who, with her knowledge, cleverness, and connections, managed to create wonderful ways for us to have fun.

Every time she went to Lily Pond, Martha entertained hordes of people. Sam, who had his own place out there, came by often to visit. He sometimes took us out in the evenings, going from one fabulous place to another, introducing Martha to many desirable bachelors who summered in the Hamptons.

So sharp with people in business, Martha could be as naive as a little girl with men. There was a wealthy investment banker with whom Martha had a passionate fling, hoping he'd leave his fiancée for her. But when Martha ran into him at a party, fiancée on his arm, he pretended not to know her. I saw her face fall, whatever buoyancy she'd had in her expression was flattened out. I felt myself hurting for her. The others blur in my mind but it became a pattern with Martha. Each time she met a man she liked, Martha heard wedding bells, and each time she suffered indignities and disappointment.

That Martha was attractive was never a question. She had looks, she had money, fame, intelligence, savoir faire. She also had a surprising flexibility when it came to bedding down with a just-met mate, but in Martha's mind, the brief affair was the prelude to the long and wonderful life they would live happily ever after. It was surreal watching one of America's most powerful women relying on strategies she'd seemingly pulled from a teen magazine. Yet how does one tell a woman like Martha to dial down "Here Comes the Bride" as she approaches the next blind date, her veil hanging from her handbag, along with the wedding guest list and the menu?

The turning point, as far as I could tell, came on a summer evening after a date full of seductive promise. Martha's first romantic encounter with The Mogul, an attractive, charismatic, and wealthy man she had known for some time, was an intimate lunch that lingered into evening, the two making their way from the table to his poolside. Seized with a spontaneity rare in the world of the seriously rich and famous, they both leaped in, only to be joined by his dog, who jumped in right after them, nearly crashing their party. I don't know if it was the addition of the sweet, brown-nosed retriever or The Mogul's competent breaststroke that did it, but by the day's end Martha had returned to Lily Pond ebullient, and proceeded to call all her friends to announce her next husband.

That he immediately ceased returning her phone calls was not part of Martha's script. Every rejection hit her hard, but The Mogul's lack of interest seemed especially destabilizing, as each unanswered phone call ratcheted up her obsession. We spent entire East Hampton weekends hunting down The Mogul, who never seemed to be where we thought he would be. Back and forth we went, alternatively hunched down or heads held high, on slow tiptoes or quick ducking darts, our path past The Mogul's home precisely the same every time.

And so went one weekend and the weekend after and the weekend after that, and each time The Mogul's butler came out to tell the teenagers dressed as full-grown women that The Mogul was out of town. The news sent Martha into a fast trot up and down the beach, her head down, hands sunk deep in the pockets of her jeans, the lightweight windbreaker around her waist snapping smartly in the salty breeze. And I by her side, my clothes dampened by the spritz of the sea, our feet aching with fatigue.

"Come," she said at one point, suddenly turning to me. "Let's go to his door."

As if hypnotized, I followed her, the chows trailing behind us, three waddling furry balls with curved-up tails, Max the blue, ZuZu the black, and Paw Paw the show dog, their blue tongues hanging from the effort of walking the soft beach sand on their short, velvety legs. The Mogul's pebbled driveway was veiled in a somewhat ominous *chiaroscuro*, the twilight shadows of trees lining it on the stretch before the bend where the mansion came into view. And then, as if rising from the riot of vegetation that lined the high driveway wall, a woman rose like a spirit, her wraithlike form wrapped as in a shawl by the fog of early night. Her hair, in tints of poured champagne, sparkled in the glow of an outside lamp.

She started moving toward us, her footfalls utterly silent. My heart started clattering in its cage and a fear seized me that Martha may become driven by demons as the truth dawned on her.

"Hi," Martha said, her tone as calm as could be.

"Your dogs OK?" the unreal but very real woman said back.

Martha asked her if she were waiting for The Mogul, in the soft tone she used whenever she wanted information from a potentially unwilling subject.

The woman nodded, smiled slightly.

"Do you know where he is?" Martha asked, her voice rising a bit, belying the desperation that lay beneath it.

Listening to their exchange over the rhythmic sound of crashing waves on the beach just beyond the house, I kept stealing glances toward the street, thinking that any moment he might pull up in his finned dolphin-gray Mogul-mobile, his eyes narrowing with displeasure as he saw Martha on his private grounds.

"He said he'd be back soon," I recall the woman saying, or something to this effect.

"When did you talk to him?" asked Martha, her put-on nonchalance straining with the sound of a scraping hinge.

The wraith-woman leaned toward us, clutching her scarab-blue vest closed at her thin throat. She was attractive yet quite different from the women I had met at The Mogul's parties. Neither typical femme fatale, nor worldly academic, she appeared gentle, unguarded, and anonymous, just about everything that Martha was not.

"He said," she nearly whispered, "he might be late."

She looked up at the sky, dazzled with sprays of stars, and then back at us. "I have often had to wait for him," the woman said, obviously unaware that she was talking to the other woman.

"You should leave," Martha told the woman. "He is out of town." Now she spoke forcefully.

Martha tried her best to dissuade the woman from waiting for her date. But much as my friend tried to cajole her, the other woman wouldn't give up what Martha couldn't have. At long last we were the ones who left, ambling with a pretend-careless gait down the terribly long drive, or so it seemed. I could barely keep myself from breaking into a gallop. Who knew what a man like The Mogul might do if he found himself pushed just a tad too far by Martha's in-your-face desperation. *Harassment. Trespassing. Stalking.* Had we been caught, the trouble would not have been Martha's alone. I'd have been drawn in as a partner in crime.

Martha's distress at her failed sentimental escapades made my heart ache. Her despondence as we walked in silence back to Lily Pond made me want to protect her. I took charge of coaxing the chows away from the fancy cars that passed us by, filled with suntanned couples on their way to romantic evenings at all the Hamptons hot spots where we wouldn't be.

8

Two Women

AS MY HUSBAND and I slowly drifted apart and the chill in our marriage began to fossilize, Turkey Hill came to seem like a sanctuary to me. We had been married for more than a decade. We had had two beautiful children together. Still, they were not enough to mitigate the pain of a failing relationship, and why should they be? Children are not sent to us as salves. That's what friends are for.

It was during these days, and nights, that my friendship with Martha began to change, to deepen, partly because of my desire to get away from the man with whom I now had no thoughts or stories to share. At first he and I agreed on little and then we began to disagree on just about everything. Even when it came to feeding the girls, we had different opinions: he tried to banish butter and cream and cheese from their diets, ignoring my conviction that children need calcium to grow their bones. He would say that as a doctor, he'd seen what cholesterol did to the heart. A valid point, but still. The idea that my children would not know the taste of butter, the pleasure of ripe strawberries beaded with cream and sprinkled with sugar—do you not think pleasure gives back in benefits twice the risks it may impose? In secret, I fed my children butter and cheese and fresh cream, delighting in the fur of wet white that formed over their lips.

My husband was a man who forwent sensual delights, was perpetually in a hurry, impatient in everything we did. He took great pride in being so speedy, a valuable trait for a surgeon but not one that spoke to my preference for a slower pace. He went skiing in the winter, rowed whenever weather permitted, criticized every day, and certainly had no time to talk about our marriage. As a wife, I played the roles that I thought my husband needed of me, and didn't require praise, but I could have done without the criticism. When the strained silence became too much, I'd head for Turkey Hill, for comfort.

Martha was calmer now. The slew of brief affairs and possible Mr. Perfects had stopped. As something settled in her and her business kept growing, she sported a new self-possession that made her look lovely to me. I thought she had come into her own, had hurdled over something very high, landed hard, and had finally found a way to stand solid.

And thus it was natural that I sought solace in her home, or just generally in her company. She was living proof of something I needed reassurance of, a woman who had lost her mate and lived to tell the tale. I was terrified to step over that threshold. A single mother? How would I support my children? Statistics were certainly grim about the earning capacity of someone in that situation.

I had been working in real estate for a few years, and I especially liked the art and psychology of the deal. It was a seven-day-a-week job, but it offered me the luxury of making my own hours so I could schedule my clients around my children's school and after-school activities. I worried, of course. What if the market slowed down again? Who would take care of the girls if I had to work another nine-to-five job?

"I will!" Martha would say with her characteristic exuberance, as we sat at her table sipping green tea. "You can get any job you want, Mariana. Look at how good you are at real estate."

What my real estate job brought me even more than money was

the knowledge that I had a knack, something Martha also admired, particularly since her efforts at being a Realtor years earlier had fallen flat. In her presence, I began to feel a tiny tingling at my shoulder, as if indeed wings were starting to prickle beneath my skin.

We talked and talked. In her enclosed porch, the canaries sang in their antique cages. The cats leaped soundlessly onto the table, brushing by me with the suggestion of silk. Her army of chows stood sentry at our feet, guarding us against the stars and everything beneath them.

What a pleasant surprise it was for me to find that Martha could actually provide emotional support. I confided in her my unhappiness in my marriage and she did more than listen. We traded tales, swapped stories, some so funny that on occasion we both would burst out into luxurious laughter. Martha is one of the people in my life I have laughed my hardest with.

Women's laughter together is unlike any other kind of laughter in that it is often in response to something tragicomic. Women do not laugh *at* jokes, like men tend to do; they laugh *within* jokes that are often the punch line to the story of their compromises, yearnings, fears, failures. As such, women laugh in humility, and as such Martha's laughter was the one way in which she could be humble, could accept that she was in and of the giant joke called *being who you are.*

Over time, then, as my marriage was failing, my bond with Martha was growing. While much of my emotion was focused on figuring things out, I never worried that I would lose Martha even though my fear of loss stemming from the loss of family and friends in Romania, and now the loss of my husband's love, was deeply embedded in my psyche. I've often thought, in the years since, that women *should* worry about losing a female friend, or any friend, just as much as one should worry about losing a mate. It seems criminal that women have no ready-made vehicle in our culture to support and celebrate the essential role friendships play in women's lives. That we fail to worry about losing friends is not a sign of the security we feel in these relationships but a sign of deep disregard, and even disrespect, for that which could sustain us through all the other seismic shifts that women experience, for better or for worse, in sickness and in health.

It seems to me that a haven might really exist inside the shelter of a female friendship, if only we could honor its value. Then, perhaps, we might think to protect our female friendships with our own rule of law—like spousal privilege—so a court could not permit one friend to testify against the other when snoops come to pry. In our trot toward the finish line, we lose our superficial beauty, raise children so that they can leave us, and often lose our mates even when we are the ones to do the actual walking away. If we are lucky, it is our female friendships that help us hold back time.

I don't know if I would have left my husband, or left him when I did, had it not been for Martha. She placed a strain on our marriage with the wave of her post-Andy demands, and then, when my husband and I recovered from that, we found a distance had sprung up between us. Martha also gave me the guts to leave. I came to appreciate friendship as a safer haven than a turbulent marriage.

I did not leave my husband all at once. We tried this and that, the late nights, the bleary eyes, the questions questions questions, continuing on and on until I finally had the guts to do the only thing left for me to do—divorce.

ON AN AUTUMN afternoon in 1994, after the girls came home from school, they put on their new Halloween costumes and we went to Turkey Hill, where Martha was filming a TV special.

"Come, my darling butterflies," I said, ushering my daughters inside Martha's barn, across the path from the *palais du poulet*.

"Mammy, how long do we have to keep our costumes on?"

"Ask Martha."

The barn appeared especially dark after the incredibly bright day, dark despite the cameras and the lights. I had never much liked that barn. It reminded me of my grandparents' barn, and the idea of gentrifying it seemed a sacrilege. On summer nights, as a child, I was allowed to sleep on fragrant hay piled atop the rafters, watching the stars through the big window while in the stalls underneath my grandfather's beautiful horses neighed softly. The large steamer trunks stored standing by the far back wall were whispered to have traveled with my family. Their brown outer shells were sprinkled with V's on top of L's among little beige flowers, their insides filled with smooth wooden hangers and pale leather-lined, gliding drawers. But we were not allowed to talk about the trunks, as they were evidence of a past considered "unclean" by Communist standards. After being thrown out of college when the new regime came to power, my father worked in a coal mine to purge suspicions that he was a member of the "potential opposition"—the aristocracy, landowning nobility, or people who had travelled abroad and come under the influence of western ideas. As I grew up, those people were referred to as "the bourgeoisie," and we were taught that they were "the enemy of the people." My grandparents' barn was cleaned and aired every day, and as I watched hay dust coming down from the rafters in fine swirls, floating on light rays that streamed in through the open barn door, I could dream of the entire world and imagine everything in it. Martha's barn had no such soul.

"Did you make these costumes?" Martha said as soon as we walked in.

"No, I'm not that good. I designed them but my friend Luiza, the fashion wiz, made them," I told her, knowing Martha would keep asking until she knew every detail.

As Martha's crew set up outside on the deck, I helped the girls get out of their costumes and slip on the ones that had been prepared for a face-painting scene. Peeking through a window, I watched Monica, dressed as some doglike critter with a black coat and white dots, having her beautiful face painted by Martha in front of the camera. I had made it clear to both the artist and Martha that only hypoallergenic products could be used on my daughters. They had reassured me that the paint was safe, but I was never the kind of mother who totally trusts others with her kids. So, craning my neck so as not to be seen by the camera, I tried to find an angle from where I could check on Lara and Katherine, her kindergarten friend who was also to be in Martha's Halloween scene.

When I finally saw Lara, the cameras were rolling. I could barely contain my anger. My six-year-old daughter's eyes, stinging from the face paint, were filling with tears she made a visible effort to hold back. She stood still so the professional artist, who appeared somewhat uncertain, could finish painting a butterfly design on her face in black and yellow lines. Then, the young makeup artist turned to the camera and said: "Never put red near the eyes, because that color is not approved for use close to the eyes." This despite the fact that big splotches of red had already been colored in above my child's eyebrows and high on her right cheek. I was biting my lip trying to calm down, blaming myself for trusting Martha's judgment. But I realized that had I let my displeasure be known, it would have caused a scene, ruined the picture, and embarrassed Lara. So I did nothing then; however, from then on, whenever my children were with Martha, I always did my best to be in the room.

It wasn't the first time Martha had put me on the spot in that barn. A year earlier, on the very day that I was serving my husband with papers, I picked up my children from school, and we went to Martha's. My lips felt flaky, dry with fear, and a stone sat in my throat, its presence palpable to me every time I swallowed. We pulled into the driveway at Turkey Hill. Martha was having a Christmas party filmed for that year's holiday special, which at that point was already de rigueur, though the filming had the odd effect of sucking the spontaneity from the event while heightening the seeming significance of it in a way that made the whole experience unnecessarily intense.

The girls and I got out of the car and walked across the grounds to Martha's barn. I gazed longingly toward the sangria-red leaves of the azalea bushes blazing in the autumn light. They had been Martha's gift to Andy for Father's Day once upon a time. I had read the announcement of his and Robyn's marriage the previous spring. Was he happy?

The candlelit tables were beautifully set in the great room of the barn. While Martha has always liked being late for parties, and thus we often were, my daughters' preference is to be more or less on time. The filming had not yet started, and Martha, as usual, was running around.

"The girls look great, Mariana. I'm so glad they are here. I haven't seen them since I came up to the lake. It's been more than a month already! Monica, Lara, come," Martha said, clapping her hands high. My girls ran over.

"Remember you must help me make the gingerbread house for the TV special. I'll let your mom know when. It'll be fun," Martha said and hugged them hard and with an affection so real I felt tears burn my eyelids. I grew up with grandparents, aunts, uncles, cousins; the only family my girls had in America were my friends. The children went to play outside in Martha's walled-in, sunken herb garden, which was sprinkled with man-made snow and festively decorated for the filming of outdoor holiday scenes. Martha asked me to sit next to her at the table near the window to the side of the large fieldstone fireplace.

The filming started. I was paying little attention.

Between shoots was when the real party happened. People talked and laughed; some drank mulled fresh pressed cider from Martha's collection of patterned glass punch cups, others had wine.

"What's new?" Martha said to me at one pause in the filming.

I bit my lip, looked down at the ground. I wanted to tell her how scared I was, but something in me knew not to. For Martha, "fear" is a four-letter word.

"Listen, Martha," I said, and as though on cue we leaned our heads conspiratorially toward each other, as close as we had ever been, so close I could smell the fragrance of her makeup and see the fine line where her subtle lipstick ended and her mouth began. "It's over. I did it."

Martha pulled back, looked at me with an expression at once quizzical and full of mirth, as if she knew something good was coming.

"Did what?"

"I hope this party lasts for a long time because I'd rather not go home too soon," I said, but I thought, *Had you asked me all those years ago if I would or could ever leave my man, I would have told you: No. Absolutely not*, and then I felt fear flash in me again, because who would I be, where would I be, without my marriage?

"Right about now," I started again, "the sheriff should be down the hill, serving divorce papers."

And then, to my surprise, Martha took a silver spoon and tapped it against a glass, the crystal ringing clearly in the room, which was abuzz with talk. There was something about the sound that carried within it Martha's determined hand, her authoritative call to attention. The room hushed as Martha rose from her seat.

"Everyone," Martha said to her audience, all of whom now had their eyes turned toward her. As she stood there, one curved-fingered hand raised in front of her chest, her long and fleshy earlobes suspended above the draped shawl that fell from her shoulders in undulating folds, Martha looked to me like that monumental gilt bronze figure of Maitreya, Buddha of the Future, at the Metropolitan Museum of Art. "Listen, everyone."

Then she paused, her pause perfect, practiced, not long enough to let a single person rustle but just long enough to let the pressure build.

"Right now," she said, and I felt her hand hovering at my back, not her touch but just the presence of her hand inches from my skin, as if to push me forward into a limelight I did not ask for. And then that hand at my back seemed to drop away, and she continued, quickly now, "At this very moment," I heard Martha say, "Mariana, my best friend, is having you-know-who served with divorce papers. Brava for Mariana," she nearly shouted, emphasizing the soft rhyming *a*'s that married *Mariana* to *Brava*.

I was totally taken aback and embarrassed, and so must have been many at the party, because even those who applauded made it short, probably as baffled as I was by Martha's turning my agony into a stage-worthy scene from the theater of the absurd. I sat there, flushed and flustered by Martha's divulging my personal information without consulting me first, while the cameras shot her, serene and friendly, delivering her impeccable hostess lines.

THE DIVORCE WAS final the spring of 1994, eleven years after our wedding. My husband preferred not to leave our home—either because of his deep attachment to its mortar, or, more likely, as a stonewalling strategy rooted half in rage, half in a fear very similar to my own. I, however, could not cave in to that fear. So our family home became his house and I left to make a new home for me and the children. Something, it seemed, was standing straighter and straighter in me every day.

The girls got in the car; we buckled up, I turned the keys so the engine kicked on, and within a matter of minutes we were soaring down the streets, passing the boundary line that set off tony Westport from its neighbor, Weston, where we were headed. I had chosen Weston because I liked the school system. I bought the best house I could for the money. It needed a lot of TLC, which meant tearing down all the drywall that separated one room from the other; yanking cheesy kitchen cabinets from their positions on soot-stained walls; throwing out decrepit windows; and pulling from between the crumbling rafters dry, flaky insulation full of mouse droppings, themselves so dried they clattered when they fell.

Some of the fun I had had exploring with Martha helped me learn about architecture, construction, renovation, furnishing styles, gardens, and landscape, and now that knowledge, which developed further with my real estate experience and benefited my clients, came in handy. Besides, I had an eye; I had some taste; I was willing to put in the work and the time. Martha's carefully formulated advice kept me from creating something like the mansion in F. Scott Fitzgerald's *A Rose for Emily*: "A big, squarish frame house that had once been white, decorated with cupolas and spires and scrolled balconies in the heavily lightsome style of the seventies."

Martha, who had begun to lovingly refer to my girls as her "goddaughters" even though they were not, grew incensed as she watched me struggle to make a living and support my children. She even called my former husband to excoriate him. Not that he cared what she thought, but her defense meant a lot to me. Martha and I joked about him having become my most formidable opponent; after July 1994, when comet Shoemaker-Levy 9 collided with planet Jupiter, we began to call the fallout from his confrontations with me "collision debris."

Martha also offered to give me a ten-thousand-dollar loan so I could pay for the excavation needed to solve some of the problems at my new property, an offer I accepted gratefully and with immense relief, since I could not have afforded the job done as expertly as Martha saw fit. But, in addition, Martha wanted me to get a property cleanup, which that loan couldn't cover, so she made the even more generous offer to get the excavators to bury the brush and stumps—which she found distasteful. As Martha never mentioned terms of reimbursement for this, I was surprised when her office billed me a few months later. I figured that Martha may have thought that giving me money outright would seem patronizing. Still, I found her gesture confusing because in Romania my friends and I had implicitly understood the give-and-take of friendship. I was too proud to say anything and resolved to pay the bill in full.

After many months of my taking care of the children while working as general contractor, architect, gardener, and decorator, plus continuing to wear my Realtor's hat, we finally settled in with our boxer puppy in our new home. In its made-over state, it seemed to sparkle, as did the girls, who must have felt renewed by no longer having to bear the weight of a stressed marriage. We had set up a custody schedule so that they spent Wednesdays with their father, as well as every other weekend and alternate holidays.

Martha came over almost daily, unless we went to Turkey Hill. And there were weekends together in East Hampton at Lily Pond. She offered advice, glue guns, fun, and talk. We loved having her around, but we loved having time by ourselves too. We had a pool, a sledding trail, rollerblades and bicycles, a piano, and a host of other musical instruments, walls covered with books, the latest toys, and I had even had a heated floor installed in the large new playroom. The girls and I played board games together, baked cookies, and invented our own cake recipes. We designed extravagant Halloween costumes: princesses with wings, frogs with crowns, good witches with sparkles in their hair, bad witches with Medusa-like snakes instead of hair. My life was full, the love strong, the strongest I've had. The children gave me more than I could ever give them. I now had time to read, and think, and reread things I had forgotten, and feel them again too. I thought Anton Chekhov was right: "Perhaps the feelings that we experience when we are in love represent a normal state. Being in love shows a person who he should be." My children made me whole. They fulfilled me. They made me courageous. Our love made me feel like a winner.

In our own separate ways, Martha and I were thriving. It seemed that there was something synergistic to our independent efforts. These were good days, each one of us forging separate but independent paths. My girls got into Weston's Gifted and Talented Program and my real estate practice continued to be successful. *I am doing this,* I'd think, and blink with surprise. *We are doing this,* Martha and I would sometimes say to each other, without words, exchanging glances across a crowded room.

Martha's success was reaching new heights, and I was thrilled for her. By the end of 1994, after the Halloween special with the children, she had filmed the Thanksgiving special, then another special featuring a charming exhibit at the New York Botanical Garden. On camera, Martha visited an imaginative display of Christmas homes made with leaves, seeds, and bark with a group of children that included Monica and Lara; Kristina and Kirk, the children of Martha's brother George;

and Maude and August, the children of her longtime graphic designer, Gael Towey. It had been almost two years since January 19, 1993, when *Martha Stewart Living*, her syndicated half-hour broadcast television series, was launched. By the fall of 1993, when Martha filmed the Christmas party at her barn, and my daughters made the gingerbread house with her for the TV special, the show was reaching 82 percent of American television viewers. Meanwhile, *Martha Stewart Living*, published by Time, Inc., was one of the most rapidly growing magazines in America. Martha had by now many best-selling books to her credit, was a frequent guest on *Oprah* and *Larry King*, and was a regular on the *Today* show.

While privately my children set the scale's balance, publicly we found our equality in a different way. A new social world was opening up for Martha, and she seemed to need me more than ever. Many of the new people who entered her life were plainly courting Martha's money and success. Too smart to fall for that, Martha often counted on me to help evaluate her new acquaintances. She knew she could trust me, that I cared about her, not about her money. The fact that Martha, one of the most powerful women in America, valued my opinion about so much of what she did really boosted my self-confidence. She was femme financial and I was femme fatale. On nights when my children were with their father, I would shed my jeans, or my more conservative Realtor attire, and join Martha at Manhattan's grand restaurants. I liked the fact that Martha ate. Many women eat like birds, but Martha and I both had good appetites. We ordered only what we really liked and we ate everything, neither one of us packing on weight yet. We dined on exquisite food, surrounded by tantalizing company, many of them men who spent part of the evening engaged with Martha in some discussion of business. Once they realized she wasn't about to reveal the secrets of her success, they were more than ready to welcome me into the conversation, which I knew how to make less intense, introducing subjects of life and spice. With Martha next to me, I felt myself at once exquisitely feminine and powerful in the presence of those people. It worked perfectly. Martha was recognized for her strengths and inclinations, I for mine. Everyone relaxed, Martha and I laughed, the men laughed, and when Martha got tired we each went to our own homes.

In late December, I was faced with my first New Year's Eve as a divorcee. My children were to spend the holiday with their father. Martha and I, each in our separate abodes, were alone. She was at Lily Pond. I had a few invitations to friends' homes around Westport but wasn't sure what I wanted to do, or even if I wanted to celebrate my new singlehood. Martha, who is "not a loner," kept calling, asking me to come to Lily Pond and spend New Year's Eve with her, maybe go to some of the fancy parties to which she had been invited.

Late in the morning on December 31, I got into my car and drove to East Hampton. New Year's Eve with Martha Stewart. It couldn't get much better than that, right?

By four p.m., the street lights were on, the grimy paths of snow lay here and there like dirty throw rugs. The sun was so small it seemed like the star it really is, fading fast. She welcomed me at her door. Lily Pond was perfection incarnate, filled with furniture that was elegant and restrained in its beauty, luxurious and refined, reflecting Martha's genius at mixing styles, like hanging Venetian mirrors and chandeliers in a room filled with cool-linen-upholstered Chippendale and Duncan Phyfe furniture, some touches of the Aesthetic Movement, and lots of stuffed fish and birds looking at you from a wall-mount or an under-glass display.

"We should go out," one of us said.

"Yes, we should," the other one of us replied.

Yet neither of us moved to get dressed. There was no excitement or buzz in the air, and we could not imagine what we needed to do to get it back. Darkness fell, the night progressed, we could hear the hooting celebrations from nearby parties, but it seemed we couldn't shake the catatonia that had come over us.

Finally, I said, "You know what? I don't want to go out. Who says that if it's New Year's Eve we have to make it an event? You know what I read somewhere that this pretending to be happy on holidays is called?"

"What?" Martha asked, one eyebrow raised half in mirth, half in curiosity.

"'Noel syndrome.' That's what. We don't have to suffer from some holiday disease to be happy."

"No?" said Martha, smiling.

"That's right," I said. "Who says we even have to be happy?"

"Let's be utterly miserable," Martha said. Now she laughed, and the sound lightened both of us.

So we settled on that, and immediately began to laugh and to talk. We had been set free. Suddenly the shadows that had darkened us lifted.

"What kind of hostess are you? Where's the BOOZE? It's Réveillon!" I shouted.

As midnight approached, we settled into the deep linen-upholstered chairs in front of the living-room fireplace with its perfect mantel, between us a vintage marble-topped iron coffee table set with antique English porcelain plates and silver, a generous-size caviar serving bowl filled with golden Ossetra on crushed ice, just-made blinis and crème fraîche served on twelve-point-star Corning glass cake-tray and bowl, and delicious Cristal Rosé—Martha's favorite—in her perfectly proportioned champagne flutes (these I prefer to cups because they hold the bubbles longer, and being a slowpoke who rarely finishes a glass of wine, I can enjoy the fizz for almost as long as I can nurse a drink). The rare caviar was so delicious, our favorite anyway, fresh—fresh how only Martha knew to find it; the luscious, golden-yellow eggs small and pleasantly firm, rich and nutty when they burst with the tip of the tongue against the palate. The cold, delicate bubbles of pinkish nectar warmed quickly in my mouth. We listened to the CDs I had brought as gifts, raising toasts to Shirley Horn singing *Here's to Life*, to Leonard Cohen's *I Am Your Man*, and to us: "May we not spend next New Year's

Eve together!" thereby wishing each other a romantic evening one year hence.

By some standards, we had everything. But although it was the top of "having," it also was the bottom of "being."

We had made of that New Year's Eve what we wanted, but on that night it was as if we had a hole in our leaky skins, letting out all the air. We slumped as quickly as we'd been plumped, because compared to what we wanted from life it was not good enough. We wanted to live the living life. I don't know how many minutes went by before the robust mood left us, but when it did, it seemed we had nothing. Martha began to look pale, almost ghostly, in the firelight. A huge somnolence came over me as I watched the champagne bubbles playing inside the narrow bottom of my flute. I set down my glass.

While toasting and talking, trying to persuade each other that we were having a good time, the pauses in conversation became longer and longer. I then noticed that Martha had dozed off, so I closed my eyes and fell asleep. We woke up in the middle of the night. The fire had gone out and it was cold. It was the only time I remember that Martha and I did not clean up the remnants of our feast before going to bed. We just set the fire-screen in front of the dying embers and left. If we said very little it was because there was no need to talk. As we went to our separate rooms, we both knew that we were together at a dead end, that indulging in our petit bourgeois feast was great, but not exciting for either of us.

When I awoke, the sky was dressed in a crisp blue suit, the black branches of the trees enlivened by the contrast of the clouds sailing behind them. I opened a window, sniffed. The air smelled of snow and salt with just the hint of spring, of tulips deep beneath the ground, still buried in their bulbs, but something was stirring.

My sleep had been short but revitalizing. I felt the surge of energy one sometimes gets when the air is clear and the sun shines its amber light out everywhere. We ate a breakfast of fragrant fruits still carrying on their rinds the scent of the countries they'd come from—Ecuador, Guatemala, Ethiopia.

Martha and I went for a walk on the beach then quickly dressed to go out. Our plan: Sag Harbor, where there was an artsy "First of the Year" brunch party. I knew the party would be filled with painters, editors, writers, friends of Martha's superb editor, Carol Southern, people who have nothing to do with one kind of wealth and everything to do with another. We went.

Lively conversation, more good food, everyone's plate full of plenty. I roamed throughout the rooms, talking less than I usually do, listening, soaking in the sights and sounds: conversations about color, art galleries, cubism, Klimt, the properties of stone, the architecture of post-postmodernity, a man who'd lived with the grizzlies—fascinating, all of it.

I came to a group of people engaged in animated conversation. Martha was with me. The conversation caught our attention exactly at the same time, and we leaned in to listen. What was this? A house . . . a friend . . . buying . . . maybe . . . no . . . now . . .

Martha and I eyed each other. We kept listening.

On Georgica Pond. A house . . . on Georgica Pond. *Desirable*, they were saying. *Of course. Georgica Pond is gorgeous. A house . . . for sale . . . friends trying to buy . . . East Hampton . . . Modern . . . no one knows, we wish . . . who would, how much . . .*

As if on cue, Martha and I both backed out of the circle of conversation, which was dwindling into a string of question marks indicating something secret was afoot. Apart from the group, Martha turned to me. "Find out what you can," she said.

I knew exactly what Martha meant.

Immediately, with no more discussion, we split up and began to work different parts of the room, employing our superior sleuthing skills. Inside of me, and Martha too, was a giggling ten-year-old girl writing secret messages with her spy pen. It was glorious. Our goal was to gather as much information as we could while seeming to idle casually by the brunch bar, popping maraschino cherries into our mouths, all the while drawing every tidbit of information about that house toward us.

Martha's task was harder than mine. For starters, I was an experienced Realtor by then. But also, people noticed her, and clammed up in her presence. Still, to the degree that people knew I was friends with her, they clammed up in my presence as well.

We met, back in the center. What have you got? Modern house. Yes, Bunshaft house. Georgica Pond. Right, Georgica Pond. No one lives there. "No one lives there?" Martha asked, a smile spreading over her face, and mine too.

"That's right," I said. "No one."

We raced to her car—"Let's go," she'd said—and we were out of there, walking down the path as fast as we could, trying to restrain our impulse to break into an all-out gallop.

We got into her car. Martha always drove; she was an excellent driver, fast, making quick tight turns with an expert whisk of the wheel. Thrilled by the chase, Martha and I drove around Georgica Pond, passing many famous people's summer homes, like Steven Spielberg's Quelle Barn, we turned inside the narrow path to Calvin Klein's weathered-shingle hideaway that peeks between dune grasses and tall pines, and followed each road with access to the pond, looking for the house. There was snow everywhere, and as the day was dying, the light looked a diluted gold on the clean snow, the Georgica Close Road partly frozen, clumps of slushy ice under the wheels.

Finally we found a neglected-looking yard separated from the street by a chain-link fence. We parked the car, got out. The snow had been piling up here all winter, and the home screamed emptiness. Saying nothing to each other, we moved forward as one into the snow, which was nearly knee-high. Clumps of it fell, freezing, in my boots, but I barely registered it, so immersed was I in our quest. The chain-link fence receded behind us. We saw a low-slung building, a windowless façade, a flat roof. A bungalow buried in snow. Impossible that this could have been the home of an architect who designed some of America's most famous, sleek, modern skyscrapers. We looked at each other, a look at once grim and confused, followed by a curt nod—*keep moving*.

And then suddenly, before us, in the single snap of God's invisible fingers, we saw it, plunked before us in majestic, heavenly space. The Pond. Visible through the wide openings between stark-boned trees that rimmed the property's winter-white landscape, its blue lagoon was separated by a narrow strip of a sandbar from the immensity of the Atlantic Ocean. The house on that side was a harmonious play of rectangular travertine blocks and large panes of glass, fronted by a garden dotted with stately trees and breathtaking modern sculptures powdered with snow. A giant Henry Moore gestured from the side of the house, a major Joan Miró and a refined Isamu Noguchi veered toward the guest house, and closer to the water's edge, a monumental bronze, also by Henry Moore. The travertine house was a 1962 modernist gem that the famous architect Gordon Bunshaft, an icon of American architecture, had built for his family. He had died a few years earlier, in 1990, and his wife, Nina, who had been a fine painter, had just passed away. The house and all the art had been bequeathed to the Museum of Modern Art.

Martha and I were both awestruck at first and then giddy with excitement. I looked at Martha and said, "You have to get it."

We had made so many finds together but none of those treasures, nor the hunts themselves, could compare to finding the Bunshaft house. Soon afterward, Martha made the offer under her corporate name, and the Museum of Modern Art chose to accept her bid of over $3 million, rejecting a few other offers in the process. It was no surprise to me.

Martha always won.

9

To the Ends of the Earth

A ND THEN MY house caught fire.

Actually it went up in flames. It was March 1995, only months after the children and I had moved in. Well after midnight, the fire alarm began to shriek. I called 911. The woman said, "Take everyone out of the house."

I mustered all the calm I could to wake up the children without frightening them. Shawls quickly wrapped over pajamas, boots on naked little toes, blankets grabbed off beds.

"Where is Harry?"

"I got him, honey."

"And Horace?"

"Keep going, darling. I'll get him. Don't run, girls, just walk fast. Go open the front door. I'll be right there."

I flew back to the bedrooms to rescue their favorite stuffed animals, then caught up with the children and yanked our winter coats out of the hall closet and threw them over our shoulders.

"Ginger. Mammy, we must get Ginger!"

"Please, girls. I must first know you're safe. I'll come back for the puppy."

We ran out as the first fireman came. We got in our car and I drove to a safe distance down the street. Leaving the children inside, I ran back, tripping through the snow. The Weston volunteer firemen were already pulling their hoses through the front and back door, so I opened the garage door. At the far right, flames were pouring through the wall behind the kitchen. Something came over me. I ran inside, using my fingers to tear through the smoke, cleared my way to the left toward the door to the laundry room, where our puppy slept as she was not yet housebroken. The flames were hitching higher and higher. I could hear them. I never knew until then how much noise flames make.

I found our puppy down by the dryer and picked her up. Her body was a slumped sack full of rattling puppy bones. I held her in my arms, and dashed back out, the flames biting at my heels.

Great jets of spray from the firemen's hoses throttled and soaked our shelter—all the work, the sanded floors, the new furniture, the beautiful beds I'd bought for my daughters to sleep in. The hoses were snorting like stallions.

As for the puppy, no sound. I threw my coat on the ground and put her on it, then pried open a mouth too small to be believed. I was frightened I'd crush her jaw, which seemed to be made of marshmallow. We had only had the puppy for about a month but of course we loved her as if for a lifetime. I slid my fingers down inside her lower lip, and then pushed up, levering her slack, useless jaw open. I put my mouth on the puppy's mouth and breathed. I forgot about the flames, or the sound of my girls' beds burning. Beneath me, I could feel the puppy's blood begin to move again, the soft stirring of her heart, the meeting of my mouth to her snout. The tiny animal coughed and coughed, and suddenly was standing. She shook herself off, then she looked at me. It was as though we had an unspoken understanding. In that moment, having crossed the boundary of my species, I saw how utterly flexible is our human capacity to connect.

Inspectors and investigators and all kinds of agents came to find out the source of the fire and they concluded that some computer glitch in our brand-new kitchen stove was to blame. Our home was so damaged that it was condemned.

But we were all alive. I had my girls, thank God, my dog, thank God; I had all my breathing beings, and that made the loss of the objects, severe though it was, much easier to bear.

Our insurance company grossly underassessed the damage (though to be fair I had not been in the habit of keeping receipts and had no proof of the value) and paid me a pittance compared to the losses we'd sustained—the loss or near-destruction of most material things under our roof—some irreplaceable, like the Louis Vuitton trunks that survived Communism hidden in plain sight inside the horse barn. My parents had brought these, filled with objects and memories of our past, when they came to visit me in 1990, after the regime fell with the Berlin Wall. Lost were the ornaments that had been in my family for generations and still enlivened our holiday when Christmas was banished by the Communists and we would close the curtains so they wouldn't see our beautiful tree. Among the few things that survived was a superb dress once worn by my grandmother, but it was only because Martha had not returned it after borrowing it to use as prototype for the bridesmaids' dresses she was planning to develop for her weddings business.

Friends of mine, China and Pierre, generously offered to let me stay in their guesthouse, where we lived until we found a rental. Martha's daughter, Alexis, was a godsend as she took our puppy to live with her bulldogs, Homer and Cleo. The year after, the Venice Opera House, La Fenice, was destroyed by a fire, too. I took my girls there to celebrate survival. From our princess suite near Plaza San Marco, we roamed the cobblestoned streets, and took gondolas along the canals of the world's most romantic city, where spirit and beauty have triumphed throughout history despite numerous bouts with destruction and tragedy. We attended an opera at La Fenice's temporary home, an auditorium under a giant tent erected to keep music alive and the memory of the fire at bay. I did all I could to help us forget that frightening, disastrous experience, yet, even today, when the girls and I pass a fire engine with flashing emergency lights, fear knots in the pits of our stomachs.

My mind was full but my purse was empty. Summer came, and while my daughters went to camp, I worked hard as a Realtor, showing people this house and that house, earning commissions as best I could, but they did not add up to what I had lost. That summer, Martha invited me to move in with her at Turkey Hill. I was very grateful, but, reluctant to intrude on Martha's privacy, I insisted on staying in her guest apartment over the outside kitchen, steps away from the main house.

Among the things that escaped the fire were my family photographs. The albums, which I kept in a vintage medical cabinet made of enameled metal and glass, got their covers damaged, but most of the pictures were saved. One morning, when Martha came to see me at the guest apartment, I was sitting on the floor, piles of pictures all around me. I had just finished making new baby albums and was designing the one for the wedding. Martha looked at the mess and said, "You know what. Give those to me. I'll have someone at the office make you a nice album. It'll be my gift for your birthday." I thanked her profusely. Going through those particular pictures then, after the divorce, the construction, the fire, was very stressful. Her offer was such a relief. However, although I asked on several occasions, she never returned the wedding album, or my grandmother's dress.

By the fall of that year, our homeless days were over. Our house was more or less restored, our puppy was back home. We had all fallen back into a rhythm of normal life by then, and it was at this point that Martha suggested we all travel together over the winter holidays to the Galapagos, a place of pure magic.

The Galapagos expedition promised to be rich in a real nonmaterial way. Having grown up in a restrictive Communist country, I longed to see the world, and I wanted my daughters to experience it in a way that had been forbidden to me at their age. Since the divorce, I had taken them to London, Venice, Jamaica, and Turks and Caicos. I also went on interesting trips with my friends, like touring Italy for opera performances and biking among vineyards in France, and had been on fabulous vacations to St. Barth, where my friend Maggie generously invited me to her extraordinary house. But what I dreamed of was to share with my children the wonder of exotic exploration and adventure travel. I felt very lucky that Martha wanted to go on those kinds of voyages with us.

Martha reveled in such adventures. She had climbed Mount Kilimanjaro and had just been on an expedition to Sikkim with Sandy Pittman, who was reportedly planning to climb the world's seven highest peaks. An attractive socialite married to Bob Pittman, the famously successful businessman, Sandy, whose keen intelligence, striking manner, and over-the-top lifestyle had been the subject of magazine articles and New York gossip, had become a trendsetter for outdoor adventures. After their mountain escapades, Martha had more stories to tell me about Sandy's eccentricities than about the splendors of the great outdoors.

Inspired by Sandy's way with luxury—according to Martha, she hired two guides and ten porters for the climb in Tanzania—Martha insisted that we rent a private boat to live on during the trip to Galapagos. I avoided reminding Martha that while she made millions, and Sandy had a husband reputed to be making millions more, I was a divorced mother with two young children, with no steady income to count on as I worked as an independent contractor, doing my best to hold things together after my house had burned down. But Martha pressured me, and finally I had to confess to her my financial situation, which she resolved by offering to give me an extension on the $10,000 property improvement loan, due in January, so I could afford the vacation. I was relieved. Still, Martha wanted to sail on a high-end luxury boat that was really beyond my means, but she generously offered to cover the premium for me and the girls. She also brought along four of her nieces and nephews—Sophie, Kristina, Chris, and Kirk—who were friendly with and close in age to my children, and Martha's publicist, Susan Magrino, whom I had known for a while and liked a lot.

It was a superb experience. Prior to leaving, I made sure my girls were primed to take advantage of the incredible adventure awaiting us. Monica read about Darwin's "living laboratory of evolution," and couldn't wait to see giant turtles, spiny marine iguanas, seals, and sea lions, to snorkel and dive among schools of friendly fish in the middle of the ocean. Lara wrote a paper on the Galapagos for school. I, too, read excerpts from Darwin's work, learning about the seminal discovery of the different finches' beaks and its implication for evolution, his theory about natural selection, and the outrage his pronouncements caused.

It had been a long time since I'd been able to luxuriate in knowledge for the sheer sake of it. Reading about Darwin made me think that life is so interconnected. When you lift off the human skin and get a look inside, you are reminded that we exist side by side with millions of other magnificent species, from tiger beetle to cheetah, from butterfly to elephant, from coral to whale.

The trip was fantastic—more exciting than I ever dreamed it would be—even if some of our adventures were more than I bargained for. One day, when we were still on land, we went riding across the picturesque landscape near Hacienda Cusin, where open vistas were backed by mountain ranges with snow-capped peaks. Along the way, our mares attracted the lustful pursuit of two wild Criollo horses. Although we barely escaped a dangerous encounter, it was fascinating to be so close to those untamed horses of South America, allegedly descendants of runaway equines that came to the New World with the Spanish conquistadores during the sixteenth century. Known to be well adapted to the altitude and cold climate, resistant to disease and drought, they roam freely among the expansive natural grasslands of the high *páramo* plains (above sixteen thousand feet). The other serious jolt I got happened when Martha and I were watching from the sandy beach of a Galapagos island as Susan and the kids swam in the crystal-clear water far from the shore. We noticed a huge rogue seal bull swimming near them at menacingly close range. The animal left as suddenly as it came, and our swimmers returned to shore safely, albeit excited by the experience of being touched by what they thought was a companion's flipper only to see a patch of glistening dark fur.

We spent six days navigating under sail on the *Ahmarã*, one of the two most luxurious boats that cruise the Pacific waters of the Galapagos archipelago, six hundred miles away from the mainland of Ecuador. *Ahmarã* was a high-performance catamaran, with beautiful sleeping cabins, an inviting lounge, full bar, delicious shipboard meals, and all the equipment we needed to go diving or visit the incredible islands with our guide, Ron, a scientist from the Darwin Institute. It was like living in a floating school. Martha had her own cabin, the largest of *Ahmarã*'s elegant wood-paneled guest rooms. The girls shared one. The boys shared one. I shared a cabin with Susan.

We disembarked on small boats (stored on the *Ahmarã*) and sailed to fish-rich spots where we snorkeled through schools of fish both big and small and of unbelievable variety. Once, as we were returning to the big boat from a daily excursion by dinghy, my sunglasses fell in water so clear I could see straight through to the bottom, the world below the world. The kids welcomed the opportunity for one more dive. So they all got back in wet suits and jumped in looking for my glasses. Ron, who went with them, said there were sharks down there but, wearing his Darwin hat, explained that since they had never been given motive for aggression against man, they would never attack.

We wet-landed on beaches colored pink, ocher, black, or mossy green. We watched Darwin's finches; stepped among seals basking in the sun; came inches close to equatorial penguins, the only members of their species not to live at the poles; and watched marine iguanas dive into the ocean, which they do nowhere else on Earth.

On Barrington Island, we saw large Santa Fé land iguanas sunning their bumpy hides on huge boulders, impervious to our chatter and the clicking of our cameras. On Genovesa Island, male frigate birds gave quick displays of their inflated, blood-red neck sacs as they practiced for their yearly end-of-spring courting ritual. On Albemarle Island, we walked for miles in the giant turtle preserve and, seeing Martha munching on small, orange-red tomatoes that grew wild from the hardened volcanic ash, we trusted they weren't poisonous. We marveled at those huge turtles, studying their elephantine legs, watching their long, leathery necks rise up once in a while, and the black sheen of their large eyes atop their smallish heads. We walked next to chattering birds, boobies that stood in pairs, trusting us to not step on their webbed orange, red, or aqua-blue feet as we trekked among the rocks under the watchful eye of the Galapagos hawk.

Martha surprised the kids with funny bathing caps, each topped with an assortment of icky-wiggly creatures. The kids wore their caps the entire morning not only in the water but during breakfast and lunch and while they played their afternoon games.

Come New Year's Eve, Martha and I opened a bottle of champagne, and under a starry sky raised the toast we were to raise on each of our holiday trips to follow: "May we NOT spend next New Year's together!" Galapagos was the experience of a lifetime, and, like the kids, I never wanted it to end.

A few days after we returned from the trip, Martha's office sent me the bill for our travel expenses. I then asked Martha for the outstanding balance due on the $10,000 property improvement loan we had already discussed, as I wanted to pay it off, and forgo her generous offer of an extension. Martha's office presented me with a complex invoice that stated the payback terms, including interest calculations. My eyes stung when I looked at the document. The invoice felt like a violation of the unspoken tenets that make female friendship sacred. But I had already acted upon my acceptance of Martha's idea that I would borrow money to fix my property as she saw fit, to go with her on the Galapagos trip, and to some extent, to afford her friendship—a friendship that encompassed our worlds of pleasure and pain, while it bestowed protection and power on me. Being friends with Martha enabled me and my daughters to travel places where we did not feel safe going by ourselves. No matter how many interest points each dollar I borrowed from Martha cost me, it was little payment for the importance of that experience in my children's lives, and the priceless joyous moments that I shared with them. *Forget it*, I ordered myself. And I did. *Pay whatever it says*, I thought. And I did. I also perceived a practical advantage in accepting the invoice, as I felt it protected me from unexpected future demands.

Few others have ever matched me in my enthusiasms. While Martha and I were very different, and in many ways opposites, our friendship was like a third entity, with a vibrant life of its own. It reminded me of that science-class experiment with a battery and two wires, one attached to its positive pole and the other to its negative one; when the free ends of the wires simultaneously touch the metal contacts at the base of a lightbulb, electric current begins the flow and the bulb lights up.

That year after Galapagos, we went here and there and everywhere together. "Let's go!" one of us would say, and the other was always ready. I gladly kept up with Martha's grueling schedule of hunting for content to fuel her media empire: gardening, hiking, antiquing, entertaining for breakfast, lunch, and dinner. The fever of activity was fun, especially in the Hamptons. Martha created an unbelievable concoction of highbrow life and lowbrow entertainment: morning departures, afternoon walks, beauty salon visits, estate sales, stops at clothing boutiques and bookstores, drinks at the Blue Parrot, dinners at the finest restaurants, savory lobster cookouts on fire-pits buried in the sand. We played in the surf and took long walks on the beach a block away from Lily Pond Lane, indulged in massages at Martha's house, shopped for rare tree peonies in gorgeous greenhouses, and searched antique shows for perfect specimens of stuffed birds and fish that Martha displayed at Lily Pond, large turquoise-glazed pots to grow decorative succulents on the terraces and around the pool, utilitarian or decorative items for Martha to reproduce and sell, a hostess gift so special it could become part of her Lily Pond collection (the East Lake period mirror I gave her passed the test and she put it in the front hall). Martha was a generous hostess, who once even let me and my girls use her Lily Pond house for a week when she traveled to the French Riviera with friends.

We visited walled-in mansions for dinner parties and over-the-top soirees. We traveled short distances or across the country in her leased private plane, like when Sam joined us to see the Vermeer exhibition at the National Gallery of Art in Washington, DC, just before it closed in February 1996.

Sam, the dashing charmer who knew everyone in New York society circles and the Hamptons, was Martha's closest male friend. Handsome and generous, a doctor of immunology and an astute businessman, he looked out for her. Often partners at social affairs, occasionally at state dinners, sometimes in a boardroom, Martha and Sam frequently saw each other or talked on the phone, and she highly valued his friendship and advice. Martha rarely made a business decision without conferring with Sam, who also had a lot of influence in Martha's personal life. She paid attention to his comments, opinions, and even his criticism, something Martha rarely accepted from anyone else except her daughter.

We took helicopter rides to East Hampton year round. On several occasions, Martha and I cut our Hamptons visits short, skipping afternoons of glamorous gatherings in order to drive to the shipping post in Connecticut, where we picked up crates of rare baby chicks sent to Martha from across the country. We took them to the *palais du poulet* and placed the wobbly, fragile creatures on sheets of newspaper under heat lamps in a space separate from the other fowl. We would sit on the floor playing with the fluffy chirplings, making sure that each of them had survived the long trip.

ONE OF MARTHA'S greatest talents was her bloodhound-like ability to scent out talent. She knew the smell of competence and, with unswerving confidence and relentless dedication, could trace its trail through to the end where there would be a unique, indispensable individual who would contribute ideas as good as gold to her growing empire. Thus it was that Martha found Sharon Patrick. A consultant with McKinsey & Co., Sharon had been creating media brands since the early 1980s. She had innate talent tempered and honed on the grinding wheel of daily experience. The two women had met during the arduous five-day trek they took with Sandy Pittman in the foggy, snowy mists of Kilimanjaro in late September 1993.

When Martha came back from that trip, she kept talking about this extraordinarily smart woman she'd met up there, a woman who said that Martha should buy her magazine back from TimeWarner and become "the world's first true multimedia brand."

"Maybe I should do it," Martha mused.

I wondered how thin the air was at 19,340 feet. I'd certainly heard that altitude alters one's judgment.

"Do you have that kind of money?" I asked.

My concerns dissipated when, at the beginning of summer 1994, I met Sharon Patrick, whom Martha had by then hired as a consultant. They would sit for hours in the Lily Pond kitchen, reshaping Martha's company. I listened to them talking, wisps of ocean breeze softening the sharp-edged, fast-paced conversation, which quickly became a duet of dreams and ideas. Sharon, whose competency rivals that of the quickest computer, immediately set about organizing the day-to-day operations, making plans and knotting ends. That summer, I went to East Hampton regularly, one weekend with the children, the next without. From morning till night I watched these two brilliant businesswomen at work.

Charlotte Beers, chairwoman of Ogilvy & Mather Worldwide, Inc. and one of Martha's friends, once said that "Martha fell in love with Sharon's mind." I fell in love with Sharon's energy, was fascinated by her life story, was charmed by her independent spirit, and was captivated by her unpretentiousness and sense of humor. I couldn't stop laughing when she talked about her youthful adventures, when she swam with the dolphins at Sea World before she got her Harvard MBA. I knew immediately that she had an ego as strong as Martha's, but, as I discovered one evening when Martha chose to stay home and Sharon and I went with Sam to a Hamptons party, Sharon was capable of great kindness.

I was next to Sharon in the line of guests waiting for drinks, when we heard the sounds of a fistfight. Curious, we pushed through the crowd, and could hardly believe our eyes when we saw Sam furiously hitting another man. We managed to convince him to take us home. On the way, we learned that Sam had fought with the other guy for having said something nasty about Martha's daughter. For the first time since I had known him, I loved Sam not for being a spellbinding erudite man, or a sarcastic bad boy, but simply for being human. By the time we got back to Lily Pond, Martha had already retired to her room. The three of us sat together outside on the back steps at Lily Pond late into the night while Sharon tended to Sam's cuts and cleaned the blood spots off his shirt.

Sharon traveled and socialized with Martha extensively, and on those occasions I saw her often. She was fun to be with and we laughed a lot together, at ourselves, at each other, and at life. I told Sharon things I would not have even dreamed of confiding to Martha. But I was careful not to cross the line: Sharon worked for Martha, and I watched from the sidelines as Martha, the "expansive visionary," did the driving, and Sharon, the "detail-minded executor," did the planning. They made a great team.

MARTHA WAS ACHIEVING the American dream and then some, and I watched with rapt fascination as the extremes of capitalism played out before me in ways I could never have imagined back in Bucharest. Money begat money, friends begat friends, success begat success. In addition to Sharon, who ran the business, and Martha's publicist Susan, who controlled her public image, Martha had numerous people working around the clock, a different person covering each of the quotidian tasks that consume more ordinary lives. There were parties, cocktails, dinners, shows to attend; invitations, confirmations, pickups and drop-offs in and out of town and on location; arrangements to be made for cars, boats, helicopters, and planes; packing and unpacking luggage;

changing batteries on hundreds of gadgets; even a weekday driver and a weekend one to take her back and forth to the office, home, meetings, visits with friends, beauty salons, doctor appointments, personal trainer sessions, massages, and frequent physical therapy treatments with Dr. Christian Rachitan. Add to that dogs, cats, canaries, chickens, gardens, and houses to look after—Martha really did need help caring for what had become a very complicated life. And that was just the maintenance part; Martha was always involved in some construction project that I found inspiring.

When MoMA accepted Martha's offer for the Bunshaft house, their trust that she would respect and preserve the integrity of the building was expressed verbally, at least that's how I understood it. After MoMa removed the sculptures, we went to Georgica Pond together, and Martha talked about the necessity of renovations.

Soon after that, Martha retained John Powson, the famed English architect of the modern, to plan the restoration. He had just finished the sharp-looking Calvin Klein store in Manhattan. Martha became so infatuated with John's talent that she named her new puppy chow Paw Paw after him. Some time later, the relationship between Martha and the architect ended in a legal entanglement. Martha hired other professionals to finish the Bunshaft renovation with improvements dictated by her personal taste. However, midway through the job, Martha's neighbor, Harry Macklowe, a famous New York City real estate developer, sued to stop it, reportedly claiming that some building addition blocked his view of Georgica Pond. Martha thought that was a ridiculous assertion, but the work at Bunshaft house halted and the neighborly dispute went on. It was not dissimilar from arguments Martha had had with her Turkey Hill neighbors except that there were many more lawyers involved.

At this point, she owned a number of houses: Turkey Hill in Westport; a pied-à-terre on Manhattan's Fifth Avenue; Lily Pond in East Hampton; and Bunshaft on Georgica Pond. In the early 1990s Martha purchased a spectacular 29.76-acre parcel of land on Bronson Road in the prestigious Greenfield Hill area of Fairfield, a town neighboring Westport. The land had frontage on two prime streets and used to be part of the once-extraordinary Baekeland estate. According to a local legend, it had belonged to the family after which Tom Wolfe had modeled the WASP-ish tribe of Sherman McCoy, the master-of-the-universe character from his novel *The Bonfire of the Vanities*, who, after taking a wrong turn, ended up in jail, losing his reputation and facing public trial. The old estate, which had also been a golf course for the Greenfield Country Club, was subdivided, and one of its pieces, a 29.76-acre parcel of land, was owned by a builder who had invested many millions in it but had been slammed by the real estate decline of the late 1980s and now the bank was selling it at auction. Martha acquired the large property for just $1 million from the bank.

In the spring of 1994, the old estate's main house, a graceful 1937 colonial built by the area's most famous architect of the era, Cameron Clark, and situated on 4.7 acres of land contiguous with Martha's parcel, also came up for sale. Excited to bring the old estate back together, Martha made an offer. I was her agent, and when she gave me her last bid, Martha made it conditional on the fact that once she became the owner of the Bronson House, my real estate firm and I would be her rental agents without taking a listing commission. I spoke about it with Wade, the owner of my office and a good friend of mine. We contemplated Martha's request—face value, cheek, and all—and acquiesced, because she was a friend, even though I was in the final stages of my divorce and could have used the commission income. After she completed the new purchase on March 31, 1994, Martha chose to name the reassembled property, the largest in the area, Bronson Fields.

It turned out that my loss of commissions for helping Martha rent out Bronson Fields was made up for many times over, by unquantifiable gains, as all of the people who had become tenants also became my friends. That's how I met Skip Bronson and his wife, Edie, who have been among my best friends since. In fact, after getting to know and like the area, they bought Hillside, a property I found for them, and one of the most beautiful mansions that Cameron Clark ever built in Greenfield Hill, with original gardens so superb they were listed in the National Register. With respect for historicity and impeccable taste, they made it into a home for their family and an epicenter for fun gatherings of friends. In a way, Martha and I again became part of a foursome, as we spent the most joyous years of our friendship with Skip and Edie. The four of us were inseparable. Their presence in our lives added an abundance of sparkle to my friendship with Martha. Those were the times when we had most of our laughs.

Some years after Martha became the Bronson Fields' proprietor, the antiques dealer who had surrendered the candlestick to Martha at our first joint tag-sale was moving to Florida. By that point, I visited his gallery with some regularity, and we had become quite friendly. He asked me to help place his three koi fish with someone who'd take as good care of them as he and his partner had done for the past fifteen years. On a clear spring Sunday morning, Martha and I drove to their house in her Suburban. They helped us transfer the large, shiny fish—two red and one golden-pink—to the lobster cages immersed in big, water-filled tubs that Martha had brought along. Then she and I went to Bronson Fields, where Martha had done little to renovate the buildings but spent great effort and money reviving the property and redesigning the landscape.

We carried the heavy cages from the driveway to her two ponds, through the grove of newly planted tall evergreen magnolia trees, over the hilly fields, among a flock of Canadian geese. There must have been a few hundred of them. We walked around the larger pond, the one with an isle in it, trying to decide where and how to release the fish.

Finally, I pointed to a soft sandy bank and said, "How would you like to meet your mustached koi right here, Onogoro?"

We laughed hysterically. We both had read Alison Fell's book *The Pillow Boy of the Lady Onogoro*, about a concubine who, insensitive to human caresses, finds ecstatic satisfaction from the quivering lips and whiskers of a giant carp in a pond.

As we walked through the pond carrying the heavy lobster cages, Martha said to me, "Are you okay, Mrs. Caliban?" which had us laughing all over again. A few years earlier we had discovered Rachel Ingalls's novel about the romantic transformation of Larry, a sea monster from the Gulf of Mexico, into the fantasy lover of the main female character, to whom the title, *Mrs. Caliban* alluded in an oblique reference to Shakespeare's *The Tempest*. Martha and I both liked Ingalls's writing and had read all her books.

It was lucky that we were so giddy, because the job was quite complicated. We dragged the cages near the mossy island and placed them on the muddy bottom, submerged and on the side, so the doors wouldn't open toward the surface and make it easy for geese to get inside. We propped up the koi's new houses with rocks, then opened the doors and buttressed them with some more stones, hoping the geese wouldn't attack. We waited until the koi came out. When they finally did, and we saw them swim about, Martha and I, drenched to the waist and covered in mud, made our way up the hill through the field of wet goose guano without saying a word.

Something about the koi adventure got me thinking that while Martha and I each wanted to find the right mate, I doubted I would encounter mine while being with her. She seemed to regard our "looking" not as a mutual endeavor but rather as a competition over who would be first to find a mate. And since my finding a mate meant I might not have been available when Martha needed me, I wasn't so sure she really wanted me to find mine.

Yet it was all friendly, and we had fun. Martha and I had perfected the art of living separately but with an interdependent bond. In her circles, I was the inside outsider—"any friend of Martha is a friend of mine." She invited me to Big-Names-whose-faces-I-remembered cocktail parties and to Big-Names-whom-I-had-met-before dinners.

"Get dolled up," she'd say.

For the most part, the eyes of available men who ran in Martha's entourage did not much flash "single man looking for long-term monogamous relationship with woman, wealthy or not, whose kids come before all else." But through Martha, I met many men like Sam, whose friendly company I cherished.

Though Martha and I had the same dream—to settle down with a wonderful man—our approaches to achieving that dream were radically different. In keeping with her more restless, risk-taking nature, Martha tended to leap into any relationship provided the potential fling that came her way was a rich man. Being less adventuresome and only capable of loving a man for himself, I just dated a few men. The one I liked and trusted most lived on the opposite coast, and I couldn't put such distance between my daughters and their father. Nonetheless, I enjoyed the glittering social whirl that came with Martha's growing fame.

While we attended events together, we did not do so as equals. A single mother, I increasingly felt a financial strain of keeping pace with Martha, whose massage bill in one month exceeded the amount of my child support, and could have made half my mortgage payment—our home was more than I could easily afford, yet I wanted my children to go to good schools and live near their father. But as Martha's fame grew, I came to feel more and more that what I really couldn't afford was our friendship. Sometimes I thought I should pull away, if only to save my wallet, but I did not.

As heady as it was being included in that social whirl, and as fulfilling, too, I think I must have felt the noose tightening, and sought some escape that would lead, at least, to an outline of my separate self, no matter how faint and no matter how painful. However, time seemed to drag without Martha. At first, in my house in Weston, we loved when Martha visited and were happy by ourselves when she didn't, but gradually, I came to seek the comfort of her presence, even if it was barbed at times.

With Martha, I got capitalism, plus American nobility and pureblood royalty, surrounded as I was by refined people who valued education, the pursuit of humanitarian goals, scientific development, the arts, and who were unpretentious, well-mannered, considerate, and tolerant. We had some fabulous times in a whirl of constant high-powered parties in the Hamptons, where I was Martha's guest. I gave Martha plenty of elbow room to socialize while I enjoyed conversations with many interesting people, such as Kurt Vonnegut, one of my favorite writers. I went to beach parties at Calvin Klein's home, was razzle-dazzled on Tommy Mottola's boat, and lunched at art dealer extraordinaire Larry Gagosian's house, a Charles Gwathmey modernist landmark. Barbra Streisand prepared fresh lobster and her favorite angel food cake with Cool Whip and hosted us for lunch on her terrace overlooking the dunes and the ocean. Some of my favorite parties were at Sam's, where his family and friends mingled comfortably with celebrities in a sort of mix-it-up intellectual slam dance where his friends, like the elegant British actor Terence Stamp or Mick Jagger, might run into Martha's friend Charlotte Beers.

Charlotte, often referred to as "the most powerful woman in advertising," was CEO of one of Madison Avenue's top advertising firms, Ogilvy & Mather. "Brand stewardship"—by which advertising cultivates consumer recognition of a particular product with taglines like "Don't leave home without it" for American Express—was her idea. Charlotte had such an uncommon talent at using the English language that listening to her talk was an absolute pleasure, and I often suggested she should write a Charlotte Says phrase dictionary so that we could all learn to express ourselves like her. There were many extraordinary facets to Charlotte besides having broken the glass ceiling and turning around the famous advertising agency. She was a solicitous and dedicated friend who supported Martha, gave her good advice, great introductions, and sometimes her superb balcony seats at the Metropolitan Opera, which Martha often shared with me. Charlotte got Martha into a paid American Express ad, and about the time when Ogilvy's award-winning ad campaign for Jaguar was glamorizing that car to Etta James's "At Last," Charlotte, who drove a blue XJ6, got one for Martha in pale silver-blue.

Charlotte, who came across as provocative and flirtatious, which well matched her beauty, was also fun and had a superb sense of humor that, combined with her incisive mind and candid manner, made her one of my top favorites among the handful of people around Martha whom I truly liked and cared for. Charlotte's longtime friend Memrie, an elegant, soft-spoken lady with buckets of Southern charm, was another. I had met Memrie at the Christmas party at the Turkey Hill barn organized for cameras and guests before the publication of *Martha Stewart's Christmas, Entertaining, Decorating and Giving*. Coincidentally, it was my friend China, who had known Memrie for years, who introduced us. Memrie invited Martha to her house in Aspen for the holidays that year, and they became good friends. A talented landscape designer, Memrie was a gracious hostess, her parties were fun, her guests were interesting, and I always felt she was a genuine friend to Martha.

10

A Queen Among the Pyramids

I SOLD THE HOUSE that was restored after the fire, and the girls and I moved to a new one, situated on three and a half acres of land next to a meandering river. It was hidden from view by curtains of poison ivy that hung from a decade of overgrowth. I rebuilt the whole place—buildings and property—and made it our home, featuring a new kitchen opening into the family room, and wired so our music played in all our common rooms. I added bookshelves everywhere, modern baths with steam showers, a fun playroom with a doggy-door and one for us that led out to a brick terrace and steps to the river, and a pergola-covered breezeway designed to connect the kitchen with the garage and our new herb and cutting gardens.

New windows transformed the waterside walls at the back of the house into floor-to-ceiling glass. Every light-filled room had glass doors that gave access to a deck running along the entire house on the river side. From everywhere we could see down a hill, green in the spring and gold in the fall, a river valley strewn with wildflowers and ferns, and the river that chuckled to itself all day and night and beyond which the wooded hills came alive at sunset and sunrise.

I decorated the formal rooms with classical Biedermeier furniture. Its clean architectural lines and honey-hued veneers showed off against a few antique lacquered pieces. In the kitchen and family room, all furniture was vintage 1950s American modern, like the comfortable, long Dunbar sofa and its matching chair, which I found at a local auction; it had come from the estate of their designer, Edward Wormley. I had them reupholstered in Scalamandré's *Chinese Vase* fabric, which horrified Martha, as the pattern was not consistent with the style of the era when the furniture was made, but I liked it.

It was a happy home where we and our boxers—Tigger the brindle and Ginger the fawn—enjoyed every moment, and our lives were filled with love, laughter, friends, music, books, and not many rules.

One spring, late afternoon, the windows were open and the sound of the river mingled with the lyrical sounds of Anne Sophie Mutter's violin playing the final harmonics from Édouard Lalo's *Symphonie Espagnole*. The girls had come home from school and tossed their backpacks onto the family room side tables. It was a day like any other day in mid-April, special only because after school my children, nine and twelve years old by then, were free of their usual extracurricular activities. Sitting high at our kitchen island, the girls did homework while we made one of our favorite cakes, a layered torte whose recipe we had been "perfecting" for years.

We unwrapped the fragrant, thin wafer-cake layers that came in packaged stacks of ten twelve-inch diameter rounds. I bought boxes of them every time I shopped at the Hungarian or Bavarian specialty stores where I got my baking supplies. They are my shortcut for making such delights as a Dobos torte, the Hungarian seven-layer cake that took my mother hours of standing in the kitchen to bake. If Martha were to make a chocolaty-layered cake, she'd do it as my mother did. I have neither their talent nor the patience to bake such cakes.

To make the filling, I opened the top of the Nutella jar and tipped it so the girls could each get a finger-dip. Then I said, "Check it out," imitating the tone from Mel Brooks's parody *Robin Hood: Men in Tights*, one of our favorite fun movies.

"Hey!" the girls answered, responding to a game we had been playing since they were little. According to the rules, I had to then pick a line from some verse we would sing to that rhythm, so I intoned, "'tis time! 'tis time!" The girls giggled, and, holding the hip-hop tune, responded to my line from *Macbeth*'s Witches' Spell with:

> *Double, double, toil and trouble;*
> *Fire burn, and cauldron bubble.*

I joined in as I emptied the creamy Nutella paste into a transparent Pyrex bowl:

> *For a charm of powerful trouble*
> *Scale of dragon*

While I mixed in sour cream and crème fraîche, Monica and Lara, ladles in their hands, kept playfully humming verses from the Witches' Spell, and each time I said, "Check it out," they tasted the instant ganache, because we don't have a precise recipe, so we make this mixture, literally, to taste.

Careful not to break the crispy wafers, we began to spread the smooth concoction on layer after layer, piling our cake gloriously high, licking our fingers in between, finishing with a thick coating of chocolate-hazelnut mixture as frosting on top, and sprinkling a few packages of vanilla powdered sugar for decoration.

The cake had to be refrigerated for a few hours before serving, until the wafer-layers became chewy and delicious, but we always had a few slices immediately, and refrigerated the rest. Just as I was preparing to cut, I heard *clink clink clink* through the unconcerned barking of our dogs. We had not heard Martha's black Suburban drive down the pebbled driveway, but I could see her through the window above the kitchen sink. I looked at the clock on top of my stainless Wolf stove, which Martha had given me when, during the renovation work at my house, she had decided to replace the wonderful cooker from her kitchen at Turkey Hill with an out-of-this-world Aga stove. It was after five o'clock already. Those afternoons with the girls went by so fast. Martha must have been stopping by for sustenance on her way back from work. Her car door open, she was about to get out, keys left in the ignition. *Clink clink clink.*

The girls grinned: Martha! One never knew what would blow in with Martha—a guest, a puppy, tickets to a sold-out show. Almost every week since we'd moved there, Martha would stop by on her way home from filming segments for the *Martha Stewart Living* television show produced in Westport. The visits provided a much needed pause between the endless demands of her two worlds: her studio, with its beautiful, life-size filming kitchens, all the cameras and lights and scripts and screens; and her houses, which, because they were always being filmed, had taken their own adornments to new heights. Not a thing was out of place within the confines of Martha's world. The table was always set for a party of many, although she lived with only her regal chows and darting cats and the canaries cooped in gilded cages on her glassed-in porch. Martha had a hard time going home. If I lived where she lived, I would have, too.

"Coming," I shouted, and swiping my Nutella-smeared hands on the nearest towel, I headed toward the door, palming the handle until it rotated and clicked. The breeze did the rest, opening the door in increments, as if obeying Martha's command, for Martha loved a dramatic entrance.

"Ta-da!" she called out when she was there before me.

"Come in!" I said, just as I'd said a few days prior, and the week before, and the week before. She came in. We kissed on both cheeks. I smelled her perfume, but it could not hide an odor at once fainter yet more pronounced: fatigue. And a splash of dread.

"We were just making cake."

"'Making'?" Martha asked, emitting one of her small snorts and lowering her voice: "You make cakes like I make love."

We laughed. The girls were still in the kitchen and couldn't hear. Martha did not have a beau and neither did I at the time. Though I wanted to meet a good man, I was content and felt no inclination to settle for Mr. Right Now.

"Well, I'm doing my best," I said.

"Let me guess." Martha smiled, her eyes filled with playful irony. "Store-bought ingredients. Tsk tsk."

"Tastes good," I said, "but if Her Highness wants top quality, I can serve you true Shi Feng Dragon Well Tea. You can drink it while *you watch* me eat the cake."

I smiled at her. She smiled at me. "Smells good," she said, and in the light of the front-hall lamp I saw a shadow fleeing from Martha's eyes. The girls. Her own girl was grown. Her home was empty.

"I want to take your girls with me on Bring Your Daughter to Work Day," Martha said and then, without waiting for my response, because she didn't need to, she entered our kitchen calling out, "Monica! Lara!" as my daughters ran to her open arms, the dogs close behind.

"Next week," she said. "Tuesday. You girls are coming with me." She paused and then added, "All day."

A treat for my kids, a treat for Martha, a treat for me, because they would come back enriched with an experience neither I nor their school could ever give them. It takes a village to raise a child, they say. Martha had become like a surrogate mother to them.

"Stay for dinner," the girls said.

But Martha veered, as she often did. Her ever-curious gaze snagged on Monica's notebook, open on the kitchen counter. Her eye scanned the page, then Lara, who was standing before her, grinning ear-to-ear. "Come here," Martha said sternly. Lara giggled, then went to Martha, who drew her into a quick, fierce hug, then let her go.

"What's this?" she asked Monica, gesturing toward the schoolbook.

"I'm writing a paper on the Rosetta Stone," Monica answered, unperturbed by Martha's challenging tone. My girls knew that Martha's commanding manner was just her style. I had on occasion talked about it with the girls and also about how one doesn't have to be controlling in order to be in charge.

"We should go to Egypt," Martha said.

Monica's face lit up. Lara giggled and did a little Isis dance, which made us laugh. As the dogs jumped up to dance with her, Martha began rifling through the pages of another schoolbook. Watching her turn the book over, reading the blurb on the key to Egypt's hieroglyphs, I thought of how similar was our longing to escape the confines of ordinary life, how similar our yen for wonder and discovery. Martha was planning to climb Mount Everest with Sandy Pittman, whom she had arranged to meet at the base camp in a couple of weeks. She was excited and prepared for the Himalayan expedition on the Stairmaster every day. While Martha trained hard, setting the treadmill at the highest incline, I was telling her not to go. If my persistence didn't irritate Martha, I'm sure my reasoning did, as I based my exasperating assertion on a bad premonition, something I couldn't understand myself.

I stood in our kitchen, and watched Martha, her curiosity engaged for a split second before something else snagged her attention: a new cerulean pot added to my Longwy faïence collection. My vintage Knoll kitchen stools. My shoes. It could have been anything. Her eyes wandered around the family room and stopped at the large abstract painting on the wall.

"Is that the Jim Dine you just got?" Martha asked. "It's not a robe."

"It's about autumn. The title is on the back, and a gallery record on the stretcher," I said. "By the way, has Lexi kept in touch with his son?"

"She hasn't talked about him since boarding school. They only dated for a while at Putney."

"Would you, please, cut us some cake slices, Martha? I'm not too good at it," I said. Stacking plates and a few cutting knives next to the cake platter, I thought of Andy. He often talked about the school in Vermont where Alexis went. That's where he had gone, and loved it. "I'll make tea," I told Martha, and turned away to lift the boiling kettle off the stove. I poured hot water to warm up two cups from my collection of antique white ironstone and the small teapot with a built-in ceramic strainer I had gotten at an estate sale. Martha had said it was a good one. At Martha's urging, we once watched a movie about the Japanese tea ceremony, which, while a truly complicated ritual that included a good deal of tradition and cultural heritage, helped refine my manner of preparing tea. While the kettle cooled down—since water that is too hot is said to make green tea taste bitter—I discarded the pot-warming water by practicing pouring from the pot with my left hand, which was how I understood one is supposed to serve tea.

I opened the pouch of pan-fired, flat-looking, yellow-green tea leaves, and gave Martha a whiff.

"Hmm! Where did you get that?"

"Jean Marc's gift from his trip to China. Tender first spring imperial camellia shoots," I said. I sprinkled a heaping teaspoon of leaves inside the pot, and submerged them in moderately hot fresh water from our well, which had a good iron content. I'd read somewhere that this enhances the taste of green tea. The merchant had told my friend to brew the tea leaves for one and a half minutes. Meanwhile, I watched Martha tackle the cake cutting, a difficult task for a non-dexterous person like me, because when the cake is just made, the layers slide from the knife.

"You should sharpen this," she said.

"I know."

All eyes in the room were now on Martha's hands, the left one held in the air just above the cake, fingers bent, ready to grab, the right one maneuvering one of our large knives with the precision and dexterity of a top surgeon as she cut out four neat slices and placed them on the plates without the slightest smudge. Our dogs took their eyes off Martha's hands and moved them to her face, then to mine, with reproachful looks, then walked over and slumped their large bodies on the family room carpet with annoyed sighs. Our laughter filled the room.

"Oh, Tiggy, Gingy!" the girls called out, remorseful. "Chocolate is bad for dogs!"

"Let's sit down!" I said and picked up the tray with cake plates, forks, napkins, and teacups.

Martha nodded and followed me into the living room. Whenever she came to my home, I was especially conscious of this moment when she followed me, somewhat gratefully, the slumping of her shoulders and spine almost audible; relieved not to be in charge, to let herself be led.

I was leading her toward the deep Russian Biedermeier armchair, because I knew she needed it, and because, once settled in, I knew we would talk in the easy, fluid way close friends do, exchanging bits of news that would be utterly uninteresting were they delivered in any context other than this one: closeness. The news is more important in the fact of its exchange than in its actual content. There was nothing chitchatty about our chitchat. When we made chitchat, I felt that we were somehow demonstrating—to ourselves and the universe—that we were tethered against all odds.

"How did you manage to keep this lime-green cymbidium alive?" she asked.

"Without a greenhouse?" I smiled, both of us knowing I was teasing her for her insistence on proper tools for every task. "I move all my orchids under the deck for the summer. They like the humid river breeze. The cymbidiums and dendrobiums I bring back in last, exactly twenty-eight days after the first fifty-five-degree night. Phillip, my hair stylist, knows everything about orchids," I said. Martha swiveled toward the next thing, and then the next, and then the next, until I had to practically push her down by her shoulders. Once I did, she collapsed into her seat, crossed her long legs at the knee, which told me that Martha was comfortable and didn't feel she had to assume the proper ankle-crossing pose, but while her fatigue was palpable, her face still sparkled, plastered with a big grin. I grinned back.

We drank tea and forked the cake into our mouths. Darkness fell. I had to get dinner for the girls.

"Do you want to stay?" I asked.

No matter how many hours she worked, Martha always had energy for some high-end sushi in the city, but we both knew I wouldn't go out with her that night, since, when my children were not with their father, I always wanted to have dinner with them. If Martha did not want to sit at a simple table, she'd find a dining partner in her phone book, have her driver transport her to the city, sleek and elegant, seeing and being seen, and then she'd come home, too tired to feel the pressure of so much space surrounding her in her lonely home. She'd sleep for a few hours and then startle awake at dawn, moving, moving, moving, reaching for the phone, who cares that it's five and dawn has barely broken?

"Want to see a late movie tonight?" Martha asked.

After I turned down her invitation, Martha told me that she was having a dinner date at Turkey Hill. The man was known to and liked by many in Martha's affluent circle of friends. As elated as we were at the prospect of the right man possibly about to enter Martha's life, we still devised a plan: I would call her that evening, about half an hour after her romantic prospect was due to arrive. Martha would answer the phone, and, if the chemistry of attraction was there between them, Martha wouldn't say anything about dessert; but, if things were cool between them, then Martha would say what she was serving for dessert, our coded understanding for me to come to Turkey Hill and join them, giving her a good pretext to suggest an early evening.

When I walked in, later that night, and pretended to be dropping by, the handsome, WASP-y gentleman, who had not been told of my planned intrusion, appeared ill at ease. The kitchen, where they were having dinner, felt cold. There was indeed no vibe.

But we soon found out that we shared a love of good desserts, music, horses, and gardens. He talked about his record collection, thousands of them, and about playing the piano. Then he talked about his black Shire draft horses with great affection, and said how he liked to get his hands dirty in the soil and gardens, experimenting with plants. The man was more and more perfect with every word he said.

We were beginning to relax and the conversation had taken a more jocular tone when, out of an upper kitchen cupboard, we noticed a little animal peeking at us. It looked like a cross between a squirrel and a chipmunk. For the next ten minutes or so, the three of us ran around the kitchen trying to shoo the creature outside. But it disappeared as mysteriously as it came. And it gave Martha's date a good reason to take his leave, which was fine by me: I came for the emergency call but didn't like to leave my kids alone for so long.

Years later, I met Martha's date again at a party given by some of my best friends who live hundreds of miles from Martha's house at Turkey Hill. He was there with a beautiful woman. When it happened to be just us near the dessert table, I said, "We met once upon a mutant."

"I know." His voice was soft, secretive, letting me know he didn't want the new date to learn of his previous escapades.

I decided not to tell Martha about that encounter.

MY ATTEMPTS TO dissuade Martha from joining Sandy Pittman on the Mount Everest climbing expedition in the spring of 1996 had been ineffective. The evening before her departure for Kathmandu, we were celebrating Martha's pending adventure at a fashionable New York restaurant with a group of friends.

"The two weeks of pre-monsoon season in early May are the best to climb Everest," Martha declared.

"Still, the jet stream is lurking high up there," I said. "What if it slams the summit with a storm earlier than usual?"

"They say the weather on the mountain is better than it's been in years," she retorted.

"Hence the caution for the unpredictable," I insisted.

"Oh, Mariana, don't be such a party pooper," Martha said, laughing.

"Giggling won't stop the jet stream."

"Sandy has been in the Himalayas a few times. She says one must go up to the summit no later than May 10. She's very organized. She knows the ropes."

"She's also an ambitious woman," I replied.

"She already climbed six of the world's seven highest peaks!"

"But she's got a book contract, television hopes," I said, disregarding the annoyance in Martha's voice. "This is her big chance to become the Martha Stewart of mountaineering. Wasn't it Bob who said that? Are they divorced yet? He's handsome. And fun."

"And very, very rich," Martha chuckled. "I think he'll end up with an older woman, like me, or a much younger one, like Lexi."

"Well, Sandy obviously has her own agenda."

"Blaine Trump is coming too!" Martha said.

"Yes. I saw the picture in the newspaper of you serving them crêpes Suzette in that pasha tent in Sikkim."

Martha rolled her eyes. Dan Shedrick, who was sitting on Martha's other side, and who had been unusually quiet that evening, said, "You can do anything, Martha. Everybody knows that. But Everest is a totally different game."

"Year after year people die on that mountain," I said.

"Keep after her, Mariana," Dan said. "I've tried," he added, looking pointedly at Martha.

"It's a once-in-a-lifetime experience," Martha snapped.

"Undoubtedly," Dan replied.

"You had a great time when you went to Sikkim," I said. "But this time is not just about trekking between base camps and procuring *shahtoosh* pashminas! As you said, knowing now that Tibetan *chiru* antelopes are endangered animals, and that three to five of them are killed to get enough fur for one shawl, you can't in good conscience buy more *shahtoosh*es, anyway."

Martha gave me a steely look, so I tried to change the subject. "By the way, did you find anyone to fix the holes Teeny and Weeny chewed in that beautiful *shahtoosh*?"

Martha shook her head.

"I'm sorry that your naughty kittens have such good taste! Of all the pashminas you brought back from Sikkim, that was perhaps the most beautiful."

A new toast was raised to Martha's conquering Everest, and I stopped my pestering to join in. But I felt that Martha had her own doubts about the trip. Had she not, she would have, by then, said something to silence me.

So, as soon as I got a chance, I continued, "Remember your trek on Kilimanjaro when you got lost in the blizzard alone? What if you are caught in an Everest storm? If you stop, you freeze to death up there. If you keep going, you can lose your footing and slide down in a crevasse."

"Mariana, stop it! It's too late to cancel this trip! It's all arranged. All paid for."

"Screw the money, Martha!" Then, lowering my voice, "I told you I've been having a bad dream. It begins with a Vermeer painting, the one I stared at for days in Vienna. *The Art of Painting.* In my dream, the background is flooded by an eerie light where I clearly see a figure looking like the woman in that painting. The Vermeer light is on her. The woman stands still, her eyes are looking down, her lids lowered, her skin is smooth like yours. As I look at her, I realize that all her features are yours, and she's dressed like you, in a puffy blue-gray jacket with a silky sheen. You look serene and calm in my dream, which is what scares me most because in real life I never saw in you the peacefulness of the woman in the painting. Eventually, the map behind the woman becomes mountainous peaks, and it snows and you never raise your eyes, you don't move, you just disappear, dead calm, in a dark, blizzardy image and I wake up."

"Sandy already has people waiting for me in Kathmandu."

"I read somewhere that Sandy's got a number of Sherpas carrying electronics and satellite equipment for her. If she can send dispatches about bringing Dean & DeLuca coffee to Everest, she should be able to receive a message that Martha Stewart is skipping the playdate."

Dan and I did not succeed in dissuading Martha from going on that trip. In fact, she seemed upset with me when we parted at the end of the evening. So I was surprised when mid-morning next day, my phone rang and it was Martha. She was supposed to be on an airplane. But, to my relief, she was calling to say she had canceled the trip. As it transpired, Blaine Trump also didn't go. Then, it was on the news: on May 10, 1996, eight climbers died during a storm on Mount Everest, the most people ever to lose their lives there on a single day. They had all been members of the expedition that included Sandy Pittman, who, luckily, survived.

"Had you come to America earlier, you'd have been burned at the stake," Martha said to me.

"I know. The caption would have said: *Martha Stewart's Witch Flambé*. I'm so glad you didn't go, Martha."

"Can you imagine?" Martha shook her head, stunned.

"Those poor people!" I said.

BY NOVEMBER 1996, Martha and I had to face the fact that one more year had gone by without either of us having found the man of our dreams to share the winter holidays with. Once again, we found ourselves making plans for a vacation together, Martha renewing her suggestion that we go to Egypt. Maybe traveling to the cradle of civilization would be exactly what we needed.

For such a special destination, people usually plan their travel months or sometimes years in advance. As we were up against an extremely late start for organizing our vacation, and since Martha, who was put off by the fact that the Abercrombie & Kent agent suggested that "due to crowds already booked in Egypt" we should change itinerary, didn't want to use a travel agency, I came up with the idea that we call Dr. Weeks at the American University in Cairo and ask for his advice.

We had met Dr. Kent Weeks, the distinguished archeologist, in Sun Valley, Idaho, that spring at the American Academy of Achievement, an annual event dedicated to inspiring outstanding students who are given the opportunity "to meet and discuss issues with eminent adult achievers from every facet of American life, the fields of sciences, business, the professions, sports, literature, entertainment, the military, the arts, and public service." I had been going to that event with Martha since she was inducted into the academy, and I had had the privilege to meet the most informed and nicest people one could ever hope to meet. Of all the parties and all the events and all the exclusive places where I went with Martha, I coveted that invitation above all. Each time we went, I ran from one round-table discussion to another. I was like a child in a candy store, listening, asking questions, learning, taking notes, making lists of things I should read about. Dr. Weeks received the Academy Golden Plate Award to honor his discovery of the biggest tomb in the Valley of the Kings. It was mesmerizing to listen to him tell us the story of how he squeezed his way through a door that had been unopened for more than three thousand years to find himself in a corridor leading to the burial chambers of the sons of King Ramses the Great.

As luck would have it, Dr. Weeks, whose grown children were visiting him and his wife in Egypt for the holidays, obligingly invited us to tag along. How much better could visiting the lands of pharaohs get than being hosted by the eminent professor? We were elated. Dr. Weeks promptly sent me his family's itinerary so I could make flight and hotel arrangements. It was difficult, not only because of the last-minute decision but also because we were a pretty large party and Martha kept changing trip dates, finally settling on December 26 to January 5. Because of a cancellation, I lucked out and was able to book us the last rooms available, at the Winter Palace Hotel in Luxor, a place of which I had a very romantic image thanks to various movies I'd seen and novels and travel books I had read.

It was already December when Martha decided to change plans again. She had made an appointment to visit a cotton factory near Cairo, so I understood how the change was important for her and made the trip a valid business expense. However, that meant inconveniencing

Dr. Weeks and my being on the phone with Egypt at three in the morning, East Coast time, trying to find in-country flights and hotel rooms for our group of eleven people. Fortunately, Dr. Weeks and his family graciously made some changes to their own plans so we could still spend part of the time with them and learn firsthand about the treasures of Egypt, and having lost the opportunity to stay at the Winter Palace, all I was able to book in Luxor was a three-star hotel, The Pharaon.

Barely a week before our departure for Egypt, Martha said to me, "What do you think, should I ask that guy I like to come with us to Egypt?"

"The one from Microsoft?" I asked.

"No. Not him. Bobby. The one I met at Thanksgiving at Joel's. I told you."

"You mean Billy Bob's friend? You liked him that much?"

"Yes. He seemed to like me."

"Fabulous. Why not?" I said, delighted that for the first time in all the years that had passed since Martha had dated that handsome journalist, soon after Andy left, she had chosen a man not for his oodles of money but for himself.

Our traveling party consisted of—besides Martha, myself, and my girls—Sharon and her nephew Daniel; Susan; and Martha's two nieces, Sophie and Kristina, and two nephews, Chris and Kirk. Bobby, whom Martha did invite, had accepted and was a perfect addition to the group. A sensitive and supremely talented photographer with a career as a film director and producer and a permanent abode in Beverly Hills, Bobby, who was quite a bit younger than Martha, always seemed to appear out of some theatrical blue, his chiseled face nearly perfect, his persona mysteriously enhanced by the fact that he was just emerging from a long relationship with a very sexy Hollywood actress whose perfume one could practically still smell on him.

I had not seen Martha so smitten in quite some time, and it worried me. I remembered the unhappy string of desperate days and obsessive nights and compulsive stalking.

• • •

LIKE ME, MARTHA had grown up in an environment where nobody could afford to travel but we watched movies and read books that made one dream of far-off lands. That romance held an irresistible attraction for both of us. Thus, with the trip to Galapagos, we began a tradition of year-end adventure voyages, after which came Egypt. We also established a method for sharing the cost of these trips. I paid for my children and myself, and Martha paid for everyone else. Before departure, I purchased plane tickets for my family. Once we landed, Martha, as a matter of convenience, put all expenses on her credit card. When we returned to the States, Martha's office calculated what our group had spent on the trip and, dividing by number of vacationers, determined the dollar figure representing the cost for the three of us. There were many more expenses, and between vaccinations, special equipment, and traveling gear, each of those trips cost a small fortune. While the payment system was favor-based, everyone traveling contributed in some way. Susan, especially, did tons of research, and generously shared information and lists of books, as well as tips on what to do and where to go.

Before we went to Egypt, Martha's company had forwarded us a Department of State Consular Affairs warning about the area. "In several incidents, extremists have sought to cripple the Egyptian economy through attacks on tourists, tour buses, and sites frequented by tourists." The statement also said that "Islamic extremists have threatened to target foreign investors and tourists." As a mother, I read the document quite carefully.

The plane ride was long but with Martha by your side, every hour was winged. My daughters were flush with excitement and jam-packed with their pretravel research. Monica and Lara were just thirteen and almost ten, but old enough to fall utterly for Egypt's beauty, mystery, history.

Only hours after we landed in Cairo, Bobby saved the trip. The

Egyptian travel agency that had booked our plane tickets for the short flight from Cairo to Egypt's southernmost town of Aswan had somehow made different arrangements from those they confirmed with me by fax. Ultimately, the airport staff got us on a plane not just because I had all that paperwork with me, but because Bobby knew how to tip them.

It was already dusk when we arrived at the Aswan Oberoi, where I had made hotel reservations for our first two nights in Egypt. I was very pleased with my arrangements, since the spa retreat was as luxurious as my research had described it, tasteful and charming, well situated on the Elephantine Island, a garden enclave surrounded by the blue waters of the Nile. After having already marveled at the pyramids on Cairo's horizon, we were pinching ourselves to make sure we were really there in the shade of tall lebbek trees.

We checked into our comfortable rooms with balconies and views of the Nile and the history-filled rocky desert beyond, then gathered for a late dinner at the Tower, one of the hotel's restaurants with spectacular views, to discuss our plans for visiting key historical sites like the majestic temple of the falcon-god Horus at Edfu, the Temple of Isis from Philae, which had been threatened with submersion after construction of the Aswan dam and so was moved to another island by a UNESCO-organized international effort, and, farther south, the Colossi of Ramses at Abu Simbel.

I had already noticed that Martha had really fallen for Bobby. But I only realized how smitten she was when she came up next to me and, out of the blue, started to tell me intimate, personal things about him, her voice a low hum, as though she were a chanting worshiper at the temple of the divine masculine in the Elephanta Caves of a faraway island in the Arabian Sea, its scenery said to recall the setting of an Indiana Jones movie.

I sometimes think that if Martha could have been someone other than Martha, she would have been Indiana Jones. While she represents to America the ultimate in domestic gentility, one need not know her long to encounter her craving for an exciting life, adventuresome discovery, horses in a lathered gallop, boats sailing by the stars at night, all of which I loved about her. But I erred on the side of prudence, especially since I had become a mother.

The fact that we were so different was, I believe, part of the reason that we'd bonded. It seemed that Martha felt grounded by my commonsensical caution, while I admired the unfailing self-confidence that led her to take such large leaps of faith. She was so audacious and uninhibited that, when I was with her, I felt free to be in love with life, liberated from my usual fears and constant concerns.

Still, I had some moments of high anxiety, like when we first arrived in southern Egypt and Martha, who became edgy and possessive around Bobby, going to extraordinary lengths to impress him, announced her plan to spend the night in an Egyptian felucca boat sailing the waters of the Nile—contrary to the U.S. Department of State warning. Martha pursuing a romantic movie vision from *The African Queen* or *Cleopatra* with Bobby was her business, but reenacting some fantasy at the risk of everybody else's safety was more than I was willing to venture into.

"I think it's stupidly dangerous to do that," I said. "Your own company has warned us!"

"You're either with me or out," she spat, her eyes narrowed with rage.

I had seen her like this before. I knew that short of walking out on her, there was no way to make her stop. Martha seemed desperate to me.

"Out," I said. I gathered my daughters and we spent the night in the safety of the Aswan Oberoi Hotel while Martha, Bobby, and the rest of the group, including the children entrusted to her care, Susan, Sharon, and Sharon's nephew, slept beneath the stars on a boat on the Nile. I could not sleep that night. I sat on my balcony and looked out over the glittering lights of the island's old Nubian villages into the Arabian night. Toward the east, across the dark curve of the river, was the village of Aswan, an old trading post and strategic military point,

My wedding day. Westport, May 1983. *Courtesy of the author.*

With Martha and Andy at my house, spring 1984. *Courtesy of the author.*

Holding Monica before her first Easter egg hunt, Turkey Hill, 1986. *Courtesy of the author.*

At Lara's baptism with (from left to right) her godmother, Maggie Kromer-Moszynski, Martha, me, and my friend Gabriela Iliescu. St. Luke's Church in Westport. Spring 1987. *Courtesy of the author.*

At home with the kids, Thanksgiving 1989. *Courtesy of the author.*

Visiting Monet's garden at Giverny for Maggie and Andy Moszynski's twentieth anniversary, May 1990. *Courtesy David Long.*

My birthday at the Walhalla lake cottage, August 1995. *Hat and photo courtesy Linn Cassetta.*

Stranded in Miami Beach by a Northeastern snowstorm on our return from the Galapagos. January 1996. *Courtesy of the author.*

Sea-kayaking in Newfoundland, September 1997. *Courtesy Rich Deacon, www.sobek.ca.*

Fundraiser lunch at Hillside, the home of Skip and Edie Bronson, 1999. Seated left to right: Sharon Patrick, Dayle Haddon, Richard "Skip" Bronson, Martha. Standing: unidentified guest, and me. *Courtesy of the author.*

Ringing the opening
bell with Sharon Patrick,
October 19, 1999.
Henny Ray Abrams/AFP/
Getty Images.

Sam Waksal flanked by his lawyers, leaving Federal Court, October
2002. *Spencer Platt/Getty Images.*

the immensity of the desert stretching beyond and the sacred island of Philae that used to house the Temple of Isis. On the west bank of the river, steep cliffs were surmounted by tombs where local dignitaries had been interred for thousands of years; the mausoleum of Mahommed Shah Aga Khan; the cupolas of the great Coptic monastery of St. Simeon; and, farther south, eight pairs of sphinxes standing guard by the Temple of Ramses II, built and rebuilt by Ethiopian kings and Greco-Roman emperors.

I listened to the silence, an occasional sound rising up from the Nile's waters. Then, near dawn, came the muezzin call to early prayer.

As it turned out, Martha and the group arrived back safely the next morning, the only excitement they were faced with having been hosting friends from New York who came for drinks on the *Moon River*, the felucca that Martha had hired for the night. They were television personality Charlie Rose, whom Susan represented in her professional capacity as publicist, and his longtime companion, Amanda Burden, a charming Manhattan socialite.

Martha seemed to have forgotten all about the dispute. She was flying high, powered by her passion. But I had no regrets about my decision.

On the third day of our trip, we met Dr. Weeks in Luxor, once the city of Thebes, capital of ancient Egypt. The Pharaon hotel was a distance away from the luxurious Winter Palace, and they had no extra free rooms, so with the new group configuration, Sharon and Susan had to share their room with me. While the staff was installing an extra bed, the three of us went out on the bare balcony with a view of the back courtyard and a claustrophobic vista of sun-washed buildings. When we walked back inside, the room had been transformed into what looked like a mattress showroom, not exactly what we were used to.

"We won't be spending much time here anyway," I said.

Susan looked as though she might burst into tears. Already, the airline had lost her luggage, and the black cashmere and winter clothes she had left New York in didn't quite work with the brutally hot Egyptian sun. Since our arrival, she had been wearing my clothes. But I knew that wasn't what preoccupied her most. We were all exhausted by Martha's raging jealousy.

"I am going to walk away any time Bobby comes near me," one of us said.

"The problem is that he tries to be polite and make conversation," said another.

"I'll pretend not to hear."

"I will simply not respond, just walk away."

"You can't talk to him anyway. Every time he comes close to one of us, Martha runs over and starts talking, taking over the conversation."

"If that were all, it would have been bad enough. But it's her relentless attacks. I might lose my cool and say something back."

Since Bobby was the prince-in-residence, Martha bestowed a generous daily dose of offenses on every one of us. I got my share as the target of Martha's griping about hotel arrangements. I did remind her that she was the one who fooled around with the itinerary and caused us to lose our rooms at the famous hotel, but reason was not what Martha was about on that vacation. We resolved the problem by spending every waking minute on the superb stone terrace at the Winter Palace whenever we were not visiting some extraordinary site. From there, our group of twelve watched the magnificent golden light of the Nile and the Valley of the Kings beyond, having drinks, talking, reading, planning our days, and having those special moments immortalized in pictures, especially the beautiful ones that Bobby took of us.

We went to a camel market where we were the only Westerners among Bedouins amused by our wondering at their goods and unafraid to pet their poisonous spitting cobras. Kristina took a picture with a snake draped around her neck. She looked cool, so Martha also posed for a snake-necklace portrait. At the spice market, we tasted the mildly perfumed hibiscus tea and bought handfuls of the fragrant cardamom seeds prescribed in the *Kama Sutra*, and pouches filled with wrinkled fruits of black peppercorn, whose pungent aroma holds the mysteries of *The Perfumed Garden*. We wandered among serene ancient temples, walked along alleys flanked by rows of stone lions, and stood at the feet of Colossi of Memnon, the seated giants calmly facing the Nile. We marveled at rich museum collections, and Martha took a picture of Bobby separated by only a sheet of glass from the funerary mask of Tutankhamen. We hiked the sandy hills in the Valley of the Kings, honeycombed with mysterious and solemn great tombs where dry heat and diffuse light silently preserve earthly remains. We sailed up and down the Nile under out-of-this-world sunsets and saw *fellaheens* working their silt-rich lands. We rode donkeys and camels on village lanes along fields of tall papyrus growing on the Nile banks, where among the reeds and invasive water hyacinth live purple gallinule water birds, whose short bills are similar in color to the brick-red chests of Egyptian barn swallows. Riding splendid Arabian horses among the sand dunes, with the Pyramids of Giza in the background, was an unforgettable experience. No matter how jealous or high-strung Martha behaved, this setting and these experiences certainly trumped everything.

Our New Year's Eve in Luxor could have ended badly, as Martha, Sharon, Susan, and I, blissfully ignorant of local sentiment and custom, got on the restaurant's stage after the belly dancer's performance, happy to swing and shake our shoulders, torsos, and hips, giggling and jiggling the bazaar copies of traditional bejeweled ornaments, which we had bedecked ourselves with for the occasion. Our unabashed behavior was unwise, given the rising anti-Western climate at the time. A number of tourists had been killed in incidents over the previous few years. Luckily, we were with Dr. and Mrs. Weeks, whose knowledge of Arabic and local customs helped them catch wind of an imminent and dangerous plot against our group. They got us and the kids out of there just in the nick of time, then quickly into a felucca that swished through the inky waters of the river in the dark, taking us to safety. (We only later realized how fortunate we were, when, in September 1997, not long after our trip, a busload of German tourists were attacked and killed in Cairo. In November, more than sixty people, most of them tourists, were killed by Muslim extremists at the Temple of Hatshepsut, quite near the place where we had celebrated New Year's Eve.)

On the first day of 1997, Sharon, Monica, and I woke up at four in the morning to get in line for tickets so our group could visit the Temple of Nefertari, in the Valley of the Queens, which did not open its gates until much later in the day. The reason for the crowds and the predawn ticket lines was that the temple, famed to be one of the most beautiful among all the tombs in Egypt, had only recently reopened after having been closed since 1986 for restoration. Nefertari, the favorite queen of Ramses II, was known to have been the most beautiful queen ruler of Egypt. She shared political power with her husband, the pharaoh, thirty-three hundred years ago. We had seen her colossal, thirty-plus-foot statue on our first day, at Abu Simbel, next to her husband's. Flocks of white-crowned black wheatear birds, which nested in stone crevices, flew around their majestic heights. We had seen her portraits in many temples, and everyone wanted to see her tomb, painted throughout with beautiful frescoes showing her figure, clad in long, white gossamer gowns and always wearing a headdress of gold in the shape of a vulture with two long feathers hanging over it, and over-the-top jewelry. Not much is known about her private life beyond her being also a priestess and mother-in-law of Tutankhamen. Seeing her tomb was a must.

By the time most of our group had joined us at the Queens Hotel restaurant across the street from the entrance to the Valley of the Queens, the gates were still closed.

Monica and I were chatting and drinking fresh pomegranate juice when Martha joined us and suggested we should hire one of the unofficial drivers who offered to take tourists through a back gate, over the dunes, so we could be first to enter Nefertari's tomb before it became stuffy with the breath of all those people waiting in line. I quickly ran to Susan and asked her to take care of Lara, who was having fun with the other kids, while I took on Martha-duty. Leaving the others at the restaurant, Monica and I followed Martha, who was already across the street negotiating a ride, and we got in the back of an open jeep, and started driving through the desert, surrounded only by huge hills of sand. I was talking with Monica when Martha began arguing with the driver.

The handsome Egyptian stopped the car in the midst of that intimidating landscape, turned an emotionless face toward us, and said, "Here you get out."

"But where is the tomb?" I asked.

"Here," he said.

I tried to plead with him in French so Martha wouldn't understand that I was apologizing for her, and I thought I saw a flicker in his eyes when I asked him please not to punish my child for my friend's mistake, but all he said was: "I'm sorry, you have to all leave my car. She must get out, now."

Left under the blistering sun, in the middle of the desert, we began walking. From the corner of my eye, I saw the jeep speeding away toward the hazy horizon, its wheel marks wiped out by the steady wind blowing over the sands of the Libyan Desert. I handed Monica the water bottle.

"But I'm not thirsty, Mom!"

"Please, keep hydrated, love," I urged her, both so she'd stay alive and also so I'd get a moment to speak with Martha, alone. I turned to Martha and in a low voice, so my daughter wouldn't hear, I said, "You got us into this, you find the way out. And pretend that we know what we're doing. We can't panic Monica."

Martha didn't answer me with words but our eyes told each other that we would pull together. We began to sing, and skip, and take pictures of each other. It was the first and last time Martha and I sang together. We walked in file, Martha in front, then my child, then me behind. I remembered *The Little Prince*, marooned in the desert, and Saint-Exupéry's descriptions in *Wind, Sand and Stars* about his own ordeal in the Sahara, the dehydration, seeing mirages, hallucinations. I nudged Monica along when she began complaining of fatigue, my imagination vivid with imminent danger, horrified that we wouldn't be

found by kind Bedouins but by a tomb robber or other unsavory ma-
rauder, if we were found at all.

But, with God's help, and Martha's extraordinary sense of direction, she managed to find our way out of there. All of a sudden, as
we passed a very tall dune, the hopeless landscape changed and we
came upon civilization. There on our left was a walled-in village, its
exterior the color of the desert with turquoise-emerald painted shut-
ters. On the steps in front of the village's gates sat, alone, a matriarch
dressed in black, her head slightly bent, looking down. For a moment I
thought I was experiencing a mirage, but quickly realized that Monica
and Martha were seeing what I saw. The woman smiled when she saw
us. She welcomed us into her house, and proudly showed us how her
people lived. Then we went to her kitchen, which was not extravagant
but clean, and she let us take pictures, gave us her food to eat as well
as little cloth dolls she had crafted herself. The Egyptian lady spoke
no Western language, and we didn't speak Arabic, yet we talked about
many things and understood each other perfectly. I thought that perhaps Martha was right to dismiss the State Department warning about
that area being dangerous. I no longer knew what was right or wrong.
The lady called upon her grandsons, kind-looking young men, and she
had them drive us in a van back to the entrance to the tombs in the
Valley of the Queens. There we met the rest of our group, just about to
go through the gates and catch an official ride to Nefertari's tomb.

"Mom, don't squeeze me like that," Lara protested, as she usually
did when I hugged her in public. But, each arm around one of my children, I didn't let go.

"Mammy, were we in trouble?" Monica asked.

"Yes, my sweet. But we are fine now."

"What are you talking about?" asked Lara. "The only thing Susan
said was that you went with Martha to the tomb."

"She almost got us there. We'll tell you later. Oh, my darlings, I'm so
happy we are all here!"

Later, when we went to Cairo for the last days of our vacation,

Martha, who always mixed pleasure with business, had us go to a cotton factory, visit museums, and wander through the markets where we smelled and tasted everything. Martha was disappointed that she couldn't climb the pyramids. We had to remind her these were historical artifacts, not personal peaks set there specifically for her to summit.

When, on the last day of the trip, Martha and I exited the secret chambers of the Great Pyramid, only my girls and three of Martha's nieces and nephews were with us. Our group had disassembled inside the claustrophobic darkness, its inscrutability barely lit by a pinhole at the top, through which a cone of fading daylight came in. Martha wanted to find Bobby, so we searched for him in the crowd. When we didn't find him, she insisted that we skip the Sphinx, which was just steps away on our right. We had walked by it earlier as we rushed to the Great Pyramid, but that wasn't seeing it. I could hardly believe that she was saying we skip it just because she wanted to hurry back to the hotel. She said we couldn't be late for dinner. If there was a time when Martha made the least sense to me, it was then. I decided to let the sea of people divide us, so Martha could return to her suite at the Mena House hotel while I took my girls to see the Sphinx.

Across a strip of sand pounded down by human steps was a cafeteria terrace with tables and chairs, which faced what is undoubtedly one of the greatest wonders on Earth. Not long after we sat down, Sharon and Daniel came to join us, then Susan, Chris, and Bobby appeared, one by one. We sipped our bottled Egyptian water in silence, and gazed in awe at the mysterious Sphinx, impassive amid the spectacular crimson glow of a breathtaking sunset.

The visit to the cotton factory resulted in a line of towels for the beach, bathroom, and kitchen, which Martha sold by mail and through Kmart.

By the time we arrived home from Egypt, Bobby had decided to move from Los Angeles to Manhattan, and, as Martha described it, to become her permanent beau. For her part, Martha had promised

Bobby not only her companionship but a permanent place in her company, which both Martha and Bobby were excited about. They had, as Martha told me, spent much time discussing and daydreaming what his role in the business would be. She had figured it out while on the trip. Trips, I suppose, are always breaks from reality. The return from a trip can sometimes feel like emerging from a movie into the stark suburban afternoon of a dull Sunday. The movie ends. You stand up, stiff. You walk out, and the glare of your "real" life hits you full in the face.

Coming home was a downer for Bobby most of all, although I had a few rude reminders too, the most notable when, just days after touchdown, Martha's office called—same call I would get after every trip—to announce they had figured out the Egypt bill by simply splitting everything twelve ways—between five adults (Martha, Bobby, Sharon, Susan, me) and seven children—then multiplying by the number of people in my party: three. My share of their stated total came to more than I had calculated, as I didn't think I should subsidize the extravagant costs of Martha's hotel suites with room service and balconies overlooking the pyramids, or felucca rides into the night. But I paid Martha the amount I was told, grateful for the opportunity to have given my family such an unforgettable voyage.

Bobby moved from his Hollywood home to Martha's pied-à-terre on Fifth Avenue. It looked as though finally Martha was getting the lover she had wanted for so long. However, once Sharon crunched the numbers, Martha saw that Bobby's joining her company would not work out from a fiscal perspective. Martha thought about it, talked to me about it, but in the end she said no. Everything fell apart. Bobby left.

Martha had gone back on her word before. Martha had hired her friend Kathy Tatlock to direct her first how-to videos. Well into the project, Martha decided not to pay Kathy for tens of thousands of dollars in expenses. But Martha was used to people she reneged on sticking around in the hope that she would ultimately honor her promise, so she didn't understand why Bobby left so precipitately. If I thought she really wanted an answer, I might have simply said, "Don't climb pyramids.

Don't give other people pyramids to climb, especially if they're not even real." And had I said that, she would have looked at me long and hard, snorted, and turned swiftly on her heels and left, for she was very busy at this point, and had no patience for foolish metaphors. I wondered if she even remembered that day when our large group was walking the pressed desert sand of the wide path leading from the bottom of the steps of a palace built against high rock, the temple of Queen Hatshepsut, who had, in fact, declared herself not a queen but a king.

Hatshepsut is famous for, among other things, establishing one of the first royal gardens known to have been created with imported specimens (large and small) from all over the world. In that arid climate, three and a half thousand years ago, Hatshepsut cultivated exotic trees and shrubs, fragrant flowers, and rare woods that came from the mysterious land of Punt. She had myrrh trees planted in front of her temple, where you may still see their roots. Her flowers were spiky and flamboyant and under her care the courtyard flourished.

As we listened to Dr. Weeks talk about Hatshepsut's botanical adventures, it was hard not to think of Martha. Both women had green thumbs or knew how to hire them. Both women were confident in their creation of beauty, believing that they knew what beauty was and bold in their attempts to appropriate it. Both women occupied powerful positions not expected of their gender. Hatshepsut, however, was political in the literal sense of the word. When her husband died, she became the regent of her nephew, the nine-year-old Thutmose III, but shortly crowned herself pharaoh during Egypt's Golden Age. As the first important woman ruler in history, she had a long, peaceful and prosperous rule, expanded the trade routes to western Asia, Punt, and the Aegean Islands, built impressive monuments, and shared her bounty with the denizens of her country. In the sculptures, friezes, and murals I have seen of this remarkable woman-king, she has no breasts or breast buds, and they are desexualized, as the shield she holds steals the show and marks her not as a woman but as a warrior who wore the crowns of Upper and Lower Egypt, dressed in male clothing and sporting the false beard traditionally worn by the pharaohs. After twenty-one years, Hatshepsut's reign ended, the cause of it as mysterious as her death. The double crown of Egypt went to Thutmose III, under whose reign the greatest oppression of the Hebrews took place. His destruction of her achievements included the beautiful temple we visited, where he smashed her statues and erased her name and image from monuments.

As we were leaving Hatshepsut's temple and gardens, or what survived of them, Martha said out loud, in a decisive, well-controlled voice: "I am Hatshepsut."

At first I thought she was joking and searched her face for a smile, but there was none. I looked at Sharon, Sharon at me. You could hear the silence. Bobby looked at Martha, and then he turned abruptly away, looked down at the sand, and kept walking.

11

Skylands

Martha Tried Hard to convince herself that she had done the right thing when she risked losing Bobby. She even became critical of those she perceived not to be as inclined as she was to choose money above all. I remember one summer weekend in East Hampton when we hiked the few miles distance from Lily Pond to Bunshaft. After some weeding and checking her neighbor's plantings on the property line, we took a canoe ride on Georgica Pond. We were paddling along the shore when Martha noticed a gathering of people at the house of one of her neighbors. He was someone she socialized with mostly for business, but she decided we should canoe inside the cove fronting his property. And, so, even though we were unannounced and in our gardening outfits, Martha cheerfully welcomed her neighbor's gracious invitation to join him and his elegant guests for lunch. We had such a good time that I was ultimately glad she had accepted.

We did dress properly for dinner, which we were invited back for. It was an interesting and lively evening, and I was totally caught up in the conversation and in admiration of Martha's ease at establishing tycoon-ish terms of endearment with the famous guests and our handsome host, the powerful owner of a business empire and the former husband of a good friend of mine. Some years back, before their divorce, she was the mistress of this extraordinary estate, although I didn't know her well, if at all, then.

We were asked to stay on after dinner to screen a new movie with our host and his houseguests in the luxurious home theater, comfortably wrapped in cashmere blankets that were thoughtfully offered each guest to protect us from the chill of air-conditioning. During intermission, Martha wanted to explore the place so that she might see as much of the spectacular house as possible. We were ambling through the mansion's inner sanctum, admiring the modern art and impeccable details, when Martha turned to me, and said, "What a jerk she was to leave all this!"

Martha saw my friend, the ex-wife, socially on occasion and knew that she and I were close. I didn't think Martha meant to take a stab at my friend. I thought she was simply trying to convince herself that it had been a "good thing" to have given priority to her passion for the fiscal over the personal, since, for Martha, who always aimed to win, feeling that she won seemed to be at least as important as the winning.

Of course she encountered opposition, because for someone to win, someone else has to lose, and when her adversaries stood their ground, Martha screamed. In fact, after Bobby left, she screamed quite a bit because an unauthorized biography of her was about to be published.

She screamed at her neighbor at the Bunshaft house, Harry Macklowe. When Martha didn't like the shrubbery that grew along the border of their properties, he built a fence that Martha disliked even more. She hired lawyers, reportedly to the tune of hundreds of thousands of dollars. And then Martha apparently screamed at Harry Macklowe's landscaper on May 21, 1997, at about nine thirty p.m., or at least that's what the police report said when the landscaper, a recent college graduate, filed a complaint, which said that Martha allegedly pulled her Suburban into Macklowe's driveway and screamed at him about the fence. Then, as she backed up her car out of the driveway, she pinned the young man with her vehicle against an electronic security box.

In a uniquely Martha turn, Martha responded to the criminal complaint by suing the young man for libel. He had to get a lawyer to defend himself, resulting in an expense he certainly could not afford as easily as Martha could. The incident ended with a "Statement of the Suffolk District Attorney's Office" on July 25, 1997: "It is beyond doubt that the incident was initiated by Ms. Stewart," it said. However, because the man's injuries were deemed by the court to be minimal, the "confrontation," which, "as objectionable as it may appear, does not warrant arrest and criminal prosecution." To the best of my understanding, the situation with the landscaper got resolved when "she did pay him an undisclosed amount to preempt a civil lawsuit," according to an article by Jeffrey Toobin in *The New Yorker*. At the time, I believed Martha's claim that she just hadn't seen him.

The media were abuzz and, although Martha wasn't charged in that case, her sense of triumph was blunted by the publication of Jerry Oppenheimer's *Martha Stewart: Just Desserts, an Unauthorized Biography*. Susan, Martha's brilliant publicist, quickly assembled a carapace of shields around her client.

Meanwhile, Martha and Sharon had been working day and night gathering the "internally generated capital" of about $75 million needed to close the deal agreed upon in February for Martha to buy herself out of her contract with TimeWarner. From what I understood, Martha put in her own money, as did Sharon, and together they devised a plan to leverage Martha's profits from Kmart.

Ever since 1987, when she began working with Kmart, Martha complained. She even found fault with the handbag Kmart's chairman, president, and CEO, Jo Antonini, and his wife had given her as a gift when she invited them to her fiftieth birthday party in 1991. Martha was angry that she didn't know where they had purchased the bag, because she wanted to take it back to the store—all so she could find out how much they had spent on it, I thought. She probably suspected it wasn't expensive enough, proof positive that Kmart didn't value her highly enough. Was she being petty or insecure? As her friend, I tried to believe the latter. A year later, when Martha's contract with Kmart came up for renewal, she was still criticizing them for not appreciating her enough, and kept postponing the signing.

But then Sharon came along and helped smooth Martha's relationship with Kmart, and things got better. So good, in fact, that Martha and Sharon were able to renegotiate her Kmart contracts a few times. And those newest 1997 contracts gave Martha not only upfront money for the TimeWarner deal, but also gave her latitude to have better products to sell in Kmart stores.

In August 1997, Sharon was in New York finessing all of those deals, while Martha went on vacation in Maine. There she and Charlotte Beers celebrated their respective Leo birthdays and socialized with Memrie, who introduced Martha to the exclusive Mount Desert social world. Memrie showed Martha Brooke Astor's beautiful garden in Northeast Harbor, and invited her to a cocktail party given by the elegant Mrs. Edward Leedes at Skylands, which she and her husband had acquired about twenty years prior from the estate of Edsel Ford.

It was then, shortly before Martha's TimeWarner buyout was due to close, that Martha had come to visit me on Golden Pond in New Hampshire, and told me about Skylands. Martha wanted to bring me to see this new wonder property. As I recall, we watched the Perseid meteor shower late into the night, while Martha talked about her mansion dreams. After midnight, Martha said we should go in and call Charles, her new beau. By Martha's calculation, it was early enough in Seattle, so we could phone and ask Charles to come in his plane the next day and take us to see Skylands.

Charles Simonyi was a top executive and all-around genius at Microsoft. They had met the year before at a high-society dinner party in a palatial apartment overlooking New York's East River. As Martha described him to me, consistent with the manner in which she always rated people by their wealth first and their accomplishments second, he was "fabulously wealthy," a billionaire, good friends with Bill and Melinda Gates, had an extraordinary high-tech house filled with paintings by Roy Lichtenstein and Victor Vasarely right on the water in Medina, near Seattle, and piloted his own jets and helicopters. Charles had pursued Martha but she had been lukewarm, particularly after Thanksgiving when she had her sights set on Bobby. After the post-Egypt debacle, when Bobby left Martha and her litter of failed promises, Martha turned to Charles, and it was not long before she was introducing him as her boyfriend.

Before Charles came to visit us at the cabin on Golden Pond, I had already spent quite a bit of time with him and Martha. I liked him from the start. Handsome, brilliant, and comfortable with himself, Charles was the archetypal WYSIWYG—what you see is what you get. A true self-made man and a proven genius, at the age of seventeen Charles, who grew up in Communist Hungary, landed a one-year job contract in Denmark. I suppose the Hungarian authorities allowed him to go, thinking he was likely to return, since his defection would have had dire repercussions for his family, especially his father, a renowned member of Budapest's intelligentsia with an important position at the University of Budapest. However, it was his father who encouraged him to remain in the West, despite the punitive consequences that his family was subjected to. A few years later, Charles was in the States, working as a programmer while studying at Berkeley. As he was taking his doctorate at Stanford, Charles worked for Xerox, where he developed Bravo, the first WYSIWYG text editor and also a break-through step in personal computer development. He joined Microsoft in 1981 and was the lead architect for Word and Excel, then became responsible for Microsoft Research new programming technologies. Charles was not only a superb technical mind but also a generous person who donated a good chunk of his fortune to educational institutions, having endowed two university chairs, one for theoretical physics at the Institute for Advanced Study at Princeton and another for a professorship for public understanding of science at Oxford University, chaired by the famous evolutionary biologist and science author Richard Dawkins. A renaissance man, Charles read philosophy, spoke several languages, collected art, liked good movies, was a great dancer, and had a wonderful sense of humor.

Unlike her prior relationships, Martha had spent a good few weeks going on platonic dates with Charles before she became intimate with him. A few months before our Golden Pond vacation, Martha and I had flown with Charles on his luxurious jet to Bilbao, Spain, for the weekend. Our dear friends Skip and Edie Bronson, who were on their way to Paris, also came with us. We all wanted to visit the Guggenheim Museum, that famous example of magic architecture designed by Frank Gehry.

After checking in at the marvelous hotel where Charles was hosting us, Martha expressed her preference that I take the room next to hers and Charles the one across the hall. As soon as we got in, we opened the door between our adjacent rooms, going in and out of each other's space as we unpacked, showered, and prepared for an elegant dinner. Wrapped in a towel, I walked into Martha's bathroom and waited for her to finish folding a bath towel into a turban, then we began sharing her large assortment of cosmetics, which she always generously let me use. While making ourselves pretty for the evening, looking at each other in the mirror as we talked, Martha said, "If Charles asks you to switch rooms, say yes."

I kept my cool but was startled by the ice-queen manner and unmistakable meaning of what she had just said. Not only was Martha telling me of her calculated intention to receive Charles in her bed, she was, just as inelegantly, implicating me in her manipulations of their intimacy. I mostly felt sorry for her embarking on a romantic journey with such little passion.

Later, Charles was quite embarrassed when he pulled me aside and said that Martha had told him he should ask me to exchange rooms. When we came back from dinner, the hotel staff had discreetly moved my things to the room across the hall from Martha.

The evening when Charles arrived at my cottage in New Hampshire, in mid-August 1997, he sat down with Martha and my girls at our kitchen table with the checkered oilcloth, overlooking the lake. They were playing Scrabble—Martha's favorite board game—while I tried to find some food to make a meal. I had few dinner choices to offer Charles, who didn't want restaurant food, didn't feel like chicken, and turned down the cooked fresh lobsters. After cheeses with toast and crackers, I gave him a bowl of sour cherry compote, a Hungarian dish he had not tasted since childhood.

Martha was the best and most competitive Scrabble player I had ever met. Charles, the proven math and computer genius, was stumped. As I leaned from behind Charles to place the bowl of compote on the table, I discreetly reached with my left hand and shifted around two groups of letters on his game tray. But Charles's eyes widened in recognition of the words he could make, and I got caught.

"Get your ass in a fucking canoe!" Martha protested.

My daughters had heard Martha say words she wouldn't utter on camera before, but her cursing always startled them. To diffuse the tension, I started to laugh. We all laughed, I brought some more food, and let Martha surprise him with those two-, three-, and four-letter words she knew were in the official Scrabble dictionary.

The next morning, we got into Charles's plane and headed for Skylands.

Charles had clearly not been impressed with my humble cottage and its spectacular sunsets, but Skylands pierced his hide. Who could ever see Skylands and remain untouched? It was a time capsule from a glamorous past, its grounds nearly rustling with the ghosts of the distinguished men and women who had danced and dined and written and wept on its green and never-ending acreage.

The property stood at the top of Ox Hill, and at its highest point was a large megalithic rock with bench-like ridges at the top, which might have once been the place for council meetings for Abnaki chief Asticou and his peers, scanning the Wabanaki horizons beyond Skyland's huge perimeter across still more green toward the deep blue and white caps of Penobscot Bay. Farther south, the New England summers could be sticky, but up there cool winds scrolled off the mountains and down trails to meet salty ocean breezes.

Skylands itself, designed by Duncan Candler, architect of renowned Manhattan buildings as well as of famous residences of the Rockefeller family, was all restrained elegance: a twelve-bedroom, pink-stone manor approached by a mile-long driveway covered in crushed pink granite so precious it was all raked and stored for the winter then spread out again in the spring. Alongside the drive were the perfect guesthouse and a playhouse with an attached squash court, accessed by a charmingly rustic footpath. Farther away were the magnificent stables with servant quarters upstairs, a garage with its own gas pump, a canning kitchen, terraces, and gardens, and an outdoor lobster-cooking area. The wine cellar was deep and stocked with bottles that went back through decades. The manor house overlooked the island-sprinkled, deep-blue ocean on one side, and miles of its meandering private trails on the other. The trails were bordered by trees and fans of ferns and covered in layers of dry pine needles, fragrant and velvety under the hiker's step, and took you through the most remarkable topography, most of it natural and some designed by Jens Jensen, best known for his prairie-style work on private and public spaces. There was also a church at the bottom of the hill, which Mr. Ford had built for his favorite cook, a pious Polish lady, and which was later desanctified.

We stood on the large hand-cut pink granite stone terrace and watched the setting sun paint the surface of the bay. When the upper edge of the fiery sun-disk disappeared in the sea, and the horizon turned that illusory emerald-green, Charles whispered in my ear that he'd buy the place if Martha decided not to.

But Martha wanted it, and badly. Later that evening, back at my cottage, music playing, we shared s'mores that my girls made in the flames of our great stone fireplace, and toasted Martha's hope with a fragrant red Bordeaux: may she become the mistress of Skylands! While eerie loon calls echoed across my beloved moonlit lake, we debated what Martha should bid for the property. Skylands was being offered for sale either unfurnished or, for considerably more money, furnished and decorated with the lovely things that once belonged to Mr. and Mrs. Edsel Ford. Martha wanted the exquisitely elegant furniture, the dining room rug—likely an original William Morris—the ample collection of fine linens, the tasteful silver, the classy crystal, the abundance of fine and stylish porcelains, the grand piano with its lean ivory teeth, the well-stocked wine cellar, the assortment of cars, and the church. Not only was Skylands larger than all her other places put together, but the treasure trove of the Ford family's fine things by far outshone Martha's famed collections.

She told us what she could pay to get Skylands. What did we think of the offer?

I thought, after having successfully negotiated by then many real estate deals, that the offer should be closer to what the owners were asking for in their unfurnished price. Martha, nervous, wanted to bid higher than I thought she should. Charles had no price opinion but he said that Martha should let me, the real estate professional, handle the transaction. Then, when my girls went to bed, he went to the downstairs guest room, which Martha had asked me to give him, while she slept in the small bedroom next to mine upstairs.

The next morning, before she left with Charles, I asked Martha, whose tired eyes were evidence of a sleepless worried night, "What are you going to do?"

"Just get me Skylands. It's a perfect wedding house," she said.

Charles's startled eyes met mine. After they left, lifting off in Charles's plane, Martha determined to get herself a mansion, I felt sad to be leaving my life-size cottage soon. I thought about how different Martha and I really were.

. . .

ONCE AGAIN AS a favor to Martha, Wade, the principal of my Connecticut real estate office, gave me permission to negotiate the deal without commission. I called the owner of the property and, after I told him I was a Realtor and he told me he wasn't going to pay me a commission, I presented him with a persuasive offer on Martha's behalf.

A few hours later, the children and I were driving home from the lake when my car phone rang. The offer for Skylands was accepted, conditional to an immediate closing and an additional sum for the church building and the wine collection. Not wanting to lose momentum, I agreed to their price, since, when added together, the initial offer and the supplemental request came to a few hundred thousand less than Martha thought she wanted to offer the night before.

When I gave her the news, Martha could not stop cheering.

There was only one small problem: Martha didn't have enough liquid assets for the down payment, which she had to produce immediately for the deal to take place. Rita, her sister-in-law and business manager, called me.

"Mariana, Martha's telling me she bought a more than $3 million house this weekend? Where am I gonna find the money to pay for it?"

"Rita," I said, "I am not familiar with the market there, but what I am sure of is that to build that place today, it would easily cost $10 million, anywhere."

I scrambled and was able to find an immediate buyer for a little-used two-acre parcel Martha owned in her neighborhood on Turkey Hill—the Easter Field, where she grew flowers and berries, and sometimes held her annual Easter Egg Hunt.

Barely a month later, Martha was the proud owner of Skylands.

As a token of her gratitude, Martha invited me to choose any rooms I liked where my girls and I could stay whenever we wanted. I didn't want to impose, so I chose two smaller rooms connected by a bathroom—not prime rooms with fireplace, balcony, or water views.

Immediately, Martha started to restore the manor, outbuildings, and grounds to their former grandeur. I remember how, trying to help her, I weeded the carpets of moss and trimmed off saplings so far and so fast that I developed carpal tunnel syndrome, which made my wrists throb through the nights I spent in "my" Skylands bedroom, listening to the gloomy hooting of the owl that lived in the nearby woods, which seemed to echo Martha's mood. She was disappointed that Alexis did not want to have her wedding at Skylands. Alexis married John Cuti, a lawyer and an outstanding young man, on September 26, 1997, in a judge's chambers in New York. Martha, who was among the five witnesses present at the ceremony, invited everyone to a celebratory lunch at the exclusive Jean Georges restaurant. But the newlyweds did spend their honeymoon at Skylands. Martha said that, while they lived in the guesthouse, they loved having that whole property all to themselves.

IT WAS A busy September. Martha and Sharon had secured the money to fund the TimeWarner deal. In the late 1980s, when Martha first wanted to publish her own magazine, Condé Nast's chairman, Si Newhouse, did not appreciate her appeal. The powers that be in Rupert Murdoch's magazine empire also turned her down. Finally, in 1990, Time, Inc. approved two test issues of her magazine, *Martha Stewart Living*, the first print run of half a million copies in November 1990, and the second in March 1991. Those issues did well, so Time, Inc. committed to publishing six issues a year, and Martha entered into a contract to create a jointly owned corporation, Martha Stewart Living Enterprises, a subsidiary of TimeWarner, Inc., with Martha serving as its chairman and chief executive officer.

By that agreement, TimeWarner provided the funds and Martha contributed her ideas and her famous name. The magazine, the books that they spun off it, as well as her new television show, *Martha Stewart Living*, which launched in 1993 and was syndicated all over the country, were all part of the joint venture. (Martha's other books, her lectures, and her Kmart royalties were not part of that agreement.)

When Sharon began consulting for Martha, the two women worked day and night, then worked some more on weekends, in Martha's kitchens at Turkey Hill and Lily Pond, devising a plan to change things. I tried giving them privacy when I was around, but as they continued their business conversations over breakfasts, lunches, and dinners, and as Martha often wanted me to help them organize the mounds of papers covering the long, marble-topped Lily Pond kitchen table, I understood that Martha's arrangement with TimeWarner was a success, but not as profitable as she and Sharon wanted it to be. Martha, whom I never knew to like being told she'd done something that was less than perfect, rarely frowned at Sharon's insistent questioning. The work was very stressful for both of them, and I was there ready to pitch in as I could, going with Martha for a beach walk when she wanted a break, or taking a dip in the pool with Sharon when Martha needed a nap. Sharon asked questions, wrote pages of notes, chewed on her pen, bit around her nails, drew flow charts and diagrams, crumpled them into balls she tossed across the room in perfect two-point shots into the garbage can, all of which would have elicited Martha's strong reprimand under any other circumstances. The fact that she never once reproached Sharon told me how utterly important was the contribution she was making to Martha's business. I watched her analyzing, organizing, planning, coming up with brilliant ideas, leading Martha toward all media ventures.

By 1995, Martha was making weekly appearances on the *Today Show*, over four million copies of her books had been printed, and her magazine, *Martha Stewart Living*, which was selling more than a million copies per issue, had earned the "Magazine of the Year" distinction from *Ad Age*.

Then, with advice from Charlotte Beers and a team of lawyers—including Allen Grubman, the prominent entertainment attorney who had been at Martha's side for years—Martha and Sharon renegotiated with Time, Inc., the contract that Martha had originally signed with them in the early 1990s. Definitely a step ahead for Martha, which brought her in better position on Sharon's flowchart figures.

Part of their plan was to expand Martha's market reach with *Martha by Mail*, which was, at first, just an insert in *Martha Stewart Living* magazine. The public response was astounding and gave a clear picture of market niches that Martha could penetrate through her audience of 2.2 million people. In 1996, Martha was named by *Time* one of "America's 25 Most Influential People."

Then in February 1997, with a dazzling strategy, which Martha and Sharon had worked out step by painful step, Martha took an unprecedented plunge, proposing that her partners at TimeWarner expand the business the way she wanted or agree that she buy herself out. Time-Warner preferred the latter, for the reasonable sum of $75 million.

The move, as it turned out, was executed with incredible acumen and brought about much good fortune to Martha and Sharon, who immediately created a new company, Martha Stewart Living Omnimedia, in which Martha had majority interest and exclusive control over all her publishing, television, and merchandising ventures. She had become, in many senses, the author of her own life, the master of her fate.

The launch of Martha Stewart Living Omnimedia that September, with Martha presiding as chairman and Sharon as chief executive officer, produced quite a stir. Both Martha and Sharon received great accolades in the business world and the media. But Martha didn't seem particularly thrilled that Sharon was being credited as the business brain.

"Remember, I'm a businesswoman too," Martha said.

Martha didn't deny the fact that Sharon deserved credit for their joint business coup, yet something about that credit appeared to bother her. Her displeasure manifested itself in odd ways I was familiar with by then, as Martha had a tendency of pointing out things that weren't perfect about anyone who might upset her, willingly or not, and always in that person's absence. I did what I always did under such circumstances: I half-listened to Martha's litany of Sharon-imperfections. There weren't many to find, so it was rather funny to hear Martha criticize Sharon for not having disciplined her pet bulldog, Norman, who had chewed some of Sharon's beautiful East Side penthouse molding and, according to Martha, was so spoiled that Sharon's cat got fed up and jumped out the window, committing suicide. I knew the cat had somehow fallen off a ledge. Sharon was understandably upset about that when it happened.

It seemed that Martha also had an issue with how she and Sharon had distributed company titles, particularly "CEO." From what I understood, it had been strategic to have Sharon hold that position, especially with all the many analysts' talk regarding possible risks involved with Martha's being the company's main asset. As that made sense, I was surprised to hear Martha say she should be CEO, but Sam Waksal apparently agreed with her, and I knew he was one of the people whose business acumen Martha relied on. By the time of Martha's buyout, they had known each other for more than ten years. During that time I had seen a lot of Sam, with Martha, and had met his daughters, Elana and Aliza, refined and attractive young ladies in their twenties. Sam had a lot of experience with structuring, developing, and leading companies, having helped bring more than one of them public. He was owner and CEO of a biomedical company, ImClone Systems Incorporated, whose stock had been trading on Nasdaq for years, since its initial public offering in 1991. Knowing all that, when Martha reclaimed Sharon's position as chief executive officer at MSLO just three months later, I thought it had nothing to do with the flattering press Sharon received regarding the buyout.

Martha was in her car, being chauffeured to be a guest on the *Tonight Show* with Jay Leno, when she called Sharon and said, "Titles. I'd prefer if we didn't have any." It was so nicely put, it sounded to me like something Charlotte Beers, the master of elegant expression, might have said in such circumstances. Martha became CEO. Sharon did not contest the decision.

In her new position as president of MSLO, Sharon continued to dedicate her work and talents to the successful company, ready to make of it "the world's first true multimedia brand," just as she had said to

Martha when they were climbing Kilimanjaro. Sharon was on the way to help Martha Stewart become the world's premier mega-brand, with myriad subsidiaries. They had already launched Marthastewart.com, a Web site that they had long been working on, which became a successful marketing tool.

From what I understood, the floral business got better after the introduction of Marthastewartflowers.com. Martha had been trying to make that a profitable venture ever since we visited the rose gardens near Hacienda Cusin, in Ecuador, where hundreds of roses grew to be picked and their thorns removed so as not to harm the precious hands of rich American buyers. It was amazing, the way that our trips would spark an idea in Martha that she would so brilliantly execute upon returning home.

Martha's television show, which began as a weekly syndicated series, became a daily half-hour show. Martha Stewart Everyday at Kmart was dressed up and nicely displayed. Everywhere we traveled around the country, Martha made sure we stopped to check the local Kmart store and see that they were doing the job according to her standards. Martha worked hard. Many were the late nights when on our way back from parties we talked about some article she still had to write before the morning, either for her "Remembering" column in the magazine, or for her newspaper column, "Ask Martha." I often worried about her being so overworked but she seemed to thrive on the pressure.

And then came Martha's joint Skylands "inauguration" party and belated Leo birthday party. Before the extraordinary occasion, Charles called Martha's assistant to find out what Martha might want for a birthday gift. Martha's exact specifications were passed on to Charles as a suggestion. When Martha opened her gift in front of everyone at the party, all of her friends knew how delighted she was to have finally found a man willing to give her extravagant jewelry. Although Martha had told us that Charles would give her gold South Sea pearls, we were still surprised by the size and luster of the gem-quality beads, especially considering the name on the box they came in, which placed them in the same price range as a house might sell for in many American neighborhoods.

The party also marked a first in my relationship with Martha. She stood up to make her speech and, to my surprise, and for the first time in our friendship, she publicly acknowledged my role in her life and how instrumental I was in helping her buy this place. Martha did not say that I never took a commission, but the simple thank you, for me, was more than enough, and it brought tears to my eyes.

The evening after that great party Martha gave her excellent Skylands crew the time off while Skip, Edie, Charles, and I were going to prepare dinner with her and have a friendly evening with a high-society couple whom Martha had also invited. According to Martha, the "who's who" of Mount Desert's summer society were not pleased about her public fame invading their cranberry bog retreats and quiet sailing playgrounds. Martha shared with us her suspicion that her Philadelphia invitees were coming to dinner at Skylands to check her out.

As it got close to their arrival, Martha became nervous. She worried about not having help that evening, while entertaining people who had butlers and cooks. But she had us there, her closest friends. And we came to the rescue. Edie, Charles, and I offered to fill in as the staff, and since, try as he may, Skip could not impersonate a domestic, he'd join Martha and her guests in the living room. Then we'd play it by ear.

When the couple arrived, Martha, who had donned a demure outfit, offered to show them around the legendary house. Eventually they came to the kitchen. First they were introduced to Charles, Martha's "butler," who, dressed in jeans and a fine Italian sweater, was struggling with a wine bottle in the butler's pantry, the bottle propped between his thighs, a corkscrew in one hand. The group then stepped into the kitchen and met Edie and me, who Martha laughingly said were the caterer and the chef. But the society lady was not to be so easily fooled. She asked Edie if she catered full-time.

Edie, who was an art director for *Saturday Night Live* and a well-known photographer with an impressive art portfolio, smiled her well-brought-up smile and said, "I offered to be catering tonight."

Then the society lady turned to me and said, "Are you a professional chef?"

"Well, I cook, and Martha is giving me a chance to be the chef."

Puzzled and amused, her gaze took me in, the spike-heeled shoes, the Roberto Cavalli jeans with roses the same deep red as my lipstick, and the low-cut black cashmere sweater which, as I had just then noticed, gaped quite revealingly when I reached to stir the pot simmering on the stove.

Martha invited her guests to sit at the table, Skip at the head across from the glowing fireplace, Martha on the long side to his right, the lady next to her, and then her husband. The table was set with Mrs. Ford's exquisite plates and silver, and fresh flowers. Charles poured the wine into crystal glasses. Edie and I went around serving everyone, then the three of us also sat down, across from Martha and the fancy guests. The conversation was lively, the lady was sharp, and so was her husband; the subjects discussed were interesting.

Finally, the lady said, "Wait a minute. You are not the help. You are all friends."

We laughed, and told them the story of how we just wanted to raise Martha's stakes with the neighbors, and the lady, who had a great sense of humor, let down her guard, and so did the husband, and we all had a wonderful evening.

Later, I went with Martha to visit their place and I understood why Martha had wanted to impress them. The lady had impeccable taste.

12

Courting Danger at Machu Picchu

A S THE END of 1997 was looming without either of us having made definite plans for our winter vacations, Martha proposed that we should go to Peru and Machu Picchu. When she first began talking about this trip, I determined that I could not afford the price of the first-class hotels and restaurants that Martha would frequent, to say nothing of all the costly incidentals like gratuities. When Martha said she would lend me $10,000 with three percent interest, a loan she would extend for three years or longer, I decided to accept.

Martha had her office make arrangements with a travel agency that booked us a trip from December 26, 1997, till January 4, 1998. Our traveling group was small that year, and included my girls and Martha's four nieces and nephews. Martha had invited Sharon and Susan to come, but they weren't able to join us. Which was too bad, because when those women worked, they worked tirelessly; when it was time for fun, they knew how to party and laugh. Martha's life was full of "good things" but I never had any doubt that Sharon and Susan were among the best things that had ever happened to her.

"Remember! You are in charge of The Asset," were Sharon's last words to me before Martha and I left on that trip.

It was an allusion to the fact that Sharon had recently arranged, as a security measure, to have Martha, the company's main asset, protected with a $67 million life insurance policy and $55 million in disability coverage, which insured Martha's body parts, per eye, per hand, per limb.

"Watch out for the 'D' things," Sharon said.

"What are the 'D' things?" I asked.

"Death, dismemberment, disappearance . . ."

"You know she can go extreme on me, Sharon. This is a lot of responsibility."

"Do your best."

Had she not been under strict doctor's orders not to fly because of an eye injury, I am sure Sharon, conscientious as she was, would have come to Peru to watch "The Asset" herself.

Martha, whose fame had risen to new heights, reveled in any kind of adventure. Her desire for risk seemed to grow right along with the rise to fame. Tending sometimes toward risqué, she flirted at the edge of acceptability.

I remember one night when Martha and I were having dinner at one of New York's poshest restaurants. By this time I was on the fast track to becoming one of Connecticut's top-rated Realtors, with clientele who were buying seven-figure homes, and the commissions allowed me to keep up with Martha's expensive taste. The restaurant had the sort of satiny silence of many upscale venues, with perfectly folded white napkins and sterling silverware. Martha and I were seated on a banquette facing the elegant dining room. Between us was a good friend, very handsome, recently divorced, and known to be looking for a new mate. I knew from Martha that he took his search seriously and that she would have liked to be considered, especially since there was so much money to go around that both he and his former wife continued to live very, very well. Sam, who was also there with us, was seated across the table from him. Martha told me on the side that our handsome companion, who was hosting us for dinner that evening, was allegedly affected with some post-divorce erectile dysfunction.

How she came by this knowledge I do not know. It might have been via her phone chatter at five every morning, when she would start her daily round of dawn calls, collecting gossip from each recipient, which she would add to her bucket and then spill the contents for the pleasure of her next phone companion. Or so I thought, since she spilled a full bucket on me every day around seven a.m.

In the case of our evening's host, she had either acquired information about his nether regions during the early-morning phone relay, or, worse, the man mistakenly assumed she could keep a confidence.

So there we were, Sam entertaining us with his eloquent wit. The food was delicious, the wine exquisite. Evenings like this remained exhilarating to me. And then suddenly, Martha's hand darted toward this handsome man's privates and I saw Martha dig an extended index finger in the fine fabric of his pants.

"And how is that?" she asked.

We all gasped.

The flustered man turned to me and said, "Can you believe this? Did you see what she did?"

With a mixture of laughter, compassion, and embarrassment, I managed to say, "I'm sorry." I was blushing and giggling at the same time: "It was maybe an invitation?"

He turned to Sam across the table from him. "Did you see what she did?" the man, flabbergasted, asked.

With a friendly but stern voice, Sam reprimanded Martha in the tone of a parent admonishing a child: "Mar-tha!" Sam said. "Girls don't poke! They stroke."

We all started laughing, including our host, and Martha, acting remorseful for a brief second, cast her eyes down.

. . .

AFTER TRAVELING ON planes for nearly twelve hours with six children, we landed in Cusco, once the capital of the Inca Empire and the first destination of our Peru trip. No sooner had we arrived than Martha announced that she and I would visit the Indian market at the crack of dawn the next day. We had not even finished checking everyone into our deluxe rooms, oxygen-enriched to compensate for the high altitude and overlooking the patio, at the Hotel Monasterio, a restored sixteenth-century Spanish colonial seminary with baroque interiors. Heeding Sharon's warning, I tried to dissuade Martha. The situation in Peru was unstable, and we risked being kidnapped had we gone alone, as Martha insisted. Without telling her, I discreetly arranged for one of our guides, Manolo, to happen to be in the hotel lobby at six o'clock the next morning; luckily, our shopping trip came off without incident.

From Cusco we drove to the Sacred Valley of the Inca, where we visited the large complex of ruins in Pisac, high up on a ridge. Then Martha wanted us to go see the witch doctor. She was hoping to find a cure for a spotty depigmentation that had begun tainting her perfect skin a few years before. No one seemed to have a cure, so she had to apply makeup on the spots she couldn't hide under clothing. The venerable man, who only spoke Quechua, was very nice and indulged all of us, but I am not sure he had a remedy for Martha. When he asked if she knew what might have caused her skin affliction, and Martha said she thought it had been the stress, the wise man looked at her for a long moment and then said, his words translated for us by Manolo, "What is stress? Get rid of it."

After that, I left Martha and the kids at a guinea pig farm, where the owners also served food in their own eat-in kitchen, to go in search of a place where we could eat in a homey, non-touristy atmosphere, but with a more varied menu. By the time I came back, Martha already had the kids eating guinea pig fricassee, which she told them was chicken.

Some hours later, when I had regained my appetite and the kids were hungry after walking through ruins perched atop the Andes' jagged crests all day, we were seated on a beautiful mountain-view terrace, having a candlelit dinner at one of Cusco's elegant restaurants. Martha asked the children if they'd like another round of guinea pig. Their eyes welled with tears and they cried out:

"Yuck!"

"Oh, no, how could you?"

"I can't believe I ate my friend's pet!"

"They were so cute in those cages!"

But Martha turned it all to laughter by clowning around, making herself a hat out of the starched dinner napkin, so the evening ended on a good note. She was a lively traveling companion and the kids were utterly responsive to her fun-loving spirit.

The next day we were scheduled to paddle-raft in the gardens of the Inca Empire, but that wasn't enough excitement for Martha. I gave in to going on a river-rafting adventure, just to avoid splitting the group and beginning the trip with a replay of the felucca night in Egypt. It turned out to be a breath-stopping, dangerous rafting trip down the Urubamba River, so bumpy that I had to steady myself on the boat with one hand while my other hand and both of my legs each held down a kid, because those skinny young bodies were flying in the air as our raft went down the rapids. At one point, both Manolo and I jumped to hold down Kristina, Martha's petite niece, to keep her from falling off the boat. Later that evening, Martha tried to be engaging, but I didn't feel very conversational after that risky ride.

Things got better the next day, when we visited the market in Chinchero. We bought souvenirs, and visited the massive Inca wall, famous for its trapezoidal niches, the largest ones found in any known Incan monuments. We faced a different kind of crisis when we visited an old Inca fortress, famous for having defeated the Spaniards. People lived there in multifamily quarters that had been built by the Incas hundreds of years ago, and used the still-working communal water system. They crafted beautiful alpaca garments, warm and soft like silk, and we got some, but for my girls it was a culture shock. They found the people charming yet they couldn't quite cope with the fact that those children lived so differently, and with so little hope for their lives to change, like the children they had seen in some of the places we visited in Ecuador and also in parts of Egypt. We walked the cobbled streets of the old town arm in arm, hiding our tears, and I promised them that when we got back home we'd find a way to help children less fortunate than they.

On the last day of 1997, we went to Machu Picchu. We took a scenic ride on a train with huge windows from Cusco along the narrow gorge of the Urubamba River to the 104-kilometer point, near the Inca Trail, looking forward to trekking that famous path to the sacred ruins of Machu Picchu at eight thousand feet above sea level. Kirk, Martha's twelve-year-old nephew, looked quite pale during the entire train ride. Altitude sickness is not uncommon when traveling to Machu Picchu, and most visitors acclimatize to the thin, dry air in Cusco, which is located at eleven thousand five hundred feet. Among the eight travelers in our group, Kirk had been the most affected by it. The night we arrived at the Hotel Monasterio he began suffering with acute shortness of breath, headache, and nausea, so Martha instructed the guides to get the medics to his room. Martha and I were not affected by the high altitude, which I thought was because we had been taking the schizandra berry tincture prepared by our herbalist, Donnie Yance, whom I was lucky to have met a few years before through my friend Linn. As we neared our destination, Kirk complained of altitude sickness.

"Either you pull yourself together and go up to Machu Picchu with us," Martha said, "or you take the train back to Cusco." I was surprised at Martha's "tough love" approach, but I must admit, it worked. Kirk pulled himself together, as told, and was soon feeling fine.

Martha liked fast-paced walks, so I let her and the kids take the lead on our half-day trek to the ruin and asked the guides to go with them. I wanted to go slowly and absorb the intense poetry of the landscape. We arranged to meet at the cascades, in the canyon, where the ecosystem changes to cloud forest, with wild orchids hanging from the side of the cliff. From there, we hiked together up what I thought was the "unexpected sight, a great flight of beautifully constructed stone-faced terraces, perhaps a hundred of them" described in the book I had in my pocket, *Lost City of the Incas* by Hiram Bingham, the Yale professor who in 1911 found, under centuries of jungle growth, the ruins of Machu Picchu. I called out to ask Carlos, our historian-guide, if we were, indeed, walking in the steps of the great explorer, but my voice was drowned out by the roar of the river echoing inside the deep gorge of the granite-lined canyon, and our guides, who were climbing ahead with the kids, couldn't hear me. By the time I caught up with them on a spectacular ridge above Machu Picchu, we were all bombarding him with questions. We were getting close—on the side of the trail opposite Urubamba canyon we saw peeking from between the clouds Huayna Picchu, the mossy peak that appears as backdrop in most photographs of the famous Inca ruins. It had been drizzling for the last half hour or so. Then the sun came out as if to welcome us just as we reached Machu Picchu's original entrance, "The Gate of the Sun," and walked down to the "Lost City" of Machu Picchu.

Inside the complex of dusky chambers, some tight and gloomy, others with splendidly open views, the feeling was powerful, charged with a mysterious energy deeper and stronger than the hum of the wind and the echoes of the Urubamba River. I felt as if my own self dissolved and became part of all else that "assimilated itself with its surroundings," as André Malraux wrote in *The Royal Way*, the book that had most fired my teenage imagination with desire for wonder and discovery. "Here what act of man had any meaning, what human will could conserve its staying power?"

Martha and I didn't have to talk to know that we both appreciated the physical beauty of the spectacular Inca fortress, made of polished fine-grained stone, some of it in monolithic slabs and all cut so precisely that they fit perfectly together with nothing in between, not a speck of mortar, not even "an air bubble." As we wandered through the ruins together, taking photographs—Martha wanted to reproduce the stone work at home—we felt relaxed and completely in tune with the scenery and each other. It struck me that what I valued most about our friendship was the peaceful communion with nature we shared.

It was the last day of the year and we were returning to the fancy baroque hotel in Cusco. Truth be told, we were kicking ourselves for not having paid more attention to the trip arrangements, because we would have loved to have spent New Year's Eve and the first day of 1998 at the Machu Picchu Sanctuary Lodge. It was built in the style of Spanish colonial lodges, and the only hotel within the Incan citadel, just steps from Machu Picchu. But it was all booked up.

It was a four-hour bus ride back to Cusco, with warnings of possible mudslides. Opting for a twenty-five-minute helicopter ride instead was a no-brainer. That night, we celebrated the New Year together, with the children, again. As the clock tower began to chime midnight, we raised our traditional toast: "May we not spend next New Year's Eve together!" and watched the fireworks in the Plaza de Armas in the center of town.

The last adventure of our Peruvian trip was an Andean horseback ride on Friday, January 2. After a long car trip in the countryside, we arrived at the stables, where they were waiting for us. The well-cared-for horses were similar to the ones we rode in Ecuador, fairly small and narrowly built, a mix of Criollo, Paso Peruano, and other breeds that cope well with the altitude.

Each horse had a blanket beneath the saddle, and the Western-style tack looked well-maintained. They did not use the more comfortable AW-trekking saddles that usually are outfitted with saddlebags, but, considering the alternatives, I figured the one-hand neck reining would still make it easier to manage riding up and down the raggedy cliffs of the Peruvian Antiplano than an English saddle.

We were each shown our horse, and before mounting I asked for helmets, and we were told that the stable had none. I suggested we turn back, but Martha couldn't be dissuaded. I watched her body become tense and her hands clench. Martha's voice grew raspy and she began a loud, erratic monologue accusing me of ruining everybody's vacation. When I invoked "The Asset" insurance, trying to give extra weight to my argument, Martha assured me that protecting her richly insured body parts was her business.

I disdained quarrels and I was too invested in that vacation not to do my best for it to be a good one, especially for my children. Martha knew she had me in a corner, so I doubt she was surprised when I gave in to her demands that we go horseback riding without protective helmets.

We left the stables and my heart tightened when at the end of the dirt road we turned left, up a grassy path along the edge of a volcanic cliff rising above a deep gorge on our right. There was a certain nervousness in our horses' steps, which made me think about the guidebook's warning of horseback riding in that region as a "high risk" activity. Martha's nieces were both very good riders, but her nephews' aptitude was comparable to my daughters', who had taken riding classes at our Westport Hunt Club but certainly were not proficient. I kept asking the people who came with us from the stable why the horses skipped like that, stepping left and right. But the *chagras* (Andean cowhands) either didn't hear me or maybe they were concentrating on their job, because they just trotted away without answering.

Finally, someone did answer my question.

"Snakes," the man said. "The horses hate the snakes."

I immediately told everyone, urging the kids to hold on tight.

After reaching a crest, we made our way down a narrow path in the gorge, tricky to tackle because of the steep slope and loose rocks. Having read somewhere about Pissaro's cavalry horses breaking their ankles on the stones of the riverbeds outside Lima, I was nervous about our safety. But I soon became calmer, because our horses were surefooted at navigating the rocky outcrops of the trail. It was a glorious day and the views seemed to go on forever, filled with a picturesque landscape of small farms, patchwork fields, and open expanses carpeted with Andean grasses, all bordered by mountain ranges in the background, and here and there a raptor soaring above in search of prey.

Although quite sore from the bumpy ride down that precipice, when we reached the plain in the valley below, we all enjoyed a fast-paced canter across flat terrain and through the red clay of a dry riverbed.

About an hour after we left the stables, Martha and I had just climbed the crest of a hill when our attention was caught by an acrobatic somersault in the valley below. It was one of our riders in the group ahead. We saw the body flying off the mount and hitting the grass, but we couldn't tell who it was.

We soon found out that it was not one of the stable guides fooling around, but Martha's niece, Sophie, who had been thrown to the ground by her horse. She lay on the grass with a bleeding gash on the side of her head, confused, her pupils enlarged, her body shaking, complaining of being cold. There wasn't much we could do for Sophie, except help the child stay warm. I wrapped my large Hermès shawl around the uninjured part of her head and stretched the rest over her body.

I had never seen Martha so petrified. She must have been incredibly shocked, because she just sat there, crouching next to her niece's feet, while I sat on my heels at the child's head. Martha's eyes kept moving from the open wound near Sophie's right temple, to the trickle of blood running among the beautiful patterns on my scarf, to me, all without uttering a word. I did my best to keep Sophie talking so she stayed awake until Manolo came back with help, and every now and then, as Sophie's hand reached for her head, I caressed it away, worried she might contaminate the wound.

Some time later, the guides who had run down the hill toward a nearby farming village came pushing a well-used car up the horse-riding trail. It was hard to comprehend that the scene was really happening; it felt more like being plunged in a disquieting image of magic realism than reality.

Martha went to the hospital with her niece and I took care of the group of scared children, who were too worried about Sophie to enjoy any diversion I tried to provide. Thankfully, it all ended well. Sophie had a concussion, and she needed a number of stitches to sew up the gash on her head, but our stoic young companion recovered quickly, and we all had a good time on our last day in Lima.

BACK HOME, I woke up every day loving my life. I was delighted to be a mother of happy children and felt blessed to be sharing my life with so many good friends. In the evenings, I went home to laughter and games with my daughters, their friends, our pets, our music, our private jokes. But that was also the time when most of the people who filled Martha's life during the day left her. At the end of a successful business day, Martha came home to her dogs and cats and caged canaries and the chickens in the backyard *palais du poulet* and the lights left on by the last housekeeping shift at her house.

Knowing this, my girls and I happily included Martha in our lives as if she were a family member, never feeling that things had to be perfect in order to ask her over. We never regarded her as a perfectionist who would be overly critical, but as a dear friend whom we truly cared for. She was welcome whether we were lounging around in our pajamas or the kids were playing in the backyard with their friends, for tea while the girls did homework and I prepared our evening meal, for a glass of wine or freshly squeezed juice, to eat whatever we had for dinner. The girls put on their funny shows for our closest family and friends, and Martha would laugh that beautiful laughter of hers, filled with a girlish lack of inhibition, which few not close to her ever heard. Martha came to visit us at our vacation spot on the lake in New Hampshire. She shared with me the task of parental supervision when my girls came places with us. Even our boxer dogs, Ginger and Tigger, loved Martha, and she was nice to them (although they did not allow her chows on our property, zealously dutiful as they were in protecting the girls and me from all intruders).

We were happy to have Martha enjoy family life with us, and my girls continued to care for her, even when the being-on-your-toes-so-you-would-not-disappoint-Martha got a little weary (they were also not great fans of having to worry about Martha's demerits, which she so liberally dispensed).

The girls were amused by the way Martha and I seemed to speak in footnotes. One day after school I couldn't wait to show them our first passionflower bloom. It had blossomed during the day among the stash of precious tropical plants I had gotten at Logee's Greenhouses, where Martha and I sometimes drove for their tantalizing exotics. "You must come see. Let's go straight to the deck," I said as we got out of the car.

Rid of their heavy backpacks, munching on the still-warm cookies I usually had waiting on the counter, dogs jumping, covering them with frantic boxer kisses, the girls caught up with me outside.

"Our first *Granadilla* blossom!" I exclaimed, beckoning them to look at a crimson-red flower cupped in the palm of my hand. "Passiflora Decaisneana."

The girls came closer.

"The central crown of lavender and yellow filaments is called the corolla, and in that yellowish, fat thing that pushes up in the middle, see? It looks like a fatty flower. Its five lemony petals are the stamens, and the pistil has three stigmas, those mustardy-colored things in the very middle."

The girls looked at the blossom, then looked at each other, and began to laugh.

"What? What's so funny?" I asked.

"Mom, we love you, but you're such a dork!"

"Why? I just want to share as much as I can with you. When you grow up there may not be a Martha to show you things and explain them."

"Yeah!" chided Lara. "Like on New Year's Eve when you guys gave us champagne but turned the whole thing into a lesson—'That humongous bottle is called a Balthazar. Blah blah.'"

"You'd rather be ignorant?"

"No, Mom!" Monica said. "But we didn't need to know, right then, that the bottle was named after the king of Babylon!"

"From sixth century B.C.," Lara added.

"And you don't have to point out which is the pistil and which the stamens, either, Mom."

"Passionflowers are different than most other flowers," I said. "And these particular ones need hand-pollination. How would you do it if you didn't know where the reproductive organs are?"

"Okay, Mom. But you've been showing us those things since we were so little—"

"When we had no idea that every time we went to the garden to cut flowers with you we'd also get a lesson in botany!"

"And one in bouquet arrangements."

"I love you, my meanies," I said, laughing. "And since I am so transparent, let me tell you that this particular passionflower doesn't just keel over and die, it makes a fabulous fruit."

"Oh, wow!" said one of them kiddingly.

"Imagine that!" joined in her sister.

"And you are my juicy passion fruits. Edible, too," I said, grabbing both of them in a tight hug, kissing those lovely faces which by then stood as high off the ground as mine.

Joy filled our life. Even if our dinner was late because I was working, even if our cookies were half-burned because I was juggling help with homework, calls from clients and friends, and some house or garden chore, my daughters and I made a wonderful family unit. I did my best to share it all with Martha. Her life looked wonderful on the surface, a picture easy to fall in love with, but on a personal level, Martha had little human love in her life.

I even agreed to let Martha tell people that she was my children's godmother when she never was officially. It didn't seem like a really terrible thing to do— it was just like an honorary title, I thought, which Martha could share with the children's real godmothers. However, the title seemed to be important to Martha. I guessed that it made her feel part of our family, so I explained that to my daughters as best I could, and they said that if it meant so much to Martha, then we would sort of adopt her as the extra godmother.

Martha was an important presence in my children's daily lives. She was among the few adults with whom I shared my maternal thoughts and concerns. She was part of all of our private family celebrations, from birthday parties to graduation bashes, and often spoiled the girls with special invitations to commemorate those events.

One invaluable contribution that Martha made to my girls' upbringing was the living example of her can-do attitude, which she inspired them with and encouraged them to emulate.

When we came back from our trip to Peru, I made an important real estate sale, and treated Martha to dinner at Pasta Nostra, one of our favorite local restaurants. We talked about everything, and everyone, including the volunteer work my kids were doing. I was so proud of them, and I think Martha was too.

Touched by the living conditions of children they had seen during our trips, my daughters began looking for ways to help make a difference in the lives of other youngsters. However, it was not easy to find an organization supportive of young people wanting to do that. After much searching, my friends Edie and Patricia introduced Monica and Lara to Charles MacCormack, the president and CEO of Save the Children. Believing in the impact that children can make in others' lives, and trusting my girls' potential, he encouraged them to create a new youth volunteer organization, Kids Care Too. Still in middle school, my daughters became youth initiators and the original cochairs for an innovative volunteer group of children who worked together to raise funds to help children around the world, and to raise awareness of the needs and issues confronting millions of the world's children.

Martha's help was very important to my girls' success with their venture. She and Sharon understood my daughters' longing to take action, and they supported Monica and Lara's efforts, as did Sam and all my friends. That encouragement was to be one of the most lasting contributions that Martha made to their lives. They gained priceless knowledge about humanitarian concerns facing the world community, as well as great confidence in their capability to act toward improving conditions for children and their families throughout the world. As young adults, Monica and Lara continue to do volunteer work today.

THAT EVENING, WHEN Martha and I were driving back from Pasta Nostra, I told her that, after having paid my bills, I was left with some extra money from a real estate commission, which I thought I would invest in Sam's company stock, and which I could gradually sell as I needed. To which I recall Martha replied, "If I were to invest money right now, I'd buy Kmart stock."

I didn't respond, but I thought it was a weird response, since, as she told me, Martha had herself invested in Sam's biomedical company, ImClone. I didn't understand the intricate cellular mechanism at work, but I knew that Sam was working very hard toward developing an anti-tumor drug, and I had read it involved the DNA structure and the clinical trials were reported to have had encouraging results.

That winter Sam had entered into an agreement with Merck, the German pharmaceutical company, which, as I understood, involved payment of a number of $30 million installments in connection with the cancer vaccine that ImClone was developing. Sam was so smart and dedicated to his work that I trusted him to succeed. Besides, he wasn't making silly trinkets, he was making a drug to help people.

I ignored Martha's recommendation and bought some ImClone shares, although I thought that Martha was giving me good advice, and perhaps the reason she had invested in ImClone was because Kmart was off limits to her, given some restrictive legality of their relationship. But I felt it would be unfair to ask about that, in case it was confidential. I never asked Martha legal or financial questions. Whatever I knew was because she volunteered the information to me, like when at some point Martha said she had bought more ImClone. Then she talked about buying Kmart. By then I had already sold my ImClone shares to supplement my income to cover living expenses. I ended up breaking about even on my stock-market adventure, but concluded it wasn't worth the anxiety and palpitations that went with it. I had already decided that if I were going to buy any stock in the future, it would be in Martha's company. She and Sharon were working to bring it public, and with the two of them at the helm I felt my money could not be better invested anywhere.

Part III

Death of the Heart

13

Piranhas in the Amazon

THE YEAR AFTER launching Martha Stewart Living Omnimedia, Martha was named one of the "50 Most Powerful Women" by *Fortune* magazine. She also received the Edison Achievement Award from the American Marketing Association, and was inducted into the National Sales and Marketing Hall of Fame. According to an SEC filing report, she earned $4.7 million in salary plus bonuses that year.

But Martha seemed to be further losing in peace of mind what she gained in success and wealth. She remained "with" Charles, but it was unclear to what degree they were together, as there were many intimations of the unsettled air between them, like not spending the winter holiday together, or the time when Charles spent the night at Turkey Hill, and Martha said she was already asleep in her bed when she heard this big commotion coming from the guest bedroom at the far end of the hall, where Charles was staying. The antique bed in that room, which tended to come apart easily, had broken when Charles turned in his sleep, and he had fallen, startled and bruised, on the floor. Although Martha tried her best to hold men's attention, and she certainly looked great, something was just not working in the men department.

• • •

I HAD READ somewhere that perfume holds the "secret codes of our moods and feelings and desires," and figured it must be true. While I only ever wore a few scents, for me they are ceremonial and their aromas are intimately related to the romances of my life. I also know that there are essences to which I am attracted, and there are others that simply repel me.

Martha liked floral fragrance, which is possibly the most feminine among all perfumes. Her favorite was Fracas. When I sometimes guessed it on other women, the scent was playful, like an unlandscaped garden. When Martha sprayed that perfume on in my presence, which she often did, my senses felt assaulted, as if her body chemistry turned Fracas into the literal meaning of fracas: "quarrel, fight, brawl, mêlée, argument, disturbance, scuffle."

I thought perhaps that was what men were objecting to. I wanted to suggest that maybe she should change her perfume, but it didn't feel right saying that. And then one day it became evident that Martha had also thought that a new perfume might be a good thing, because she presented me with an open bottle of Opium, the scent that had become part of my daily routine. Martha said she had bought it for herself, but thought it smelled better on me.

I was grateful for Martha's gift, yet the fact that my body chemistry had saved us from becoming a double serving of the same scent reminded me about an aspect of our friendship which I never liked, the competition that showed up in so many ways, the races I didn't want to be in, or even knew I was in.

Around my divorce, when I was searching for an outline of self-definition, I sought style. Everyone around me was wearing couture: Armani, Chanel, Christian Dior. But I didn't want to look like everyone else. Having already learned that "fashion and style are not indivisible," I decided that Hermès was what I was going to wear. What attracted me, besides quality, was its Old World feeling and the memories it brought back, starting with the Hermès silk print *carré* with its fleshy, peachy-coral lotus flowers that my paternal grandmother had given me. From a very young age, I saw Hermès as the epitome of style, and now I was ready for more: red-striped silk-lined jackets, exquisite screen-printed silk and cashmere scarves, luxurious towels in joyful animal prints, silk tunics and riding pants, which Martha called jodhpurs.

Then I told Martha how much I wanted a refined Hermès Kelly bag, a status symbol for European women, usually a gift from a husband or a lover, like a piece of expensive jewelry. Not more than a week could have gone by when suddenly Martha appeared with her own Hermès bag. Martha had not bought the particular bag I coveted but a sportier version, a Birkin, favored among rich Americans.

When I saw the Hermès bag on Martha's arm, I complimented her on it. But I no longer shared my fashion aspirations with her, so when I got my Hermès bomber jacket, I didn't tell her that being enveloped in the oversized dark brown folds of soft Cerf leather felt somewhat like wearing my man's clothes, which I always liked doing when I am in love. I just listened to her disapproval, which came out in words to the effect of, *Why would you wear THAT?*

Thus, I was surprised when, a few years later, we were going to the movies one night, and Martha said, "Tomorrow my Hermès jacket is coming."

"You got an Hermès jacket! Good for you! Mine seems indestructible. What do you mean 'is coming'?"

"Catherine [who owned the Hermès boutique in St. Barth] is sending it."

"She has fabulous taste. I wear everything I bought from her. Which style did you get?"

"I told her I want one just like yours."

"We're going to walk around in uniform now?"

"No, we're not going to wear it at the same time."

"So I'll have to call you every time I want to put my jacket on?"

She didn't answer.

While there is nothing simple or easily described about the bond between two adult women, I think a good part of the competitive tension that Martha introduced between us was due to the fact that while, compared to her, I had a pittance of cash, I had a whole string of suitors. Still we found ways to turn it around and make a joke of it. I remember one odd, hilariously fun and self-indulgent night. It was as if we were in a whirl of gowns and glamour, two princesses with two fairy godmothers floating in cartoon bubbles above our heads, sprinkling their magic dust upon us wherever we walked. We were like two pretty twelve-year-olds, walking through the playground at recess, girls who know they own the jungle gyms, the swing set, the monkey bars, every castle in the box of sand. Martha had asked me to come with her and a group of executives from her company to a meeting in a sunny Southern city. Since my girls were on school break skiing with their father, I was delighted. She often asked me to go with her on business trips to balance out the intensity and impersonal nature of the working world. This time it was a huge hotel with domed turrets, a circular drive, gorgeous gilded doors that opened and closed in a perennial *shushh-hushhhh* as bell boys, at once soundless and swift on their nimble feet, opened the doors of dark cars from which stepped gloved ladies in vermilion pumps and stockings made of lace.

Whenever Martha was free from her business obligations, she joined me for a swim through the liquid blue of the pool, diving down to touch the tiled sundial at the bottom. Later, we sat in lounge chairs, sipping this or that through long straws, wrapped in soft, thick robes, or just kissed by the sun, as it was warm outside and our private terrace, with its own pool, insulated us from the rest of the world.

We sometimes had two rooms on those trips, maybe two interconnected suites, or, if she wanted to save her company money, Martha and I shared one room, as we did on this trip. (Though I paid my way when we went together on vacations, business trips were a different story.) The bed was obese, smothered in pillows and scrumptious Italian linens, so layered and overdone its mattress was as hidden for us as was the pea for the proverbial princess. Exhausted from our long day, the hours of meetings and nonstop talk, the gourmet dinner and delicious wine, we flopped back on the bed like a pair of synchronized dolls. And that's when we noticed it. Above us the ceiling was made of a large mirror, so when you cast your eyes upward, you saw all of yourself.

Martha and I laughed and laughed at that silly ceiling. We were so ABOVE this, and yet we loved it. And then we lay there, silent and flushed, for several moments. My eyes roved the room and then came back to our reflection. My face. And then Martha's face. In the glass mirror, her whites seemed shinier, her pupils both darker and deeper, like inkwells.

"I'm so pretty," she said.

Her voice was flat and slow as though she had a battery pack running low. Her voice scared me. My reflection looked at her reflection. Our gazes locked.

"I'm so pretty," Martha said again, her eyes in the mirror now ticking from her reflection to mine, and back again.

In the mirror, I saw her lift her index finger, swipe beneath her eye, check her fingertip, blow lightly. Then, suddenly, she started to smile, moving her head so as to examine her profile from all angles—chin up, chin down, head left, head right, and she was smiling, giggling, fluffing up her hair. It was a game, so I jumped in.

"No, *I'm* so pretty," I said, my fingers fanning out my hair so the locks loosened and I bobbed in a coppery-chestnut lake.

Martha eyed my hair quickly, and then, both of us still lying side by side on the bed, she fluffed her own hair too, harder to do with her shorter bob, but she tried, and then swiftly moved on to her lips, biting down deep so blood filled the delicate membranes.

"No, *I'm* so pretty," she said.

"No, *I'm* so pretty," I said again.

We started to laugh again, and within seconds the laughter erupted like hives, spreading everywhere, and we could not stop.

"No, *I'm* so pretty!" Martha said, twirling a single strand of hair.

"No, *I'm* so pretty!" I gasped, yanking a whole hank of my hair up, letting it fall freely.

"No *I'm* so—"

"No *I'm*—!"

"No *I'm*—!"

How long did we lie there, laughing, snorting, hooting, howling? The joke was on us. *Mirror, mirror, on the wall, who's the fairest of them all?*

PERHAPS THE REASON I overlooked the competitive undercurrent Martha imprinted on our friendship was the fact that we were truly excellent at pulling together whenever circumstances required. Like on our sea-kayaking adventure in Newfoundland the fall after the Skylands purchase and the TimeWarner deal were complete.

Early one morning, a whole bus of us drove to a location I hadn't looked up on the map, knowing only that we were going to a place at the seashore where we'd kayak while Martha's crew filmed us for a television special. I was excited about the trip, having just read *Random Passage* by Bernice Morgan, which was filled with foreboding stories of expeditions attempting to explore or even reach those unforgiving lands.

We drove a couple of hours through the rugged landscape of the rocky protrusion where Canada juts into the Atlantic off the northeastern coast of North America. The foliage had already turned but the colors were different, tamer, and the landscape more rigid than our American Northeast, solemn and less populated. We had met the locals the night before, having flown in after dusk on Martha's company-leased plane, and they were welcoming and gentle. I had the impression that every single person I met could fish, sail, and do something artistic with their hands.

The kayak-landing turned out to be a narrow, short strip of sand on a rocky beach between people's houses, where a courteous but stern man, the guide-instructor, met our party: Martha, her sister Laura, Sharon, and a few women who had worked for Martha for many years, and Martha's television crew, most of them people I knew by then.

The segment was for a new venture that Martha and Sharon were exploring with Mungopark Expeditions, who were somehow connected with Microsoft. I didn't quite understand their relationship to Martha, and didn't bother to find out. Martha had received a Daytime Emmy Award Outstanding Service Show Host for *Martha Stewart Living* that year. She and Sharon knew what they were doing.

They had plenty of ideas, and I perceived this excursion as their attempt to have Martha become "the Martha Stewart of mountaineering and the outdoors." The event also had sponsors. Martha was dressed in new Timberland from head to toe. Sharon's outfit was made with much of that brand, as was Laura's. Martha had offered me a spanking-new red waterproof Timberland jacket with many pockets and black zippers. I refused it at first, fearing I might damage it, and insisted I use my own jacket, the one with a compass patch buttoned to the left arm, which I had taken to Egypt and we took turns wearing. But Martha explained that I had to put the red jacket on for the TV special, that it didn't matter what happened to it, because all the Timberland stuff was for the wearer to keep. She reassured me that her things were as good as my European stuff.

For about twenty minutes we listened to technical descriptions and watched our guide demonstrate at water's edge the skills required for sea-kayaking.

We were supposed to pair up with another inexperienced person in our group, rather than a guide. The first person he wanted in the kayak was Martha.

"Who wants to go in with Martha?" he asked. His smile turned into perplexity when no one jumped at the opportunity. Sharon declined with a smile. She already had Martha's sister, Laura, as her partner. No one else seemed prepared to be trapped in that narrow boat with

Martha, so I offered, making it clear all the while that they should make the decision based on the fact that I knew nothing about the sport. Unfazed, he helped me into Martha's beautiful kayak just as my mind began to process the idea that the boat I was climbing into was designed to capsize.

About half an hour after we left the shore, a local television crew, who had gotten wind of Martha's presence, drew up in a boat very near our kayak, competing with Martha's film crew to get close-ups of her. Paddling against the surf of the frigid Atlantic, Martha and I pulled together against two great opponents, media and nature, flashing photogenic smiles toward the cameras while we used our minds more than our skill to balance the long, narrow, and unstable boat. Doing our mighty best to avoid the pull of the boat's pitching, we leaned in tandem into the turns and lifted the bow so we could ride up the waves and descend on the other side without smashing into them.

While I concentrated on synchronizing my brain and body with Martha's, I tried not to think about the Eskimo Roll, which the guide had said was the only safe recovery option for a capsizing sea kayak. I knew full well that we could hardly count on pulling one off. I understood an Eskimo Roll to mean that, when losing control of the boat, the kayaker rolls with the kayak into the surf while being smashed by the crushing wave. As it wasn't quite clear to me how one does that without hitting one's head against the sea bed, which around Newfoundland seemed to be all rock, the recovery technique sounded more like Russian roulette.

But Martha and I were a good team. We rode on, disregarding our fatigue, numbness, and cramps from not being able to change position, our feet strapped in braces. We paddled with and against those high crushing waves, concentrating on advancing toward the far shore. It was an arduous fight, hard on each part of the body. Sharon ended up with a splintered wrist.

After about five hours of "sea-kayaking adventure in the scenic and pristine waters of Placentia Bay," as the Mungopark described it, we reached the bedrock-lined, narrow harbor of a small coastal town, an "outport," as those Newfoundland fishing settlements were called. From what I could see through the foggy dusk, the place looked as if it came straight from the pages of Annie Proulx's book *Shipping News*, which I had just begun reading.

Safe on terra firma the next day, I took a long walk with Laura. We had known each other for many years, yet it was the first time she and I had spent time alone. I liked her presence, lively yet peaceful, much like Chris, her son, a wonderful young man who came on the trips Martha and I had taken to Galapagos and Egypt. As we walked in the fine drizzle, I thought of my friendship with Martha and how it depended on our balancing skill, the same way a sea-kayak relies on its passengers' skills in balancing the craft. I rather liked that image.

Back at the inn, Martha had returned from a filmed session of fishing for cod with one of the area's expert fishermen, where I left her earlier, after she and I took a long hike along picturesque fjords, trekking over rocks, sand, and icy waters.

I also made a wonderful new friend there, Rich Deacon, one of our Canadian guides, a very nice, attractive man. He loved the outdoors, and we seemed to have a lot in common; we even liked the same books. He told me about an out-of-print account of Newfoundland, *Wake of the Great Sealers*, then later sent me a copy of it. From Farley Mowat's text and David Blackwood's soul-stirring illustrations, I understood so much more about that place and the people I'd met. But it wasn't the right time in my life to explore, because I had fallen in love. For some time now I'd been seriously dating a man who sent me exuberant bouquets of flowers every week. Not a short infatuation this time, but love.

Feeling protective of the fledgling relationship, I wanted to keep it a secret for a while, partly to safeguard our privacy, and partly because my lover was close with many of Martha's friends. I didn't want gossip to precede my telling Martha about us, particularly since I knew that Martha had hoped to become the center of his attentions when he parted with his wife. About two years later, he had not yet given any sign of interest in Martha, but began courting me with disarming charm. With her new success, Martha was invited to so many places across the country, and between that and Charles flying her around in his Falcon 50 private plane, I had much more time for a life of my own. But Martha did get suspicious when she noticed that my crystal vases held gorgeous and extravagant bouquets of flowers. Still, I wasn't ready to make her jealous, so I laughed off her speculation about my mystery man without divulging a word.

While there were many reasons why I wished to keep my relationship secret from Martha, the main one was because Martha had become so possessive that she tried to restrict me from flirting with any prospects. When I was attracted to a man, Martha seemed to instantly be aware of my desire, as if she could smell it from a distance, and she hounded me about it. For some reason, I often caved in to that.

I especially remembered one evening, a few months before I began dating my new man, when Martha and I were out together on the New York party circuit. Soon after we entered the place, we were talking with a well-known photographer when, in the middle of the conversation, Martha excused herself and left me and this gentleman behind even though she knew that he and I had nothing to say to each other. But the message was quite clear: Martha was going on a celeb patrol and she was not taking me along. As her guest, I felt I was obligated to defer to Martha charting the course of our evening.

I like people-watching, so I was walking among the glamorous crowd when I found myself face to face with Jeremy Irons. Our eyes met in one of those rare electrifying encounters, which was strange, because he is such an enormously famous star. We began to talk. I can't tell you what we said but I could describe every sparkle in his eyes and each movement of his lips. I was floating in this divine experience when, from the other end of the large, loud room, I saw Martha rushing toward us. She looked absolutely panicked, waving as she pushed through the crowds, and shouting, "Mariana! Mariana!"

When she reached us, Martha seemed out of breath.

"We have to leave now," she said curtly.

Never knowing what Martha might do, I preferred to avoid a scene, so I acquiesced. It was better to ignore the seductive plea of a man whom I felt incredibly attracted to than risk having Martha embarrass him and me both.

"Next time," I said, then I reached out and kissed his cheeks, one at a time.

I followed Martha out of the place, abiding by the rules of her deadly serious game of dominance, but I resented being cheated out of that intoxicating encounter. With that kind of history behind us, I decided I'd spare my current love Martha's jealousy for as long as I could.

With our friends and hers, and just the two of us, Martha and I socialized a lot. One evening she invited me to a dinner at renowned Nobu restaurant in New York, given by a prominent Hollywood producer whose extraordinary Frank Lloyd Wright estate she had taken me to visit a couple of times. Martha loved Japanese food and so did I, so we often went out for sushi—on my invitation, mostly, when we ate around Westport. When we went to New York, I was Martha's guest. That evening at Nobu, as it turned out, we were not the only guests. Our host had invited quite a crowd, and we arrived late.

We joined a large group, seated at a round table, near the entrance. Martha sat next to our host, then came his smart and attractive new girlfriend, and then, next to her, and across the table from me, was Jean Pigozzi, the Franco-Italian heir to the Simca automobile fortune, a man I admired, whom I had last seen at a party on his boat Martha had taken me to. I was seated to the left of Richard Meier, the well-known architect whose work I hold in high regard. He had flirted with Martha one divorce earlier, and having met him many times over the years, I knew that he could sometimes be remote, yet always interesting and often funny, as he had a dry sense of humor. On his right was the glamorous former wife of a famous actor. The dinner had been arranged with the hope that the attractive lady and Richard Meier might like each other.

But Richard decided to talk mostly with me. As if that was not enough to get me in trouble, he also kept sliding his hand under the table and resting it on my knee, and I spent much of the evening placing it, carefully but firmly, back on the table. I was irritated with Richard but I tried not to attract attention, hoping he'd soon tire of behaving like a spoiled child.

The conversation at our table was interesting and lively, the hot sake smooth, and the food delicious. We were in the middle of the dinner when Martha got up from the table, eye-messaging me with her customary *We leave right now*. I didn't think much of it, since, with her busy morning schedule, Martha often left dinner tables abruptly and before dessert. With practiced rapidity, I gathered my things and took my leave from my dinner neighbors. When I turned to kiss Richard's cheek, Martha was already behind us, her hand on the door handle, hurrying me out loud: "Mariana, we are leaving!"

By then, I had seen Martha argue with people many times, so I recognized the onset of that bizarre state of excitement that took hold of her whenever she picked a fight. Apparently, so did everyone else, because silence befell our table and neighboring heads started to turn toward us. Since Andy, Martha had never made that kind of scene in front of people we both respected. With all the composure I could amass, embarrassed by her behavior and worried about what she might do next, I began rising out of the chair. I was halfway up when Richard's powerful hand pressed me back down into the seat.

"I'm coming, Martha," I said, hoping she had not noticed Richard's move.

I got up and Richard's arm grabbed me, tightly, squeezing my standing body close to him. The only thing I knew to do was keep an idiotic smile on my face.

"Richard, she's coming with me." Martha's tone did not invite opposition.

"Why? Because you want to go home? Just go!" Richard said.

"Richard, I brought her, I am taking her back. The car is waiting."

"I'll drive her home," he said.

"Are you going to take her to Connecticut?"

"Yeah, I'll drive her to Connecticut."

"Don't be ridiculous, Richard. She has children waiting for her at home."

It wasn't quite true—my children were with their father that evening—but the ploy worked. Richard's arm loosened its grip.

"Come, Mariana," Martha said.

Mortified, I gave Richard another kiss on the cheek, I mumbled some good-nights and thank-yous, too embarrassed to look anyone in the eye, and I rushed toward the door. Martha was already in the back of the Suburban and Larry, her driver of many years, had started the car.

Martha and I never discussed that evening, but it had made it very clear that we had reached the stage where our competition in the "first to find a mate" category had reached a new low.

With each new experience, a new facet of our friendship developed. Eventually, ours became a friendship in which Martha dominated the interaction, and soon established my acceding to her needs as a major part of the goal of our relationship. I put up resistance at times, like when I confronted Martha about spending the night on a felucca on the Nile, but most often I gave in, like that evening at Nobu or on that fateful horseback ride in Peru. I didn't like myself for this, but I made the choice to maintain the friendship. A different person now, I sometimes find this hard to believe.

NOT LONG AFTER the awkward incident at Nobu, Martha gave a grand, weekend-long Leo birthday bash at Skylands, which became an annual event that Martha organized not only for herself but for her friend Charlotte Beers and me, and anyone else she knew born under that astrological sign who happened to be on Mount Desert Island at the time. It was always a party to outdo all other parties.

My secret lover, a longtime friend of many of the people at that party, had been invited by Martha to join the celebration and spend the weekend at Skylands. He arrived bearing gifts for the Leo ladies being fêted. Each of us received a beaded Judith Leiber minaudière-style evening bag. Martha immediately wanted to see mine, but I tried to put off showing it to her. There was something about the purse that bothered Martha immensely, because she kept pressuring me until I finally took it to her bedroom and showed it to her while she was getting ready for the evening's festivities. Charles, who was known by then as Martha's beau, had already gone downstairs. It was just us in the room and all those exotic butterflies, prettily framed on the walls, their beauty pinned under glass, wings spread, thorax pierced, the perfect V of antennae extending outward, perpetual witnesses to Martha's intimate world. Martha interrupted her dress-up ritual to compare my purse to hers. They both looked nice to me, but Martha proceeded to explain why she thought hers was better than mine. I knew what Martha was doing. She was trying to kill my hope. I just looked straight in her face and made a joke, but for the first time since we had been friends, I laughed at Martha and not with her.

I had a great evening of fun at that party, but happiness was not in the stars for me. My lover had had enough with the secrecy of our affair and wanted us to spend the night together. There was no place I wished to be more than in his arms but I thought we should wait until we left Martha's house. Given the recent episode with Richard Meier at Nobu, I was concerned that my emerging from my lover's room in the morning could bring on a real scene with Martha. By the time I realized that I was permitting her to bully me yet again into surrendering my chance at personal happiness, the man I wished to be with was on his way out of my life.

Having made so many sacrifices to live free, I resented allowing myself to be confined to the limits of Martha's world, which, great as it was, had become quite small. The worst part was that I was Martha's accomplice at taking away my happiness.

Late that night, after the festivities were over, and all the elegant guests had left Skylands in their luxury planes, I couldn't sleep, thinking of what I had done, how my handsome lover had insisted that we go public, and I kept putting him off, asking him to wait so I could find the right moment to tell Martha first. When he took matters into his own hands and offered the best way to tell her about us—by spending the night together under Martha's roof—I panicked at the thought that she might create another embarrassing scene. Seen at face value, my action could have easily been read as though I cared more about Martha's feelings than his. As much as it hurt, I had to accept the fact that I had been both weak and not very smart, and the man I could have been happy with had very good reasons to be disappointed and was likely to disappear into thin air.

Not long after that Skylands Leo birthday party, Martha proposed that my daughters and I go sailing the Brazilian Amazon, as her guests, to celebrate the New Year. Generous as it was, Martha's offer only included the boat trip along the Amazon, which meant I was still responsible for flights, hotels, and all other travel-related expenses for the three in my family on a trip to Brazil, Martha Stewart–style. There were also gratuities, especially considering that I always tipped generously, often for both of us. I once confronted Martha about it, and she said her company had made a donation to the Darwin Institute in the Galapagos, which is commendable but it's not the same as tipping the people who personally help you have a good time. I didn't mind doing it, but it could get expensive, particularly since besides appreciation for good service the tips included attempts at smoothing the feathers Martha ruffled along the way. I had enough experience traveling with Martha to know that the trip was beyond my means, so I told her, "I'd still have to spend quite a bit of money, and I don't have it, so I can't go."

To which Martha said, "Yes, you can. You have the Judith Leiber bag, and you can borrow the rest from me." Then, as I didn't really understand, Martha proceeded to explain that I should give her the birthday present—from my now-departed lover—and she would lend me the money for the trip. She would return the Judith Leiber beaded evening purse to the store, and deduct the price of the bag from the cost of my family's plane tickets, which she'd advance me. I was quite taken aback by her proposal, and for so many reasons, of which I only shared with Martha my distress that though the Judith Leiber *minaudière* was a bit fancy for my lifestyle, I didn't want my friend to hear that I had exchanged his gift for money. Martha dismissed my concerns by saying that she would also return the Judith Leiber that he had given her.

I knew Martha was experienced at returning gifts. I still remembered how hard she tried to exchange that handbag gifted to her by Kmart's Mr. Antonini and his wife on the occasion of Martha's fiftieth birthday. But I was unsure of Martha's motives in creating the complicated plot involving my purse. She had never once before offered to treat me, or my girls, on our year-end trips. Out of the blue, Martha was offering me a form of creative financing so I could cruise the Brazilian Amazon with my daughters, which she knew I would have loved to do.

I realized, of course, that the little beaded bag was, in many ways, proof of my having been more successful in the mating game than Martha. So, given her competitive nature, of course, she wanted to take it away. In fact, Martha wanted it so badly that she was offering to pay for chartering a boat down the Amazon just so she could relieve me of my gift. Here is the hard part: I accepted the arrangement Martha proposed.

So it was that, a year after I had taken a loan from Martha, with interest and a contract, to go with her to Peru, I handed over my purse so I could go with her to Brazil.

Partly because I felt it was the tribute she demanded as the price of peace between us, partly because I thought that, under the circumstances, had I not relinquished to Martha what to me was a memento, to her a trophy, I would have been like the naturalist in the old joke, who was lost in a remote jungle and caught by cannibals. Before having his skin peeled and made into a canoe, to be followed by a tribal feast on his body, the scientist was given a final wish. He asked for a fork, which he immediately turned on himself, punching holes in his body and yelling at the top of his lungs, "Now, now I am getting back at you. I am sinking your canoe."

Boarding in Manaus, we traveled the Amazon by chartered yacht, marveling at the lush jungle along its banks. We were traveling with the same group of six children who came with us on all our trips, Martha's nieces and nephews, and my daughters. Brazilian-born Necy, Martha's set designer, and Sharon Patrick were also traveling with us, possibly to protect the Asset.

We headed up toward the Rio Negro and the animal- and bird-rich Xixuan Nature Reserve, whose transparent waters we scanned for endangered manatees and *boutou*, the large, pink Amazon River dolphin. We saw rare giant river otters, turtles, and huge schools of fish, including frenzied, flesh-eating piranha and giant pirarucu. We explored the largest river archipelago in the world in motorized canoes, watching swarms of egrets, colorful macaws, parrots and toucans by day, and at night, we piled into dugout canoes to search the submerged jungle under the stars, among pairs of phosphorescent eyes and myriad eerie calls, as the fearless local guides pointed out to us large black caiman, or alligator, and on the river banks elusive greenish-yellow flashes of the puma, jaguar, and ocelot watching us.

While we admired its wonder and beauty, we stayed clear of the river's water because of the piranhas, which were everywhere, the electric eels we saw sometimes at night, the giant anacondas we had seen in movies, and the small, transparent parasite catfish, *candiru*, which penetrates fish and human bodies to feast painfully on blood and tissue. We fished for the peacock bass, called *tucunaré*, and marveled at how carnivorous piranhas attacked our fighting catch. Necy, who was good with the fishing rod and also a great cook, caught piranha and prepared it deliciously for our Amazon feasts.

Before we went to Brazil, I had recommended that everyone watch the film *Fitzcarraldo*, a great movie about a man obsessed with two ambitions: making his fortune and building an opera house in the jungle. As he travels the Amazon wilderness in a huge steamship, his megaphone plays famous operas, the music floating above the impassivity of nature and the struggle of men. We played opera on *Amazonia II*, a truly spectacular experience.

Martha and I were in perfect sync, and the doubts I'd had about the trip faded. We continued our adventure upriver, to the mouth of Rio Branco, then we turned down the Rio Negro. We toasted the change of the year with champagne and our usual "May we not spend next New Year's Eve together!" On the first day of 1999, we watched the Meeting of the Waters of the Amazon, where the black waters of Rio Negro and the brown waters of the Solimoes River meet but don't mix. The exoticism of the experience—and my daughters' awed enjoyment—made it seem worth the worry later on.

Except a few nights in hotels and when we slept at the Xixuan Reserve in *maloca* huts built in the tradition of people indigenous to that area—where we didn't dare to use the baths at night although we were told that the shadows among the tree branches were harmless monkeys and sloths—we lived on the water the whole time. *Amazonia II* was our home base for most of the trip. I shared a queen-size bed in the master stateroom, the largest of the yacht's air-conditioned cabins, with Martha, who had the habit of monopolizing the bathroom, so I went to take a quick shower while she prepared some of her delicious caipirinhas with fresh limes and the best cachaça. I rushed back to catch the sunset—my favorite time of the day—on the deck, where I had left Martha in charge of my daughters, then fifteen and almost twelve years old. I found my children jetting around our boat, both of them in bathing suits and T-shirts, standing on one water-bike, which I had noticed on the boat ever since we boarded but no one had risked taking it for a spin. Monica, who had never driven a moped or a car, was driving the bike, and standing behind her, Lara was holding on to her older sister's body, their bare feet skimming the opaque surface of the piranha-infested waters. I was outraged.

Everyone was watching for my reaction. I looked at Sharon, who looked away. I knew there was nothing she could have done; she wasn't there to protect my daughters. Concerned that my fear would panic my girls, I put on a fake smile and, without a word of reproach, took a sip of the iced caipirinha Martha had waiting for me and met her gaze, not bothering to hide my disgust at her sinister manipulation of my children. On some level, I knew she wasn't motivated by wanting to endanger her guests' lives. It was simply part of her effort to escape the confines of ordinary life. But these were my children, and that made all the difference. It was the beginning of the end.

I stood there watching the waves made by the speeding water-bike dissipate in the water turned blood-red by an ominously large setting sun. My children were laughing, intoxicated by their perilous adventure, which, as all six kids confirmed to me later, Martha had goaded them into. While I waited for their flirtation with danger to end, I realized that I'd been in denial about how challenging my friendship with Martha had become and faced the fact that we were, after all, quite dissimilar in our desire for wonder and discovery.

14

The Barefoot Contessa

THE SPRING AFTER we came back from Brazil I embarked on an ambitious project to transform my river-house property. My vision of fields covered with wildflowers was inspired by a romantic expanse of narcissus blossoms from a scene in *Dr. Zhivago*. It was also intended as an homage to Van Gogh, whose enchanting swirls of greens and yellows had captured my imagination the previous fall.

Just after I had let Martha take away my beaded purse, she rewarded me with a very special invitation. The National Gallery of Art in Washington had agreed to let Martha film the Van Gogh exhibit for one of her TV segments. It was one of those special events at which, if lucky enough to get an entry ticket, one had to share the space with as large a crowd as allowed by fire and security code. The filming was done one morning before the exhibit opened for the public. I was there with Martha, her sister, her crew, and the curator. As I had no obligation to be in the segment, I walked ahead of the group, looking at the paintings for as long as I wanted and from as close as I could. Martha joined me between shoots.

My gardening adventure had been influenced as well by the way

Martha had borrowed from artists in planning her own gardens—for example, the Christo-inspired burlap-dressed bushes, or the rose arbors at Lily Pond, which so perfectly imitated those at Giverny. Martha and I had visited Claude Monet's garden at the end of May 1990 to celebrate our friend Maggie's twentieth wedding anniversary. Martha came back with lots of pictures of the famous rose arbors. I, like many others, file away pictures, magazines, and piles of books, in private stashes to return to someday, usually never. Not Martha. She had those arches immediately reproduced by an iron-works master. She had them painted that aqua-teal predominant at Lily Pond in contrast to the Giverny green, and she grew her own old-fashioned roses along a walk-through of those arches that resembled the archways of the central pathway at Giverny.

To create my art-inspired acres of garden, I had to plant thousands of daffodil bulbs and foxglove seedlings. I decided to start with three hundred, which seemed feasible as it was the same number of bulbs Martha had planted at Lily Pond in just one morning. Three days later, my knees raw, the inside of my right thumb covered in blisters, I was still digging holes, and not really minding it. As I kneeled among gnarly roots of weeds and crab grass, I imagined myself in the middle of a real-life version of Van Gogh's unforgettable *Blossoming Almond Tree*.

I WAS WITH Van Gogh in my garden when I received the most extravagant invitation I ever got over the years of my friendship with Martha. Actually, it was not from Martha but from Charles, Martha's sometime companion. He offered to treat his friends to what he called a "Fantasy Echo" four-day trip to the French Riviera. The hand-rendered invitation included an itinerary of elegant parties, each one with a cinema-inspired romantic theme. This generosity so fitted Charles, who unlike some people with great wealth didn't seem to mind spending it, and also never expected you to sell your soul for his fabulous invitations, which made them easy to accept. Charles refused to disclose the reason for his sublime gesture but he had confided in Martha his plans to leave Microsoft to open his own software company, and I assumed the party had something to do with that.

Charles's entertaining philosophy was simple: he settled for nothing less than the very best and made his friends feel grand. In the late afternoon of May 12, 1999, Charles's pilots greeted Sam, me, and an attractive blonde near Charles's Falcon 50 at the White Plains Airport in Westchester County, New York. We sauntered onto the plane that would fly us to Nice. The glamorous lady friend of Charles's, whom we had not met before, turned out to have many shared acquaintances with Sam. Karen, Charles's efficient private secretary whose pleasant manner and competence were as impressive as those of Martha's two personal assistants—Julia, who worked in Martha's Westport office, and Annie, in New York—had kept us all informed of the details of his "Fantasy Echo" trip.

I brought my red crocodile Hermès Bolide along, secretly enjoying the idea of taking a purse modeled after a racecar to, as the invitation read, "Brunch and sipping champagne on the yacht *Andale* while watching the prestigious Grand Prix Final of the Formula One championship." Ever since I was a teenager and saw *Grand Prix*, a romantic movie featuring a 1960s motor-race up and down steep elevations and around tight corners in the narrow streets of Monte Carlo and the harbor of Monaco, I had dreamed of being there one day to watch candy-colored Ferraris and Lamborghinis compete. The Monaco Grand Prix had so much sparked my imagination that, when I finally could have my own Hermès handbag, I chose the Bolide, which was inspired by Bugatti, the car that had won its inaugural race.

The first thing I did when I walked into my hotel room was open the window to catch a glimpse of the golden-coral Mediterranean sunset. Bouquets of fragrant fresh peonies in beautiful vases dotted the room. The elegant side table was set with a feast of delicacies: a silver cooler holding champagne, a tempting box of chocolates from Nice's famous patisserie Maison Auer, an opalescent bowl overflowing with aromatic ruby globes of wild strawberries.

The room phone rang with an old-fashioned chime.

"Ready for the soirée?" Martha asked, affecting a French accent.

"Almost!" I said, although I was far from it. "Where are you staying?"

"Charles's new apartment."

"Is it nice?"

"Needs work. What are you wearing tonight?"

"Give me a second. I'll tell you."

Holding the phone with one hand, I reached with the other to unfasten my old-faithful Gurka travel bag.

"Why did you and Charles not stay in the old apartment?"

"Charles put up some of his friends there."

"Tonight is black tie, isn't it?" I asked, mostly wanting to gain time to undo buckles and zippers.

"Optional."

My luggage was finally opened and, as simplicity is easy when you travel light, I put an outfit together at a glance, while reciting for Martha: "My favorite little black dress . . . the red Fortuny shawl . . ."

"What shoes?"

"The Christian Louboutin open-toe pumps."

"When did you get here?"

"About an hour ago. Charles had us flown in on his plane—Sam, me, and a blonde I haven't seen before."

"How's Sam? What's his room number?"

"I don't know, but Susan might," I said, thinking that, as usual, Martha's publicist had all the information.

"Charles says, 'Get dolled up!'"

"Please give him my love."

"Au revoir! See you on the *Orient Express*."

I was immersed in my dress-up ritual, when, through the open window, a strong scent of acacia plunged me into a Proustian reverie about the delicious *beignets* my mother used to make with acacia blossoms. I could see her hands gently breaking each flower from the grape-like bunches, then dipping the blooms in an egg-and-flour batter, to which she added beer for fluffiness and rose water to enliven the fragrance. Not surprising that such a tasty memory would come to me just when one of my childhood dreams was coming true: spending an evening in the fantastically elegant *Venice Simplon-Orient-Express*.

Our fête began at eight o'clock in the evening. Sam, Susan, and I arrived at Monte Carlo's Monaco Train Station, where we met Charles and the rest of his entourage, thirty or more people, some wearing black tie, others in evening suits, all friends of Charles who had flocked there from around the world, delighted to make one another's acquaintance. The classic shine-and-brass *Orient Express* chugged to the platform and welcomed our private party. A beautiful 1920s carriage, with the recognizable red front bumper and bronze monogram, had been chartered by Charles for our private use. In the style of a bygone era, a steward rolled out the red carpet on the platform, and we were greeted with the same formality that had been extended to the most noble of guests for more than a hundred years.

The intimate confines surpassed my romantic vision of the fabled train. The magnificent original décor was similar to the *Etoile du Nord*, famously used as a setting for the film *Murder on the* Orient Express. I couldn't be sure if our carriage was also one of those classified as "historic monuments," but given the exquisite 1920s wall paneling with stylized veneers of inlaid precious woods, splendid Art Deco glass designs, polished bronze light fixtures, dusty rose and deep dark burgundy of Côte d'Azur armchairs, and gold-trimmed midnight-blue carpeting, I presumed we were in a premium-class Blue Pullman.

A jazz pianist dressed in coattails enlivened the luxurious atmosphere. Comfortably spaced dining tables were festively set with starched white linens, heavy crystal, light porcelain, and the subtle spark of silverware. Outside the window, day was giving way to a starry night over the open vistas of small French villages, vineyards, high plateaus, rugged gorges, castles, and rocky ruins. Charles's guests were engaged in animated conversation boosted by a superbly stocked cocktail bar.

Charles looked particularly handsome dressed in an impeccably cut evening suit. He moved through the crowd, happily floating in the pixie dust of Martha-by-his-side. The creamy silk of Martha's evening dress enveloped her closely as it flowed down toward her ankles, just above her splendid café-au-lait Manolo Blahnik sandals. She was wearing the magnificent multiple-strand necklace of golden South Sea pearls that Charles had given her. Their opalescent glow softened her smile and intensified the deep luster of her eyes. Attentive and solicitous to each guest, Charles and Martha were advancing slowly toward our group at the far end of the dining car, where Sam, Susan Magrino, and I were mingling with new acquaintances, making conversation, sipping champagne, and waiting for them to join us.

The always-fetching Susan looked alluring in her haute couture dress from Arnold Scaasi, and beautiful ear clips offset her sun-kissed tan, and blond, Frédéric Fekkai–styled hair. Her intelligent, golden-hazel eyes sparkled with amusement as Sam entertained us with the latest New York high-society gossip. Next to him was an attractive, interesting brunette in her thirties, a friend of Charles's, whom we had just met. A journalist who lived in London, she had come on the trip alone, and held her own very well in that brainy crowd of beauties. She wore a sleeveless indigo dress that accentuated her slim body, alabaster skin, and sexy eyes.

I felt a light tapping on my shoulder and turned to face Martha and Charles.

"Let's see!" Martha said, pushing me back slightly for a full body appraisal. "How elegant." After nearly twenty years, I knew the way she said *eeleegant* to mean that, although she looked beautiful that night, Martha might not have felt so.

"You look fabulous!" I whispered in Martha's ear, as we touched our cheeks in greeting.

When I turned to Charles, his arms were already open for my hug. I quite adored Charles and thought of him as a brother.

"Oh, Charles, you are the mostest, perfectest host! And so terribly handsome!" I said, as he gave me one of his tight, paralyzing clinches.

Next to Martha and Charles stood a tall, dark, and handsome man in his mid-thirties. Charles introduced us by our first names. His name was Gyorgy. He had a charming smile and greeted me with a polite bow. I responded with a slight curtsy and, when I gave him my hand, he bent over with the ease of practiced custom, and brushed the air above my fingers with the warmth of his breath. His English was impeccable and he had a stylish intensity about him.

"He's the crown prince of Hungary," Martha whispered in my ear, while Charles introduced him to Susan, Sam, and the journalist.

"What a splendid Habsburg specimen," I murmured back.

Martha agreed with a flash of eyebrows and an appreciative nod.

"Young, too," she said with a giggle.

"Didn't he get married recently?" I asked quietly.

"Yeah! To some duchess. Remember? Charles gave them his plane for the honeymoon."

"Uh-oh, yes."

I remembered. It happened the previous autumn. Charles's generous gesture had irritated Martha no end because it meant that they then had to fly on a rented plane to some White House dinner. She had told me that Charles had lent his plane to a friend of his, some prince who was going to the islands on his honeymoon. Charles had told me a bit more about his friend Archduke Gyorgy von Habsburg of Austria-Hungary, prince imperial of Austria, prince royal of Hungary and Bohemia, grandson of Emperor Karl I, the last emperor of Austria and last king of Hungary. From Charles, I learned that Prince Gyorgy, the representative in Hungary for his father, Otto, the former pretender to the Austro-Hungarian throne, was not just some prince, but quite a special man. The prince was Hungary's ambassador for NATO integration, and, together with his German duchess wife, they were well-known personalities from Hungarian television. In fact, the very friendship between Prince Gyorgy and Charles was a symbol of emancipation, as it overrode the well-known anachronism of mutual dislike between "elephants" of aristocracy and nouveau riche "lions."

"So, what are we celebrating?" Sam asked, the jocular sparkle in his eyes intensified by the dark color of his elegant evening suit.

The hint of insinuation in Sam's voice must have raised Charles's suspicions, because his blue eyes turned a steely gray when he threw Martha a furtive look. Charles was probably concerned that she might have revealed his secret to Sam, but he kept his cool.

"It is just a party!" Charles said.

I began to worry that if their discussion did not stop, Charles might find out that Martha had told Sam his secret. To protect her, I hurried to change the subject. I barged into their conversation, slipping my left arm under Charles's, my right under Sam's, and, pulling them both close to me, I said with a greedy whisper, "I can't wait for the Louis XV praline!"

Everyone burst out laughing at my unrestrained gluttony.

"Laugh all you want! I promise you that he who eats chocolate last, laughs best."

Suddenly, the train stopped and the joyous sound of voices in the room was reduced to silence. Outside the window, lonely distant lights flickered in the night. We looked at each other inquisitively, maybe startled, but not alarmed, because this was May 1999 and there was no reason to panic.

"Murder on the *Orient Express*?" asked someone jokingly.

"It's the surprise," Charles said mysteriously.

The doors opened and I recognized Jean Pigozzi as soon as he began to emerge from the dark. With him walked the young and distinguished Prince Albert of Monaco, his step accompanied by the piano with arpeggios from "The Entrance of the Emperor and His Court." Charles invited the newly arrived guests to join our group.

One of Europe's beloved royals, Prince Albert, of the House of

Grimaldi, the family that has ruled the Principality of Monaco since 1297, is a humanitarian, progressive, and effective environmental "green prince." His American-accented English and open manner reminded one of his mother, the Hollywood icon Grace Kelly, who became a European princess when Prince Rainier III married her in 1956. Prince Albert greeted us with an open smile.

"Hello, again," he said when I was introduced to him.

I was a bit annoyed with myself for being so flattered that Prince Albert remembered having met me at a party the year before, where I was with my friends Skip and Edie Bronson.

Jean Pigozzi, known in his social circles as Johnny, was a dashing bachelor, a friend of European royals, high-society Americans, famous rock singers, and movie stars. He had an imposing presence—tall, with dark hair and an aquiline nose, deep brown eyes keen and penetrating but kind, a deep voice, and a smile as charismatic as his ever-ready wit. The gravity of his manner was combined with great brilliance and endearing charm. He greeted Martha, Susan, and me with friendly embraces, then Sam, Charles, and Prince Gyorgy with hearty handshakes.

Before long, Prince Albert was swept away from us by the graceful solicitude of seductive beauties with luminous smiles, slim bodies, and gleaming, scented shoulders. Shortly afterward, the music stopped and Alain Ducasse, the famous chef and essential star of the evening, walked in from the kitchen. He accepted our applause with modest gratitude and invited us to sit down and enjoy the dinner that he and his crew had especially prepared for our first sumptuous affair of "Fantasy Echo."

We accepted Johnny's gracious invitation to join him next day for lunch at his house in Cap d'Antibes, one of the paradisiacal spots on the French Riviera, then went looking for our assigned seats.

As Sam, Susan, the British journalist, and I were settling down at our table, the farthest away from the kitchen, I saw Martha and Charles walking toward us, while the famously trained Alain Ducasse restaurant staff, dressed in elegant couturier-tailored charcoal gray jackets and trousers, began their efficient, carefully choreographed service.

The tables were beautifully set according to French custom and table etiquette. The fork prongs were facing down, revealing the etched *Orient Express* coat-of-arms on the back. Delicate vases held fresh flowers at lower than eye level so diners could see one another across the table. The wines were poured to fill the glasses exactly one third: Bonneau du Martray Corton-Charlemagne, the prized white Burgundy, and a delicious red Pauillac, Château Mouton-Rothschild.

When Martha and Charles reached our table, she sat down facing the room, while he remained standing as he volleyed witty replies to our jokes and compliments. I was under the impression that he would sit with us next to Martha, but evidently they were splitting hosting duty that night, because soon thereafter Charles went to sit at the opposite end of the dining car with Johnny, Prince Albert, and Prince Gyorgy, and those ladies with the fab figures and shapely cleavage.

Sam was in good spirits. His gift for conversation galvanized all of us and the subjects ran from serious to very funny. The Monica Lewinsky scandal was the conversation icebreaker. Around the table, the jokes were dispersed with particular gusto.

"Give that woman, Ms. Lewinsky, a cigar!"

"Loose lips sink ships of state!"

The wineglasses were attentively refilled, there was animated conversation at every table, the sound of the piano in the background was soothing, the appetizer plates of "Thinly rolled fresh pasta with herbs, raw and cooked asparagus" disappeared, and elegantly presented delicacies of "Breton lobster cooked in a court-bouillon, served warm, with bitter and wild herbs, squid, small broad beans, coral sauce" were set in front of each guest. Tiny portions of cider-flavored, iced sorbet followed to refresh the palate before the main course. At our table, the exchanges on the Clinton-Lewinsky scandal continued.

"To be widz another woman, dzat is French. To be caught, dzat is

American." The line from the movie *Dirty Rotten Scoundrels* had us roaring with laughter.

I glanced over at Martha and noticed that she looked tense, far-away, and absorbed in thought. I knew that look on Martha's face. I could almost hear her brain-wheels turning as she watched Charles. At his vivacious table, the cabal of princes and handsome dashing men of the international jet-set were enjoying their dinner under the spell of beauties with a powerful arsenal of charms. When he looked back at Martha, Charles's imperturbable calm was devoid of any tension, his eyes revealed no more than that detached blankness of the supremely confident.

Sam, who, as usual, barely touched his meal, must surely have noticed Martha's sulking. I had known Sam for almost thirteen years by then, during which time we had mainly kept in touch through our intricate drama of mutual accommodations with Martha. Besides the chemistry of friendship, Martha and Sam shared the alchemy of money. Their latest experiment at turning the magician's rock into gold involved the multimillion-dollar takeover of an online cosmetics retailer, ibeauty.com, which Sam and Martha had told me a few things about.

Trying not to let Martha's funk ruin Charles's memorable dinner, Sam spiced up our conversation with friendly teases and stories.

"Monica Lewinsky is not getting enough credit."

"You must be kidding!"

"No. She helped bring notions like DNA and DNA testing into the popular culture."

"It was O. J. Simpson who did that."

"O. J. Simpson was the reminder that you must be careful when choosing whom you break bread with."

"That's harder to learn than the DNA."

The after-dinner champagne rosé had delicate bubbles that burst on my palate, thin and small, just the way Martha and I liked them. The spirits were high, and while everyone sipped champagne and savored chocolaty, crunchy, "Crispy Louis XV praline croustillant," its gold leaf melting on the tongue, I raised my champagne flute in Martha's direction to make a toast:

"Let's make it sparkle, Martha!"

She returned the toast with a forced smile. Clearly, something was wrong between her and Charles. But she said nothing that night.

The guests were starting to move around, mingling with that informality of lively musical chairs that marks the end of friendly parties. Many stopped by to greet Martha because wherever she was, people, regardless of their age, gender, or profession, invariably gravitated toward her. I loved to watch her connect with people, to see how, when she wanted to make herself accessible, she used all her charm and intelligence. Making his way through cheers and compliments, Charles came to offer Martha his arm and, together, they went visiting from table to table.

The next day, the "Fantasy Echo" guests joined Charles for lunch on the boat *Andale* in Monaco's famous port, while Martha and I, along with Sam and Susan, went to visit Johnny Pigozzi on Cap d'Antibes.

We passed through Antibes, the "luxury yacht capital of the world," on the way to the picturesque peninsula of Cap d'Antibes. Following the coast, we drove along the walls of the nineteenth-century fort. Martha insisted we make a stop at the famous Eden-Roc Hotel, whose opulence seemed shrouded in melancholy just before the beginning of the season. Then, guided by Martha's keen eye and great sense of direction, we navigated the narrow roads bordered by high walls that guard some of the world's most famously elegant seaside villas, and arrived at Johnny's magnificent place, a world of quintessential luxury and perfect harmony of place, architecture, and landscape.

The interior was bathed in light, which came in through generous windows over the sea. The sophisticated splendor, the suggestive modern art collection, and the elegant furnishings, all tastefully displayed, evoked so many emotions that I felt as if I were inside a "white telephone" villa of the Italian cinema.

We lunched on home-cooked traditional Provençale food on the seaside terrace under the shade of a giant fig tree. The fish was suc-culent, the vegetables fresh and hearty, and the olives had an inde-scribable sweet yet bitter taste. It felt as if the soothing breeze coming from the Mediterranean, where so much history still lies hidden on the bottom, bestowed upon us the blessing of those who had lived and loved there before: ancient mariners, fearsome pirates, Ligurian tribes, Greek colonizers, Roman protectors, barbarian invaders, French rulers, Russian émigrés, geniuses, artists, magnates, bohemians.

We spent the afternoon talking and sipping a fragrant local rosé wine while Johnny led the conversation away from customary banali-ties. Having been afforded exceptional opportunities, our jovial host appeared to have made the most of his personal experience. Johnny an-swered all of our questions and was a pleasure to listen to as he talked about the local vineyard that produced his delicious rosé, his short in-cursion into film acting, his esoteric collection of African masks, the bio-sustainable project he was developing in Panama, and his various business ventures. What struck me most about him was that he did not project a persona but seemed comfortable in his skin—a rational and intelligent man with a capacity for emotion, sensibility, and passion.

As I chatted with his lovely Scandinavian girlfriend, I saw that Martha had let down her guard. I remember wishing that she were like that more often. Smart and flirtatious, she talked business with the men, enjoying the attention lavished on her, as both Johnny and Sam were gifted with that rare flair of men who focus exclusively on the woman they are talking to for an entire conversation.

As far as I was concerned, we could have stayed there forever.

There was little time to prepare and get into the mood for Charles's next event, a "Soirée Grecque," that evening at the Villa Kerylos, the superb art nouveau copy of a classical Grecian villa. The invitation read, "Toga costumes will be provided at Villa."

The sun, the sea, the friendly afternoon, the high expectations for the fun toga party, had heightened my spirits. Such a mood deserved a heavenly perfume. I decided to splurge for Charles's "Soirée Grecque," and chose Amourage, a precious spicy Oriental made with silver frank-incense from trees growing in the Arabian mountains near the famed Incense Road, which dates back to the beginnings of antiquity's per-fume trade.

Never wanting my fragrance to enter a room before me, I followed my grandmother's perfume lesson, and dabbed sparingly so as to share my scent with those close to me, while people at arm's length would barely sense it. I put on a light dress made for easy slip-off, and was ready to go.

When I arrived at Villa Kerylos, Martha, who couldn't resist visiting its beautiful Mediterranean garden, insisted we walk first among the specimen trees and down the path leading to the point where one can view the sea around the cliff on which the villa stood.

Quite late for the party, we had to change into the last costume gowns left in the elegant ladies' changing room. The outfits featured a tight-fitting satin tunic that wrapped snugly around the body to form a calf-length tube gown with a long side slit, baring the shoulders and décolletage. The top edge of each satin gown was decorated with em-broidered ribbons. Satin shoulder straps, with small clasps at each end, secured the gown from sliding down. A loose-fitting tunic worn on top of the gown was modeled after the shape of an antique chiton, or *palla*. This part of the costume, sheer and sleeveless, was fastened to the straps of the satin tunic underneath it with button-like ornaments, sewn shoulder-high to replicate the fibulae, those jeweled brooches worn by ancient Greek ladies.

Martha took the gown made from peachy-pink colored silks, while I settled for the pale yellow one. It was a color that didn't love my skin tone, but I hoped its mossy-green, gauzy *palla* wrap would neutralize its unflattering cast. Our backs turned to each other as we dressed, I heard steps in the hallway coming toward us.

When the attractive blond woman came into the room, Martha was still fighting with the side closings of her gown. I recognized the in-truder as one of Charles's guests. She was barely in her thirties and quite stunning, her svelte body closely hugged by the slinky silk of her "Soirée Grecque" costume. Her sandals and hairdo were perfect for the occasion.

Without saying a word, she brazenly looked Martha straight in the eye. Watching the two women out of the corner of my eye, I noticed the startling duality of their appearance, their similar height, coloring, and cheekbones. But the differences in age, curves, and suppleness made Martha appear stout next to the tall blonde whose eyes seemed to say, *"I am younger than you, I am thinner tha · you, I am better than you."* Or perhaps I was thinking of the movie *Dirty Rotten Scoundrels*, which was filmed nearby.

Not quite knowing what to do, I took my cue from Martha, and we tacitly agreed to disregard the intruder's unfriendly pantomime, pretending to be exclusively absorbed in getting dressed.

The woman walked out of the room as abruptly as she came, leaving the door wide open behind her.

When she was out of sight, Martha said, "Enough fussing. Let's go!" She was clearly annoyed.

"Who's she?" I asked.

"Eh. Ohhh. Getting over some hot love affair . . ."

"Who's she here with?"

"Ask Charles. Are you ready? Let's go! We're late."

I couldn't blame Martha for being snappy, considering the unpleasantness she had just been exposed to, but I was surprised that she didn't tell me more. I was used to Martha being secretive about money, but not when it came to personal matters. Something was going on that Martha didn't want to tell me.

The click-clack of my heels on the mosaic floor barely keeping up with Martha's angry clomping, I followed her inside an elegant dining salon with frescoes and rare stone mosaics of famous Greek mythology scenes adorning the walls and floors, all lit by impressive bronze torches. Among Doric and Corinthian columns, cool gray-veined Carrara and sensual mauve Sienna marbles and rare fruitwoods, Charles and his guests, everyone in costume, were seated around large, circular tables.

Charles stood in polite welcome as we approached. The men at his table, dressed in white togas, all rose, waiting for Martha and me to be seated. I had known Charles for long enough to recognize a note of irritation in the forced gaiety of his laughter as he invited us to take the two empty chairs at his table, offering Martha the seat on his left, and me the one across the table from him, between Sam and a friend of Charles's from Seattle. Feeling guilty for having arrived so late—as Martha and I not only missed cocktails but we also kept everyone at the party waiting for dinner—I tried not to linger standing. The men at our table sat down as soon as Martha finished a graceful little speech.

Charles, in his Greek regalia, looked like an ancient portrait figure in a medallion, his short-cropped hair surmounted by a laurel wreath. The artfully folded toga was knotted on his right shoulder, draped across his chest, and fell over his back. Seated at his right was his longtime friend who had known him since he left Hungary at seventeen. Having kept in close touch for all those years, she had come from Denmark for his "Fantasy Echo." She teased him with amused familiarity and undisguised fondness. Seated at his left, and looking good in her ancient Greek outfit, Martha showed no such lighthearted, affectionate behavior toward Charles. She welcomed the newspapers touting Charles as her beau, and approved of social columns reporting their joint outings, but her connection with Charles seemed to lack the spark of passion. Their involvement appeared more like a pact between financially equal moguls, in which they were not a man and a woman, but trophies for power dinners and social occasions.

Within our view of the discreetly lit atrium, a live band played, inviting our mélange of draped bodies to dance under the stars around the lit water fountain at the center.

I noticed that Charles's eyes frequently traveled somewhere behind me. Curious to see what was drawing his attention, I took a discreet look over my shoulder and *Oh-la-la!* The statuesque blond woman who had confronted Martha in the changing room sat at a neighboring table, smiling saucily at Charles over the curve of her bare shoulder. Turning my gaze back in his direction, I saw Martha as her eyes glossed over the woman, then moved through Charles to the frescoes on the wall.

To break the mood, I turned to Charles and asked him to dance. We had danced together many times before. Martha did not much care for dancing, while my body moved by itself to the music. He smiled his boyish grin and, excusing himself to the ladies at his sides, started walking toward me just as the band began to play that longing tango from *Burnt by the Sun*, one of my favorite movies. Growing up, I knew that song as the *Suicide Tango*.

Charles was a great dance partner with a disciplined yet flexible step, whom I could trust to bring me back into the rhythm every time I strayed. As we were the first couple to start dancing, the ample mosaic floor and fresco masterpieces felt like our private ballroom for a while. Our lithe swaying freed and inspired by bittersweet lyrical chords, we stepped up the attitude, combining tango walks, slinging promenades, spins and pirouettes around the star-lit atrium. By the time we were rock-stepping in a double hand-hold tango, Charles was counting out loud a precise calculation of paces, which he sometimes did while dancing, and he appeared much more relaxed.

"Charles, did you invite all your past, present, and foreseeable girl-friends?" I chided him.

"Might not have been a good idea." He smiled wickedly.

"Smooth move, my friend." Although I felt terrible for Martha, who had to compete with women less than half her age, I gave Charles a peck on the cheek and joined in his laugher, because, in that setting, his answer was so reminiscent of the harem sequence in Fellini's movie 8 ½, depicting the idealized male fantasy of being absolute master over all the women he ever desired. It was a perfect setting for the "playboy of the scientific world," as Richard Dawkins once described Charles.

Soon, there were many couples tangoing under the stars. When the song ended, Charles thanked me for the dance with a polite kiss of the hand, then helped me back to the table, where Martha sat looking forlorn, weary, and not a bit amused.

I had barely sat down before Sam invited me to dance.

"Are you going to the after-party, on the boat?" he asked.

"No. I'd rather go to the hotel. I want to call the children back home."

"Then I'll make sure you get a taxi."

"Sam? How about Martha?"

"She'll be all right. Charles will see to it," he said, giving me a friendly squeeze and a kiss on the forehead.

We left the dance floor in the middle of the song and went back to the dining room, where many people were standing and talking loudly. The party was breaking up, and Martha was ready to call it a night. Charles urged me to take the costume-gown as a memento of the evening. I did.

The festivities continued the next evening. The "Fantasy Echo" gala on Saturday, May 15, was a black-tie event that began with cocktails in the garden of the opulent Monte Carlo Hôtel de Paris. We dined amid the splendid surroundings of the Salle Empire, under frescoed ceilings and walls with gilded stucco–framed medallions painted with sensual portraits of famous courtesans who had been lovers of Louis XV.

We sat at intimate round tables, adorned in starched fine white linens and signature Louis XV vermilion chargers. I was seated next to Charles, with Martha across the table from me. Susan and the attractive brunette British journalist were also at our table. Sam, who had business to attend to, had left already. We feasted on delicacies prepared for us, again, by Alain Ducasse, whose large crew of maître d's, sommeliers, and waiters bestowed upon us their impeccable service, with *amuse-bouches* in Murano crystal glasses and courses served under silver *cloches*, while the Cristofle silver, gold-plated china, and glassware were changed throughout the meal along with each serving of food and wine.

During dessert, which was served in customary Louis XV manner with blue silverware, blue candles, and blue dessert plates, Charles seemed slightly distant. I thought there could have been many reasons for him to be preoccupied, not the least of which was concern that his guests had a good time. For a number of us, dinner was followed by the notoriously racy *Crazy Horse* show at Le Cabaret du Casino, while the rest of the group was invited to a party organized on the *Andale*.

Giggling, Martha, Susan, the British journalist, and I climbed the stairs to Le Cabaret du Casino. Scanning the audience through the diffuse lighting, we saw Charles. Next to him, looking like a top model, was the gorgeous young blonde who had flirted with him at the toga party. With them was a group of Charles's friends, including Prince Gyorgy.

Looking straight at us, Charles made a show of ignoring the fact that he had not saved us seats. I could hardly believe Charles's master-of-the-universe attitude, his eyes focused on Martha's face like two large pools of intensely blue ice.

Their confrontation lasted for many long seconds before Martha turned to me, her eyes wide with exasperation. I threw Charles a *What are you thinking?* glare, angry with him for making her suffer the ignominy of being publicly traded in for a new model. Pretending to be cool, he calmly dismissed us, fixing his gaze on the boudoir-like stage.

As I expected, Martha was not about to turn tail and run in order to make Charles more comfortable. She began walking down the red-carpeted stairs toward the stage. Her entourage followed Martha in silence, and with each step we came nearer to the cabaret stage, in front of which a few tables were waiting for privileged guests.

Martha pulled out a chair for herself and gestured for us to join her. The auditorium lights began to dim, announcing the imminent emergence of half-draped performers who were sure to engage in uninhibited contortions and undulations. My anxiety up a notch, I paid no attention to the sotto voce conversation between Martha and the waiter, who was bent in a posture unusually ingratiating for a European member of staff serving at tables. When he departed, Martha told us that we were asked to leave our table, as it had been reserved for an important party. We gathered our shreds of dignity and rose to join Martha's shame parade, climbing back up the red-carpeted stairs.

Turned from spectator to spectacle, the only gesture I could manage was to put one foot in front of the other until, all the way in the back, we found some empty chairs. Fortunately, our spectacle was soon eclipsed by the *Crazy Horse* ensemble ready to put on their "Teasing in Monte Carlo" show.

From sumptuous burgundy velvet seats, we watched sex kittens who looked more than naked as they trotted their wares on the stage. Making sure no one saw me, I peered into the darkness at Charles, who sat a few rows in front of us, enjoying the show without Martha.

I felt terrible for my friend. In the two years I had known him, Charles had never given me reason to believe he was a cruel man. I wondered if his disrespectful attitude was part of a bigger contretemps with Martha, which, judging by her behavior, may have started before the evening on the *Orient Express*. Though she played it cool, I knew that Martha was seething. But I admired her. Not many women could have mustered that much sangfroid in the same situation.

My thoughts were interrupted by the waiter bringing our drinks along with the surprise addition of a bottle of Cristal Rosé. I asked Martha if she knew who ordered the champagne.

In her most matter-of-fact voice, she said, "I did. I asked him to give the bill to the gentleman over there," she said, pointing to Charles.

The queen is not dead! Long live the queen! I thought. I tried to delight in the rosy bubbles, but the fact that the heavenly liquid was procured as punitive measure took away some of the appeal.

I knew there was more than a remote possibility that Martha would even her score with Charles, and that she was already thinking up intricate ways to create the opportunity for revenge. Charles, apparently, knew it too. Although he seemed to be absorbed in the sensory world of velvet, silk, and flesh, I caught him stealing glances toward us a few times. As chess players say, "The threat is stronger than the execution." While neither Charles nor I could have known how Martha was going to retaliate, I was convinced that she would do her best to destroy the other woman, somehow using Charles's party, with thirty or more guests, to deploy her strategy and use them as mere pawns of her offensive.

When the show was over, the off-stage drama unfolded with Charles, Prince Gyorgy, and their companions unceremoniously abandoning us as they headed off to the next stop on their fun ride, Jimmy'z, the famously exclusive discothèque. Charles probably expected to shake off Martha that way, since few beside royalty and their friends could get into Jimmy'z, the "premier nightclub" in Monte Carlo, without booking reservations well in advance, especially during the week of the Formula One Race and the Cannes Film Festival.

Drained by all the embarrassment we had been subjected to, when Martha suggested that we go visit the casino we all agreed. It was a sensible choice, as Le Cabaret was inside the extraordinary baroque building of the Grand Casino, one of the oldest and most famous buildings on the Cote d'Azur. We followed Martha as she, chin held up high, looked straight ahead, leading us down corridors to the side door of the Casino de Paris.

"So, please tell me, Mrs. Gates, what would you like to see?" Confusing his Microsoft executives, the manager mistook Martha for Mrs. Bill Gates.

Susan, the British journalist, and I looked at each other in surprise, then at Martha, who straightened her back and smiled coyly. Cool as a cucumber, she did not correct him. Instead, with her poker face held a little higher than usual, Martha listed some rooms she wanted to see at the Casino. I immediately knew that Martha was plotting some scheme.

"This way, Mrs. Gates."

I felt my cheeks burning, but knew not what to do.

Martha ahead, the three of us quietly avoiding eye contact and walking as if there were Molotov cocktails beneath our feet, we continued

the embarrassing charade. I kept cringing in expectation that something terrible was going to happen any second. The anxiety became
exhausting.

We were shown through a succession of spectacular private gaming
rooms—European and English Roulette, Trente et Quarante, Chemin
de Fer, Black Jack, Craps. Walking amid stained-glass windows, paintings, sculptures, bronzes, period furniture, ornate mirrors, and amazing bouquets of flowers, we ambled through the casino's inner sanctum,
the stylish private gaming rooms populated by men in coats and ties
and women in evening gowns, some sitting down at the roulette wheel,
others standing.

Martha kept chatting with the manager in her sweetest, most engaging tone, but I never once looked at him, afraid that my face might
give us away. That's when I heard the manager say, "May I do anything
else for you, Mrs. Gates?"

"We want to go to Jimmy'z," she answered loud enough for all of us
to hear.

It wasn't long before a black Mercedes was summoned.

"Are you sure we should go?" I said.

Martha disregarded my interference, and walked toward the car,
her jaw squarely clenched. The manager himself drove "Mrs. Gates"
and her party to Jimmy'z, where soon thereafter "Mrs. Gates" and
her coconspirators were escorted through the entrance of the mood-
lit, über-kitsch confines of the famous discothèque. Martha stormed
in looking for Charles. Thankfully, we were not in the States, where
Martha would have been instantly recognized. The clientele on and
around the dance floor paid little attention to her.

Martha's hawk eye scanned the crowd and, there, lo and behold,
she found Charles, the blonde by his side. He watched our Trojan Army
advancing. Despite the semidarkness, I saw confusion flicker across his
face, and I could practically hear his brain trying to put *this* puzzle together. One expects people in Martha's position to throw money at a
problem, not themselves.

And then Martha was all over him. She roared in a sustained display of Martha wrath. Ready to take Martha's challenge, Charles stood up. Martha had succeeded in turning the argument into an athletic event—like she did with cooking. The confrontation was definitely now taking a turn from bad to disastrous.

Things were happening fast. While Martha and Charles were working at making each other infamous, Susan, the tireless watchdog who had forever guarded the publicity gates of Martha's empire, stood alert on the sidelines, scrutinizing the crowds for the camera that might turn yet another one of Martha's private matters into public record. Susan knew as well as I did how the perfect Emily Post etiquette and all the airs and graces instantly went out the window when Martha lost control—a well-guarded secret within her privileged world. But being close to Martha, I had been subjected to embarrassment, gaffe, and humiliation before. There was nothing that I knew could be done to help her when she got like that. Nothing, besides waiting for her rage to subside.

The British journalist, who had by then understandably abandoned the spectacle, was finishing Charles's drink, sighing with relief for having finally extricated herself from Martha's world of no boundaries. I located Prince Gyorgy in the crowd. The expression on his face was that of total amazement.

It occurred to me that if Martha and Charles's confrontation involved the police, then got into the press, I certainly had reason to worry about my family, since my livelihood depended on my reputation. I couldn't make a living if my most basic asset for someone in my business were to be negatively impacted because Martha involved me in some public scandal.

Martha and Charles, their chests nearly touching, screamed in each other's faces, their screeches underscored by the pulsing soundtrack. As Martha backed her body toward the door with slow, ungainly shifts through the noisy crowd, whenever she stepped back, Charles stepped forward, as though they were tied to each other by some invisible chain.

Unaware that he was being played by the master of obfuscation, Charles followed Martha farther and farther away from his prize. We all wound up outside the discothèque, where, with the arrogance of emperors and the desperation of lonely people, Martha and Charles let their guard down even more, standing on the curb near a lamppost, hurling invectives at each other. Susan and I stood back in horror. I think Susan had her hand over her mouth, slowly shaking her head. Charles might never have been in a bar brawl before, but he argued with abandon, his body bending toward Martha's. Her hands seemed to have a life of their own—powerful, aggressive. I can't be sure if she was hitting him or just gesticulating. Not that he did not deserve a little spanking. Martha's shrill was getting louder and louder. People were watching. Monegasque law enforcement agents could have appeared any minute, as they are famed to be quite strict. Suddenly I saw a woman rushing out of Jimmy'z, the breeze blowing through her evening gown as she ran down the front steps like Nike, the *Winged Victory of Samothrace*. It was Charles's beautiful blonde.

Caught in the crossfire between the two women, Charles took a step back, his head shaking with fury as he faced them.

"What on earth are they thinking?" I said.

Susan answered with a slow, dispirited shake of the head.

Finally, Charles threw up his arms and stormed back up the stairs to the invitation-only club, abandoning the two women at the driveway's grassy edge.

The young woman started to follow him, but Martha grabbed her shoulder and was talking to her, the two of them standing in the semicircle of the wide driveway, among the file of Mercedes taxicabs dropping off and picking up people in front of Jimmy'z.

Since we couldn't hear what they were saying, I was concerned that Martha might begin a new round of hostilities, but she relieved my apprehension when she waved at us.

"Come, come, let's go to the boat!" Martha's voice was strangely animated with a joyful urgency. "Everyone is waiting for us at the party!"

she called out excitedly. Walking among the cars, she cut in line, grabbed open the door of a moving taxi, and hurriedly helped Charles's other woman inside.

I thought the way Martha whisked that girl into the taxi was very similar to how she had rushed me out of that party when I met Jeremy Irons.

"Susan, go if you want. I'm Martha-ed out for the day," I said. "I need a break from friendly duty."

Before Susan had time to answer, Martha was already seated inside the taxi, waving us a quick *suit yourselves, good-bye* and closing the door as the car took off, losing itself in the fleet of black Mercedes sedans.

I would have loved to dance off the stress of the day, but I did not want to risk making Martha feel betrayed. So I decided to share a ride with Susan instead, and go back to the hotel. Before we parted, Susan said she was worried about having left Martha alone.

"I'm sure she'll be okay. They are nice people, Charles's friends," I said. "Anyway, Martha should have had her fill of arguments for today."

The next morning, my phone rang at seven. It was Martha.

"Are you up?" Her voice tingled falsely with put-on joy.

"Not yet. How are you?" I replied. "What did you end up doing last night? You left with that girl?"

"I told her that Charles would join us on the boat. They had a party arranged for those who didn't go to *Crazy Horse*."

"How was it? Did Charles come?"

"He waited at Jimmy'z for a while. Then came to the apartment. I wasn't there. He went looking everywhere. He got to the boat around five this morning," Martha said, then she urged me to bring my passport and come downstairs. When I did, she dangled a key in front of her face, a wicked look in her laughing eyes. What was this? The key to Charles's Ferrari, a car he loved so much he barely dared to drive it. As revenge for the previous night's insults, Martha suggested we take the car for a jaunt.

Martha's brazen plan to fizzle Charles's sizzle was, in a way, funny, yet the ploy seemed disrespectful. I regarded Charles as my friend. He had worked so hard to make himself what he had become. Illustrious degrees. High-pressure jobs. Diction lessons. French lessons. Dance lessons. I hoped he found someone who liked him for himself. Get married. Have children. Have a life.

I certainly understood Martha's feelings. Charles had been acting like a pasha, entertaining one harem favorite while expecting the other to stand by fanning him. I would have liked to support her, but the adventure she proposed, making me a party to absconding with his beloved car, was a bit extreme. Which didn't mean that I couldn't appreciate the brilliance of her strategy: once I got in that car, I would have become a partner in her mischief and compromised myself. I would have lost on two counts while Martha would have gotten the full benefit of revenge against Charles at the discounted price of only half of the responsibility, or maybe even less if somehow Charles was persuaded to think that it was my idea to take the car.

"Are you coming?" she asked, then pushed the seduction up a notch. "We could drive to Italy or go to France. They have open markets on Sundays."

My imagination and wanderlust were piqued at the thought of riding through picturesque scenery, peaceful villages, medieval hill towns. It sounded so wonderfully romantic, an absolute *Barefoot Contessa* movie fantasy. But the beautiful images running through my mind were interrupted by the realization that one unspoken part of Martha's plan was to keep up the intensity of pain she inflicted on Charles in order to allow him no time to regroup and think up some romantic escape, much like a boa constrictor that wraps itself around its prey and keeps tightening the grip of its coils until the victim ceases to struggle, at which point the boa unwinds and swallows it up.

For once I stood my ground.

"Sorry, Martha. I don't feel like it. Last night was very difficult. I haven't recovered yet."

Wanting no part of Martha's car scheme put me in a difficult position, because I couldn't very well refuse her and go watch the Grand Prix with Charles, as if nothing had gone awry. Under the circumstances, going to sip champagne on the yacht with Charles and enjoy the grand finale of that splendid trip would have meant compromising my friendship with Martha.

I felt completely out of my depth, but I didn't want their games to involve me. So I flew home early, the only way I could think of to make a graceful exit in a graceless situation and send Martha a message that I didn't want to be caught up in her intrigues.

Back in Connecticut, with the soothing sounds of the river, I thought how those quests for something out of the ordinary that I went on with Martha seemed always to bring me home, where I was happiest to be with my kids, who are, for me, both the extraordinary and the terra firma.

15

Martha Goes Public

BACK HOME, MARTHA and I never talked about what happened in Monaco. Martha's work pressures were so intense that I didn't want to burden her with my criticism. Then, too, we had reached a point in our relationship when it seemed impossible to discuss charged issues without doing damage. So the only thing I could do within the boundaries of friendship—at least friendship between two women who were on one hand so close and on the other so far apart—was to swallow my disappointment.

My ambivalence also sprang from the fact that only a month prior to Charles's trip to the French Riviera, there had been another incident when Martha's behavior did not quite fit her persona, when she appeared on Conan O'Brien's late night show, smiling at the cameras as she sipped on a forty-ounce bottle of Old English beer. I thought that appearance would do terrible damage to her image, but it turned out to have been a brilliant move on Martha's part, said to have solidified her popularity with millions of fans. Charles seemed to also understand that for Martha the end justified the means, because while he may have found himself conflicted in Monaco, he remained "with" Martha.

Martha and I still had some good times together. I could still bring out the silliness in her, such as when she mimicked me walking on stiletto heels, swaying her hips. That would crack us both up. When she was at ease, Martha laughed so beautifully—her voice pealing, her head thrown back—that no one could resist joining in. She did an American Express commercial that depicted her retiling a swimming pool with credit cards, showing everyone that she could take a joke. Lately, though, Martha seemed too preoccupied to laugh much. She maintained her grueling weekend schedule of flying to Maine or East Hampton, gardening, hiking, antiquing, yoga, and entertaining at breakfast, lunch, and dinner, but the fever of activity seemed less fun now.

In September 1999, in keeping with the "omnimedia" business model created by Sharon Patrick, Martha launched a new TV series, *From Martha's Kitchen*, a repackaging of cooking segments from her regular TV show, which aired on the Food Network. Martha's company had reported $763 million in retail sales for 1998, double its previous year's merchandising figures. But the biggest news had come in July 1999, when Martha Stewart Living Omnimedia filed plans for an initial public offering, which was eventually set for Tuesday, October 19.

The Saturday before the IPO, Martha and I were in California, at the Beverly Hills Hotel, celebrating the marriage of our friends Skip and Edie Bronson's son, Jon, to his lovely bride, Leslie, a wonderful young actress. I danced all night with my friend Richard Baskin, while Martha enjoyed the attention lavished on her by Los Angeles high society. I didn't know who most of the people were, so Martha kept a running commentary for me as they came and went from our table. "[He or she] is very rich," she'd say about the ones who were.

To my surprise, Martha seemed to be in good spirits. Usually, every time someone's child had a wedding, Martha was reminded that her own daughter, Alexis, had refused to have a big wedding. It was as if Martha's book *Weddings*, which had brought her so much money and public success, had taken away from her the very happiness that a wedding can bring in a mother's life. At Sam's daughter Elana's wedding in March the previous year—a happy, weekend-long, luxurious dance-filled party at the Four Seasons on the exclusive Island of Nevis, where Charles had flown Martha and me in his plane—Martha had been in a deep funk. I figured that the IPO cheered Martha up enough to smooth over any pain she might be feeling.

After Jon and Leslie's elegant black-tie wedding dinner, we went back to our rooms at the Beverly Hills Hotel. I woke up to the telltale shaking and swaying of an earthquake in the wee hours of the night. Immediately, my phone rang. It was Martha. It seems the seismic tremor might have affected the best-view rooms more than the rest of the hotel, because she had been thrown out of bed. Our sleep was over for the night, but we had to get up early that Sunday morning anyway, because Martha had a chartered plane flying us back home.

We had spent the previous weekend at Skylands. Before leaving Maine, Kevin Burger, a solidly reliable man whom I had known and liked for years, a talented painter whose rose-hued landscape done in his signature pointillist-like manner was so good that Martha had it hung in full view in the Skylands' elegant parlor, and who, in his everyday life, worked for Martha's company, joined us for a scenic drive on Mount Desert Island. When we were heading back to Skylands at sunset, Martha received a call on her cell. She had never been one to begin a phone conversation with a greeting like most people do, so Martha didn't say her caller's name, but I saw her face fall as she said some number in the thousands, then she asked: "Why so many?" After she hung up, she drove in silence for a few minutes, while her eyes flashed that calculating *zunz-zunz-zunz* I was so familiar with. Then she glanced at me in the passenger seat for a brief second, and turning her gaze back to the road, she said there was still a bundle of unsubscribed Martha Stewart Living Omnimedia stock available for purchase. "Would you like to buy some at $18 a share?"

I hesitated. Martha had previously offered me friends and family stock options, for which I had filled out a pile of paperwork with Peter

Bacanovic, Martha's broker at Merrill Lynch, and which I could only exercise in prescribed increments over four years, and no more than 10 percent on the day of the IPO. I had regarded those shares as compensation for the commissions I'd spared Martha on both the Skylands purchase and the sale of the Turkey Hill Easter Field, the proceeds of which she used to make the down payment for Skylands. Martha had discussed the IPO in my presence, and I had heard her talk with other people about their purchasing her stock, so although I had paid little attention to those conversations, I picked up enough to understand that this transaction was a different matter, but I didn't know in what way.

I wasn't sure whether to accept, given that Martha seemed to be making this offer only as a result of that phone call, which had clearly distressed her. But when I heard Kevin, from the back seat, commit to buying a large number of shares, I decided to take the leap, convinced that someone as wise as he would only do so if it were a good thing. I signed on to buy more than $100,000 worth of Martha's stock, knowing that I'd have to borrow most of the money and that I didn't have the information I needed before consenting. But it seemed like a surefire opportunity. I was certain that with Martha and Sharon's leadership, Martha Stewart Living Omnimedia would succeed and the dividends would help ensure my children's future.

I spent the next week figuring out how to come up with that huge sum of money before the October 19 opening bell, but I didn't get the chance to contact any of the people I trusted who might have enlightened me about the pros and cons of purchasing before-IPO stock and who also would have understood both my ignorance and the fact that I was worried that if I later wanted or had to sell Martha's stock it would be disloyal. So when Martha rang me to say she needed company in New York the evening before the IPO, as she had been in meeting after meeting all day and still had a dinner meeting with a team of lawyers and bankers about the next day's big event yet to come, I decided I would ask her then what I should do.

Will Rogers once said, "Everybody is ignorant, only on different subjects." Just as I had conveyed to Martha my professional expertise on how to structure a winning real estate offer, and volunteered my negotiating skills for her to get Skylands, I figured it was only fair that she would explain to me how to make money from purchasing IPO stock, since she had been one of the first women stockbrokers on Wall Street and had a successful career working for the prestigious firm of Perlberg, Monness, Williams and Sidel. I expected her to reciprocate out of simple friendship but, if that were not enough, I thought she would remember that on the financial favor scale, I was ahead: while the friends and family stock options might have, over the course of four years, offset the commissions I'd spared her on her real estate deals, I had also saved her a few hundred thousand beyond that when I negotiated the purchase price for Skylands.

Anticipating an evening of glamorous late parties in New York, I rushed to prepare the children's dinner, got dressed and made up, and drove to the train station for the hour and ten minute trip to Grand Central Station. When I arrived at the restaurant where Martha had asked me to meet her, I found her presiding over a large private table in the back. She had an extra chair for me placed between her and a man I knew to be a big honcho in the investment world.

My presence at the table produced a long, silent pause. Sharon, who sat across from me, said nothing and the bankers smiled politely while Martha made introductions. But when Martha said, "Mariana's all right," the discussion resumed.

For me, a business meeting of this sort was tantamount to traveling to an exotic culture where the mores and the language are completely alien to my experience. I was there but I could not comprehend what was going on. They spoke bankerese and legalese—it may have just as well been the final rehearsal to deploying a space shuttle mission. I didn't understand how it all worked, and I didn't care. Martha knew that I didn't want to spend my evenings with people who talked about banking. That kind of talk bored me to such a degree that I would have rather been filing records, something I never liked doing. Consequently, since Martha didn't get up to leave with me as she had said she would, I realized this was the reason she'd invited me—she wanted me at this table to get my take on everyone there, as she had done many times in the past. And indeed, when we eventually left, Martha asked in detail what I thought of each person at the table. I told her which voice and which eyebrow had done what, and at what point in the conversation.

But when I said, "Martha, I got the money for the stock. But how does one make money on an IPO?" she answered, "Ask Peter. I can't stand talking about this anymore."

It was about nine or ten o'clock in the evening. I had already spoken with Peter Bacanovic, who had called me to confirm the stock purchase I had agreed to with Martha, the previous Sunday. Although I had met Peter on occasion when socializing in Martha's circles, and liked him very much, I didn't ask him any questions. First of all, my purchase was very small compared to what I knew he was handling for Martha. One evening she had called Peter while I was in the car with her. After they hung up, I commented on how hardworking he was, and Martha said, "He better be. I gave him $10 million of my stock. He's making a lot of money." I also didn't know if it was proper for me to ask Peter about profiting from selling Martha's shares, in case there was a conflict with his obligations to Martha. I didn't want to put him in an uncomfortable position. I had thought it best to ask Martha directly, as she had to know what was right or wrong, since she also was in control of 96 percent of the MSLO voting shares.

Oh, well, I thought. *I was wrong to think I shouldn't ask anyone else but Martha.* Yet, she was going through a stressful time, and it was okay if that evening was about Martha and her needs alone. Convinced I'd somehow figure it all out, I put the stock questions out of my mind and took up my role as Martha's companion at a fun party where someone from her glamorous circle was being fêted.

We were soon in the Suburban heading back to Connecticut, Martha asleep on the back seat. Larry, her driver, suggested we drop Martha off at Turkey Hill first, and then go back to the train station where I had left my car. They usually took me there first, since it was on the way to Martha's, but that evening Larry and I wanted to give her a chance to catch an extra few minutes of sleep, as she had to get up very early the next morning.

Martha invited me to attend the IPO ceremony. She had her staff set up an attractive tent outside the New York Stock Exchange, where a whole crowd of traders and well-wishers gathered for fresh-squeezed orange juice and pastries. Looking radiant in her light blue suit, Martha passed around a tray of brioches for a true Proustian memory of this event. Spirits were very high. At the sound of the bell, Martha's company went public under the ticker symbol MSO on NYSE's big board. The initial public offering of 7.2 million shares, which represented 14 percent of total outstanding shares, was set at $18 per share, and it kept going up at a vertiginous rate. From the tight ranks of the crowd, I watched Martha and Sharon standing high up on the podium, where dignified NYSE executives framed the image of the first two women to start a company and take it public. They were both squealing with delight at their unprecedented victory. I had tears of joy in my eyes witnessing my friend achieve what I thought was the greatest of her desires. It was like seeing my children receive awards. I thought that Martha was now free of her need to kill herself striving for more, that content with her rise to the height of riches and fame, she would start looking at life as I did, that she'd begin living instead of just doing.

Martha asked me to join her at a few of the parties given in her honor. Everywhere we went, she entered beaming like a little girl: "I am rich! I am rich," she kept saying. "It feels great." "It's a good thing." "Isn't it nice?"

Afterward we went to her office, where champagne flowed and delicious hors d'oeuvres adorned the beautifully set tables, mostly untouched. The stock had already soared to $52, which made Martha euphoric.

I was thrilled for her, but flummoxed when I went to wash my hands and found the bathroom full of women placing orders to sell their stock.

How could they? I wondered. How could women I'd considered friends for years prove so unfaithful to Martha? That's how naive I was.

I didn't want to dispel Martha's joy by tattling on those "disloyal" women, so I kept my peace as I followed her from one celebration to the next. The finale was a lavish dinner at Le Cirque. On the way to the restaurant, I climbed into the front seat of Martha's Suburban next to Larry so she could lie down in the back. She was exhausted from all the excitement.

"Did you sell your stock?" she asked.

"I didn't," I answered, a bit offended by her question. Didn't she know I was trustworthy, too loyal a friend to risk diluting the value of her stock by selling it like those women in the bathroom?

"I sold mine," I thought I heard her say as she yawned. "I made a lot of money today." Shortly, she was asleep.

On that day, Martha's company was said to have a market value of $1.7 billion, and Martha had become mega-rich, her personal fortune estimated to be $1.2 billion. While Martha took one of her invigorating catnaps, I gave it some thought and realized that everyone who bought low, then sold high on the day a company went public, making a tidy profit, could then later repurchase the stock at a reduced price. It was the capitalist game, which had nothing to do with fidelity and loyalty.

I felt idiotic for not understanding what I was supposed to do, and, even worse, my ignorance had cost me a lot of money. Martha knew I needed money. She gave me the chance to make a killing on her stocks, but she was well aware that I had no idea how to do so.

As she had to be up very early the next day for numerous interviews, many of which would include tough questions like the ones from those analysts who kept talking about Martha's company being overly dependent on one person, Martha was staying at her Fifth Avenue pied-à-terre that night. She invited me to stay with her in the airy, high-ceilinged apartment that she had transformed, since she bought it in 1988, into a true masterpiece, with elements of 1940s modernist style. As seductive as the idea of waking up in Martha's fabulous place was, taking in the views of Central Park and sharing a morning latte at her Cuban pedestal dining table, I declined the offer. I agreed to my daughters' taking the school bus once in a while, because they wanted it so, but I cherished the time in the car with my girls in the morning when I drove them to school. Soon it would no longer be possible, as Monica was about to turn sixteen.

The hour spent in the car as Larry drove me home gave me time to reflect on the events of that day. I started to think that Martha's caring for me might be an illusion. But perhaps I was being unfair. I could still sell my shares the next day, since the price was quite a bit higher than what I had paid initially. From what they said on the news, Martha's stock had ended the first trading day at $38 or $35 per share. But I decided I shouldn't sell; even though Martha didn't want to advise me, I wasn't going to behave badly and then feel guilty for being disloyal. At any rate, I trusted my investment, thinking her stock could only go higher.

My feelings were truly hurt when, a couple of weeks later, Martha told me how disappointed she was that my ex-husband had sent her only one bottle of champagne, not even a Cristal Rosé or Dom Pérignon, after he made a pile of money on her IPO. That Martha thought it was okay to keep in touch with him behind my back while she had insisted that I erase Andy from my life was upsetting enough, but what annoyed me most was that he had made money and I had not. I knew he watched his investments like a hawk.

I figured out that on that Sunday evening after we got back from Maine, after Martha and I had shared the delicious Chinese fare prepared by Lily, the wonderful lady who took care of Sam during the week and of Martha and her menagerie at Turkey Hill on weekends, and after I had left to go home, Martha had probably gone through her phone book to sell her not-yet subscribed shares. And that's how it was that "at the last minute," as she had put it, she called him. So I focused on the fact that Martha was not only racing to sell her shares but doing so in competition with other companies whose IPOs were set for that same day: the Indian Internet service provider Satyam Infoway Ltd. and World Wrestling Federation Entertainment.

THE HOLIDAYS THAT year confirmed how much Martha and I were growing apart, but I wasn't yet ready to see it. As we were not taking a trip overseas, and my children were to spend New Year with their father, our plan for the last day of 1999 was to go trekking to the top of Cadillac Mountain in Acadia National Park, the easternmost point in America. At 1,532 feet above sea level, the highest point on the Atlantic Coast, its summit receives the sun's first light as it rises over the United States. We were going to start the year 2000 watching the new millennium's first rays of sunshine. As December approached and the reality of icy, steep, treacherous terrain sunk in, our plans began to change. Eventually, Martha proposed that we book a relaxing stay at the Golden Door Spa in California, where she would have us fly in her leased plane. But from the moment we checked in, I felt uncomfortable. Not only were we immersed in what felt to me like a sea of vain, unapologetically hedonistic pampering but also it was a women-only week, which, regardless of how much I liked many of the guests, gave me the chills. I felt like I had been plunged into the terror of Margaret Atwood's *The Handmaid's Tale*. The idea of ushering in the new millennium with my only company women on diets didn't work for me.

I told Martha I was going to leave, and she decided to go home too. I don't remember what Martha did, but I spent New Year's Eve with my friends Angela and David and their friends in Westport. At midnight, we went outside and, under the starry sky, alive with fireworks, we said our prayers, made our wishes, laughed, and teased each other until the cold chased us back inside.

It was the first New Year's Eve in a long time that I hadn't spent with Martha. Somehow I survived.

16

The Queen on Her Throne

THE IPO BROUGHT Martha, who owned 34.1 million shares in her company, more than $1 billion overnight. In 2000, Martha Stewart Living Omnimedia reported profits in excess of $21 million with annual sales of over $285 million. That year, Martha's television show earned its fourth Daytime Emmy Award; it was by now a daily show syndicated nationally through King World Productions, the same company that distributed *Oprah*. The hourlong program aired five days a week plus an additional half-hour edition on the weekends. Martha reached millions of American households through the monthly *Martha Stewart Living Magazine*, the quarterly *Martha Stewart Weddings*, special interest magazines like *Entertaining* and *Martha Stewart Baby*, as well as her company Web site, Marthastewart.com, which would launch on September 8. *Vanity Fair*'s list of the top fifty leaders of the Information Age ranked Martha in the forty-second position, and she was named for the fourth time to *Fortune* magazine's "50 Most Powerful Women" list. 2000 was also a very good year for my business, as I earned high six figures in real estate commissions.

And the year brought another whirl of extravagant parties and travels. Martha and I crisscrossed the country on Charles's plane or in Martha's leased corporate jet. We went to Chicago so Martha could appear on *Oprah* with her mother, Big Martha, as we called her. We met Oprah Winfrey and her crew behind the stage, where everyone seemed in a good mood. I couldn't imagine Oprah angry and screaming at them, the way I saw Martha yell at people who worked for her, shrieking "Don't give me that shit!" I traveled with Martha and her crew to North Carolina when they filmed a segment on deep-frying turkey at the amazing Frank Lloyd Wright estate owned by one of Martha's Hollywood friends, and went there again, as her guest, when she was invited to spend Thanksgiving. At least once a month, I flew with Martha to East Hampton and shared fun-filled weekends at Lily Pond, where my daughters often joined us.

Monica and Lara were exposed to some very well-known personalities in the arts and business. I particularly remember the weekend Eric Fischl, the contemporary realist painter and sculptor, and his wife, April, came to Lily Pond for lunch. Martha and I were both excited to spend time with the talented and handsome artist, but, not wanting to make Monica and Lara nervous, we didn't tell them that Eric Fischl had often been compared to Degas, and we certainly said nothing to the girls about his paintings being known for giving the viewer an awkward feeling of embarrassment, as if catching oneself in a voyeuristic-like experience.

We set the table outside on the covered porch, and indulged in a wonderful, Martha-made meal, sipping delicious "perfect margaritas," frothy as only she knew how to make them. Eric Fischl seemed very much at ease among mature female admirers as well as polite but indifferent teenagers. He took the conversation wherever he wanted, and was actually quite funny. And there were many such occasions. My girls had a world open to them that would contribute to their education in all kinds of ways that were valuable and special, even as awkward teenagers. Plus, life with Martha was fun. Martha was always ready for an adventure. One day, she suggested we take the girls and sail her brand-new small sailboat out on Georgica Pond. We managed to get stuck in the silt and had to carry the sailboat back to Bunshaft's sliver of sandy beach, with Martha and me pulling it as we walked in chest-high water along the shore and my girls pushing it as they swam behind it. The hardest part was keeping a straight course because we were laughing so hard.

On April 9, 2000, the girls and I went with Martha to see her nephew Christopher in the role of Figaro in the Yale College Opera's production of *The Marriage of Figaro*. Besides having taken those amazing adventure trips together, Chris and my daughters had also shared musical experiences. An accomplished musician, he had been Lara's first viola tutor, and had encouraged both her and Monica, who played the violin, to audition for the rigorous Norwalk Children Symphony Orchestra, where the girls played for a few years. But that opera performance was the first time we heard Chris's beautiful baritone voice.

The evening was doubly fun because we had some news to share with Chris. He had suggested that Monica apply to the American Academy of Achievement and she had just received her letter of admission, which made her one of the 450 high school honor students from around the country selected to participate in the thirty-ninth annual Salute to Excellence program that was to take place in Scottsdale, Arizona.

On June 15, Charles flew Martha, Monica, and me to Phoenix. We all stayed at the Phoenician and in a way it was like a family reunion, because Charles, chief architect at Microsoft, was to receive the American Academy of Achievement Golden Plate Science Award for his accomplishments as a "computer software pioneer."

During the four days of the event, Monica had the chance to meet many exceptional people, some students her age, others prominent American professionals like Brendan V. Sullivan Jr., the attorney who defended Oliver North during the Iran Contra hearings; award-winning composer John Williams, whose work includes the soundtracks of *Star Wars*, *Raiders of the Lost Ark*, and *Schindler's List*; and Dale Chihuly, the famous glass artist. My daughter had the honor of speaking with Colonel Eileen Collins, USAF space shuttle commander of mission STS-93, which had deployed the Chandra X-ray Observatory. In their conversation, Monica learned that Collins, the first woman to pilot a space shuttle, always took with her on space flights a scarf that belonged to Amelia Earhart.

If Monica had any doubt about the profession she had wanted to pursue since childhood, after the lectures and discussions with Dr. Baruch Blumberg, a Nobel Prize–winner in Medicine, and Dr. Bernadine Healy, the president of American Red Cross, my daughter was certain now she wanted to become a doctor.

As parents don't normally get to be with their children during the program, I was extremely grateful to Martha and Charles for having invited me. Monica and I ran together from one seminar to another like two little girls.

Shortly before this trip, we had gone to Washington, DC, where Monica, who had been selected as state representative for Connecticut, received a national medal from the Prudential Spirit of Community Awards program to honor her achievements in youth volunteering. The year before, Monica and Lara's work with Save the Children had garnered them a presidential award from the White House, and during that earlier trip we had visited the Vietnam Veterans Memorial, so it was extraordinary to have the opportunity to meet the architect of the monument, Maya Lin, at the American Academy of Achievement, where her artistic talent was being recognized with a prestigious award for her contribution to arts.

I was convinced that my daughters had learned their poise in front of microphones and cameras from Martha, from being filmed with her in so many segments, including the recent "Take Your Daughters to Work" or the fun one on homemade doughnuts. Because the work Monica and Lara did with Save the Children often involved participating in public discussions, hosting social events and functions, distributing and receiving awards, and being interviewed by journalists, the early media exposure Martha had given them had been invaluable.

My daughters liked doing things with Martha. She called them "beautiest" and "my pet," and when they went to Skylands, the girls kayaked with her on Somes Pond or joined her for afternoon private Iyengar yoga lessons, practicing Downward Facing Dog and other postures with Roseanna, the most patient and thorough instructor. Martha had transformed the lower-level "pub" room at Skylands into a home theater and bistro-like area that doubled as a yoga room when the yoga mats and blocks came out of the elegant storage bin with the belts and bolstering blankets Martha liked to use as knee support.

They took hikes along spectacular trails in the Acadia National Park through majestic woodlands and along the shores of crystalline lakes and the rugged seacoast. The girls liked going with Martha up Jordan Pond Shore Trail, a moderately difficult hike that often included a rewarding stop for some famously delicious popovers at Jordon Pond House. But sometimes hiking the pristine Acadia trails with Martha could get adventuresome, and just in case she decided to climb her favorite, Beehive, I wanted to be there with my kids. Less than a mile long, the trail was fun to hike but quite strenuous, and the iron rungs up the steep, exposed ledges were rather far apart in places. I had joined Martha more than once when she took executives applying for positions with her company to the Beehive, proposing it to them as a great hike. By the time we'd get to the boggy descent, the hike would become more of an endurance test, their breath growing short with the exertion and their designer polo shirts becoming sodden with sweat as they answered Martha's interview-like questions.

Martha and I had even followed our outdoors enthusiasm on a wilderness adventure organized by Torie, the house manager at Skylands. We climbed the rugged, steep inclines of the most abrupt and northerly of the Appalachians, Katahdin, the highest mountain in Maine, immortalized by Henry David Thoreau in *The Maine Woods*. Camping in a simple, rustic cottage in the scenic wildlife sanctuary at Baxter State

Park, our small group went canoeing on pristine lakes and climbed sparingly marked rocky trails among large boulders, some of them as big as a house. Careful to avoid sprained ankles and broken legs, feeling our way through the cracks and crevices, we sometimes had to slide down on our butts to keep from falling off the edge of a boulder following Clare, the most experienced climber in our group. I had known Clare and her husband Allan Stone, a well-respected art dealer, for years. Kind and unassuming, Allan was a charming storyteller and a wonderfully unpretentious, amazingly modest man who adored his wife and daughters. A delightful couple, Allan and Clare were the type of people you'd expect to meet with Martha, who hated routine. They had a remarkable array of interests and an extravagant way of displaying their collections of all kinds of art—abstract, tribal, folk—all over the large expanses of their living spaces in Connecticut and in Maine.

Even with all the excitement already in her life, Martha was always coming up with new undertakings for herself and the people around her. Laughing at those who struggled to keep up, she maintained a game-like atmosphere while making everyone yield to her wishes. Each challenge she survived seemed to feed her hunger for something still more demanding, and further from what I was comfortable with. Her cravings often struck out of the blue, like the life-risking horseback ride in Peru or the folly in Monaco.

One lovely summer morning, when we were at Skylands with Memrie, Charles, and a few other friends of Martha's, Torie, the wonderfully knowledgeable woman who had worked for the mansion's previous owners, "the Leedeses," as Martha referred to them, served us a delicious breakfast. We chatted, comfortable in the Ford family's seventeenth-century Italian chairs arranged around the long antique dining room table set with Mrs. Ford's American sterling flatware and her Copenhagen porcelain set decorated with hand-painted irises, roses, and carnations. Martha had acquired numerous tableware treasures along with the property. The butler's pantry, which had been designed and fitted to be suitable for splendid entertaining, included felt-lined drawers filled with tasteful silverware, like the Tiffany set, and a storage closet where a plethora of finest vintage tablecloths and exquisite runners were hung on removable wooden dowels, while divided drawers held sets of starched napkins and table linens.

We delighted in the fresh breeze that blew in through open windows, fragrant with pine and sea, sipping perfectly foamed cappuccinos and freshly squeezed citrus juice, wolfing down just-made wild blueberry waffles and bowls of fragrant fruits.

"Dheelicious," Martha said with the charming inflection she always used when pronouncing that word.

Presiding over the table from her favorite seat at the fireplace end, which afforded a full view of the dining room, the property outside and the ocean beyond, Martha told us how lucky we were that we would be able that day to go up the Precipice, a trail often closed from spring through mid-August to protect endangered peregrine falcons.

I had no idea that the Precipice was considered the most challenging trail in Acadia National Park, and I doubt that any of Martha's guests knew, but about an hour later I am sure we all wished someone had warned us. We grappled with slippery iron rungs, climbed unsteadily up steep ladders, and clutched at flimsy tree trunks as we tried to keep our footing, the sweat pouring off our brows, Martha cajoling, *Come on!* perched as we were on the protruding rim of a vertical cliff.

As we advanced, hugging the smooth surface of the sheer rock face, someone's small scream echoed down into the gorge hundreds of feet beneath. Memrie began crying quietly. I guessed that the nauseating fear of heights had lodged itself in the pit of her stomach as deeply as it had in mine. Martha rolled her eyes, but said nothing. Charles, who showed no sign of panic, led us along the narrow ledge. In the end, the view was spectacular at the top, but we never went back to the Precipice. And we never confronted Martha about her recklessness. Only too late did I learn the cost of this silence.

∙ ∙ ∙

MARTHA HAD A very particular vision for Skylands. In a *Vanity Fair* profile, she told a wonderful tale about the Romanovs' hundreds of estates, including one that no one in the royal family had visited for 110 years. "Then this one prince finally decides, 'I will visit that one,' and he gets in his coach and spends weeks traveling up to the place and there's no way to communicate, because it's 1900 or something. And when, after the grueling journey, the prince finally arrives, all the candles are lit, the beds are made, and dinner is ready. The servants have been waiting for 110 years for a tsarevich to show up, and every night—they have enough money to do this—they prepare just in case the Romanovs come. And one shows up! That's how I want [Skylands] to be."

Skylands, a 20,000-square-foot mansion, came with so many accoutrements that Martha immersed herself in acquiring the skills for living like American nobility. Even the laundry room at Skylands was a far cry from the crowded, painted-cement-floor basement at Turkey Hill, where Martha's clothes were cleaned and her contingent of Himalayan cats got washed. The laundry room the Fords had built for their staff was in the basement but the similarities ended there: it was immense and outfitted on three sides with windows affording gorgeous views of the property. There were finished floors, tiled walls, four deep white porcelain sinks for hand-washing, drying racks, built-in ironing boards fitted at various levels to accommodate the different heights of the laundresses, and a linen room the size of a galley kitchen, also with a window and fitted with drawers, cupboards, and a drop-down folding table. Martha added multiple sets of washers and dryers.

Every aspect of Skylands' ownership showed that Martha had arrived. And among the ones to be faced with it first were the Skylands staff who had previously worked for Mr. and Mrs. Leedes. When they sold the property to Martha, I believe that they had accepted the low bid because she had agreed to their request that she keep on the people working at Skylands, and at the same salaries, bonuses, and increases that the previous owners had paid them.

After Martha took ownership, it became evident what a gift it was having Torie manage the house, Peggy and Gretchen as house caretakers, and Bruce as property manager, each one knowledgeable of how everything worked and excellent at their jobs. There was also Greg, an expert at landscape and outdoor maintenance, and Kevin, who knew all about trees and whose grandfather had worked for Edsel Ford. He shared pictures and stories from the time when the property was being built.

Capable, trustworthy, dignified, and well-mannered, the Skylands staff, who over the years had become accustomed to that lifestyle, began introducing Martha to it. Perhaps it was because she was enthralled by all those details that Martha decided to reclaim the use of Skylands' staff quarters, an area reserved for the people who worked in such mansions. She began referring to the staff rooms off the kitchen as the "servery," which implied a lowly status for how the staff dining room, sitting room, and office had traditionally been used. When Martha completed her redesign, they were no longer the Skylands staff quarters. But she made excellent use of the space for her own purposes.

The staff dining room walls were beautifully covered in a paper with faux-bois motif and then became Martha's "map room." She had started collecting area maps—many of them antique, vintage, and rare—which were piled in an organized fashion on a large table that also held guide books. After some trial and error, she found that she liked the maps displayed in cherry veneer frames, under glass, with acid-free matting and lined up at the base above the chair-rail cherry wood paneling. Later, a pair of parson's benches were placed along the walls, offering perfect seating for putting on and taking off shoes, which earned that space another title, "the pre-hiking room." The built-in mid-1920s refrigeration unit, which had been used exclusively by the staff, was reassigned mostly for storing bottled water and soft drinks that Martha thoughtfully shared with her guests.

The expropriated staff sitting room was transformed into a multi-desk office space, with state-of-the-art computers, various electronics, office equipment, and storage. It became the "communications/control room," allowing Martha to do both.

The upstairs help-wing was transformed into quaint guest quarters. Originally finished with ship-like wood paneling, the area lent itself nicely to a nautical themed décor, and incorporating mission furniture and arts-and-crafts style elements, Martha, who, unlike the Fords, had no staff living at Skylands, gained four or five extra guest bedrooms all sharing a spacious hall bath.

MR. AND MRS. Leedes had given Martha all of the Skylands architectural drawings, including the original plans done for Edsel Ford by Jens Jensen, the details of what had been completed, and what still needed doing. Martha went to work. She replaced yellow marigolds and red and blue geraniums on the great terrace borders with mosses, ferns, and succulents. She kept the kiwi vines that climbed the pink granite façade on the main terrace side, adhering to a schedule of drastic pruning after the ripe fruits were harvested and the leaves, which turned golden in the autumn, had begun to fall.

Near the entrance to what used to be the staff quarters was an area where Edsel Ford had begun Jensen's project for building a Councils Circle, designed as a continuous circular bench made of thick slabs of granite surrounding a fire pit built from a big chunk of pink granite with a foot-wide rim. I went with Martha to the quarry to pick the right pink-speckled gray monoliths to cap the benches so people could gather for campfires. Her chows especially liked it there.

To finish off the side of Skylands' back entrance, Martha also ordered the stone artist to make granite containers in which she planted mosses and succulents, although I don't remember if those were on Jensen's plans.

One beautiful element in Jensen's drawings was a reflecting pool set not far from the Councils Circle and fed by natural underground springs. When Martha bought Skylands, the pool was almost dry. That turned out to be lucky for Sharon's bulldog, Norman. One night she and I took him out for a walk and Norman fell into the reflecting pool with a yelp. Sharon jumped in after him. As I lit match after match in an effort to illuminate the darkness, Sharon found Norman, his nose peeking above the foot-or-so of dead water. Soon thereafter, Martha restored the reflecting pool and the fountain, which were beautiful to look at from the Councils Circle as well as through the diamond-shaped, leaded-glass panes of the dining room windows.

The area near the reflecting pool had been home to the Leedes grandchildren's swings, but Martha took those out and designed a shade garden there, planted with many varieties of ferns and mosses and accented by cool-blue Himalayan poppies.

In honor of her restoration, Martha set three rows of long tables and many chairs on the pebbles of the back driveway, off of what used to be the entrance to the staff quarters, and invited Mount Desert summer society to an early lobster dinner. I didn't understand the gesture, as of all places one could have dined at Skylands, that was, I thought, the least appealing, without views, little breeze, and, although I loved all the spruces and white birch trees Jensen had planted, the branches hanging over the driveway hid the majesty of Maine's starry skies. But whatever Martha's reasons for entertaining in the Fords' servants' driveway, David Rockefeller seemed amused and the evening was a success.

SKYLAND WEEKENDS WERE filled with interesting guests whom Martha entertained with grace, and loads of fun. We weeded the moss gardens, studied seacoast gardens with landscape architect Patrick Chassé, went antiquing in Northeast Harbor, and picked wild blueberries. We read books and learned about the history of Mount Desert Island, visiting the Historical Society as well as the local natural history and Native American heritage museums. We traveled around Maine as Martha filmed segments for her shows about potato harvesting, diving for scallops in frigid waters, crabbing, making studio pottery, or crafting sea-glass jewelry with artist Lisa Hall.

We even rode in a horse-drawn carriage competition against experienced drivers from all over the country. Dressed for the part, I got inside the gleaming vintage carriage next to Martha, who insisted on driving despite the fact that she had just begun learning the sport. Our carriage wobbled, leaned ominously to the side, and we barely missed scraping its precious frame against the large granite coping stones, also known as bear teeth, that flank Acadia's miles of historic carriage roads, the gift of philanthropist John D. Rockefeller, who personally oversaw their construction and design. But Martha summoned all her skill to interpret the messages sent by our superb equine from Wildwood Stables, and we smiled coolly for the cameras filming us for Martha's television show. It was impossible not to be utterly captivated by these summer days and it was easy to overlook what was less than perfect in our relationship.

Among the priceless treasures Martha had acquired with Skylands was a superb antique Steinway grand piano with a player mechanism, which, after being restored, could play any of the Ford family's closetful of music scrolls. There was a rare Zeiss telescope on a tripod, a fine observing instrument that Edsel Ford had placed in the Great Hall aimed at the skies and sea. And last but not least, there were two deepwater moorings in the harbor a couple of minutes' drive away.

After one weekend when real estate business had kept me in Connecticut, Martha came back from Skylands asking to have dinner with me at Sakura, our local Japanese restaurant. She was very cheerful as we sat at our sushi.

"I'm getting a picnic boat," she said.

"What's that?"

"It's sleek, just glides with no propellers. It has a jet drive."

"Like a motorboat? You get a face-lift when it flies against the wind?"

"It feels more like a sailboat. And there is a lot of room inside. You can fit quite a few people. You must come sail with me."

"Yeah, we make a great team. Remember how well we walked your sailboat in Georgica Pond?"

She punched me lightly on the upper arm with her knuckles, her "you're funny" gesture. We laughed.

By the summer of 2000, we were taking lunch and sunset rides aboard *Skylands II*, Martha's thirty-six-foot wooden Hinckley picnic boat with a hull painted to match the ivory-colored shell of an egg from one of Martha's exotic chickens. When my girls came, they loved sailing by the ledges off Baker Island to watch harbor seals sprawled on the granite slabs or the puffins on the cliffs of the wildlife refuge at Petit Manan Island. Once, on a cool late afternoon sail, we saw bands of aurora borealis glowing across the sky.

Everyone who visited Skylands went on these magical picnic boat rides. Martha even took the chows. It could get a bit tense getting everything together for these excursions, everyone organized and wearing non-marking rubber-sole shoes as per Martha's request, arranging the caravan of cars to take larger groups to the Harbor Club, and loading people and dogs and cargo hampers brimming with delicious picnic goodies and ice-filled coolers with drinks. But once the boat left the dock and we approached Sutton Island, Bruce, Skyland's property manager and also the captain, would point out the decades-old osprey nest perched on top of an enormous pile of rocks where we sometimes glimpsed the rare birds. Once he drew our attention to the top of a lady's bathing suit hanging from the raptors' nest. Enjoying the spectacular ride, we delighted in exquisite picnic lunches prepared by Torie and her crew. Martha spread the tablecloth and set up elegant trays of individually wrapped lump-meat crab salad sandwiches made with the delicately flavored pink flesh of Maine Atlantic Peekytoe, fresh lobster rolls, and Torie's delicious oatmeal cookies, crunchy and chewy with chunks of toffee, chocolate, and dried cherries.

We sailed many places in Martha's Hinckley picnic boat, going southwest along the coast and across the bay to find antique treasures in Blue Hill, or northeast by the old lighthouses that perched on rocky islands just off shore. We visited researchers from the College of the Atlantic at the whale study station, and once even dared the spray and fog all the way to Canada, where we visited President Franklin Roosevelt's summer retreat on Campobello Island.

We always sampled the local food, and, as we had done everywhere we went, we bought local spices as souvenirs. In a small gourmet shop where we had lunch we found a jar of chocolate-brown tea-like leaves, hand-labeled *Dulse flakes*.

"Twenty-two milligrams sodium per teaspoon," Martha read out loud from the label of a commercially packed version of the same product on the rack. "A leafy sea vegetable that grows on the shores of Grand Manan Island. Hand-picked and sun-dried."

"So, it's a sea plant that sounds sweet and tastes salty," I said.

Umami. The thought popped into my head perhaps as randomly as the one that hit Japanese chemist Kikunae Ikeda in late 1800, when he ascribed to the traditional *dashi* seaweed soup that he so loved a fifth taste, which he named *umami*. Neither sweet nor sour nor salty nor bitter, but savory. A flavor that stands alone and also, when combined with others, enriches their bouquet.

I sometimes felt that way about my friendship with Martha.

ON AUGUST 5, 2000, Martha gave the annual Leo birthday party at Skylands. The invitation, which pictured in scientific detail the external anatomy of a lobster, indicated casual dress and cocktails beginning at seven p.m., followed by dinner at eight thirty p.m. and "featuring the Rock Hoppers."

Martha and I went to pick Sam up at the tiny Hancock County–Bar Harbor Airport. While we were waiting, we noticed that the airport was crammed with a fleet of private planes parked next to one another as close as bicycles, a regular sight in East Hampton but not something we had seen before in Maine.

Sam's chartered plane arrived, and we were able to catch up in the car as Martha drove us back to Skylands. Sam would be leaving that night after the party.

Back at the house, Martha unveiled her first art purchase since she had become a billionairess: a very large, voluptuous bronze nude by early twentieth-century French sculptor Aristide Maillol, which she placed on one of the lower terraces where it doubled as a glorious headstone atop the grave of her late chow Blue Max, who had recently died and been buried there. Martha told me she paid $1 million for *La Rivière*, the languidly reclining woman, whose face and body were animated by a mysterious and tormented ecstasy. It had the effect of rendering some of her male guests as giddy as teenage boys. I had the impression that Carlos, Martha's friend and talented curator, was trying to figure out how to fix the way that Martha had chosen to display the piece, trapped on a hidden terrace, so unlike Maillol's *Prometheus* in its deserved public setting at Rockefeller Center.

Martha's previous sculpture acquisitions had been considerably more modest. The pair of glazed six-foot terra cotta sphinxes designed by Emile Muller that resided on the back terrace at Skylands had come from an auction. I was doing the driving the day she acquired them on our way to East Hampton, because Martha had a lot of calls to make. With a copy of the *Newtown Bee*, an antiques and auction newspaper that she had subscribed to for as long as I'd known her, open on her lap, Martha took the call from the auction gallery where she had put in a phone bid based solely on the black-and-white photo reproduced in the *Bee*. To her surprise, she was the top bidder. Martha immediately became concerned that they might be too gaudy.

"Don't worry," I said, "I'll buy them if they are too gaudy for the queen of taste."

When the sphinxes arrived, they were indeed quite extravagant and large. Martha kept them in storage for some time, but eventually decided to display them on the terrace at Skylands, flanking the entrance into the Great Hall. They looked strange for a while, but not at all bad. Fortunately, after that, Martha had interior designer Kevin Sharkey help her with redecorating, and no more sphinxes made their way to Skylands.

* * *

AT THE LEO party, it soon became time for Martha to open the gifts everybody gave her for her fifty-ninth birthday, most of which came in fancy boxes from stores like Loro Piana or one of Martha's favorite antique galleries. Sam came with an armful of presents for her, including a brown Hermès bag, about which he said modestly: "I thought you might like a Garden Party tote." Martha accepted it graciously, and confirmed that it was indeed the right bag for her new prosperity, but in truth she paid little attention to it. Made from socially and environmentally responsible rubberized canvas known as vegetable leather, produced through a process traditionally employed by indigenous people of the Amazonian Rainforest, the hard-to-find tote was modeled after a gardener's bag for carrying gardening gear. It was waterproof and came with individually packed towelettes for maintaining the rubber, which could get discoloration spots if splashed. My friend Eleanor had given me essentially the same bag for my birthday that year, so I knew that. When Martha saw me carrying mine, she said, "I thought it was just for the garden, but if you wear it, I will." We just didn't know that she'd be carrying her Hermès Amazonia Garden Party tote, together with her Birkin, into a courtroom.

Martha particularly loved the lobster trophy I gave her. I had scoured the antique shops to find something special for Martha's first birthday as a billionairess, and I didn't know what I would get until I found it at the Antique and Artisan Center in Stamford, where she and I often went shopping. Ron, one of the owners, had just shown a lady the extravagant 1960s vintage blue lobster trophy. Rare as it was—only one in 2 million lobsters is blue—the lady decided not to buy it. The thirty-two-pound beast had huge claws, and was mounted on board and burlap thirty-two inches across and twenty-eight inches high. Not a Damien Hirst, but still "beautiful in my mind," as one Hirst exhibit was called. The lobster was a bit pricey, but I was never frugal when I found unusual things for my friends. I thought Martha, who unlike most people in her tax bracket, collected artifacts and taxidermy, not art, would like it, and it would end up in one of her houses, not in her huge storage depot, chock-full of things. Martha placed the framed lobster over the mantle in Skylands' Great Hall, which pleased but also worried me, thinking she might start filling her extraordinary mansion with taxidermy trophies, as she had done at Lily Pond.

"Most people don't have the imagination to mix and match bed sheets," Martha had told *Time* magazine in 1997, the year she purchased Skylands, ready to share her decorating expertise with Kmart clients. "We're going to bring them along." While Martha did that for others, Kevin Sharkey helped her make Skylands into what it had become, polished but not too shiny; designed but not overly ornamented. When Martha enlisted him to the Skylands project, Kevin had only been with her company for about a year, yet he had already proven himself to be a tirelessly dedicated worker with impeccable taste. I knew that with Kevin's savoir faire, the Skylands mansion, the Georgian-style guesthouse with its own terrace overlooking the ocean and a large living room with a great fireplace, the rustic playhouse with its indoor squash court, would not become trophy display cases.

I always tried to lend a hand in some way, whether it was organizing the library or helping sort and store the hundred or so vintage French bistro posters that used to be the unifying decorating element at Skylands before Martha. There were various tasks that Martha needed help with, like checking for cracked or broken glass panes on the many old lampposts that lined the mile-long main driveway.

My favorite job was doing flower arrangements. Skylands, like every great old mansion, had a large flower room accessed from the front hall and the kitchen. I liked working at the spacious counter with the generously sized soap-stone sink, surrounded by cupboards and shelves filled with every imaginable kind of vase and protective liner, frogs to hold the stems steady, all sizes of basket to carry blossoms in from the garden, and various cutting shears, some of which Martha had brought back from her Japan trips.

I outdid myself for Martha's 2000 birthday party. Having Kevin Sharkey around certainly helped. For us, the party started much earlier, with the fun of making the massive arrangements of tall blue delphiniums, sunflowers, ferns, and blueberry branches. We wanted to show off the beauty of our friend's place to the local garden society, whose upper-crust members were coming for seven p.m. cocktails on the majestic terrace.

They came all at once, punctual, more women than men. Their surnames would be familiar to anyone well versed in American history, their ancestors having contributed to building this great country. Surprisingly unpretentious, the garden-society guests paid Martha and Skylands a bounty of compliments. While the guests enjoyed their drinks on the terrace with the eagle's view over Martha's domain, I was inside, straightening the collection of Mount Desert antique books on the large Great Hall round table. That's when one of the ladies, whom David Rockefeller had introduced me to minutes before, came in from the terrace. She looked every bit the way I imagined the original owner of my beloved lake-cottage in New Hampshire would have looked.

My visitor was happy to learn that Martha had restored the Steinway player-piano, whose music she had listened to as a young girl when she visited the Ford family with her parents. Then she asked about the many stones that were mixed in with the books on the center table. I told her how Martha's guests had collected them from the beaches and hikes. The woman told me that we shouldn't be removing the stones from their habitat. I thought she was joking—there are so many stones in Acadia. In reply, she asked me to imagine what would happen if every one of the millions of people who came to visit Acadia Park every year left with a rock. I promised never to remove a stone again. When I told Martha about it later, she said: "Oh, those crusty old ladies." However, today, it is illegal to remove stones from Acadia, and punishable by fines.

. . .

LIKE EVERY PARTY organized by Martha, the sit-down dinner she gave to celebrate her birthday unfolded like a grand opera with an endless flow of the best food and a large crowd of guests. The only unusual feature was the live band, The Rock Hoppers.

The great Skylands terrace was set with many round tables of various sizes, seating four to twelve people each. Sam and I had been placed at a small table and with us was Annie, Martha's personal assistant, who had previously worked for Isabella Rossellini and Dustin Hoffman. Very discreet and rather shy around big crowds, Annie was a voracious reader and a theater buff, and once you got her talking about that it was a pleasure to listen.

We had not been sitting for very long when Martha came by our table to visit. Pulling Sam and me close, she asked us to do her a favor and squeeze another chair between us for a friend of hers. I had never met the woman, a very successful finance executive, but Martha had told me about some amazing things she had done.

"She just had a face-lift and the poor thing looks terrible," Martha said with that amused little laughter I was so used to. Then, smiling all the while, she continued mocking the woman, saying her husband had been spending time with a lap-dancer, and how she needed company.

Martha laughed, but I didn't find her mockery very funny. This woman was supposed to be a friend. And when she joined us shortly thereafter, Sam and I were spellbound. She was interesting, funny, and extremely smart, so much so that I realized that Martha was probably envious.

That evening, Martha retired immediately after dinner, soon after Sam left. No one minded it. All of her houseguests knew that she had been up since dawn, way before any of us had gotten out of bed. Unlike the weekends at Lily Pond, where she invited you to come exercise with her the next morning, Martha became more tolerant of her guests' morning dallying. I could wake up mid-morning, have a delicious cappuccino, and catch up with Martha, who had already done a day's work on the property.

"Good night, Martha," everyone called, as my friend disappeared up the stairs, the chows following close behind.

It was understood that once Martha went to her room, I took care of her guests. I turned on Cesária Évora, poured drinks for everyone, and danced with Carlos, the fiery curator of classical art.

When we went back to the couches, Charles wanted to show us the blueprints for his new boat. Sitting on the floor, he had neatly laid the large scrolls on the coffee table, describing the myriad details and subtleties of his new toy. The luxury yacht was being built in the Netherlands by a German builder. Called the *Skat*, a Danish term of endearment bestowed on Charles by a former girlfriend, the boat was 233 feet long, making it the sixty-fourth largest in the world. It had four levels, reached by an elevator; a gym; and a helipad complete with helicopter. It was going to be a jewel of craftsmanship, a floating building the size of a large home, with minimalist-style finishes and designed in the same shade of gray as his high-tech house in Medina.

Then ABBA, the next disk I had put in Martha's music tray, began playing. Soon everyone was dancing near the large windows in the Great Hall, between the Steinway piano and the Zeiss telescope, when we saw a meteor streaking over the sky and we all went outside hunting for early Perseid fire, which the next day Martha said she had also watched from her upstairs window, and I was sure she did. My friend's life had, by then, become so complicated, no wonder she didn't get much sleep.

The more accomplishments Martha piled up on her publicly visible success trajectory, the more she was compelled to go for, and the less satisfied she was with what life brought her. Martha had just found out that the upcoming September 2000 issue of *Forbes* would place her at number 274 on the "400 Richest Americans" list, and she was unhappy that her $1 billion fortune did not place her in a higher position. I first thought she was kidding, but when Martha declared that her only consolation was that Charles was ranked at the same position, I just smiled but could barely hold Arthur Schopenhauer's words from slipping off the tip of my tongue: "Wealth is like seawater; the more we drink, the thirstier we become; and the same is true of fame."

BY THE EVENING of August 12, Martha's weekend guests had left. She and I were the only ones still at Skylands. I was sitting on the back porch, cell phone in hand, listening to that evening's messages on my real-estate answering machine, when shortly after midnight, the ground alarms went off—intruders! Martha came flying out of the house, a beauty mask slathered all over her face. She was screaming invectives and rushing to her car.

"Where are you going? Wait, Martha, wait for me, you can't go alone!" I called out and began running behind her.

It could have been a bear, but I was more concerned about people having taken a wrong turn, since Skylands' back driveway was as wide and long as a country road. I worried about bad press and feared that barely a few years after becoming the owner of Skylands, Martha might strain her relations with the neighborhood, like she had at Turkey Hill, where she was perennially involved in arguments with her neighbors, and at Bunshaft, where her neighborly disputes involved expensive lawsuits, or at Lily Pond, where Martha raised a few eyebrows with her complaining about neighbors who played tennis on their own court, on their own property.

From the high vantage point of the SUV's front seats, I saw rear car lights in the distance to the left. Martha began racing her Suburban down the curving gravel driveway in that direction. I started dialing Kevin Burger's cell. He had helped arrange the Leo party and was still at Skylands, staying in the quaint guest quarters that Martha had made out of the maids' bedrooms over the stables. When Kevin answered his phone, it was obvious that I had woken him up, but, with his usual solicitous manner, he offered to come.

Honking her horn, Martha overtook the trespassing vehicle, a limousine, by a mere car length, and with a wild swerve turned the wheel to the left, and backed up, forcing the limo to stop. We jumped out through my door, because the Suburban was so close to the limo there was no room to open hers, and Martha began berating the intruders. Standing next to her in the dark Maine night, I saw the lights go on inside the trespassing car, first in the front near by the driver, then in the back, where a group of young women, all prettily dressed, began apologetically explaining how they were coming from a nearby bachelorette party and the driver took a wrong turn. Martha raged at the polite driver and the girls, throwing her body forward toward them, her fists pounding the air. She then called the police from the cell phone. Eventually, Kevin came and we persuaded Martha to walk back to the house with me, while Kevin stayed behind with the Suburban blocking the limo, waiting for the patrol officer. Martha wanted to press charges.

The midnight fracas hit the news, but it was deemed a matter "of privacy and personal safety when in the sanctity of her own home," as her publicist's statement said, with what I thought was a dash of Alexander Pope: "Get place and wealth, if possible, with grace; If not, by any means get wealth and place."

WHEN I RECEIVED my invitation to Charlotte Beers and Billy Beadleston's wedding, I immediately called Martha to tell her how beautiful I thought it was, on a tri-fold card with pictures of Tiffany stained-glass windows at St. Jude's Episcopal Church in Seal Harbor, depicting a Maine-like forest, the sea, and a sunrise. The ceremony was to take place Saturday, October 7, at eleven o'clock.

Charlotte and Billy had been together for years. There were seventy-five guests in attendance, and a wedding party that included Charlotte's five bridesmaids, her longtime friends, all successful career women: Martha, Frannie Dittmer, Memrie Lewis, Judith Wheelock, and Darla Moore—president of the private investment firm Rainwater Inc. and the first woman to have a major business school named after her, the Darla Moore School of Business at USC. Darla was married to the famous dealmaker Richard Rainwater. She and her husband were among the few brainy, stunningly attractive couples I met in Martha's world of the rich and famous who were also personable without a trace of pretentiousness.

Martha thought that Charlotte's idea to have her attendants wear long taffeta skirts and cashmere sweaters was brilliant for a wedding celebration at a country home in the fall, and she immediately called on talented young fashion designer Michael Kaye, who made five superb bridesmaids outfits, each different yet all in harmony with one another. Then, shortly before the wedding, Martha decided to improve on Charlotte's idea and accessorize with shawls, which she worked her magic to get in matching taffeta and cashmere.

Good will and love filled the beautiful chapel as our misty-eyed group of friends, relatives, Charlotte's daughter, and Billy's four children, all young adults, watched the handsome, elegant groom and his beautiful bride, smiling affectionately at each other, take their vows. Billy was wearing a boutonnière of wild berry and thistle, and Charlotte, as radiant as the luminous multiple-strand pearl choker on her graceful neck, wore a simple, elegant, creamy-white cashmere sweater set with a long burnt-orange silk taffeta skirt, and on her chestnut hair a diadem of small white roses and barley spikes.

It was wonderful to see Charlotte so happy. She hadn't been herself since her mentor David Ogilvy had died, near her birthday, the year before. Martha didn't quite know how to deal with her friend's sorrow, and also didn't seem to approve of Charlotte's decision to step down from the helm of the advertising giant Ogilvy & Mather either, but, in a true Martha fashion, she was generously hosting a champagne brunch for Charlotte and Billy's wedding.

Horse-drawn carriages waited outside the chapel to take the wedding party to Skylands, where Martha had her Maine and Connecticut crews prepare delicious foods for a festive party that showed Skylands as "a perfect wedding house," just as Martha had said years before. She also published a wonderful article about the wedding, with beautiful pictures, in her magazine.

After a hike on Jordan Pond trail with Martha, Sharon, and the bridesmaids, all of whom were staying with Martha at Skylands, we got ready for the wedding dinner at Isis, Billy and Charlotte's new home in Northeast Harbor. It began with the memorable blessings-of-the-house ceremony. There were so many friendly toasts to the newlyweds that the clinking of tulip-shaped champagne glasses drowned out the music for a while. Then we danced and it was soon evident that most of the powerful and revered friends of the Beadlestons were as good at partying as they were in their professional fields.

All that cheer may have been a little too much for Martha. That evening, while the party was still in full swing, Martha went to the front parlor and fell asleep on the couch in plain view of everybody. It was a bit awkward, but no one said anything. Charlotte just smiled understandingly. The rest of us continued to dance and dine on the romantically lit porch overlooking the ocean below.

17

Martha Moves to Bedford
and Goes Global

ONE GLORIOUSLY SUNNY Thursday in early August 2000, before Charlotte and Billy's wedding, I went with Martha to visit the Abby Aldrich Rockefeller Garden, in Seal Harbor, Maine, created by American landscape designer Beatrix Farrand for its namesake and her husband, John D. Rockefeller Jr. Walking on the wooded bluff near where the Rockefeller Tudor-style hundred-room "cottage," the Eyrie, used to be until it was razed in the early 1960s, we followed the woodland path that meandered along the coral-colored stucco wall framing the garden. It was a tall wall, capped with glazed yellow tiles salvaged from a demolished part of the legendary wall in China that surrounds the Forbidden City.

We went inside the garden through the visitors' entrance, near a large, circular moon gate and walked among colorful English-style flower borders, toward the lawn at the center of the sunken garden. At its far end, near the pool, surrounded by members of his family, was David Rockefeller, whom Martha had arranged to meet. After introductions, he took Martha and me on a private tour along the Spirit Path, separated by a wall of bayberry from the annual and perennial beds, sharing with us the story of this special place, begun as a sculpture and cutting garden and inspired by a trip through Asia his parents had taken after traveling to China for the opening of the first Western medical school there, built and endowed by the Rockefeller Foundation. The collection of Eastern sculptures and the "Korean tomb procession figures," acquired from fine American dealers, were placed among native Maine shrubs, natural pools, carpets of ferns and mosses.

I couldn't tell if it was the unusual combination of Western and Eastern, of essence and magic, or maybe it was the tenderness in Mr. Rockefeller's voice as he reminisced about moments and places in the Orient that he'd shared with his late wife, Peggy, but this walk along the Spirit Path was transformative. I felt as if we were in the garden from Giuseppe Lampedusa's historical novel *The Leopard*, with David Rockefeller looking as handsome and dignified as Burt Lancaster when he played the powerful prince, descendant of an ancient Sicilian family, in the movie version.

When we reached an overlook at the end of the path, where a fifteen-hundred-year-old sandstone memorial stele stood tall, I looked at the glorious view beyond and watched the glow of light on Mr. Rockefeller's forehead as he told us about having created the lookout point with his wife, as an addition to the original design. And, for the first time, the words of Lampedusa's Sicilian count had meaning to me: "For things to stay the same, they have to change." I thought, *For Martha and me to stay friends, things have to change.* That became my new goal.

Martha also took inspiration from our visit, albeit in a different way. A few days later, she launched a new line of decorative fabric collections for the home, one of which was called "Miss Farrand" after landscape gardener Beatrix Farrand. Two other fabric collections Martha introduced at that time, "Capability" and "Miss Jekyll," paid tribute to two other garden design greats: English landscape architect Capability Brown and English gardener Gertrude Jekyll.

As Martha's fame grew, her brand visibly placed "in all media windows," as Sharon would say, her name entered the language as a metaphor for everything and anything that was in good taste. "La Martha" of local Westport catering fame became Martha, a diva on a first-name-only basis with America. There was a negative side to the fame, catty publicity, mockery, and gossip, but Martha usually brushed these off as "crap," or "c-r-a-p," depending on whom she said it to.

Even with all the grandeur of Skylands, Martha wasn't finished on the real estate front. After thirty years in Connecticut, she decided it was time for a new home base, and at the end of spring 2000, she had paid $15.7 million for about 120 beautiful "horse country" acres on Girdle Ridge Road in Bedford, New York. An area in northern Westchester County famous for its large estates, Bedford was once home to the esteemed statesman John Jay, one of the nation's founding fathers, whose 1801 homestead was built there as a retirement home. Martha fell in love with a property that some called Sycamore Farms, but she preferred the name Cantitoe Corners, after the wife of Indian chief Katonah, who had lived in the area three hundred years earlier. Ralph Lauren's large estate was next door. Other famous area residents were billionaire George Soros, real estate tycoon Donald Trump, music industry magnate Clive Davis, and film stars like Glenn Close, Chevy Chase, and Christopher Reeve. Martha said we'd meet many interesting people, and calculated that through making friends with them she'd find the active, rich man she had always wanted.

The Cantitoe Corners spread included a number of buildings. The houses were small, and built in close proximity to well-traveled roads on two sides of the property line. Martha referred to the 1925 farmhouse as the Winter House, and the 1770 colonial house the Summer House. A "boxwood room" adjacent to one of the houses was my favorite structure on the property. Before she gave her final bid, we walked the land for hours, through snow and mud, with her Bedford broker, Muffin

D'Ambrosio, looking for the perfect location to build the perfect house. Far in the woods, near the stone wall that separated the property from the neighboring hydraulic company land, we found it: a hilly area that could be approached from the main road by a long, meandering driveway. I suggested renting a crane to figure out exactly which perspective would offer the most picturesque views of the large property and the nearby reservoir.

Martha immediately wanted to restore and renovate the property, building new additions, including a huge greenhouse and amazing stables. She hired renowned architect Allan Greenberg to work with her on the project. Meanwhile, she started bringing in construction materials and architectural artifacts from her other properties. From the Gordon Bunshaft house on Georgica Pond, she had the slabs of travertine and marble pried out and cut to create the "harmonious" pattern she wanted for the kitchen floor at the Winter House. More of the white and gray marble came from a house that had been demolished in Vermont in 1995. I had heard about it from my builder Daniel, who knew how much I liked antique architectural elements, and when I shared the secret with Martha, we bought large portions of the site, including architectural antiques and building materials, which Daniel and his crew then transported for us to Connecticut.

I bought the hundred-year-old roof, or, rather, all the beautiful old Vermont slate that it was made of, every tile of it, because I loved the depth of its color and the quaintness of its cut, and it still had the copper snow guards. I was sure that one day I would build myself a cottage, and give it a slate roof. Martha offered to store it on her property at Bronson Fields. But after she purchased Bedford, Martha's movers came and mistakenly took away the crates filled with roof slate together with all the architectural artifacts that belonged to Martha, and moved everything to her property in Bedford, miles away, leaving me without a roof. Martha said that a slate roof didn't fit my house. I knew then that I would never see my roof again. And I didn't.

Martha persuaded the town of Bedford to approve a zoning variance for her to build a higher-than-permitted stone barn, which would offer her both the utility of a barn and a high wall to screen out traffic at Cantitoe Corners. There were insinuations that she won three out of five zoning members' approval because she passed around homemade cookies the day of the hearing, but I think it was really because first, they knew Martha was not going to subdivide the property, and second, that indeed she would improve it.

Martha's Bedford project was advancing in many ways. She planted tens of thousands of daffodil bulbs, thousands of new trees, and lots of peonies, which she loved as much as I did. And she became socially active in her new neighborhood. Muffin was the one who introduced Martha to Seema Boesky, whose large sculpture garden housed a fabulous Maillol collection, which, when we went to visit, Martha liked so much she said that was what she should get for Skylands, and she did buy *La Rivière*. Seema invited Martha to numerous elegant parties, some of which I went to as Martha's guest.

The first time I met Seema was at a benefit at Caramoor, an estate just down the road from Martha's property, which hosted a highly regarded annual music festival that my former husband and I used to attend every summer. Everything about the event was a rare treat, including the company of our hostess. The open-air concert was beyond expectation. Seema had reserved front-row seats for every one of her guests, and before I could open the program, I saw, the width of a garden path from me, my favorite cellist, Yo-Yo Ma. I would have been happy with anything he played, but he regaled us with Vivaldi's "Concerto for Two Cellos," a lovely piece for a summer afternoon, which Mr. Ma played with a young cellist, and Elgar's "Cello Concerto in E minor." I must say, Martha could bring about the loveliest of surprises.

The residents of Westport, however, might not have thought so. A remarkable misstep Martha made was the way she chose to announce her departure from Connecticut, in an article she wrote for the April 9, 2000, *New York Times* magazine, called "Fed Up in the Burbs." In the piece, she more or less trashed the town, claiming it had lost its small-town vibe and that everybody lived behind high walls and locked gates, which was true of Turkey Hill. The locals didn't take her comments well. Martha had told me she was writing an article about Westport, but I read it at the same time as everyone else. Many people called me to say how disappointed they were; some even said I should no longer be friends with her, as her having made so many Westporters so angry could affect my business. What gave me the biggest pause was the fact that Martha's gesture was the repetition of what she had done to Andy when, after he was no longer part of her life, she made terrible public statements she had to retract. I didn't want to think of what she'd do if we somehow stopped being friends, because while the things I didn't like about Martha had been piling up, my friendship with her, although eroded, was still strong.

MEANWHILE, MARTHA WAS also busy reinventing the Bunshaft villa on Georgica Pond on Long Island. The house Bunshaft built in 1963 had massive concrete walls covered in travertine. Enormous windows faced across the pond, the dunes, and the Atlantic beyond. It had been home to the Bunshafts' art collection, from which the garden sculptures were removed by MoMA, when Martha purchased the house.

"When I buy a house, I must do something to it, to change it," Martha said. When MoMA accepted her offer, Martha told me, they said they trusted her more than the other bidders to respect and preserve the integrity of the building. But when she described to me the changes she envisaged making to Bunshaft's home, I worried about what might happen to that gem of modern architecture. It couldn't possibly satisfy Martha's ambitions.

As she had written in her high school yearbook, "I do what I please, and I do it with ease." Still in the middle of litigation with her neighbor Harry Macklowe, Martha set about tearing apart Bunshaft's original design and remaking it into something altogether different. She had originally hired John Pawson, an architect from London, for the make-over of the master's work. Artists have a long history of altering the work of their peers. Titian is said to have painted over the mysterious *Feast of the Gods*, a masterpiece of the great fifteenth-century artist Giovanni Bellini. But, as it transpired, Martha's concept of gutting the elegant pavilion, a unique piece of art designed by one of the most revered American architects, whose inspiration was the great Le Corbusier, was to Pawson more like melting a Michelangelo bronze down to make a cannon (this actually happened). When Pawson stopped indulging Martha, she ripped out various elements of the house and moved some of them to Cantitoe, including the floor and the marble blocks, not long after the lamps and most of the built-in Bunshaft-designed furniture were cleaved away and moved to Martha's daughter's, Alexis's, stark, monochromatic penthouse apartment in Tribeca.

I visited the Bunshaft house every time I went to East Hampton. Looking sadder and sadder each year, it eventually became a derelict shell. I did a little weeding here and there, and that's how I discovered a multitude of rocks that had been painted with faces by Mrs. Bunshaft. Coming in all sizes, the largest about ten inches across and others only pebbles, some with happy faces, many looking sad and a number of them kitten-like, they were placed among the plantings, painting-side down. I searched for them everywhere, concerned they'd be crushed during construction. I found in the neighborhood of a hundred stones, which I left in the protected space by the side door. Martha, who said that Chris, her nephew, had also found quite a few, took them all to Bedford.

Martha would end up selling the gutted house in 2003, the ambitious renovations never done, for $9 million, about three times what she'd paid for it a decade earlier, proving once again that whatever she touched turned to gold, even when her touch ruined and destroyed. The new owners had not much choice but to tear down this once-important monument to American art and culture and start over.

A few years before she sold Bunshaft, Martha agreed to pay more than $6 million for another modernist dwelling—the top two floors of the North Tower of Richard Meier's glass-walled building going up on Manhattan's Perry Street overlooking the Hudson River. The building would have amazing views of the Empire State Building and the Statue of Liberty. Many of the rich and famous, including Calvin Klein, Nicole Kidman, and Hugh Jackman, had already bought space there. I thought it was a great idea. Martha needed a new place in Manhattan, since her beautifully restored apartment on Fifth Avenue was too small for entertaining on the scale she had grown to enjoy.

Martha also entered a real estate transaction in which I helped her in a professional capacity—the sale of Bronson Fields, her thirty-seven-acre property in the Greenfield Hill neighborhood of Fairfield, which she decided to sell once she closed on the farm in Bedford.

Martha had assembled Bronson Fields from three adjacent parcels, which she purchased over the years for a total of $2.9 million. Although the market indicated a substantial appreciation of property values in that prestigious area, the highest sale in the neighborhood was just under $7 million, which had also been my listing, and was a record-setting sale. While that was a much smaller single parcel, it had a beautiful home in great condition with well-maintained guesthouses. The Bronson Fields house and auxiliary buildings needed total renovation, but the three large parcels of land were picturesque, and the opportunity to own them together was unique. Martha, who was an educated seller, understood that while the market did suggest a value of around $10 million for her property, the demand for such a large parcel with so few amenities was not very high. We listed Bronson Fields for $10.5 million.

I began working on the sale of Bronson Fields with a sustained and intensive marketing campaign: advertising, calling brokers in the area, throughout the state, all over the country, builders, architects, golf-course investors. I was happy with the response, as the property was showing a few times a week and the bottom fishing started. Most of the interest came from builders, which concerned me, because I was reluctant about the property being subdivided; I would have preferred that a new owner preserve the natural landscape.

One of the areas with likely buyers for Bronson Fields was Martha's new neighborhood in Bedford, where people appreciated large properties and also would not have gotten sticker-shock over the asking price. One of the Bedford Realtors I called regularly was Muffin, who had sold Martha Cantitoe Corners. I liked her, I thought her trustworthy; she worked hard, knew her market, and had a good client base. As real estate business is dependent on referrals, we negotiated a co-brokering agreement and sent each other clients. That's how I found the buyer for Bronson Fields. Martha was delighted. I was already having a very good real estate year, which had afforded me the down payment for the beach cottage in Westport, but that had also added another large mortgage to my bills, so the sale of Bronson Fields, which had brought Martha very nice proceeds, was of great help to me. It also made it possible for me to repay the loans I had taken from Martha so I could go with her on the trips to Peru and the Amazon. Of course, she was a wealthy woman for as long as I knew her, and after her company IPO she became one of America's wealthiest people, a billionaire. Still, I was glad to be able to pay her earlier than we had agreed I would, if only by a couple of months. Immediately after the sale of Bronson Fields, at the beginning of November 2000, I asked Martha to have her office calculate the payoff amount on my loan.

My clients usually thanked me with a variety of beautiful gifts after closing their deals. That's why, perhaps, I was so astonished when Martha's office sent me a new contract for the $10,000 I had borrowed from her for our Peru trip, to supersede the original one we had agreed upon at the time. The accompanying bill stated that I owed the $10,000 loan, plus the cost of plane tickets to Brazil for me and my daughters, minus the price of the Judith Leiber bag, plus the per diem accumulation of the interest at a new, higher rate, for a total increase that came to an amount close to the cost of the last gift I had given her. I was flabbergasted by her hubris and complained to Heidi, the employee whom

Martha had instructed to send me the new contract, but I decided not to raise the issue directly with Martha. There is a Romanian expression that translates something like "being too embarrassed to shame someone." It is possible that arrogance may have impeded Martha from understanding why I wrote a check for the sum she demanded. She might have thought that I paid simply because what else could I have done? Who would have believed that Martha would go to such lengths for a handful of dollars?

In many ways, Martha and I were so close at this point, it was as though we were symbiotically tied, and to sever her from that push-me-pull-you was to sever myself. Yet, keeping our friendship had become so much work that it had turned into a job. But you can't offer your resignation from friendship. So I did my best to find excuses for what she did.

Perhaps Martha had done that because she was remorseful for having just given me her first-ever true gift. Not a book from her shelf, nor an item from her catalog, not an open perfume bottle or an old stove she no longer had use for, but something she bought specifically for me from an antique store in Maine. One weekend when we were at Skylands, Martha had wanted to bid on some items that we had gone to see at the local auction gallery. But she had to get back to the house to give a cocktail party for someone from New York. I offered to stay in town and handle the bidding for her while she entertained. Kevin Burger accompanied so he could help me load the auction items into the car. As we had an hour or so before the auction began, Kevin and I went to a nearby antique store, where I saw a very large, rolled-up canvas with a mixed-media painted scene. The image depicted two women sitting on rocks facing each other against a background of sky and people working the land. The store owner said she had gotten it in Belgium and that all she knew of it, as it wasn't signed, was that it used to hang above the bar of a country inn. It was so large that it would not have fit comfortably in the cottage I had bought at the beach. I also couldn't afford these kinds of added costs, while carrying two homes and expensive mortgages. So I went to the auction, I got the items Martha wanted for a song, and never gave the painting another thought. I was truly surprised when on my next visit to Skylands sometime after Charlotte's wedding Martha presented me with that canvas as a gift. It was, she said, for everything I did for her, for helping her with Skylands and Bunshaft and Bronson Fields. I was overwhelmed by what I perceived the gift to imply—not only the cost, but knowing that Martha had to have asked Kevin's advice about what I might like and then to actually get it. That was a lot of effort for Martha to make for someone else, and it impressed me when she gave Charlotte the champagne wedding brunch at Skylands, but having done it for me could only mean that Martha was finally beginning to be the kind of treasured friend I had always wanted her to be. I presumed that, without us ever discussing it, Martha also thought of Lampedusa's "For things to stay the same, they have to change."

Then, when Martha raised the interest on the loan, I figured perhaps, for reasons I didn't know, she was having doubts about having given me the painting, but while that was the best excuse I could find for Martha raising the interest on the loan, it also meant she wasn't beginning to be the kind of friend I thought she might become, so it was high time I acted on the resolve I made when visiting Mr. Rockefeller's garden. *For Martha and me to stay friends, things have to change.* I decided that to begin with, the change I'd make would be not to accept a gift or a loan from her ever again, so we could continue being friends without my having to confront her. I was aware that I was basically stalling, as my taking gifts or loans from Martha were rare occurrences, but that was all I was ready to do then.

ON NOVEMBER 18, 2000, Martha was one of the guests at the wedding of Hollywood couple Michael Douglas and Catherine Zeta-Jones, held in the Grand Ballroom of New York's Plaza Hotel. Martha told me she danced with actor Anthony Hopkins and asked me if I found him attractive.

"Very," I said. "There is something about the Welsh. Look how gorgeous Catherine is."

"Should I date him?"

"Isn't he seeing someone?" I said, which was the best way I could think of to remind her what most people know: that you can't possess everything you touch.

A few months later, before one of her trips to California, Martha was really excited about seeing Anthony Hopkins in L.A. Her people had apparently called his and arranged for the stars to have lunch or dinner. When he had to cancel at the last minute, Martha, familiar with the athletics of scheduling business deals, was willing to meet him for a breakfast at his house. At the meal, Martha said that Hopkins behaved weirdly detached. But breakfast at the house of such a famous and private man was enough to fire imaginations, and soon thereafter the tabloids picked up the story, making the assumption that the two were dating. Martha would put her own clever spin on it when she appeared on the *Howard Stern Show* and said, "I would have probably had a very nice relationship with Anthony Hopkins, but I couldn't get past the Lecter thing."

Around this time, in February 2001, the sun was experiencing some bizarre behavior of its own. Its magnetic field flipped, so the sun's magnetic north pole was pointing south. "This always happens around the time of solar maximum," said David Hathaway, a solar physicist at the Marshall Space Flight Center, as quoted by Tony Phillips of Science@NASA. A complicated web of magnetic lines affecting the solar atmosphere and interior create magnetic fields which produce cyclical activity on the sun's surface. The sun's cycle is eleven years, during which the sun's surface activity goes from minimum to maximum. The solar maximum is the time when the sun's magnetic fields are most dynamic and their changes shape the churning plasma at the surface of the sun, causing the most explosive activities, like sun flares, solar storms and violent ejections of the sun's own plasma, and the most sunspots. "The magnetic poles exchange places at the peak of the sunspot cycle." The changes in the sun's magnetic field are carried by solar winds.

"When a gust of solar wind hits Earth's magnetic field, the impact causes the magnetic field to shake. If it shakes hard enough, we call it a geomagnetic storm," Hathaway said. "These storms can create power outages, interrupt cell phone service, or knock out communications satellites, and make compass needles swing in the wrong direction." I wondered if somehow Martha was affected by the solar storm phenomenon, which had been reported to occur throughout the prior year. It certainly seemed like the MSLO stock was being affected; it had fallen as low as $13 a share in March 2000, well below its $18 IPO price the previous October.

NONETHELESS, THE ACCOLADES poured in. On Thursday, March 29, 2001, Barnard College, Martha's alma mater, honored her at its fourteenth Annual Awards Dinner, a black-tie event held at the Grand Ballroom of the Waldorf-Astoria. Martha was the first Barnard graduate to receive the Iphigene Ochs Sulzberger Award, named for the alumna and civic leader, and given for "contributions . . . to our society and to the city," as Barnard president Judith Shapiro said in the press release for the event. Martha had received Barnard's Woman of Achievement Award a few years earlier. Shapiro went on to say that Martha had "demonstrated how domesticity and entrepreneurship can be combined to extraordinarily powerful effect." It was a really special evening capped off with dancing to the Michael Carney Orchestra. And it raised more than $1 million for the school's scholarship fund. The evening was particularly wonderful for me, since Martha had invited my daughter Monica to join us. As the party went on, Monica told me she felt guilty that the president of Barnard was so nice to her that night, because Barnard had accepted her application for admission the following autumn but my daughter had chosen to attend Columbia University across the street.

Next, Martha was the honorary chairperson of the bicentennial ball committee of the Friends of John Jay Homestead in Katonah, New York, a historic site that had become a nonprofit educational center near her new home in Bedford. She invited me to the black-tie ball held on April 21. We got there in time for cocktails, and I had a chance to meet more of her new neighbors. It always impresses me how civilized and unpretentious wealthy Americans are. We had a lovely time and stayed for the elegant sit-down dinner. As for dancing to the Starlight Orchestra, we just watched other people, then went home.

I was one of the sponsors for the Save the Children Women's Empowerment Forum that was held at the Pierre Hotel on May 11 in celebration of Mother's Day. The forum was designed to discuss its recently published study of mothers and children in ninety-four countries. The discussion was followed by the Women's Leadership Award ceremony, which was honoring Kerry Kennedy Cuomo for her efforts on behalf of human rights around the world. The award was presented by Fox News anchor Paula Zahn. Queen Noor, who had been the 2000 recipient of the award, passed the torch to "another remarkable woman and mother." Martha came as my guest.

IT WAS A fantastic spring. My older daughter, Monica, was accepted to almost all the colleges she had applied to, my younger daughter, Lara, was admitted to the Groton School, in Massachusetts, and I began construction of my beach house in Westport.

And Martha continued to be on fire. Just when I thought she'd done everything possible, she managed to do more. A profile of her in *Time* magazine that June described the current state of her empire: her six-day-a-week television show on CBS, *Martha Stewart Living*, replaced the syndicated program. She had given up her twice-weekly guest spot on NBC's *Today* show for a weekly slot on the competing show *CBS This Morning*. Instead of appearance fees, Martha controlled the advertising for her segment. Her show would follow *CBS This Morning* in most markets. "Sometimes you have to do things for an economic and brand sensibility," she said in an interview. "I have more fun with Katie [Couric] and Matt [Lauer]. But on CBS I got an amazing lead-in to my show. It only made sense." Her new daily national radio show, which had the same name as her nationally syndicated newspaper column, "askMartha," was introduced the same day as her TV show. Her twelfth book, *Martha Stewart's Healthy Quick Cook*, was scheduled for July with the publisher's largest printing ever. Her Web site averaged more than half a million visitors every week. Also in July 2001, she debuted a new quarterly magazine for families, called *Kids: Fun Stuff to Do Together*. And Martha made a deal with Bernhardt Furniture Company for a Martha Stewart Signature collection.

Amid all the frenzy of Martha's corporate expansion, the traditions carried on. In August, Martha threw her annual birthday party for the Leos at Skylands. That year marked her sixtieth. Among the guests that weekend were Charles; Martha's entertainment lawyer Allen Grubman and his wife, Debbie, a successful Realtor in New York with the Corc-oran Group; Memrie and her fiancé, Charlie Duell, whose foundation owned and operated Middleton Place, an eighteenth-century planta-tion that had been in his family since long before the Civil War; and Sharon Patrick.

During one of the delicious dinners, served while guests sat on staggered-height stools at Martha's long, zinc-topped kitchen table, the conversation turned to the situation in Afghanistan. On the menu that evening were lobster and corn. Martha had placed large bowls along the middle of the table for the shells. The sound of cracking crustaceans got louder as the conversation got more animated. The Taliban, which had been in power since the mid-1990s, had murdered thousands of Afghan citizens in an effort to retain its control of the country. Women were forbidden to work outside the home, or even leave home without a male relative, and forced to wear a burka; girls were kept from school. Men were required to wear beards of a certain length or face beatings or imprisonment. The Taliban also went after Afghan culture, ordering the destruction of all ancient Buddha statues in the country, including those in museums. Just a few weeks before the Leo party, the Taliban had detained two dozen international relief agency workers and were threatening to execute sixteen of them, all Afghan citizens, for allegedly converting to Christianity from Islam.

Of course, that was just a prelude compared to the jolt of September 11, which came not long after the Skylands' weekend. Martha was in Japan at the time. She called me from there soon after the news broke. We were relieved to learn from each other that our daughters, Alexis and Monica, who both lived in New York at the time, were well. Martha called me often and we exchanged news and rumors and bewilderment over the five days or so while she remained in Japan. She had recently done a merchandising deal with Japan's Seiyu, a retail chain of more than two hundred stores. Seiyu was slated to carry a broad range of Martha's branded products and collaborate with her company on a new magazine called *Martha*, published in Japanese. She had gone global.

But when *Fortune*'s list of the four hundred richest Americans came out later that month, Charles had moved up to #236 in the rankings while Martha dropped to #381, barely making the list with a personal fortune of just $650 million, down from the previous year's billion.

18

The Beginning of the End

IN OCTOBER 2001, weeks after the horrors of September 11, Charlotte Beers was appointed by Secretary of State Colin Powell to be undersecretary for public diplomacy and public affairs. Her mission was essentially to launch a marketing campaign to counteract growing anti-American sentiment in the Arab world, a job she conceded was going to be much more challenging than the product branding for companies like American Express, which she was so famous for.

We celebrated her appointment at the elegant Manhattan restaurant Le Cirque, with Martha and Sharon. Charlotte and Billy, who had now been happily married for over a year, were accompanied by former ambassador to Syria Chris Ross, a young and very handsome diplomat. Charlotte had just come back from a fact-finding trip to the Middle East and told us in general about her plans and responsibilities. Part of her mission was to persuade millions of Muslims that Osama bin Laden wasn't a hero but a mass murderer. Every morning she would read the anti-American transcripts and headlines sent to her by American embassies around the world. In addition to spearheading a radio and leaflet propaganda campaign overseas, she was accompanying

Colin Powell, Condoleezza Rice, or Chris Ross to the Al-Jazeera studio in Washington, DC, to respond to the latest developments, including the release of any new bin Laden tapes. Plus she had to wrangle with Congress to get funding for her efforts. It was an exciting job. I was so proud of Charlotte and convinced she would succeed.

By then, my children had left home: my older daughter was a freshman at Columbia University and my younger daughter had just started boarding school at Groton School in Massachusetts. I was home alone, an empty nester in a large house on the river in Weston, with a smaller house under construction at the beach in Westport. Martha had been talking for years of building a big compound where she and I could live and grow old together if we never remarried. Originally, the compound was to be built on Bronson Fields, but after she had bought Cantitoe Corners, her Bedford property, Martha talked about building the compound there, a self-sufficient farm with everything one might need, Martha-style.

The fervor of property renovation at Cantitoe was in full swing. Martha was reconstructing her Winter House, adding thousands of square feet to make it into three floors of living space with dormers and porches. Everything was going to be finished in a palette of gray paint that Martha would then sell through affordable national outlets, which by now numbered so many that I could barely keep count.

My favorite building on Martha's property, the new greenhouse, was drop-dead gorgeous. Martha's focus was on the stables. Eager to have her own mounts at the ready whenever she felt like riding, she had already bought horses. The breed she chose was the elegant Friesian horse, big, well-behaved trotters whose size once enabled them to carry knights in armor into crusades. Martha would look much better on them than she did on the smaller Criollos we rode in South America. Besides, it was important that they fit the aesthetics of Martha's color scheme, which the Friesians were sure to do with their lustrous all-black coats. There were four or five of them, and she was paying for her horses to live somewhere in Canada for a few years, at their original Ontario stables, until the Bedford stables were ready.

"Do they have long tails and manes, and long furry socks?"

"Yeah, they wear black socks, like you, just no high heels," Martha said, laughing.

Martha busied herself studying, sketching, designing, and building. She'd fantasize about the library she'd build at the Cantitoe Corners compound, filled with glorious books. Sometimes she'd say, "I am not a loner," and her wistful loneliness reminded me of the high-society American divorcee played by Vivien Leigh in the movie *Ship of Fools*, set aboard a luxury liner traveling from Mexico to Germany a few years before World War II. Tragic and sad, she worries about ending her life "sitting in a night club with a paid escort who tells you the lies you must hear." I wondered if, had I ever considered living in Martha's imaginary tale, I'd dance in secret, like Leigh does in what I think is the saddest scene of the movie.

Seductive as it was, I could have never lived in Martha's compound. Truth was, the whole idea of living in a compound was not right for me, despite the profusion of money and luxury. I knew that I would much rather be alone, live the way I wanted, free to do as I pleased. The way I told Martha *Thank you, but no thank you* was to make a joke of it. "I love living," I'd say, quoting Neil Simon. "I have some problems with my life, but living is the best thing they've come up with so far."

Then one evening late in 2001, we were in her car going someplace or other, and I heard myself say, "The children are out of the house now. It's time I paid attention to my life. What I really want is to find that man whom I wish to spend the rest of my life with. I don't think that I will find him in those super-wealthy circles."

"That's not true. You've met many good men. You didn't go for them!"

Inside the dark car, Martha's voice went on listing names of people I had met in her company who were, indeed, good men whom, in her opinion, I had allowed to pass me by. She also mentioned the man I loved and lost because her jealous and competitive behavior prevented me from committing to the relationship, which made crystal clear the fact that I would not find the man I was looking for in Martha's world.

Be that as it may, I decided that I had to be more proactive about planning my own future. I had finally started to make real money as a Realtor, having cleared high six figures in the last two years, but I was watching it fly out the window with my high mortgage payments and construction costs for the beach house. Then came September 11, which shook me deeply. As for my private life, I returned each night to my river house with my two dogs, guardians of my secrets, listening to Placido Domingo with the volume turned up high. It became clear that I needed to turn my life around.

AT THAT POINT, Martha and Charles were still "dating," but their relationship, which was never passionate, now appeared distant, mostly cerebral. I had been single for seven years and Martha for thirteen years, and neither of us had found the man of our dreams. I had fallen in love with one man; it had been a heart-pounding adventure but it hadn't worked out.

The changes from modest circumstances to fortune had no noticeable effect on the way I felt about life. I wanted to put my head on the chest of a man with whom, when I looked up into his eyes, I could feel safe and loved. Martha's billionaire lifestyle, seductive as it was, felt terribly empty to me. I could make clever conversation and dance the dance and play the social games, but my heart was not in it. Martha had only ambitions, and I had only aspirations—this major gap in our characters had been driving a wedge between us ever since we met.

I began to face the fact that I had grown tired of being a participant in Martha's life, and longed to be living a life of my own. I was expending too much energy and effort on her world, conforming to what was expected of me, and, in the process, was neglecting my own passions and dreams. Yes, living in Martha's world had its rewards, but they were becoming less and less satisfying.

I put my river house up for sale and decided that, once that was done, I would also sell the house I was rebuilding at the beach. Then I could put aside money for my kids' college tuitions, buy a small place with a garden in a less expensive location, and try to go back to school or volunteer at one of the wild animal rescue shelters, which had piqued my interest.

One of the first people who looked at my river house was Eartha Kitt. Her Realtor, Dorita, who was a friend of mine, thought Eartha would like it. She danced in with her toy poodles, and her beautiful daughter Kitt. "Let's do it," she said in her distinctive "Santa Baby" voice. I had expected to get more for my place, but I could not resist Eartha's candid offer. Without playing any of the games people sometimes do during the sale of a house, we agreed on everything. We soon signed a contract by which we agreed that the passing of title would take place six months later, the following spring.

I sold my MSLO stock to make sure I didn't get caught when and if it went down to $13 again, as it had done that March. I needed every penny.

ALTHOUGH EVERYONE TALKED about the need to show restraint after September 11, glamorous events and extremely elegant Christmas parties went on as usual. On November 13, Martha did the official lighting of the magical windows at FAO Schwarz in New York, with cocktails and sugarplum princess delights.

On the evening of November 15, Sam was honored for his work in cancer research and received a "Corporate Vision" award at Gilda's Club in New York, presented to him by Gilda Radner's former *Saturday Night Live* costar Chevy Chase. Comedian and talk show host Rosie O'Donnell was a special guest. Martha and I missed the cocktails and silent auction because we both worked late but we got there in time for the black-tie dinner and award presentation hosted by Joy Behar of ABC's *The View*. The performance after dinner included music and stand-up comedy.

Sam gave his annual holiday party on December 6 at his recently renovated loft in SoHo, the walls covered with superb modern art. Among the two hundred or so guests, Johnny Pigozzi came with his friend Mick Jagger. On December 14, Martha had her own Christmas party, a sit-down dinner for almost a hundred people at Chanterelle. Charlie Rose and his companion, the ethereally beautiful Amanda Burden, sat at Martha's table. Martha's daughter, Alexis, was there also, which made Martha really happy. Sam had been invited to the party but he only came by to pay respects, as he had other engagements that evening. At my table were a group of lawyers who worked with Martha. They all seemed to know each other, but as I didn't ask and they didn't say anything about it, I had no way of knowing if they were working on a class-action suit that was filed that December against MSLO and its board of directors, claiming they had artificially inflated the price of the stock in the immediate aftermath of the IPO, allowing certain investors to make a huge profit when the stock price skyrocketed.

After the party, Martha asked me if I noticed that Sam sort of dragged one foot. I had not. But Martha never missed a thing. All I saw was that Sam, although smiling and courteous as usual, looked a bit tired. But who wouldn't, with all the stress involved in heading a publicly traded biomedical company, ImClone, whose new anticancer product, Erbitux, had gone through all kinds of test trials. From numerous articles in the national press, I understood that Sam's company stock was expected to go sky-high upon FDA's approval of Erbitux, which was pending.

MARTHA AND I had so many amazing experiences together. Much of the time we were with other people, most of them fabulously interesting, complicated, each in a special relationship with Martha, each friendly toward her but protective of themselves at the same time, most of them high achievers and public figures. All these friendships were highly symbiotic, and there was never a question in my mind that each and every one of Martha's friends sincerely cared for Martha and liked being in her presence and doing things with her.

Yet, most of Martha's friends seemed to avoid spending long periods of time with her. For almost a decade, I, alone or with my children, appeared to be the only adult who spent real time with Martha, days on end, on vacation or not. When we got together, we looked at each other, we talked to each other, and I momentarily forgot what we "knew" of each other.

When I told Martha how annoyed I was that my children would be spending New Year's Eve with their father, she proposed we go somewhere together.

"Where should we go where we would have fun? Somewhere in South America, so there is no time change," Martha said. "Call this travel agent in New York. She came to a White House dinner. It would be good to get to know her. I'm sure she knows lots of nice people."

I called the travel agent, who turned out to be extremely knowledgeable and professional. She put together a fantastic itinerary.

I wanted to go trekking in the high plains of Chile. Perhaps I harbored some hope that if we used our bodies, we might forge a way back to some common ground, impossible to accomplish if we turned our vacation into a decadent bash with Martha and her wealthy tribe.

But Martha insisted we go to Mexico's Las Ventanas al Paraiso resort in Cabo San Lucas instead. As she became less concerned about gathering great riches, Martha was increasingly attracted to the comforts exclusively enjoyed by the very wealthy. When I asked the travel agent about the resort, she laughed and said, "Posh, five-star? I thought you wanted to begin the New Year with outdoor adventure, glorious views, pink flamingoes, mountain air, and a good hike!"

To convince me, Martha reminded me that Johnny Pigozzi was expecting us on his boat in Panama to celebrate his birthday, that Sam would join us there, that she would lease a jet to fly us to Mexico, then Panama City and back home, and that she and Sam would pay for helicopter flights in Panama. All I would have to pay for were the on-location expenses. Martha and I would share a suite at Las Ventanas.

In the end, I accepted, even though the hotel turned out to be so expensive—$1,500 a night—that the six nights would cost me as much as if we had gone to Chile for twelve days flying on a regular airline, and I knew it would be much more once the meals and extras started to trickle in. It's hard to be on a budget when you're traveling with someone with limitless funds. At the last minute, Martha also invited Kevin Sharkey. It was her Christmas gift to him for all his hard work at Skylands, she said. I was delighted, as I liked Kevin and enjoyed his company.

On December 27, 2001, early in the morning, Larry, Martha's driver, took us to Million Air terminal at Bridgeport Airport, where we were to meet Kevin. Martha spent the ride shouting into her cell phone, as usual. I had no idea that just about then, a drama was playing out for Sam that would forever change all of our intertwined lives.

We boarded Martha's leased Hawker, fastened our seat belts, and enjoyed the airplane fare Martha had prepared for us with champagne and leftover Christmas delicacies: caviar, foie gras, and fresh Viennese bread toast. Then, as Kevin napped, Martha showed me some of her writing projects and asked my opinion on some pictures she planned to use for an article.

Having lived in friendship with Martha for so many years, I was used to the soundtrack of the ringing phones, the detached, multi-subject conversations that she carried on. When Martha started to scream on the phone, I simply tuned out, or walked away, not wanting to know whom she was demeaning or why. Which is exactly what I did when we stopped in San Antonio to refuel.

Later, we landed in Los Cabos and were whisked out to Las Ventanas al Paraiso. As we checked into our luxurious suite, Villa 401, Martha realized she had forgotten to make a reservation for Kevin. She offered to order a roll-out bed for him in the living room, a generously sized common space that separated our bedrooms, Martha having taken the one farthest away from the entrance, which also happened to be the larger one, but they both had king-size beds. My heart ached, because Martha seemed to not see, or worse, not to care about his reaction.

"Kevin," I said. "We can share my bed. See? There is plenty of room for both of us." I showed him the large bed that occupied most of my bedroom. Kiss kiss. Both cheeks.

To give us both some privacy, I spent evenings on the terrace adjacent to our suite until Kevin went to sleep.

One night I lay on a chaise lounge, reading under the stars, the fire going in the terrace fireplace. I had scented the fire with some copal tree resin, a kind of incense the Mayans used in all their mystical ceremonies and sacred rituals. When I asked the wrinkled old lady in the marketplace what kind of ceremonies, she said, "Confession of misdeeds."

I wasn't sure I understood, so I asked again: "Was there death?"

She smiled and said, "Confession."

As a precaution, I put only one little chunk of the copal amber on the fire every night. I figured that, burning it outside, the fumes would dissipate, and indeed by the time Martha joined me on the terrace only the slightest trace of the sweet smell remained. She was coming from a massage in her room, where she usually had them at night. We both sampled the various types of massage treatments offered at the spa, but Martha often indulged in more than one each day. She took a sip of my drink, which was made with the aromatic fresh juice of a Yucatán aloe, maguey. I had been given some during a massage and I liked it. From my pretravel reading, I knew that maguey was an agave plant much revered by the Aztecs for its medicinal properties. This warrior culture also used the prickles from the plant for piercing fleshy body parts, like the ear, in order to draw sacrificial blood to smear on the faces of their idols. The Aztecs stored these blood-stained aloe thorns in urns in their temples to prove that the blood-offering had been made.

As we lounged in comfortable chaises, wrapped in our luxuriously soft, white hotel robes, watching the Sea of Cortez, we ordered more of those drinks, and I asked Martha about her friends, and how they were spending the New Year's holidays.

"Memrie," she said, "is in Aspen again."

Charlotte and Billy were in Seal Harbor, and Charles was in Seattle.
"And his yacht? Is it finished?"

"Everything exactly the same gray as his house in Medina and the apartment in Monte Carlo."

Martha's negative take on Charles's boat, one of the largest and best-engineered yachts in the world, warned me to change the subject.

"How's Sam?"

"He disappeared again," Martha said with that inflectionless voice and those raised eyebrows that told me she wanted to dish.

I wasn't going to let her take me there, so I said, "Maybe he just needs a break. He's been working so hard. He's probably peopled out."

"He's with some woman."

As far as I was concerned, Sam's private life was Sam's business, so I glossed over it, but Martha felt like talking, so she did. I heard her say something about Sam walking funny at her Christmas party, his daughter selling stock, and that Merrill Lynch didn't want to sell Sam's stock, and I thought, *Why is she talking about this? I don't want to talk about money. I don't want to think of money. I'm on vacation!* I tuned Martha out. I was watching the waves in the moonlight and was only half-listening when I heard her say, "I sold mine."

I wondered why she had bothered to tell me that and what it was supposed to mean, but knowing how much Martha hated when friends kept secrets from her and how she always took it as a snub, I thought maybe she was telling me that she had sold her ImClone shares to punish Sam for having dropped out of her life for a while. It crossed my mind that maybe Martha felt guilty for having sold Sam's stock. I couldn't think of any other reason that she thought I would care about that. *Oh, well, she'll buy it back.*

We had been there a few days when Kevin introduced Martha and me to two very handsome, well-mannered European men, one of them, Paolo, a dead ringer for Richard Gere. Kevin had met them a few years before, while sailing off the coast of Greece on one of his friends' yachts. They invited us to go deep-sea fishing on the last day of the year and we made plans to spend New Year's Eve with them as well.

I struck up a nice rapport with "Richard Gere," which Martha might not have liked, but she had been in a bad mood ever since we had left home, giving off angry vibes and making it hard for anyone else to have a good time. During the New Year's Eve dinner, as we sat on either side of this man, Martha, who looked stunning, had apparently decided he was her kind of a guy. Trying to impress him, she kept ordering expensive extra foils like Cristal Rosé, Ossetra caviar, and other such niceties to accompany our already extravagant feast.

He was too blasé to care. I think that hurt her feelings—Martha was used to being the center of attention—or it may have been because a wealthy man with whom Martha had a short-lived affair came by our table to greet us, a gorgeous new wife on his arm. Fact was that right after midnight, Martha simply left the dining table, walking away without a good-bye and leaving us with a very large bill, a good part of which was due to Martha's ridiculously expensive additions to the menu. Kevin and I were mortified. We decided to subtract Martha's extravagances—payment for which we would figure out later—and evenly share the remainder with our dinner companions.

On New Year's Day, very early, Martha and I went sea-kayaking. It was a gorgeous morning, but Martha still was in a bad mood. She insinuated that Paolo had slept with a woman he had picked up after I left. It wasn't the first time that Martha had maligned a man who treated her with disinterest, but I was tired of her attempts to sour me on men I might find attractive, and let it pass.

Perhaps frustrated that she didn't get a rise out of me, Martha started to criticize my paddling. Without a word, I dropped my paddle, and, resting it across my lap, I let her row alone.

The next day Kevin flew back to the States, and Martha's chartered plane took us to Panama City International Airport. We transferred to a helicopter and, about two hours later, were landing on a sandy beach where a tender from Johnny's Pigozzi's *Amazon Express* was waiting to take us to his yacht moored in a picturesque bay off the coast. Martha and I stayed for a few days before the party, and Sam joined us the day of Johnny's birthday celebration. We all had a wonderful time talking, swimming, fishing, digging for luscious oysters, spending those few days with Johnny, his girlfriend Olga, a European blue-blood princess, and her two interesting friends, an architect and a photographer. Poised, quietly confident, and gently unassuming, Olga had made all the preparations for Johnny's birthday party with the help of her talented friends. With not one thing bought, they transformed the covered porch of a bamboo cabin on the shore nearby into a magical stage set decorated with fresh flowers, leaves, and shells.

It was a stylish celebration. Johnny was unmistakably touched. With great affection and gratitude in his eyes, he enveloped Olga in a long embrace, which, although chaste, was charged with such intimacy that I turned my gaze away.

I thoroughly enjoyed that magical evening. Our beautiful hostess seated Martha with Johnny and Sam. There had been some general conversation about a delay in the experimental cancer treatment Sam's company was working on. As far as I understood, it seemed there was a problem with the paperwork filed with the FDA application, that it was not organized precisely as they required. To my mind, it sounded like something from a Communist bureaucracy, like being rejected for putting dashes instead of forward slashes in your birth date.

All of us spent the night on the yacht, lulled to sleep by the sea. I slept outside on the upper deck in that heavenly air. I remember looking up at the sky and hearing my grandfather's voice, almost as if he were next to me: "The stars," he used to tell me, "are the diamonds of the poor."

The next morning, Sunday, January 6, I was awakened by the splashing of dolphins and the swish of pelicans flying low. While we ate our last breakfast on the *Amazon Express*, Martha and I kept wondering about the fragrant whiff we noticed on the breeze. It was the scent of flowering bamboo, we were told.

Together with Sam, we climbed onto a little boat that took us ashore, where we got into a waiting helicopter that would take us to Panama City. From there, Sam would be taking his own chartered plane to a meeting in California about the failed FDA approval of Erbitux, while Martha and I were to return to Connecticut. Hundreds of feet in the air, Martha and Sam sat side by side in the cabin, and I faced them, jammed in next to all of Martha's bags and hats and other luggage. I was reading, wrapped, as I usually am when I travel, in a large scarf. Suddenly I felt the door give way under my elbow with a screeching rasp, and a blast of frigid air yank my scarf through the opening. Sky poured through the aperture, surprisingly icy considering that beyond the colorful flutter of my scarf I could see the warm and swampy country beneath us, the jungle vegetation choking in stagnant pools.

I stiffened. *God, am I going to die? My children.* I looked from the gaping abyss toward Martha and Sam.

"My door!" I said, but it was as if my voice would not work. "My door is open!" I said again, my voice choked with fear. Sam came to help. He strained against the enormous suck of pressure from the other side, and with all his might, struggled to close it. As he tried to keep his balance, I thought, *My God, he could slip right out.* I wrapped my arms and legs around him. As Sam wrestled with the helicopter door and I held him, hard, I swiveled in my seat and saw Martha. She was sitting, rigid, her expression severe, her feet on the seat, knees spread apart, her hands clawing at the tight canvas lining the copter's ceiling above her head. In that instant, I saw the limits of our friendship. No concern, no smile, just overwhelming will emanated from Martha's calm detachment, her gaze filled with cold indifference.

Despite his slenderness, Sam closed the door in a show of Herculean strength, shutting out the thrum of the engines.

Inside the copter, the silence was profound. For a few moments, no one spoke.

"So," Sam finally said, observing his position wedged between my thighs. Then he looked down the length of my body, all the way to my toes, and then up in the other direction, past my chest, and he smiled wryly.

There is nothing in the world like comic relief. I joined in.

"Now," I said, "you can say I've held you close."

Always the gentleman, Sam gently untangled himself, crossed the tiny copter, and buckled himself back into his own seat.

He looked at me and laughed. "You should have seen your face!"

Then we laughed. I heard Martha laugh too, but I could not look at her.

SOON AFTER OUR return from the Mexico-Panama vacation, Martha told me that "they" were asking questions about her sale of ImClone stock. The stock dropped more than 13 percent on January 10, the day Sam publicly acknowledged that just before New Year's Eve the FDA had rejected the application for Erbitux. The company's stock had fallen more than 40 percent since December 28. I wasn't really following the story in the papers. I hated the negativity, and thought Sam would tell us the truth if and when he wanted to. Martha didn't say who "they" were. As far as I was concerned, it was a business matter. I thought "they" were people at Martha's company whom she was bickering with, something which, judging by how much Martha complained about them to me, it seemed she often did. There might also have been, I imagined, some kind of regulatory body that oversaw stock sales, because Martha had told me one day that "they" came in and asked to see the "big kahuna," which sounded to me like one of those exaggerations Martha would make, because I never heard anyone refer to her in those terms. I wondered if it had something to do with the fact that she was being considered for the board of the New York Stock Exchange at the time.

While I listened to Martha talk about her other problems or mention "them" asking questions, and while the details of our conversations at Las Ventanas were still present in some recess of my mind, I did not fully appreciate the depth of her worries, because I was preoccupied by other things, like my empty nest, and my financial load—I wasn't strapped, as I had a successful real estate business and was happy to work seven days a week from morning till night, but I still felt a sustained level of anxiety about it. I was sure that both Martha and I would resolve our problems, and still had great hopes for our friendship, although it was harder and harder to be the sounding board for her personal problems and her seething anger.

I knew so little of what was going on that when Martha told me she could no longer speak to Sam, I thought that because Sam's public image had taken such a drubbing of late, her PR people had asked Martha to stay away so as not to risk compromising her own image. When she said she would not be attending his first-Wednesday-of-the-month cultural soirée, I figured it was a temporary situation, as Martha and I always went to those salons for the New York Council for the Humanities, of which Sam was the chairman. The soirées were held at Sam's elegant penthouse, where accomplished people in the world of arts, journalism, and politics came to listen or give interesting talks and have erudite discussions.

On one of those Wednesday evenings during the months when Martha did not see Sam, after a day when she had been taping a television segment at the Westport studio and I had been doing real estate business, Larry drove us together to New York, dropping me first in front of Sam's building in SoHo before taking Martha to some parties or meetings. Martha and I agreed to get back together afterward for a late dinner at Balthazar, one of our favorite places to eat in New York, where we usually ordered the multi-tiered seafood platter, steak frites or brandade de morue, a Burgundy or Bordeaux to go with, and, from the bakery, I would always take home delicious walnut bâtard, mouthwatering éclairs, brioches, and croissants for my girls when they were home.

Before I left her car, Martha asked me to tell Sam that he should call her on her driver's cell phone. When Martha reached into her over-stuffed chocolate-brown Birkin bag and pulled out a sticky note on which she scribbled down the driver's number, it did not occur to me that we were doing something wrong.

I took the yellow sticky message without a second thought and slipped the folded missive inside my red Bolide handbag, running my fingers over the fine saltwater crocodile bumps that went from perfect ovals at the base of the bag to small, even rectangles lining up near the top. How I loved that bag!

I am quite sure that had she given it a moment's thought, Martha would have realized that by giving me the message she was making me both an accomplice and a witness. It didn't matter to me, because Martha had told me so little about what was going on. She had never used the term "investigation," or given me any clear indication that she was worried. All I knew was that some people, whom Martha referred to as "they," were bothering her with questions about her sale of Sam's stock.

I parted with Martha and buzzed myself in to Sam's apartment, taking the elevator to the penthouse. The elevator door opened inside Sam's entrance hall, giving on to the salon-size living room with tall windows overlooking SoHo on the right. I gave Sam the folded-up paper, slipping it in his hand while giving him a casual hug and kissed both cheeks. I said in his ear, "Martha wants you to call her at this number."

Sam replied, "Why isn't she coming?"

"I don't know. She said you'd understand."

"It's silly."

I never knew if he called her or not.

In fact, I didn't understand what it all implied until the end of March, while on our way to the movies one evening to catch a late show Martha and I were sharing the events of the day, as we had countless times during the previous twenty years. As we pulled out of Martha's Turkey Hill driveway in her black BMW 7 Series, waiting for the gate to open, Martha said, "Did you read the papers today?"

"Yes. Poor Sam! I wish they had left him alone!"

I was sure that Martha was as horrified as I was to read those articles about Sam, which became more damning each day. By late January, there was a congressional investigation into whether ImClone had misled investors regarding the approval process of Erbitux in order to keep the stock price up, that maybe it wasn't just a paperwork problem, and then the SEC and the Justice Department joined the fray. Apparently, between the two of them, Sam and his brother, Harlan, who was the company's chief operating officer, had sold millions in ImClone stock in the months before the FDA rejected the Erbitux application. On March 14, the *Times* reported that Sam's daughter Aliza had sold nearly $2.5 million worth of ImClone stock just one day before the FDA decision, when the company's stock started to plummet. Then on March 22, the *Times* reported that the House Energy and Commerce Committee, which was investigating ImClone, had asked Sam for information about his daughter's sale as well as information about other relatives and his own personal accounts. It wasn't pretty. Sam's investigation was reported all over the media. We were both silent for a while as Martha slowed the car to a stop at the traffic light at the end of the road.

"I saw them again today." There was lassitude in Martha's voice. I was convinced that even if in her tireless pursuit of money Martha always knew what she was doing, she had acted on an impulse when she sold Sam's stock.

Martha so exhausted people around her that once in a while one needed to take time out away from her in order to recharge or simply live one's private life in private. Yet, it wasn't easy to tell Martha that you needed privacy. Each time I did it, I had to confront intense hostility. It was simpler not to answer her calls for a day or two. Deep down, I was convinced Martha had sold her shares to punish Sam for not having called her back those last few days of December.

"Why don't you tell them it was instinct that made you sell?"

"Stop talking about instincts," Martha said testily.

Although I thought she had sold Sam's stock because of her vengeful tendencies, I suspected Martha knew her instinct to punish was unattractive. I didn't want to offend her, so I decided to say that I was referring to one of the traits she was admired for, and said: "But everyone knows you have good business instincts. Look how far you've gotten with them!"

"It's stupid." In the glow of the streetlights, I saw anger flashing in her eyes.

She was right. Sam would have given Martha practical advice. Not being able to talk to him must have frustrated her as much as those front-page articles about him.

Breaking the silence as she stepped on the gas when the light turned green, Martha said, "By the way, I gave them your number. I hope you don't mind."

There was something so uncharacteristically meek in her voice that I turned to look at her, but she kept staring at the road.

I wasn't concerned. I was familiar with Martha's moods.

A couple of weeks later, at the beginning of April, Martha's lawyer called my cell. The conversation didn't go very well, as I got piqued that he thought I'd speak about her trips to someone calling me from an unidentified caller ID, whose voice I didn't recognize. When I told Martha about it, she confirmed it had been her lawyer, and that he had already spoken to her about our exchange. Martha was tense. Although she had been in a bad mood since that morning when we left for our Mexico-Panama vacation on December 27, 2001, I thought she might be worried about what was happening to Sam. I was. The newspapers had not only been reporting his ImClone troubles, but his star-studded personal life was becoming regular gossip fodder as well. On May 22, Sam had resigned as CEO of the compnay. His brother, Harlan, would take over.

I felt lucky, as my own troubles seemed to be easing up. Selling my river house at the beginning of April considerably alleviated my financial pressures. I reminded Martha that her office had not billed me for the Mexico expenses and Martha said she'd tell Heidi about it. Heidi was Martha's business manager. At least that's how I understood it, since it was Heidi who had sent me the modified contract on the Peru loan, and it had been Heidi to whom I had complained. I didn't like owing Martha and wanted to settle that bill. Despite the fact that the one mortgage I held was still for a staggering amount, and the reconstruction costs for the beach house were running more than triple the cost of what I had originally estimated, my real estate business was going strong. I finally would make enough in commissions to cover my expenses and follow through with my plans to reduce my living costs and be able to go back to school or volunteer while supporting my daughters and my father, whose deteriorating health had been causing us concern for a while.

I was a bit down since I had intended to spend the Memorial Day weekend with the girls and my friend RoAnn, at her summer home, as we had for years. To us, she, her husband, Jim, and their four boys are like family. But both my girls had plans to go away that weekend with their new school friends. There was also Martha, who wanted me to go to East Hampton with her instead. I decided to go, as she clearly needed company. Kevin Sharkey joined us as well, and we spent a quiet holiday weekend at Lily Pond. Martha, who flew us out on her leased company jet, found a moment when we were far from Kevin's earshot and whispered, "That . . . situation . . . it's been resolved."

"Thank God!" I said.

Unfortunately, she could not have been more wrong.

A FEW DAYS later, early in the morning on June 7, I read the following story by Andrew Pollack in the *New York Times*:

> **Martha Stewart Said to Sell Shares Before F.D.A. Ruling**
> Martha Stewart, a close friend of the former chief executive of ImClone Systems, sold all her shares in the biotechnology company a day or two before ImClone announced an unfavorable ruling by the Food

and Drug Administration, according to people close to a Congressional investigation of the company.

Ms. Stewart, chief executive of Martha Stewart Living Omni-
Media, has long been a friend of Samuel D. Waksal, who resigned as
ImClone's chief executive two weeks ago as questions mounted as to
whether he had tipped off family members or friends to sell ImClone
shares before the F.D.A. decision was made public.

The press announced that Martha had sold just under four thousand shares of ImClone stock at an average price of $58.43 a share the
day before the FDA ruling. The sale had netted her about $228,000,
which was probably about $50,000 more than if she'd waited until the
stock price tanked. Her name would be attached to the scandal from
that day forward.

Martha had spent the previous evening at a private gathering in a
palatial Manhattan apartment overlooking the East River. That day, she
had been officially named to the twenty-seven-member board of the
NYSE, which she was very excited about. It was a great accomplishment, and I was very happy for her. Dining among friends of presidents
and statesmen, Martha sat next to an influential media tycoon, someone whom she had known for a long time. Some years before, Martha
even pinned her marital hopes on him. But after that dinner, Martha
insisted he must have known his newspaper would publish an article
about her the next morning. She resented him so much for not telling
her that listening to Martha you'd think he was a real-life J. J. Hun-
secker, that treacherous journalist in the film *Sweet Smell of Success*,
blameworthy for the whole mess.

Early on the morning of June 12, Sam was arrested, charged with
insider trading for allegedly tipping off his father, a Holocaust survivor,
and his daughter Aliza, both of whom had sold large amounts of stock,
and with perjury for lying to investigators about the transactions. Federal agents had gone so far as to block "potential escape routes from his
apartment." It seemed ridiculous to be treating him that way.

Over the following days, newspapers were abuzz with talk of Martha's sale of Sam's stock. The gossip columns were even suggesting that Sam was sleeping with both Martha and her daughter, which was a complete fabrication. Reporters were chasing her. They were even calling her unlisted home number. Every article I read about Sam or Martha smeared them with innuendoes and accusations.

I expected that Martha would do everything feasible to put an end to the scandal and extricate herself and redeem her image as soon as possible. In the meantime, we continued life as usual.

On June 15, Martha and I were invited to the glamorous Connecticut wedding of the daughter of friends from the art world and film industry. It was one of those enchanted evenings that you don't want to end. The music was so perfectly chosen that I couldn't resist going to the dance floor where, although I had no date, I soon was rocking, swinging, and spinning with Steve Buscemi, an actor I admire.

Outside the wedding tent, I joined a celebrity-studded group of men smoking under the evening stars and chitchatting with that gusto particular to guys in a gossiping mood. I had barely lit my cigarette when a handsome actor whom I had seen in a few movies made a smug comment about Martha going to prison. I shot back that he was mistaken, claiming I knew better, because Martha was my closest friend. His reply was friendly toward me but filled with disdain for Martha. By the time I heard myself saying, "Gentlemen, thank you for the company. I shall let you enjoy your cigars now," I had nothing more to add. I walked away from the group and went to stand alone by the lake.

I stood there for a while, my back turned on those beautiful people, thinking I might have underestimated the gravity of the "situation" Martha was in, but kept reminding myself she had said it had been resolved. So the only answer seemed to be that the journalists were making a mountain out of a molehill just because of Martha's fame.

19

Into the Quicksand

ONE AFTERNOON IN mid-June, I was driving along, listening to Marilyn Horne sing my favorite aria, "Mon coeur s'ouvre à ta voix." My cell phone lay on the seat of my Mercedes, and at red lights I'd punch in my code and listen to as many messages as I could, saving the important ones. I was making plans to take my daughters on a safari adventure in Africa, a place I had always dreamed of sharing with them. I wanted to watch the wonder on their faces as they saw elephants and hippos, great golden-eyed cats, flamingos flying over the lake, and all the sights straight from *Out of Africa*.

This was a trip we would take all on our own, just me and my two girls, who had passed so much of their childhood with Martha, around Martha, because of Martha, Martha determining what we did or did not do. Dreaming of Africa and listening to opera, I thought of the conversation Martha and I had had just days before, when I told her, "I want a simpler sort of existence."

That had been hard to say, but once I'd said it I felt right with the world for the first time in years. I'd been feeling the gentle rush of the weather all May, portending a summer of books and breakfasts with my children. I had begun spending more time with my own circle of friends. I wasn't thinking about parties or outings or group vacations but of a peaceful personal space, without another person's consciousness impinging.

Red light, code punched. I heard a click, the pause before a voice finds its way from cyberspace to your ear. "Hi, Mariana. It's me. Did you get the theater tickets . . . ?" *Save.*

"Honey. How ARE you? How does one get hold of . . ." *Save.*

Then followed two messages from Realtors. One was asking me for feedback. *Save.* Another was from a broker who had showed one of my listings the day before, the clients nice, polite, but obviously not interested. *Erase.*

Green light. *Go.*

Red light. *Listen.*

There followed two more messages from friends, and then came message number seven, the speaker's voice at once oily and extremely distant, hard to hear. I could hear the word "commerce," and then I heard the word "Congress," and then the voice said, in a burst of clarity, "I would like to speak with you, Ms. Pasternak."

Why would someone from Congress want to speak with Ms. Pasternak? My first thought was that it had something to do with the congressman from Louisiana who'd done a cooking segment with Martha on her show. She had mentioned his name lately and asked if I had watched him barbecue but I hadn't. It was possible that someone from his office had picked my name wrongly from Martha's contact list, which meant I would refer the person from Congress to Susan Magrino, Martha's publicist. Just as I did with the reporters who had been calling since the weekend trying to get me talking about the star-studded wedding, same as when reporters tried to talk to me about Martha. The one exception was Barbara Walters, whose work I admired ever since I had watched her on Romanian television before my escape. She came to interview Martha at Turkey Hill, and I joined them for lunch in the outside kitchen. I hadn't expected her to be so personable and candid about her own life; while she led the conversation through myriad issues, I felt as if I had known her forever.

Beep. End of message.

The light turned green and I accelerated. I tried to find yet another spot where reception was better. Not waiting for red lights, I kept the phone clamped to my ear as my messages spilled forth: the hardware store, saying my custom skylights had come in; a friend saying, "Honey, I *need* to see you," for she was under the weather; and then an unfamiliar female voice saying, "Miss Pasternak, I am with the FBI. Could you please give me a call back at this number." I figured Martha's lawyer had given them my number. Perhaps the FBI wanted to confirm that I was with Martha on that trip.

A few more messages. House construction. Friends. "Sweetie, let's have lunch." And then: "Ms. Pasternak, I'm calling a second time from Congress . . ." Him again. "I left you a message a little while ago," the obsequious voice said. "I really would like to speak with you."

I was a little annoyed. Why were these people bothering me? Reporters, Congress, the FBI.

At the office, I called the man from Congress before the woman from the FBI, because he had called first. I dialed the number. It rang twice. I was expecting an operator or a receptionist. He picked up.

"This is Mariana Pasternak," I said. "I'm returning your call."

"Oh, Ms. Pasternak," he said. "I want to ask you a few questions about a trip you took to Mexico." Ingratiating at first, his voice suddenly became ominously official. "On December 27, 2001, you were accompanying Martha Stewart on a private plane. I have you on a passenger log."

"Excuse me," I remember saying when I realized it wasn't as simple as referring him to Martha's publicist. "I am only calling to let you know I have now returned your calls. I'm not sure I should talk to you without counsel. I need to think about it."

His tone changed. "Well then, Ms. PPPPasternak," he said, practically spitting out the P like a watermelon seed, then asked that I have my lawyer call him as soon as possible.

"Thank you for helping me make my decision as to whether or not I should have a lawyer. Clearly," I said, "I should."

I hung up the phone. I was shaking. I was starting to realize something was really wrong. I looked around at the four walls of my tony real estate office, decorated with beautifully framed oils of New England's summertime shores. All I could think was, *I do not have a lawyer.*

I immediately phoned Martha to tell her about the calls. Obviously the "situation" had not been resolved as she'd said. She was in a meeting when she answered her cell. She listened and said she'd be in New York late. There was a raised alertness in her voice. We agreed to meet at her house later that night when she came home.

In the glow of my headlights on Martha's tall stone wall, I punched in the Turkey Hill gate code and her painted wooden gates opened slowly with their usual hum. Entering through the back door, I walked between the chows sprawled on the floor, guarding the entrance to the dimly lit large hall, its far corner a home office. Martha was there at her desk, the computer on. While she closed up her work, I went to the kitchen and put the kettle on the stove. We had met there at night so many times before, for tea, or to enjoy Lily's Chinese cooking. Sometimes I'd be there because Martha needed help coaxing the chows to come in from outside. Whatever reason women friends might have to meet in each other's kitchens late at night, we had.

Martha made "jade dew" green tea with leaves that she brought home from her frequent business trips to Japan. I loved to watch her absorbed in the fastidious "tea ceremony." Warming up the cups and the fine, old Japanese teapot in which Martha carefully arranged the fresh Uji Yamé leaves, she picked up the kettle the very moment it came to a boil, then, as she poured on the water, she kept an eye on the clock above the stove. Precisely ninety seconds later, she filled the cups, slowly, with a gentle gradual tipping of the pot, and that was the moment I liked most, because she treated that liquid as if it were a beloved being.

We sat down at her kitchen table that evening, the same place we used to sit when we first became friends, but it no longer reverberated with the sounds of animated conversation. One of the Himalayan cats jumped on the table, rubbing softly against my arm. It was close to midnight. Both of us tired and under the cruel illusion that the nuisance that brought us together that night was a short-term affair, Martha and I filled long silences with sips of aromatic, pale green tea, the only other sound the screeching of song canaries in their antique cages on her glassed-in porch.

Martha said little, but I knew she had had a long day and was probably still half-thinking about it. I was used to her operating on different levels at the same time. Yet the silence that night had an unusual ring to it. It was as if I were watching TV and across the table from me was not my friend but Martha on a program, appearing to look me straight in the eye while, in fact, she was reading a text scrolling on a hidden screen, a text she edited while reading, taking out words that she didn't want me to hear.

When we looked in each other's eyes that night, tacitly acknowledging the gravity of the situation, all I had to go on was what I thought to be implied by the subtle signals that I had learned to read in Martha's body language during the twenty years of our friendship. But if I were to do something for Martha, didn't I need to be told in words exactly what was expected of me?

As I prepared to leave, I said I would take a third mortgage to pay for the legal expenses I'd incur with this. But Martha said that I only needed lawyers for a couple of interviews in New York and maybe a quick trip to Washington, and assured me that her company would pay for the lawyers.

"If you pay, it might come back to hound you. They'll think that I am telling them what you want me to say. I'll take a third mortgage."

"Mariana! My company will pay. They paid for everyone else," Martha said.

That was the first time I heard that other people were involved. I dreaded the idea that there might still be lots of surprises Martha had in store for me now that I was in it.

"What do I tell these people, Martha? I don't know anything."

She looked me in the eyes, her jaw squarely clenched. "Just answer their questions."

It was well after midnight when I left Martha's house. It was damp and chilly outside. In the overcast sky, the moon gave the illusion of moving toward the clouds. *Nothing is as it seems*, I thought. *Answer their questions! As if that should be a simple task. It might be for her. She has such a mission-oriented mind. But for me? Am I supposed to know the answers? What had Martha told me that I needed to remember?*

To avoid getting upset with Martha when she was rude, arrogant, impatient, critical, I had allowed myself the luxury of inattention around her. I could barely remember anything concrete. I had read the articles about Sam and understood that what they were faulting him for was selling, or trying to sell, his ImClone stock on December 27. I didn't remember which day Martha and I had that conversation on the terrace at Las Ventanas al Paraiso, but it could not have been on December 27. Martha and I were on a plane, traveling on December 27. Then, when we got to Las Ventanas, while Kevin and I were unpacking, I could hear Martha scream at the top of her lungs to someone, but she was in her room, and if I paid any attention to it, it was only because it annoyed me that we were supposed to be on vacation and she was obviously on the phone, doing business. After that we went walking around a small town nearby, and in the market I bought the copal incense. But the massage where the lady served that Yucatán-aloe drink, I was sure happened a few days later. The best I could place our terrace conversation was the night after we took a daylong hike in the hills, a few days after December 27.

I also remembered one breakfast Martha and I had on the terrace at Las Ventanas when we read the newspapers. We had gone first to the hotel boutique, which sold American papers. But I didn't recall if it had been then that we read the article about ImClone and the FDA delaying approval of Erbitux. It could have been after the deep-sea fishing trip on the last day of the year. What I did remember was walking down some steps ahead of Martha, talking. It may have been the steps toward the beach, where we took long walks every day. At some point in that conversation, I was looking at Martha over my shoulder, and she was looking at me with that fixed stare, and one of us said, "Isn't it nice to have brokers who tell you those things?" But who said it? Was it Martha? She often used the expression "Isn't it nice?" But why would she be boasting? Was it me? Why would I say that? It didn't make sense.

I was getting frustrated by the fact that I clearly remembered those words but I didn't really know who had said them. Then, I thought, *So what?*

My mind was spinning.

Just as I had begun to hope for a life of my own, without dedicating as much of it to Martha and her needs, I was being pulled into yet another Martha drama. The very thought of it exhausted me.

I felt overwhelmed. Martha must have known that. Since I retrieved those messages from the government only hours earlier, I felt as if I had stepped on quick sand, and was sinking deeper and deeper into a bottomless pit. I had to try to understand what it was that Martha had gotten me into. And the biggest surprise, after the calls from Congress and FBI, was the fact that other people from her company were involved, and that Martha had not told me.

As much as I might have wanted to protect Martha, I didn't know how to protect her, because I didn't know what she was dealing with. I did not really know what Martha was being suspected or accused of. I also knew little about the law beyond real-estate law. And from my position of ignorance, I suddenly had to deal with very powerful authorities. I thought of the story in the Bible where the soldier in King David's army rushed forward to support the Ark of the Covenant when the animal pulling the cart that carried it stumbled. When he touched the Ark, the soldier died on the spot, smitten by the Lord for his irreverent act. Only priests who knew how to deal with the Ark's immense power could touch it.

Next morning early, before eight o'clock, I was on my way to the office when Martha rang my cell phone. She had found a banker willing to give me a third mortgage. And she gave me the number to call immediately.

The banker was rushing to a meeting and conferenced me with an associate, who faxed me the loan application. Our office machine started to spew page after page. I arranged the pile of paper, scanned through the info requests—many of them on each page—enough to give me pause about what I was doing.

I was taking a third mortgage on my home to give Martha a gift. Not a gift bought with disposable cash, not even with money unwisely taken out of my savings, but out of the mortar and joists of the house that belonged to my family. On top of that, it was an uncapped expense; I had no way of knowing how much I would have to spend.

I was being really foolish offering to mortgage my life to the hilt, I thought. Martha had offered to pay for the legal bills, and that seemed to be only fair. It was because of Martha that I was being pulled into a government investigation while I was minding my own business. It had not been me who sold Sam's stock. So I decided against the mortgage and accepted Martha's offer to pay the fees. Ironically, the bureaucracy I so hated ended up saving me. My annoyance at having to fill out so much paperwork had made me stop and think.

I certainly needed a lawyer. Not for me, but so I wouldn't say God knows what to get Martha in more trouble. It was typical of her to involve me in rehearsals of her spectacular career moves and her calculated business showdowns and I in no way wanted to embarrass Martha, but of all the things I'd seen and heard her do, how was I to know on my own what was legal or not? I hadn't for a moment thought that her selling the ImClone stock would be an issue beyond threatening her friendship with Sam, but now that Congress and the FBI were involved, I was starting to doubt myself.

And if she knew that there might be the slightest reason her sale could be questioned, which she must have, since she had been a stockbroker herself, why did she tell me about it? Why did she put me in harm's way? When I was planning my escape from Romania, I was burning to tell my dearest friends that I would never be able to see them again. Yet in order to protect them from the authorities, I kept to myself the crime of my planned escape, the fear that I might soon be incarcerated in a political prison, tortured, violated. And I said nothing to the people I trusted most. But Martha had so cavalierly put me at risk, simply because she wanted to get off her chest something so trivial as the sale of a few stocks that meant nothing compared to her extraordinary wealth.

I had defied a government before, and under certain circumstances I might do so again, but if ever I were to risk my freedom for a friend, it would be because I believed that my actions would contribute to a greater good. This was not one of those cases.

I decided to follow the rules because after careful consideration, as much as I loved Martha, I could not sacrifice myself in service to her devastating problems.

There is a beginning in each ending. How can one pinpoint a day, a moment, a second, of undoing? Knots take time and often skill to tie. Their undoing is a process. I had to go against our custom of my finding excuses for Martha, and I had to take leave from my being too embarrassed to shame her. If Martha shamed herself, that was up to her. All I could do for Martha was walk the plank she had put me on as well as I could, and for that I needed good advice from someone whom I could trust to keep me from saying something to harm her.

Part IV

The End of the Affair

20

The Investigation

AT FIRST I thought the Fifth Amendment could protect me from being a witness in Martha's case, since it said that no person shall be compelled in any criminal case to be a witness against himself. I certainly remembered that Post-It with the driver's number that I delivered to Sam, but at the time, I had no idea that Martha was being investigated by the FBI, the SEC, as well as the Attorney General's office. I only learned several months later, from newspaper accounts, that Martha's office was first contacted on January 25, 2002, and that she had her first interview with investigators on February 4.

As it transpired, I couldn't be protected by the Fifth Amendment.

So I answered their questions.

Over nearly two years of exhaustive questioning, I answered as well as I could, as I knew it, as I'd heard it, as I recalled it. The possibility that I might have to take some kind of lie-detector test appeared quite real to me all along. The interviewers, who worked for various American government branches, were all very proper and intelligent, not in the least resembling the thugs I had dealt with in Romania. My interrogators worked for various American government branches and were good at their jobs. It may have been confusing to them that I could answer so many questions about Martha yet know so little about her sale of ImClone stock on December 27, 2001.

Eventually I gave up trying to understand why a question was asked or a subpoena served, and just answered their questions, as Martha had said to do when we had our last tea in her Turkey Hill kitchen. One of the very few things that became clear to me quite early on was that the idea that our friendship might survive that process was an illusion. Even before I testified in front of a grand jury—which was, for me, a very intimidating experience—I sensed that all there might be left of our relationship were our memories and my respect for Martha's work helping millions of people make their lives and the lives of their families a little nicer. I am sure Martha also knew that our friendship couldn't survive, although neither she nor I could have known that our hardest turn still lay ahead.

On Tuesday, June 25, 2002, CBS News reported that "Investigators with the House Energy and Commerce Committee are examining whether Stewart had inside information when she sold nearly four thousand shares of ImClone on December 27, a day before the announcement that the Food and Drug Administration had decided not to consider Erbitux, an experimental drug for combating colorectal cancer . . . sending the value of ImClone shares into a tailspin." Before her regular morning segment on the *CBS Early Show*, Martha agreed to answer a few questions asked by Jane Clayson on the show's kitchen set, where Martha was busy chopping cabbage. As the report said, "Martha paused from cabbage-slicing to predict that the investigation of her stock dealings will be resolved and 'I will be exonerated of any ridiculousness.'"

Martha's troubles came at a time when the media was permeated with corporate scandals. It was disheartening to learn from the morning papers the depth of the deceit and the magnitude of the hubris by which some of those white-collar criminal Hogzillas had appointed themselves masters of the universe, like the disgraced CEO of Tyco,

Dennis Kozlowski, whose ostentatious lifestyle included having the company pay for an $18 million apartment in New York and a million dollars toward a birthday party for his wife in Sardinia, a tasteless bacchanalia of rich people gone wild. Before long, Kozlowski was forced out of Tyco by his board of directors when they learned he was about to be indicted for misappropriating millions of Tyco's corporate funds, for which he would ultimately be convicted in 2005.

The Enron scandal was unfolding at the same time. *Fortune* magazine dubbed it "America's Most Innovative Company" from 1996 to 2001, but by December 2001 the $67 billion company had become one of the largest bankruptcies in American history. Company executives, including CEO Ken Lay, had reported false profits for years, managing to escape the collapse with millions in their own pockets while employees lost their jobs and their savings. Ken Lay would be convicted of six counts of securities and wire fraud.

The government went looking for the rotten apples in America's bountiful economic cornucopia and picked every one they could find, regardless of the degree of blemish. Sam Waksal, whose investigation began after Kozlowski's, was charged with securities fraud and conspiracy, and arrested on June 12, 2002. While Kozlowski's job had been nothing more than glorified paper-pushing and transferring vast sums of money across desks and countries, Sam had been investing millions in biomedical research dedicated to the discovery of an anticancer treatment. Still, the end does not justify the means.

Since those first days in June, when the media began reporting that Martha had sold her ImClone shares, the stock price of her own company began to fall. As I understood it, as CEO and chairman of MSLO, as well as a majority shareholder, Martha had a fiduciary duty to her shareholders. In that capacity, she made a number of written and verbal public statements meant to satisfy her responsibilities. On June 12, the day Sam was arrested, and again on June 18, Martha stated publicly that she had done nothing wrong. She said it again in front of investors and analysts when she spoke at a conference on June 19.

On June 20, Martha made an odd decision. She re-aired on her show the cooking segment with Congressman Billy Tauzin of Louisiana, called "Barbecue Shrimp with Billy," which had originally been broadcast two years earlier. I only connected the dots after Martha re-aired that show, realizing that Congressman Tauzin was the head of the House Energy and Commerce Committee investigating Martha's sale of ImClone stock. The person who had called me a few days earlier was a member of that committee. After that conversation, which had been my wake-up call to what was happening around me, I began to read those articles about ImClone, Sam, and Martha very carefully. One week earlier, Tauzin's House Committee had grilled Sam.

A few days after Martha's replay of the Tauzin segment, CBS News ran an article online, titled "Martha Stewart Focuses on Her Salad": "'There is something silly, desperate, and pathetic about it,' Eric Dezenhall, who manages corporate public relations crises, told CBS News correspondent Jim Axelrod. 'There is a certain *Saturday Night Live* backdrop to all this that will probably last in the public consciousness for a while.'"

On June 21, Peter Bacanovic and his assistant, Douglas Faneuil, were suspended by Merrill Lynch. According to the press, investigators were saying that Martha's phone log showed that Peter had called her on December 27 and told her that he "thinks ImClone is going to start trading downward." But Ken Johnson, a spokesman for the House investigating committee, chimed in that the stock had been heading down for a while. "Why did Mr. Bacanovic call her on that particular day?" Johnson wanted to know.

Peter had known Martha since the 1980s, when he was a student at Columbia and Martha's daughter, Alexis, was at Barnard, and the two became friends. Later, when Alexis was dating Sam, she introduced Peter to him. Peter would go on to work for Sam at ImClone as a director of corporate relations for a little while, but in 1993 he took a position at Merrill Lynch as a broker, listing Sam as a reference when he applied for the job. Once there, he did what lots of new brokers do to develop a client base, tapping their friends and relatives. Sam and Martha signed on.

As the *New York Times* reported, Peter "played a large role at Martha Stewart Living Omnimedia. When the company went public, he handled the 'friends and family' shares, which involved opening several hundred accounts. He helped administer the 401(k) retirement savings plan, and he handled the stock option plan."

While Martha continued to deny the insider trading allegations, on September 10 Congress dropped its investigation of her but asked the Department of Justice to launch its own investigation. In early July 2002, Martha had hired the brilliant white-collar crime attorney Robert Morvillo, who had famously dealt with New York Attorney General Eliot Spitzer's office defending Merrill Lynch when the company was investigated for conflict of interest.

On Wednesday, October 2, Doug Faneuil, Peter's assistant at Merrill Lynch, pleaded guilty to accepting gifts in exchange for keeping quiet about what he knew of Martha's stock sale.

On Thursday, October 3, Martha called NYSE CEO Richard Grasso to resign from her prestigious position on the stock exchange board, where she had been a director only since June 6. On the evening of her first day in that office, while Martha was celebrating in select company—friends of statesmen and presidents—the Associated Press ran a story about the investigation surrounding her ImClone stock sale. The *Wall Street Journal* published an article about the sale on June 7. In those four months since she was named to the NYSE board, her company's stock price dropped more than 60 percent.

Shortly after that, I received my first calls from investigators. A June 24 *New York Times* article by Constance Hays quoted a House Committee spokesman saying, "[Pasternak] was interviewed by the Congressional investigators last week, and confirmed that she had traveled with Ms. Stewart, referring to her as a 'very good friend.'" He also stated that a third person on Martha's flight to Mexico would be questioned, evidently meaning Kevin Sharkey, who was with us. A *New York Times* article reported that "Ms. Stewart's longtime personal spokeswoman, Susan Magrino, has come under scrutiny." Various reports in 2002 talked about several class-action lawsuits by investors in Martha's company. The suits claimed that Martha and other company executives had sold millions of shares of MSLO stock because they knew the share price would go down when news of the investigation of her Im-Clone sale became public. Not only was Martha's "situation" far from "resolved," but the lives of so many of us around her had been exposed to government intrusion.

I saw Martha a scant few times after that conversation in her kitchen at Turkey Hill, as I was concerned that I would then have to answer investigators' questions about our meetings, which could put her in even greater jeopardy.

At first, she kept calling and I didn't respond. Then one evening, three or four days after our last tea in her kitchen, I called her and said we could see each other if we didn't talk about the case. I was going to be in the office late, as I had to work and couldn't during the day because of the reporters. She said she was on her way to her brother George's for dessert but would come by after that.

When she arrived some time later, the first thing she said, in a raised voice, was, "What are you telling these people?"

I felt like saying, *Please leave*, but didn't. Instead, I said, "Let's go downstairs and talk." My office is on a busy corner and the main floors have windows all around. Worried someone might hear her shouting and it would be in the papers the next day, I figured the half-basement computer office was a better place to have that conversation.

On the way downstairs, she asked, "Do you know if I had a phone in Mexico?"

"I know I saw you on the phone, but don't know for sure you had a phone," I answered. Those were investigation issues, and I didn't know how to get her to stop. I said, "I know I had a phone. Do you want to see the bill? I have it in the folder in my car. I also have the receipt for having paid my spa charges." I realized I was giving her clues about what I would say, or had said.

Martha said yes, she wanted to see them.

I went outside to my car and saw that Martha had not come by herself. There was her black Suburban with Larry at the wheel. By bringing him there that night she was involving him also. I didn't think she did it on purpose but out of pure solipsism. However, she could have created just as much damage either way.

I gave Martha copies of my receipts at Las Ventanas. I never wanted to see her privately again. It was too risky. As expected, that meeting was brought up later during interviews with the investigators.

After that, we were mostly isolated from each other. It was hard not seeing her after so many years of close friendship. For a while, Martha continued to call me. One weekend that summer she left a few messages saying that Charlotte was visiting her place in Bedford so I should come and have breakfast with them. Martha knew it would be hard for me to refuse seeing Charlotte, as she was among the few people I both loved and admired. But I thought, *No, I'm not going to take the chance of involving the undersecretary for public diplomacy and public affairs in this mess. I know better by now.*

Then, in the early fall, a friend gave a dinner party for about ten people and invited us both. I think that Holly hoped she could help Martha and me save our friendship. She sat us at the narrow part of the tasteful dinner table across from each other. Martha did her best to appear as if she were making friendly conversation but all her questions to me involved veiled investigation issues.

I did not see Martha again, for many months. One day she was walking on the beach near my house with a friend of hers, Sharon Hoge, a contributing editor at *Condé Nast Traveler* magazine. Sharon had hiked with Martha, Sandy Pittman, and Sharon Patrick in Kilimanjaro. I had met Sharon before and liked her. I invited them in for some green tea. The conversation was guarded and neutral. We talked about the Buddha figures in my house. Although the topic was really aesthetics, it helped me bring up Jean-Francois Revel's book *The Monk and the Philosopher*, as I was trying to suggest to Martha that she might find some comfort in spirituality. I knew that she had to be under incredible stress and that my spiritual practice had been of great help to me. I prayed a lot in those twenty-one months.

The next time we saw each other was when Martha stopped by my house at the beginning of 2004. When the trial date was announced, I had called her home number to wish her well. Alexis had answered. She was polite but expressed her surprise that I would call there. I asked her to give my good wishes to her mom.

A few days later, Martha was outside my house with Lily, her housekeeper, whom she sent to the door to ask if she could come in. It was weird, since we had always just entered each other's houses unannounced before. At that point, I hadn't processed how deeply profound the change in our relationship was. Martha came in and I gave her a hug. She began to say something by way of an apology about Lexi's response to me. But I thought Lexi had been civil, and I appreciated the fact that she was protecting her mother. I was glad to know Martha had support at home.

Soon after I received those first calls from the authorities, my name appeared in the papers, making public my involvement in Martha's affair. Some reporters totally misstated the facts, saying I had also sold stock, which was certainly not true, as I had sold all my shares of Im-Clone stock years before, between late 1997 and early 1998.

Westport, the small town where I had been a successful, busy real estate agent for well over a decade, was a place where people knew me. I had listed, or sold, or showed their houses. My children went to school with their children, participated in community drives, played in the orchestra, been on sports teams. The girls made many friends whose parents I knew.

When I went to the local Starbucks every morning and again in the afternoon to pick up my usual, I often ran into people I knew and we would chat and exchange pleasantries and perhaps a little gossip, just as people do in all small communities. But after my name appeared in the papers in connection with the investigation in Martha's sale of Im-Clone stock, when I entered the coffee shop, the conversations seemed to stop. Then there was a lot of murmuring.

I was at the peak of my real-estate career. I also had huge financial obligations, which I was sure I could satisfy, as I was healthy, I worked hard, and I had quite a few clients whose houses I had listed for sale as well as customers who were looking to buy. Then came that day in late June when the first article appeared, mentioning my name in connection with the congressional investigation. Shortly after eight a.m., my phone started to ring with calls from clients. One by one, they politely expressed their regret at being unable to continue working with me as long as I was involved in Martha's investigation. They were concerned it could distract my focus from promoting their homes or finding them one—at least that's what they said. Before the end of that day, I had lost over 90 percent of my business, the only source of income for me and my family.

I decided to struggle through it, convinced that in a few months Martha would put an end to her ordeal, and hence mine. All I could do was to not get frazzled by the setbacks, stay calm, and continue to work.

Going to work also became tricky. Reporters and photographers kept showing up, often coming right into the office. Some waited in their cars parked at the shopping plaza across the street. Now I had to call first before going in.

"Is the coast clear?"

Dena, the Westport office manager, would go to the window and screen the cars.

"Can't really tell."

So instead of going to work at my own desk in the Westport office, where I had all my files, I'd sometimes go to the Nicholas H. Fingelly Real Estate's other office in Southport Village, the next town over. One day I parked my car about twenty yards from the entrance to the beautiful historic building that housed our office. I got out of the car that sunny summer afternoon, and looked toward the water and saw what I thought was a gun pointing at me from the other side of the fountain. Then I realized it was a camera I was being shot with. I began running back to my car as the photographer chased me, easily gaining advantage since I was not only in high heels but shaken by the surprise and the panic of thinking I was about to be killed. I got inside the car and slammed the door shut. As he pushed that grossly long lens to the edge of the open window, I reached for my coffee cup in the holder by the dash to throw it at his camera. Mercifully, I remembered Martha telling me how one can be sued for damaging a photographer's camera, so I only put my hand in front of his lens and started the car. As I drove away, I could see his face in my rearview mirror. He was driving some kind of sport utility vehicle, following me. I called the police from my cell phone. As I was talking to them, I saw him turn his car around and speed off in the opposite direction.

The harassment continued for almost two years. It got particularly bad in March of 2003, when an article published in the *Financial Times* erroneously reported that I had asked Martha to give me $150,000 to cover legal bills and mortgage payments on my home. While Martha did cover my legal expenses related to her case, I had never asked her to. Likewise, I had never asked Martha to cover my mortgage payments, and she never did. Yet the same story appeared in other newspapers, on newswires, and on Web sites. It totally destroyed my reputation. I didn't know the source for those lies but I needed them rectified. I thought of my grandfather, who used to say, "A great man once said that if a donkey kicks you, it would be silly to kick it in return," yet I felt compelled to have the truth told. I pondered the situation, sought counsel, and prayed for guidance to do the right thing. In the end, I decided not to go public with it. I did not want to add to Martha's grief. But I did ask that Martha put the truth in writing.

Whatever Martha's issues were, she and I had been the only people present during the conversation in her Turkey Hill kitchen, where the subjects of legal bills and mortgage were discussed, when I had offered to take a third mortgage so I could pay the legal expenses I'd incur in her case. In the event Martha had forgotten our conversation, there were two other people who knew the truth: the bankers Martha found for me. I didn't hear from her for a long time. But then, she was busy.

Martha was also fodder for the late-night talk show jokes. She'd been on the shows herself, and called "Dave, Jay, Conan" her buddies in her interview with *New Yorker* writer Jeffrey Toobin, but I was sure all the barbs hurt her feelings. There was even a fake magazine cover for *Martha Stewart Living Behind Bars* circulating on the Web, which offered hints for "Jailhouse Chili" and "Sprucing Up Your Cell for Holiday Occasions."

In May 2003, a made-for-TV movie version of Christopher Byron's *Martha, Inc.* aired, starring Cybill Shepherd as a "sledgehammer-wielding shrew," as the *New York Times* described it. The film had also tried to portray me, with Martha telling me to tip someone, which never happened. The night the movie aired, my phone rang throughout the broadcast. "You probably don't know about this but you are being played on TV!" My daughter Lara said, "Mom, someone is playing you! She's wearing pants and she's dressed in beige!" If little in that movie resembled me, I had to admit that I thought Cybill Shepherd did a very good job.

On June 4, 2003, Martha was indicted by a federal grand jury on a number of charges, and resigned as CEO and chairman of Martha Stewart Living Omnimedia, the company she worked so hard and for so many years to build.

SEC Charges Martha Stewart, Broker Peter Bacanovic with Illegal Insider Trading

FOR IMMEDIATE RELEASE—2003-69

Washington, DC, June 4, 2003 — The Securities and Exchange Commission today filed securities fraud charges against Martha Stewart and her former stockbroker, Peter Bacanovic. The complaint, filed in federal court in Manhattan, alleges that Stewart committed illegal insider trading when she sold stock in a biopharmaceutical company, ImClone Systems, Inc., on Dec. 27, 2001, after receiving an unlawful tip from Bacanovic, at the time a broker with Merrill Lynch, Pierce, Fenner & Smith Incorporated. The Commission further alleges that Stewart and Bacanovic subsequently created an alibi for Stewart's ImClone sales and concealed important facts during SEC and criminal investigations into her trades. In a separate action, the United States Attorney for the Southern District of New York has obtained an indictment charging Stewart and Bacanovic criminally for their false statements concerning Stewart's ImClone trades.

If convicted, Martha risked never being able to serve as an officer or a director of the company that carried her name, or any other public company. I didn't think Martha would be convicted. But there was a sad irony in the fact that when Martha stepped down as chairman and CEO, Sharon Patrick, who was originally CEO when MSLO was launched in 1997, until Martha took the title for herself, became, again, CEO. I had no doubt that Sharon would do a good job, and I was to be proven right about that.

But the damage was sizeable. An article in *Slate* that appeared the day after Martha was indicted talked about the impact on shareholders in Martha's company, quoting from the "risk factors section" of the MSLO public offering prospectus that was published in 1999:

> We are highly dependent upon our founder, Chairman and Chief Executive Officer, Martha Stewart. Martha Stewart's talents, efforts, personality and leadership have been, and continue to be, critical to our success. . . . Our business would be adversely affected if Martha Stewart's public image or reputation were to be tarnished.

The article went on to discuss the expensive insurance policies the company had taken out on Martha, all of which proved to be useless under the circumstances. Meanwhile, as if an invisible hand was directing this horror show, the latest Martha fiasco was immediately followed, on June 10, 2003, by Sam's sentencing.

Samuel Waksal Sentenced in Federal Court to 7 Years
3 Months in Prison, Fined $3 Million

JAMES B. COMEY, the United States Attorney for the Southern District of New York, announced that SAMUEL WAKSAL, the former president and chief executive officer of ImClone Systems, Inc. ("ImClone") was sentenced today in Manhattan federal court to 7 years and 3 months in prison for securities fraud, conspiracy, obstruction of justice, perjury, bank fraud, and wire fraud. United States District Judge WILLIAM H. PAULEY III also fined WAKSAL $3 million and ordered him to pay restitution of more than $1.2 million.

I visited Sam in his penthouse apartment in SoHo just before he left to serve his term. The feds had already attached a bracelet to his slender ankle. Sam, one of Martha's very best friends, was the bull's-eye of her inner ring, one of the few people she used to call every morning when she made her five a.m. rounds. Martha's morning phone calls had always startled me from sleep, her voice on the other end so cheery, exclaiming about star-studded cocktail parties, elegant sit-down dinners, this or that tycoon's country home and should we accept the invitation to visit?

Sam and I shared a love of books and music, and we'd traveled with Martha many times. Sometimes Martha, Sam, and I would talk for hours, or he'd talk and we'd sit back and listen to him hold forth on the pessimism of Schopenhauer or the chemical cascades of the CREB molecule. To think of Sam in some small square cell, a man with a mind as wide as Wisconsin and a love for lavish entertaining in his gracious Manhattan home, seemed impossible.

Sam's hands that afternoon were clasped in his lap. I looked at his hands, and then I looked around his recently redecorated home. His old, gracious European style had been tossed out, beautiful though it had been with the rich dark wood French Empire chairs, the long clear-cut silhouette of the couch with its curved sweeping ends, the large classical painting of a boat in the eye of a storm, and the low-lit period chandeliers. Not long before his investigation began, in one of Sam's impulsive moves, his décor had disappeared, to be replaced by a bold, contemporary style, equally as tasteful, all the furniture twentieth century now, the pictures on the bare white walls huge washes of color—Cy Twombly, Francis Bacon, Mark Rothko, Francesco Clemente, Willem de Kooning. But even the new Sam-style could not lighten the somber mood during that last visit.

Approaching his building that day, I saw clumps of people hovering about his trendy SoHo neighborhood. As I got closer, I saw they were reporters. One of them offered me a microphone; I pushed it away. "No. No!" I managed to tilt my head up and scan the windows of his building. And I thought I saw Sam up there, at his window high above the street; he was peering down, his face barely visible.

Later, inside, as we sat facing each other on his sleek French modernist couches, loss hung in the air between us. Even the sunlight flooding into his loft that early evening ominously illuminated every wall left bare by the valuable art, now gone, as if to send him a message.

"So," Sam said.

"So," I answered. "When can friends visit you?"

"I'm not quite up on all the rules yet," he said. "I'll have to find out."

He got up and walked to the window. I could hear the droning of a plane flying close by in the sky. I wanted to say how grateful I was for his having risked his own safety for mine when the helicopter door had come loose on our last trip together with Martha in Panama, but I didn't feel it was the proper time to say thank you, as that would have highlighted the imminence of his departure for some unthinkable place.

Sam then turned to me. "You should have seen your face," he said with that boyish Waksal grin.

We are making the best of the worst moment we've ever shared, I thought. Sam and I had laughed together and at each other for fifteen years. I missed him already.

On July 23, 2003, Sam began serving his sentence at the minimum security Schuylkill Federal Correctional Institution in Pennsylvania.

SINCE THOSE FIRST articles about Martha's sale of her ImClone stock were published, I had tried my best to understand Martha's strategy, but a lot of it didn't make sense to me, perhaps least of all the fact that I had heard several vague stories saying that Martha "was reported" to have rejected a plea deal. Later, in his wrap-up of the trial for *The New Yorker*, Jeffrey Toobin would explain what had happened. According to his piece, Martha's lawyers, anticipating the indictment that would come in early June, contacted the U.S. attorney's office to start plea negotiations. Martha went to her lawyer's office on Sunday, June 1, to discuss the terms:

> Stewart would plead guilty to a single felony: making a false statement to federal agents. The agreed-upon sentencing guidelines would make probation or house arrest likely, although there was no guarantee that Stewart would avoid prison. Also, under this arrangement Stewart wouldn't have to cooperate with prosecutors or give a proffer—an advance preview—of what she was going to say. . . . Would Stewart admit that she had lied to the investigators? In the end, late Sunday night, Stewart decided that she couldn't do it.

The following day, as Toobin wrote, Morvillo and his legal team "all told Stewart that she would never get a better deal. A trial was a risk. No doubt a felony plea would complicate her role at her company, but the alternative—indictment, trial, and possible conviction of multiple felonies—was far worse. But again Stewart said that she couldn't do it. A grand jury indicted her two days later."

I read reports that at a hearing in New York City on June 19, 2003, a federal judge set a date for Martha's trial: January 12, 2004.

On November 7, I watched Martha telling ABC News that she was scared of prison. "I don't think I will be going to prison, though." It was surreal.

Later that month, I was in St. Barth with Maggie and a group of friends, sitting on the terrace at Cap au Vent, scanning the papers as I waited for everyone to get ready for the beach, my attention divided between the spectacular views and the headlines. It may have been the setting, but when I read that, on November 18, Martha was in court for oral arguments and pretrial hearings, it made little sense to me.

On December 19, 2003, Martha sent me a letter "to correct the misstatement" in the *Financial Times* article published in March of that year, which had incorrectly reported that I had asked Martha for $150,000 to cover legal bills and mortgage payments. Recognizing that many other media publications had reproduced that "misstatement," Martha elaborated on the fact that I had not asked her for anything: "While I have offered to pay, and have paid, the legal expenses you have incurred as a result of being a witness in the government investigation surrounding my sale of ImClone stock, this was done at my initiative. At no time during the course of this investigation did you ask me to give you money," Martha wrote. She also acknowledged the distress caused by the false reports, and their destructive effect on me, personally and professionally.

The "distress" Martha mentioned in her letter was very real indeed. My business was nearly wiped out, my reputation was ruined, and even my friends were ridiculed for trusting me. Yet, how could I blame those who turned against me when they had seen it in print? All I could do was watch the distaste on faces of people who considered me disgraceful.

However, my children and my closest friends trusted I was doing my best with what I had to deal with. They understood I couldn't talk openly, and they stood by me, respectful of the secrecy I had to preserve in relation to Martha's case and of my wish to avoid sharing my grief that might cause them grief.

By December 2003, when Martha sent me that letter, it had been nineteen months that I'd been waiting for Martha to put an end to her ordeal, and mine.

I was financially unprepared for what was happening to me. My girls insisted that the jewelry I had given them as gifts be auctioned off along with mine. Whatever didn't fit the Sotheby's criteria, I sold to dealers. And so went the art, the furniture, the Oriental rugs, and all the things that had been hard to afford and seemed extravagant when I purchased them, but they brought back every penny, which I needed to make up for the loss of business I incurred for having been involved in Martha's trial.

I had no idea worse was yet to come.

ON DECEMBER 22, 2003, my daughters, who had come home for holiday break, were having friends over. Since we moved to the beach, our house had become party central. Every time the girls were there, it was a pleasure to see all those children I had known for so many years having a good time at our place, although by then it was quite sparsely furnished. We baked cookies and over-decorated the house. Christmas music was on full blast. I had set a buffet table on the kitchen island, and kids were coming in and out, when I noticed Tigger and Ginger, our boxers, watching the TV screen, wagging their tails. It was Martha on *Larry King*, telling him it was her "saddest Christmas ever." By the time she said, "I'd like to find time to marry again," the dogs had lost interest in the show.

21

The Trial

J URY SELECTION FOR the trial of *United States v. Martha Stewart and Peter Bacanovic* began on Tuesday, January 20, 2004. I don't know why Martha didn't accept the plea deal she was offered—we were out of touch by then—but I suspected Gillian Glover of the *New York Times* got it about right when she wrote: "Stewart did not go to court to answer charges of insider dealing, she stood trial for lying about what she was not accused of in the first place. Which is odd to say the least. And it may have been this core absurdity which tempted her to the greatest offense of all—treating the whole matter like some sort of embarrassing nuisance."

While the crimes were pretty minor compared to what her fellow CEOs at Enron and Tyco were accused of, the allegations were anything but trivial. According to the indictment, on or about Oct. 31, 2001, ImClone submitted to FDA an application for approval of Erbitux, a drug to treat colon cancer. It was publicly reported that the decision was expected at the end of December 2001. On December 27, Bacanovic's assistant, Douglas Faneuil, informed Bacanovic that Waksal and a family member wanted to sell all of their ImClone stock.

In breach of Merrill Lynch confidentiality rules, Bacanovic told Doug to tell Martha about the Waksal sale, which was not public information. Bacanovic called Martha and left her a message while we were traveling, then told his assistant to tell her about the sale when she called back. Martha called back that afternoon and spoke to Doug, who told her about the Waksal sale. Martha immediately ordered all her ImClone stock sold, nearly 4,000 shares. As a former stockbroker, Martha would have known the information was a violation of confidentially rules. After close of market the next day, ImClone announced that FDA had rejected the Erbitux application.

As I gathered from media reports, in January 2002, the SEC, the FBI, and the Attorney General's Office had started their investigation. Martha's office was first contacted January 25 and an interview was scheduled for February 4. On January 31, Martha accessed the message Peter Bacanovic had left her on December 27 on the phone log kept on her assistant Ann Armstrong's computer and altered it. She apparently reconsidered and asked Ann to change it back. During the February 4 interview, Martha told investigators that she had a preexisting agreement to sell her ImClone stock if it fell to $60 per share and claimed she didn't know if Peter's message was in the phone log. She also said she had talked to Peter directly on December 27, while evidence pointed to her having only spoken to his assistant, Doug, which I thought was strange, because the only way that made sense to me was if Martha really forgot whom she spoke with, and that made for a peculiar coincidence of faulty voice-memory between Martha and me, as I remembered looking at Martha when the words "Isn't it nice to have brokers who tell you those things?" were spoken, yet I couldn't remember who said them. She allegedly lied again in an April 10 phone call with investigators.

When the charges came down in early June 2003, Martha and Peter had been indicted on nine counts between them. They were both charged with conspiracy to obstruct justice, making false statements, and perjury. Martha was charged with two counts of making false statements, once to investigators during the February 4 interview, and again during the April 10 interview; one count of obstruction of justice; and one count of securities fraud, though the last charge was ultimately dismissed. Peter was also charged with making false statements, making and using false documents, perjury, and obstruction of justice.

Every day I read the newspapers and surfed the Internet for information on what happened in the courtroom at Martha's trial. They showed her on TV, as she came to court every day, looking more glamorous than I had ever seen her. I wondered if that was the best approach, but then I read that Martha had hired consultants to advise her on that, and thought she must have known better than I.

Opening statements in Martha's trial began on January 27. At Martha's defense table were said to be high-powered attorney Robert Morvillo and John Cuti, Martha's son-in-law. Her daughter, Alexis, was in the front row of spectator seats every day as well. Peter Bacanovic was in court with his own defense team. His parents—his mother, a retired doctor; and his father, a banker—were also there. Jeffrey Toobin, who attended the trial every day, described the U.S. attorney's office prosecution team in an article he wrote for *The New Yorker*: "Karen Patton Seymour and Michael Schachter, the prosecutors in the trial, were shrewd choices for the government in a case in which the defense was certain at least to suggest that the prosecution amounted to a government vendetta against a prominent person—and a particular kind of celebrity. Schachter . . . who looked like Seymour's nerdy kid brother, barely changed his expression (or his boxy gray suit) during the entire trial. Seymour . . . came across as more thoughtful than passionate." *Slate*'s Henry Blodget called Seymour, the lead prosecutor "as intimidating as a preschool teacher." I thought those articles were missing an important aspect of the prosecution team, because after having been repeatedly interrogated by them, I knew their minds were as sharp as razors. I was sure that Martha, so good at surrounding herself with smart people, also knew that.

Peter Bacanovic's attorney, Richard Strassberg, made the next opening statement, and tried to pin the blame on Peter's assistant Doug Faneuil.

Then Martha's attorney, Robert Morvillo, a reputed legal lion whom I thought to be a very likable man, was described to have delivered his opening statement in a loud, theatrical voice, and compared the case with something out of George Orwell. He also did a valiant job of trying to humanize Martha, who had by that point been vilified ad nauseam in the media. According to a *New Yorker* article by Jeffrey Toobin, Morvillo said:

> Martha Stewart initiated a catering business which by virtue of sixteen-hour days, fierce desire to put forward the best possible product, whether it deals with flowers, fixtures, food, furniture, expanded into a successful multimedia corporation run predominantly by women with similar goals and ideas and skills. Martha Stewart has devoted most of her life to improving the quality of life for others.

Martha's defense team seemed to believe that the ImClone stock sale was so minor that she never would have gone to the trouble of making up lies about it in the first place.

After a few days' delay, during which Morvillo asked for a mistrial because the prosecution had turned over some documents much later than they should have, Peter's assistant Doug, considered the prosecution's star witness, testified on February 3 and 4. Doug had already taken a plea bargain in exchange for his cooperation in the trial. He testified that Peter had told him to pass the ImClone tip to Martha.

A week later, Martha's assistant Ann Armstrong was called to the stand. I had known and liked Annie for all six years she had worked with Martha. I always asked her opinion on what was the best Broadway show or the latest hot restaurant in the city to take my children or friends visiting me from around the country or abroad. She came camping with Martha and me on our five-day trip hiking Katahdin and canoeing in Baxter State Park in Maine. She sat at the table with Sam and me at one of Martha's Leo birthday celebrations at Skylands. I held Annie in high esteem and respected her many qualities, including her loyalty to Martha. The poor thing burst into tears on the stand.

As Toobin described in *The New Yorker*:

> Armstrong loved her, which was why her testimony was so devastating. The central image she presented was vivid—the haughty Stewart sitting in her secretary's cubicle (something Armstrong said she had never done before) and fiddling with the phone log. Armstrong tried to minimize what Stewart had done, emphasizing that Stewart had told her to change the document back "instantly." On cross-examination, she told Morvillo that Stewart had never asked her to cover up or lie about the incident.
>
> Still, the damage from Armstrong's testimony was profound. It foreclosed what would have been one of Stewart's best arguments in a case where she had not been charged with insider trading: Why would she lie if she hadn't done anything wrong in the first place?

Meanwhile, the press was having a field day. About a dozen photographers lay in wait for Martha at the courthouse when she arrived each morning. And Martha wasn't the only one they went after. One morning, naively trusting the early hour, I braved the winter chill and went outside to start my car and let it warm up. I heard someone call from the beach parking lot across the street. My sight already blurred from countless sleepless nights, I looked toward the sound, the sun in my eyes. Ever since Martha's trial began, I barely slept a wink. When I did, I had the same nightmare that used to keep me up when I was a child. In the dream, once again I heard the gunshots as they killed the horses, and the animals' panicked screams as they were forced to watch their companions die before them.

It took a moment to make out the camera shooting me from inside a car. I would see my exhausted early-morning face smeared all over television screens and the tabloids. A picture is worth a thousand words, and it showed what the Martha-thing had made of me. All I could do was pray and hope while the circus masters paraded my haunted face around and the time approached for me to be propelled inside the ring.

On Thursday, February 19, it was my turn to testify. It was the twenty-fifth anniversary of the day when I entered the refugee camp in Austria on my way to America.

There was so little I knew, yet they had me in the witness box twice: first at the close of the day, and again the next morning, on Friday. I watched the prosecutor approach the stand and I reached for the water in the plastic glass in front of me. But it did not quench my thirst, and I had trouble rolling the vowels, which thickened my accent, making my words hard to understand, I'm sure. The thumping of blood pulsating in my ears was so intense that I had to concentrate really hard to hear their questions. All I could think was: *What am I doing here? Tell me this is not happening! Get me out of here!*

I knew I must answer the questions to the best of my recollection. Strings of words, some out of context, the facts. I had already told them to the investigators. I was so concerned that there not be the smallest error in my testimony that when the prosecutor, referring to the conversation Martha and I had that night on the terrace in Mexico, described us as having sat on chairs, I corrected him and said, "Chaises."

Without my ever meaning to, the words I spoke ruptured my relationship with Martha for good, and there would be no going back. The courtroom fell silent while I spoke. I had merely repeated words I remembered having heard in Mexico—not a word more, not one less, not a conjunction added or deleted, not changing the sentence so it made more sense, or made me look smarter.

My first day in court as a witness for the prosecution, against the woman who for twenty years had been one of my closest friends, was described accurately by *Slate* reporter Henry Blodget:

> . . . after Assistant U.S. Attorney Michael Schachter had finished lead-
> ing the auburn-haired, thick-accented Pasternak through her memory

that Stewart had mentioned the Waksals' sales, he had asked one last question:

> Q: Do you have any recollection of speaking with Ms. Stewart on the subject of brokers while you were in Mexico?
>
> A: I remember one brief statement, which was: "Isn't it nice to have brokers who tell you those things."

The government investigators knew that I recalled talking with Martha when those words were said, but that I wasn't sure if it was Martha or me who said them. I had been asked that same question before, including in front of a grand jury. I remembered being in front of Martha, us talking and me looking back, seeing her face and her hat and her eyes, and those words, but I could not recall her voice saying that. On the many prior occasions when that question was asked of me, I was also asked who said, "Isn't it nice to have brokers who tell you those things?" but that first day on the witness stand the prosecutor did not ask who said those words, so I didn't explain.

For some reason, it was reported that I had testified that Martha had uttered that damning sentence. But I never said that. Of course, for the show to be thrilling, the story of "Martha's Trial" needed a villain.

The next day, I had to go to court and testify again, and I knew the media would be back for blood-sport and that attorney Morvillo, Martha's lawyer, would be set to prove that George Bernard Shaw was right: "It is dangerous to be sincere unless you are also stupid."

The room was full of people, but I had to strain to make out their features.

Up front was the examiner's stand.

On a separate podium, to my left, a jury of grave men and women sat silent, watching and listening. I threw furtive looks in their direction because I thought I was not supposed to make eye contact with them. It was the first time I saw a jury in real life, not in the movies, and, anyway, when I watch *To Kill a Mockingbird*, my eyes are on Gregory Peck, not on the jury.

In the dimly lit rows of seats at the back of the courtroom were many faces I knew, mostly from TV. Some seemed to stare at me. Some were talking to each other. There were some whose hands moved quickly across notepads. The whole thing was surreal. Through the veil of my exhaustion, I had to concentrate on the people asking me questions. As Blodget reported, attorney Morvillo asked me:

> Q: You are not sure that the words were actually spoken by
>   Martha Stewart or whether they were words that just are
>   somehow embedded in your mind as one of your thoughts?
> A: Exactly, I do not know if Martha said that or it's me who
>   thought those words.

"OK," Morvillo said, "I have no further questions."

Then the lawyers suddenly jumped, and, bickering with each other, they rushed to the judge.

From my seat on the witness stand, I scanned the room. In the first rows, I recognized some of the investigators who had interviewed me at the U.S. attorney's office, Southern District of New York. A few rows behind was Peter Bacanovic, the stockbroker trapped in Martha's nightmare. Farther back, next to Morvillo's seat, was John Cuti, Alexis's husband.

Squinting into the crowd, I searched for Martha. Our eyes met. But when we looked at each other, all I saw was what we had done to our friendship and what our friendship had done to us. Our gaze had nothing to say, no stories to swap. I gave a brief, tiny nod, meant only for her. I don't know if she even detected it. The nod said, *You gave me no choice, Martha.* I felt like crying.

It wasn't until the next day or after, when I read Blodget's dispatch on *Slate*, that I learned what the attorneys were complaining to the judge about:

> [Morvillo] excoriated the government for intentionally creating the
> impression that Stewart had made the statement when it knew full

well that Pasternak wasn't sure she had (Pasternak, apparently, had shared her confusion with not only investigators but the Grand Jury). Then Assistant U.S. Attorney Schachter returned to the speaker stand and asked:

Q: Ms. Pasternak, yesterday you testified, "I remember one brief statement, which was, 'Isn't it nice to have brokers who tell you those things?'" And in response to Mr. Morvillo's **questions today, you said that you are not sure whether that** was something that Ms. Stewart said or that it was something that you thought.

A: Yes.

Q: Ms. Pasternak, can you please tell us, what is your best recollection, that this was something that Ms. Stewart said or that it was just something that you thought, your best recollection?

A: I really am not very sure.

Then, as if I needed to be reminded of all interviews and questions and subpoenas over the past twenty-one months, he said:

Q: Ms. Pasternak, in advance of your testimony, you met with people from the government, is that right?

A: Yes. . . .

Q: And in one of those meetings, Ms. Pasternak, fairly recently, you were asked what was your best recollection . . . about whether this was something that was said by Ms. Stewart or whether it was something that you thought, isn't that right?

The prosecutor kept asking me questions, and I kept answering, and to each question someone objected, and of each answer someone disapproved. They asked me about the same thing over and over, narrowing or widening the scope, depending on who asked the questions. I had to focus really closely.

During the last interview with investigators, I was asked again who had said those words, then again what was my best recollection, and toward the end the new question was about who did I believe had said it. While my best recollection was of the words, not of who said them, I believed all along that Martha had said: "Isn't it nice to have brokers who tell you those things?" Martha often used the phrase, "Isn't it nice to have [this or that]?"

> Q: Ms. Pasternak . . . What is your best belief, sitting here today?
> A: That Martha said it.

Even the most impartial reporting on my testimony said I changed my mind on the stand.

SHORTLY AFTER MY testimony, but completely unrelated, the prosecution's charge that Martha had lied to inflate the value of her own company was thrown out before the trial went to the jury. The judge dismissed the insider trading charge against Martha for lack of evidence. Conspiracy, obstruction of justice, and making false statements charges remained.

I read that one of the witnesses called to the stand was Martha's "bookkeeper," as Jeffrey Toobin described her. "Heidi DeLuca said that she was employed by the company but that her duties included maintaining Stewart's personal checkbook, paying her bills—such as health, life, and automobile insurance—and overseeing the payroll for her personal staff of between thirty and forty people. (Stewart reimbursed the company for a portion of DeLuca's salary.)" Toobin also said, "In an effort to prove the $60 agreement, Bacanovic's lawyers called Heidi DeLuca, Stewart's bookkeeper; but in an artful cross-examination Schachter had shown that her conversation with Bacanovic probably concerned an earlier sale of ImClone shares by Stewart, not the one on December 27, 2001."

I testified because I had to, and answered the questions asked of me, but what I knew about Martha's trial I learned from the media and the press. Many things were made public during the trial, such as the fact that Martha charged her company for her Frédéric Fekkai haircuts and her travel expenses, even the cost of a cup of coffee. That Heidi had presented the company with a $17,000 bill for our Mexico-Panama trip, which included Martha's spa charges of about $2,000, though the company had not allowed that deduction.

The defense put only one witness on the stand and Martha did not testify. Some saw arrogance in that, but I wondered if perhaps Jeffrey Toobin's theory was closer when he wrote:

> It was out of the question for Stewart herself to testify. She had no good answers for the most basic questions. What explanation could she give for altering the phone log at Ann Armstrong's desk? How did Pasternak know that the Waksals were dumping their shares? And if Stewart told her, as she certainly did, why did she deny to investigators that she knew of the Waksal sales?
>
> What's more, in a cross-examination of Stewart, the rest of her life would be open to ruthless scrutiny. . . . Even more important, [Morvillo] knew that, under federal sentencing guidelines, Stewart would face a longer sentence if Judge Cedarbaum thought she had lied on the witness stand.

On March 5, the jury reached its verdict. Martha was found guilty on all four counts: one count of conspiracy, two counts of making false statements, one count of obstruction of justice. She had been spared the securities fraud charge when the judge threw it out earlier in the trial. Peter was found guilty of four counts as well: conspiracy, making false statements, perjury, and obstruction of justice. It was reported in the press that Alexis cried upon hearing the verdict, but Martha did little more than grimace.

I was as shocked as everyone else at the news of Martha's conviction, and felt the deepest sorrow for her, her family, her friends, everyone who loved her.

On March 15, Martha resigned from the Martha Stewart Living Omnimedia, Inc. board of directors but retained the title of founding editorial director.

Soon thereafter, it was reported that the television show *Martha Stewart Living* would be suspended after the current season.

On July 8, the judge refused to grant Martha and Peter a new trial based on perjury charges against Larry Stewart, a Secret Service ink expert who prosecutors said had lied on the witness stand at their trial; he was later acquitted.

On July 16, Martha was sentenced to five months in prison, five months of home confinement, and an additional nineteen months supervised release. She was fined $30,000.

Peter Bacanovic was given the same sentence as Martha, although his fine was only $4,000. I felt so sorry that my memory, vague as it was, had hurt both of them. Although it wasn't my choice to be involved, I couldn't suppress the feeling of guilt.

The media didn't need slick *Chicago*'s Billy Flynn to transform the trial into "the old three-ring circus" that had their audience "begging for more." Martha's speech outside the courthouse that day, which must have been heartbreaking to anyone who cared about her, also reflected the Martha I knew, good at everything except saying "I'm sorry," well-intentioned but unable to resist self-promotion. As the *New York Times* reported:

> Outside the courthouse, an upbeat Ms. Stewart, 62, was greeted by a crowd of sympathizers wearing sandwich signs and chef hats who chanted "Save Martha!" Ms. Stewart, who had faced as much as 16 months in prison, told them: "I'll be back. I will be back. I'm used to all kinds of hard work, as you know, and I'm not afraid. I'm not afraid whatsoever. . . .
>
> "Perhaps all of you out there can continue to show your support by subscribing to our magazine, by buying our products, by encouraging

our advertisers to come back in full force to our magazines," she said before a phalanx of television and newspaper cameras. "Our magazines are great. They deserve your support, and whatever happened to me personally shouldn't have any effect whatsoever on the great company Martha Stewart Living Omnimedia."

The night of her sentencing, I watched Martha in a TV interview with Barbara Walters. While talking about other "good people" who had been in prison, Martha mentioned Nelson Mandela. I was glad to see that Martha's self-confidence was unshaken, although I couldn't think of much parallel between her and Nelson Mandela, who spent nearly thirty years in prison for fighting apartheid and social injustice.

There was nothing I could do for Martha but be grateful that I had paid so little attention to things she had said to me, yet the news of her conviction hit me really hard. It was my friend David who pointed out that I must seek help, because in the simplest conversation I wasn't making sense. I felt so lost as to doubt the worth of my own life, so I heeded his counsel and called my friend Diana, who said, "You need to figure out what just happened to you." She spoke with Dr. Steven Marans, the highly regarded Yale psychologist, on my behalf. He was kind and talked to me for hours and hours, week after week, until I began wanting to be my old self again.

During the time between Martha's conviction and her sentencing, I often listened to Bach's "Sarabande" from Cello Suite no. 5. Although it reinforced my sense of isolation, it gave me hope, however naive, that perhaps, like the protagonists of Ingmar Bergman's movie *Saraband*, we might in a distant future all meet again and reminisce about the wonderful things we'd done together, but also of how much we accomplished after that.

Meanwhile, I held on to my fortress and tried to withstand the vulgar Brutus label that was painted on me. I was scared to read newspapers or watch TV. But I worried that if some calamity happened, I'd be the last one to know it, so I read and watched. Martha's friend

Dominick Dunne went after me in *Vanity Fair* and on CNN, suggesting I was being personally investigated for wrongdoing and that Martha had paid for all of those trips over the years. I saw men and women gossiping about me in such a juvenile way that I was reminded of *Lord of the Flies*.

A few true journalists asked thoughtful questions, but many others preferred regurgitating the same damnations of me. When I amassed enough strength to Google my name, the character assassinations glared out from thousands of entries dispersed all over the Web, from national publications to local-issue dilutions, from "news" rags to an Iraqi newspaper article, most of them quoting the same source. To make things even worse, my knowledge of several languages made it possible for me to be slapped with words written in English, French, Spanish, Portuguese, Italian, even Romanian.

All these printed lies filled my clients with angst, and my business continued to dwindle. The harshest moment was when I fell behind on my mortgage payments and I was about to lose my house to foreclosure, along with all the money I had worked for and saved for twenty-five years. Hoping to save my house, I called the mortgage holders to remind them that in the past couple of years I had paid them more than $350,000 in interest alone, so perhaps they could lower my monthly payments for a year or so, giving me time to recoup or sell the house. But they said they couldn't.

ON SEPTEMBER 15, Martha announced that she had asked the judge to vacate the stay on her sentence, in place pending her appeal, so she could begin her prison sentence "as soon as possible" and "put this nightmare behind me." On October 8, 2004, Martha began her sentence and entered the Alderson Federal Prison Camp in rural West Virginia, as federal inmate No. 55170-054, where, as I read in the papers, she was fingerprinted and strip-searched.

The foreclosure auction on my house took place the month she went to prison, leaving me homeless and destitute. My pain from it was numbed by the sadness I felt about what was happening to Martha.

On December 8, Martha's company, which continued to function very well under Sharon Patrick, announced it would enlist the help of *The Apprentice* producer Mark Burnett to revive Martha's daily home-making show, which was going to have a new format, with a live audience and celebrity guests.

On December 22, while I was living with friends, I read that Martha posted a Christmas message on her personal Web site, calling for sentencing reform and criticizing prison food. I thought it was great that she was using her famous name to try to make a social impact.

On February 2, 2005, while Martha was still in prison, NBC announced plans for *The Apprentice: Martha Stewart*, the second TV project she was planning to undertake upon her release from prison. By then, Sharon had returned to running the Sharon Patrick Company to pursue "her entrepreneurial interests in creating new, next generation branded ventures capable of 'doing good while doing well.'" She had passed on the honor and stress of her CEO functions at MSLO to Susan Lyne, a veteran of the television, publishing, and film industries.

On March 4, 2005, Martha was released from prison and jetted in style back home to Cantitoe Corners in Bedford, where she was quoted to have said, "There is no place like home." She served out her five months of house detention there, as well as an added three weeks she received for reportedly violating the terms of her confinement.

Peter began his sentence in January 2005 at a federal prison in Las Vegas. I was taken aback when I read in the October 13, 2006, *New York Times* that Peter, who had lost his job, his professional rights, and his beautiful Manhattan apartment, was required to pay $75,000 to settle the SEC insider trading case when he got out. "In his view, Ms. Stewart could have reached her own settlement with the commission at any point between late 2004 and this spring, obviating the need for him to pay a fine." So that April, according to the article, Peter had called his old friend Alexis, Martha's daughter. "'I said, "This is harming me,"'" Mr. Bacanovic, who had to borrow money to pay his fine, recalled saying. "'And she said, "No one here feels we owe you anything."'"

While Martha no longer figured on the list of *Fortune* magazine's four hundred richest people, she still had hundreds of millions of dollars. According to the *New York Observer*, Alexis, who was divorced from John Cuti in 2004, was reported to have bought five adjoining, multifloor condo units in one of Richard Meier's glass towers in the West Village, with many balconies and views of the Hudson River, for about $35,000,000.

On January 6, 2006, federal appeals court upheld Martha's conviction. The number of lawsuits brought by investors would eventually be consolidated, and in late 2006 the case would be settled for $30 million, with Martha's personal share at $5 million. Her legal fees also ran into the millions.

TWENTY-EIGHT YEARS HAVE passed since I had first met Martha Stewart, a woman I never would have guessed might become a friend, never mind a best friend who would later implicate me in a crime, or crisis, call it what you will. Either way, it became my crime, and crisis, too, for I found myself ensnared in rules and regulations and rituals that had nothing to do with me even as they brought my castle crumbling down.

In the trail of "Martha's Trial," I had been robbed not only of my reputation, income, and material possessions, but also of something I had always taken for granted: my spirit. After Dr. Marans talked me back to the place where I began even wanting to be myself again, for about a year I searched for my shadow with Carl Jung, piled in neat stacks on the coffee table next to the couch: books by Jung, with Jung, about Jung, some of them given to me, unexpectedly, by a lady I had met in Martha's circles. I read and read, and every single word resonated with meaning, but the powerful impression left only the faintest trace. Reading Jung was like watching flying flocks of geese. Eventually, I faced the fact that before I could afford the luxury of searching with Jung, I had to try finding the basics in books like Judy Fisher's *Heaven on Earth*, which says, "the subconscious mind . . . listens to everything you tell it. If you say you will never be happy, then it believes you. It stores that knowledge, so when you try to be happy it will not allow you to be, and it will remind your conscious mind that you are never to be happy."

And here's what I've learned, and this despite my years of experience selling real estate: the real worth of a life cannot be measured by its mortar or its materials. The real worth of a life is best assessed by the pain one feels upon that life's undoing, and the lengths one will go to gather all the pieces, join the joists, and, relying part on prayer, part on muscle, and mostly on love, resurrect the roof.

So every noun a nail, every page a sheet of sanded wood, sentence by sentence, story by story, I have tried to recast my castle, tracing the shape of a new self emerging from the drama of the old, hoping to inspire other women to take a close look at the intimacy of our friendships. And as I write these words, I feel the full impact of the irony, and some sadness also. As I grew closer to Martha, I became more familiar with her façades. Is a part of closeness learning the lies as well as the truths about the ones you care for? Perhaps a friendship—any relationship—is finished when the scale tips in the wrong direction.

In the end, the loss of such a close and long friendship was the most devastating loss of all. We had shared so much, had been so profoundly intertwined that it was hard for me to imagine a life without Martha. I hardly knew who I was without the friendship that had defined most of my adulthood.

I miss Martha, my friend. I miss her laughter and our wordless communication, especially the complicity. Whether it was plotting a strategy for snagging a mansion or a stratagem to lure reporters off Martha's scent, had one listened carefully, one would have heard beneath any of our words the steady, sustaining pulse of all that went unsaid. On the surface we were discussing this or that, him or her, but beneath that we were also passing back and forth a mutual dependence of the sort you frequently see in the animal world: think of horses, standing neck to neck, grooming one another's manes and withers. We moved through the same plains, ascended the same trails, and when we were not moving, as on the night before she first took me to see Skylands, when we listened to loons on the dock, we did what all human beings who love each other do: we talked, what we said less important than the fact of its utterance, this essential volley of words that proves you see me and proves I see you. "Mariana," Martha would call, saying my name in the particular way she did. No one said my name quite like Martha. And no one said Martha's name quite like me. We constantly sparked each other's imagination and creativity.

With all that happened in those years, when times were good and I gained so much from being close with Martha, and also when times turned really bad and I lost so much for having been made a witness by Martha, it was the love and rituals I shared with my family and friends that sustained and sheltered me through grief. Does one get over the grief of the loss of such a close friend and along with it an entire life-style? I don't know. But I know that my loss was liberating. And perhaps one must go through grief to be free.

When I was a single mother with small children, I wanted to take my daughters around the world and teach them a sense of freedom, yet I feared doing it alone. I was afraid of the unknown. Afraid of the unpredictable. Afraid of violence. Martha was fearless but she was not a loner, so we traveled with her. She and I traveled together almost as much as we talked together. We rode horses through the desert dunes of Egypt and hiked the winding Inca Trail to the mysterious Machu Picchu. We were so bold we paddled at night between tree trunks in dug-out canoes in the eerie submerged Amazonian jungle, looking for the phosphorescent glow of crocodile eyes. Then, while I trusted Martha to lead me places without fear, she took me to the acme of fear. It was not a game I agreed to play, and for a while I did not realize the seriousness of the trouble I was in. But then, from that chaotic, dizzying edge where Martha took me, I emerged beyond fear. And from there to the place where I am today was a long road.

The last time I saw Martha Stewart in real life was more than six years ago, the stillness of her velvet brown eyes drilling into me as I sat on the witness stand answering questions. Occasionally I see her on the cover of a magazine or on TV, and "they" marvel at her "comeback" even as I have come to realize that true comebacks are not possible, because time does not come back. But memories do, and these are what save me. I am back by my favorite lake, on an early August morning, listening to my beloved loons calling each other across the water. My girls are still asleep, and so are my friends, and their children, who have come to Walhalla to spend with us the week of my birthday.

And as I sit in the old Adirondack chair on the dock, I watch a loon looking at me. Then, hooting softly, he stretches his left foot out of the water with a "foot-wag," the loons' way of saying "Hi." I've been flattering myself for all these years, thinking that one bird has been swimming by when I am there, coming so close that I hold my breath so I won't startle him away. I can see his red eyes staring at me. In a way, it's the same fixity of gaze in Bobby's sepia-tinted photographs of Martha, framed and hung along the upstairs walls at Lily Pond. The same look I saw in Martha's eyes as we toasted our good life over thin-stemmed champagne glasses or sipped our last "jade dew" green tea in her Turkey Hill kitchen. It's love and it's intense, regardless of how others see one's partner's peculiarities.

In the world I live in now, a mother of daughters who've grown into wonderful young women, my life neither about having, nor about being. I am not afraid. My life is somewhat less rich without the moments Martha and I used to share, but I have the deep satisfaction of feeling that it is my own, a life of my own fashioning. I'm not anyone's sidekick; I am the center of my own world. I don't live in anyone else's shadow. No longer blinded by Martha's radiance, I try every day to recognize, be grateful for, and take pride in who I am.

ACKNOWLEDGMENTS

The Best of Friends is a story of friendship, and each page is a token of gratitude to the people whose lives touched mine.

The book recounts the milestones of my twenty-year friendship with Martha Stewart, a relationship that indelibly imprinted both of our lives, but came to a precipitous—and all-too-public—demise when I was forced to testify at Martha's trial. Because the case was major news, I was caught in the media crossfire. Those were very dark days.

Yet, it was then when I, luckily, caught Gloria Allred, the famous lawyer, on the *Larry King Show*. She was accompanying Amber Frey, whose involvement with Scott Peterson, then a murder defendant, had been portrayed quite ambiguously by the media. As Allred helped Frey maintain her courage and dignity during the interview, words came to my mind from François Fénelon: "By reason of affliction the road may seem a narrow one but . . . the important thing is to suffer without being discouraged."* The strength and wisdom I saw in Gloria Allred

---

Selected Letters of Fénelon, ed. John McEwan, foreword by Thomas Merton, Harville Press, 1964.

prompted me to, eventually, call her, and it was through her invaluable support and guidance that *The Best of Friends* became a book.

The words of Fénelon also echoed in the wise counsel I received from my Romanian spiritual advisers, among them Father Ioan Cucu of St. Gheorghe Cathedral and Father Ciprian of Sihăstria Monastery.

I want to express my gratitude to Kimberly Witherspoon, my agent at InkWell Management, for instantly recognizing that my book might have a place in the literature of "women's friendships," as well as for her unwavering belief in the project. Kim also introduced me to colleagues who lent their talents to bringing the book to fruition, notably Elisa Petrini.

I am deeply grateful, too, to Gail Winston, my editor at Harper-Collins, for her enduring guidance, inspiration, and enthusiasm, as well as to Jason Sack for his great taste and welcoming manner.

My family's encouragement and selfless support have sustained me through the hard times, mostly alluded to, in my story and also through the unfamiliar exertion of writing this book. My thanks go out to each and every one of them—to my father, Constantin; my sister Adriana; my brother-in-law Costin; my niece Ana Maria; and the cousins, aunts, and uncles who are all so much a part of who I am. I devote this book to the memory of my mother, Lucica; my grandparents; and others no longer among us who remain alive in my heart.

My dear friends also generously encouraged and supported me, including Maggie Kromer, Michel Delhaise, and George Jordan, who appear in this book. I am thankful to them and to many others who have stood by me through so much, like Leslie Stone, George Chiriac, Vicky Fingelly, and all the associates at Nicholas Fingelly Real Estate.

I dedicate this book to my daughters Monica and Lara, with my love and with the hope that their lives might be blessed with only the truest and best of friends.

ABOUT THE AUTHOR

MARIANA PASTERNAK grew up in Romania and immigrated to the United States as a political refugee. The mother of two daughters, she has been a biomedical engineer and held other positions involving computer-based research and development, while volunteering for children's causes. For the past twenty years, she has been working as a Realtor in Connecticut, where she lives.